Scottish Mountaineering Club
District Guide Books

THE CAIRNGORMS

General Editor: W. B. SPEIRS

The Cairngorms

THE CAIRNGORMS, THE MOUNTH, LOCHNAGAR

by Adam Watson, B.SC, PH.D, D.SC, FRSE

Map Drawings by James Renny

THE SCOTTISH MOUNTAINEERING TRUST

EDINBURGH

ʌrst published in Great Britain in 1975 by
THE SCOTTISH MOUNTAINEERING TRUST

Copyright © 1975 by The Scottish Mountaineering Trust

First Edition   January, 1928
Reprinted   August, 1931
Second Edition   August, 1938
Third Edition   June, 1950
Fourth Edition   November, 1968
Fifth Edition (rewritten)   January, 1975
Reprinted with amendment   April, 1980

Designed for the Scottish Mountaineering Trust by
West Col Productions

WHOLESALE DISTRIBITORS
West Col Productions
Goring on Thames
Reading Berks RG8 9AA

SBN 901516 90 2

Set in Monotype Plantin Series 110 and Grotesque 215
Reproduced, printed and bound in Great Britain by
Fakenham Press Limited, Fakenham, Norfolk

CONTENTS

ILLUSTRATIONS

SKETCH MAPS *by James Renny*

FOREWORD

THE FIRST EDITION of this guide book was written by Sir Henry Alexander, a distinguished member of the Scottish Mountaineering Club, and was published in 1928. There were few changes in the area until after the war, but in 1968 a major revision was necessary and was carried out by Adam Watson, J. C. Donaldson, G. Scott Johnstone and I. H. M. Smart. This edition is out of print.

Now in 1974, on account of many changes – new roads and tracks, the continuing development of climbing techniques and skiing, our growing knowledge of the area's natural history, and not least the adoption of metric measurements by the Ordnance Survey – it has been necessary to rewrite the guide book.

Adam Watson, who was responsible for much of the work in revising the 1968 edition, fortunately agreed to carry out this onerous task. His home is on Deeside, and his knowledge of these mountains at this time is unsurpassed. Although extremely busy with other projects, he has found time to carry out the task with expedition and the greatest attention to detail, and the Scottish Mountaineering Trust is most grateful to him.

We are also indebted to those who contributed photographs, particularly Tom Weir, Greg Strange, and Adam Watson, and to James Renny who drew the sketch maps which are an innovation and will enable the reader to place the main topographical features described in each chapter. We also thank J. C. Donaldson, editor of the new metric issue of *Munro's Tables*, for checking the heights and map references from the new issue of the Ordnance Survey Maps.

Up to date information on these mountains is published in the *Scottish Mountaineering Club Journal*, issued about May each year, and on public sale.

W. B. Speirs, Killearn, June 1974

WARNING TO HILL WALKERS

The Guide Books issued by The Scottish Mountaineering Trust describe routes which range from difficult climbs to what are in fine weather mere walks. It cannot be stressed too strongly that an expedition, which in fine weather is simple, may cease to be so if the weather becomes bad or mist descends. The conditions especially arising in the Cairngorms are set out in the Introduction.

Equipment. All parties should carry simple first aid equipment, torch, whistle, watch, one-inch Ordnance Survey map, and compass, and know how to use them. Except for a few spots in Skye where the rocks are magnetic, the compass direction is certain to be correct even if it differs from one's sense of direction. Ice-axes should be carried if there is any chance of snow or ice, and a rope unless it is certain not to be required.

Clothing. At all times reserve clothing should be carried. Temperatures change rapidly, especially at high levels. Clothing should be warm; in winter a Balaclava helmet and thick woollen gloves should be carried. Well shod boots should always be worn.

Food. Each member of a party should carry his own food. Climbers will find from experience what kind of food suits their individual need. Normally jams and sugar are better than meat as more rapidly converted into energy. Alcohol should not be carried; it increases the loss of body heat and thus will worsen any case of exposure. Light meals at frequent intervals are better than heavy meals at long intervals. In winter it may be advisable to make an early stop for food in a sheltered spot.

PROPRIETARY AND
SPORTING RIGHTS

The Scottish Mountaineering Trust desire to impress upon all those who avail themselves of the information given in their Guide Books that it is essential to consider and respect proprietary and sporting rights.

During the shooting season, from about the beginning of August to the middle of October, harm can be done in deer forests and on grouse moors by people tramping through them. During this period walkers and climbers should obtain the consent of the local stalkers and gamekeepers before walking over shooting lands. In cases of doubt it is always wise to ask some local resident.

It should also be noted that many of the roads in the upper glens were made and are maintained by the proprietors, who do not acknowledge a public right to motor over them, though they may follow the lines of established rights of way. It is, however, sometimes possible to obtain permission to motor over some of them, but, as the situation is liable to change, local enquiries should be made in advance.

METRIC MEASUREMENTS
AND ABBREVIATIONS

Heights are in metres and distances in kilometres. One metre is approximately 3·28 feet, and one kilometre is about 0·62 miles or about ⅝ of a mile. Heights and distances of the more important hills and passes are also given in feet and miles,

m   metres
km   kilometres
ft   feet
ha   hectare (100 m × 100 m or about 2½ acres)
SMCJ   Scottish Mountaineering Club Journal (e.g. *SMCJ* 10, 21 is Vol 10, page 21)
CCJ   Cairngorm Club Journal
ECJ   Etchachan Club Journal
OS   Ordnance Survey

★   In the lists of hills, an asterisk indicates a 'Munro' or separate hill over 3000 ft or 914 m. All Munros are given in these lists at the beginnings of the chapters, but only a selected few of the large number of 'tops' over 3000 ft; the latest edition of *Munro's Tables* should be consulted for the others. Many lower hills that are worth climbing also appear in the lists heading the chapters.

The reader should note that all sketch maps in the book designate kilometre(s) by the Americanese spelling of kilometer(s).

ACKNOWLEDGEMENTS

I thank W. B. Speirs for his cooperation as General Editor of the Scottish Mountaineering Club's District Guide Books, and G. J. Tiso, Convener of the SMC Publications Committee, who offered prompt efficient help. When planning the book I had useful discussions with a number of Club members, especially W. D. Brooker and J. E. M. Duff. I am very grateful to James Renny, who prepared all the fine map diagrams; he freely gave up much of his spare time to do this work and thought nothing of driving up from Fife to Deeside to talk things over. This book would be much the poorer without the help of the many friends whose photographs are published here. I also particularly thank John Duff, BEM, who wrote the up to date summary on accidents and mountain rescue; T. Chasser, CVO, gave ready permission and offered police assistance for this task. G. S. Johnstone, FRSE, and D. Sugden kindly read and commented on my summaries on Geology and Landforms in the Introduction, as did J. M. Boyd, FRSE, and W. B. Prior the parts on the conservation work of the Nature Conservancy Council and the Countryside Commission for Scotland. G. S. Strange offered help and I am grateful for his comments and those of W. J. March about the sections on Climbing Routes. Thanks are due to Edith Stewart who gave up her summer holidays to type this book.

I am indebted to numerous local folk – unfortunately, too many to mention individually – for their friendship and information, and especially Bob Scott, ex-stalker of Luibeg, and in Rothiemurchus J. Grant and Mrs Carrie Nethersole-Thompson and her son Brock. In every generation we depend heavily on those who pioneered before us. We owe a lot to Sir Henry Alexander, distinguished SMC member, who wrote the early editions of this Guide, which were the biggest, most learned and most far-ranging of the Club's old District Guides. He set a high standard to try to follow.

PREFACE

Nineteen years of visiting and later seventeen of living and working in the hill country of this District Guide have taught me the humility of realising how little anyone can know of even one hill or glen, let alone such a vast tract of some of the most varied country in all Scotland. In this book there are therefore likely to be errors; let me know, and I will correct them. I have reworded and kept much of the fine historical material from Alexander's editions of this District Guide, but otherwise have rewritten the entire text and have added a lot of information that was not in the earlier editions. I have also re-organised the information into different subjects within each chapter, so that readers who have particular interests will be able to find what they want more quickly. Much more could be written to describe such an area but to do so would be a grave mistake. If too much becomes well known and publicised, whether of rock climbing routes or descriptions of walking routes, topography and views, it decreases and spoils the feeling of exploration. Exploring for yourself by your own free will, without formal courses or training, is the greatest joy the hills can give. This book tries to strike a balance. Enough information is given on routes to help any serious walker or climber who has not been here before, but deliberately not so much as to make it the equivalent of a human guide. I have also given some other information which was not in the earlier editions and which does not detract from the feeling of exploration but may well add to it. Examples are the old place names and their pronunciation, a lot of extra material on history that was not in earlier editions, and the summaries on landforms, vegetation and wild animals. The newcomer is unlikely to find much of this in the easily available local guide books. The reader who wants more detail on these other subjects is given references to other publications where he can dig more deeply, with some idea of their quality and the type of information that they contain. I merely give an introduction to these subjects, enough to make newcomers, when they do come here, appreciate better the total environment and special character of the Cairngorms country. It may help to make their days on the hill fuller and more enjoyable.

It may also help to turn them into guardians of what they experience. As I write this book, it is saddening to have to mention the countless new bulldozed roads and other affronts to the hillman's appreciation which have occurred in the short six years since the last edition. Indeed, pressures on the priceless hill country and grand wilderness described in this book are so great and increasing so fast that future hillmen will be denied the enjoyment of what we still enjoy, unless many more of us become active guardians. To write a book which may well attract more people and thus more pressures to these hills is worrying. My sole reason for agreeing was that at present there are obviously not nearly enough of us as guardians to prevent or modify the many undesirable new things which are happening, often with insufficient action to try to control them. The risk I have taken will have been justified if this book adds strength to the ranks of the unofficial guardians of the Cairngorms.

A. Watson, *Crathes.*

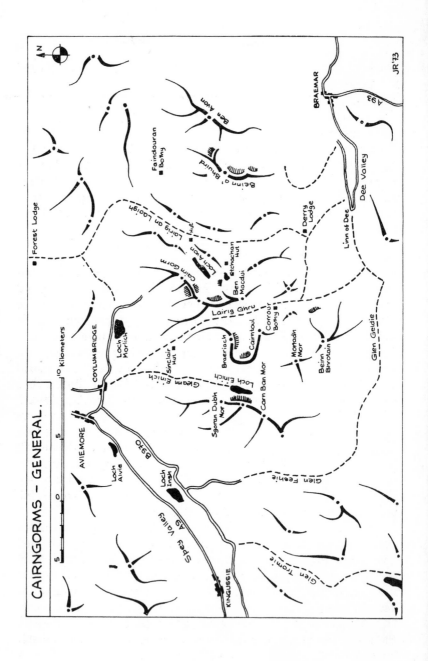

CAIRNGORMS - GENERAL.

INTRODUCTION

Area covered

THIS book covers the North East of Scotland from its arctic-like high plateaux to its wild coast. The area is bounded on the W by the Inverness–Carrbridge road, the valley of Spey and Drumochter Pass, and on the S by Garry, Tay and Strath More along past Forfar to Arbroath, and on the E and N by the North Sea and the Moray Firth.

Names of the hill ranges

The book has been named mainly after the Cairngorms, the great central dominating hill group in the North East, pronounced Cairn*gor*oms. Within the main Cairngorms massif from Aviemore to Braemar and from Glen Feshie to Glen Gairn, 30 km from E to W and 25 from N to S, you will find magnificent remote hills and a wealth of river, loch and forest scenery that cannot be matched elsewhere in Britain. Although we are so used to the name 'the Cairngorms', it is a nickname. These hills are Am Monadh Ruadh (Um Monna *Roo*a) or the red hills, distinguishing them from Am Monadh Liath (*Lee*-a) or the grey hills W of Spey; if you look from Aviemore on a clear evening, the granite screes of Lairig Ghru and Braeriach do glow a warm red in the sun. The name Am Monadh Ruadh still lives among the oldest folk of Strath Spey, but long ago, outsiders had replaced it with 'the Cairngorms', on maps and in guide books. Erroneously they had transferred the name of the best known hill in the group, Cairn Gorm, to the group as a whole.

The other main hill group is the long chain running from Drumochter in the W almost to the sea just S of Aberdeen. Many maps and books have given its name as 'the Grampians' but although children have to learn this at school, they do not learn it at home and nowhere is it used in local rural speech. Some map-makers have confused the issue by printing 'Grampians' over the Cairngorms and Strath Don hills as well! As it has often been used on maps to take in the Ben Alder and Perthshire hills far to the W of our area, it is unsuitable for this book. To add to the confusion, most local peoople now

19

associate the word with 'Grampian Television', and from 1974 with the Grampian region of local government covering lowland NE Scotland. It is therefore best not to use this vague name for the great E–W hill range. The old local name was Am Monadh, the hill range commonly called the Mounth, often spelled 'munth' in old documents and still pronounced 'mun' or 'munth' today by local people. It survives in the local names of the old 'roads' or paths that cross it, such as the Cairn o' Mount, the Fir Mounth, the Capel Mount, the Tolmount, etc. and in their collective term 'the Mounth Roads'.

Place names

The rule, as in all the SMC Guides, is to follow the latest Ordnance Survey maps for their spelling of place names. This does not mean that all the place names on the map are accurate. In some cases, long established local usage differs greatly from what appears in the OS maps, and the book mentions a few examples. However, as it would be confusing for a guide book to give names very different from the OS maps, the OS forms are used except where the map shows obvious small printers' errors. Another slight difference from the maps is that this Guide omits the Gaelic vowel accents on the names; these accents are very often inaccurate on the OS maps, for instance on the Tourist 1 inch map issued in 1972, but in any case their function is not understood except by Gaelic speakers and they are not necessary for finding locations. The full Gaelic forms of some names, however, are given, especially for the main hills when they are first mentioned in the text. These are spelled as far as possible according to local usage, with the English meanings of the names sometimes added. Vowel accents are printed here only where a name's pronunciation or meaning is also given.

You will find it interesting to scan the place names in different parts of the region. In most of the hills of Moray and Nairn, and to the W of Corgarff, Balmoral and Glen Shee, the names are virtually all Gaelic in origin. Already around Strath Don, Glen Muick and Glen Isla, many are corruptions of Gaelic and difficult to decipher, with a few in North-East Scots or English. Next to the lowlands around Huntly, Banchory and the Braes o' Angus, many are North-East Scots or English and the rest corrupted Gaelic, with none in pure Gaelic. Name-changing by outsiders still goes on. Since 1960 the Cairnwell and nearby ski slopes – all in Glen Clunie in Aberdeenshire – have commonly become the 'Glenshee' ski grounds. Even the well known Spey and Strath Spey have become the 'Cairngorm Valley' to many journalists and television announcers. This book resists such unnecessary changes that ignore well established local usage. It also gives many names of corries, burns and glens, which you will not find on the OS maps. Most of them are still used locally but a few have virtually died out, and some have not appeared in print before. Publication here should help to keep them alive, as well as being useful to visitors for describing locations in these hills more precisely.

A. MacBain, no date, late 1800s *Badenoch: Its History, Clans and Place Names.* A careful collection by an expert.

J. Macdonald 1899 *Place Names of West Aberdeenshire.* New Spalding Club. A pioneering list.

W. J. Watson 1926 *History of the Celtic Place-names of Scotland.* Includes interesting history and derivation of some words from the Cairngorms region.

F. C. Diack 1944 *Inscriptions of Pictland.* 3rd Spalding Club. Valuable material on place names, local Gaelic and local Gaelic poetry.

S. Gordon 1948, reprinted 1972 *Highways and Byways in the Central Highlands.* Authoritative glossary and list by W. J. Watson.

W. M. Alexander 1952 *The Place-Names of Aberdeenshire.* 3rd Spalding Club. An excellent list.

C. P. Will 1963 *Place Names of Northeast Angus.* Covers Glen Esk, Lethnot and Edzell. A pioneering list, but many of the suggested meanings have been criticised.

J. Milne Kirkmichael (Banffshire) place-names. *CCJ* 5, 93. A good list of the map names, but some rather speculative meanings.

W. J. Watson Some place-names in the Cairngorm region. *CCJ* 8, 133. Very good but short.

Name pronunciations
The most accurate pronunciations are given by older local people who have lived all their lives in a small area and whose parents also lived there. Many of those who know the area well as climbers nevertheless err when pronouncing a lot of the place names. Coming from temporary visitors, such errors may seem ignorant or even patronising to those who belong to this hill country. A new feature of this Guide

is to give many of the local pronunciations in parentheses, though the writer realises that in other parts of the Highlands some of these place names would be pronounced differently. The part printed in italics shows which syllable of the name one stresses in speech. As it is impossible to describe Gaelic pronunciations accurately, this Guide gives no more than very approximate versions of how some of the place names are pronounced by the most reliable older local people. The following table shows some of the main sounds that are used for indicating pronunciations later in the text:

a	— bat	e	— get	o	— got
aa	— far	ei	— height	oe	— Joe
ai	— pain	g	— go	oi	— boil
aw	— dawn	i	— hit	ole,	pole,
ay	— say	ie	— corrie	ome,	home
c	— can	igh	— high	one,	bone
ch	— loch or Bach	ng	— hung	etc.	etc.
				ow	— howl
				u	— but
				y	— yes

The 'y' sound often comes after a consonant, a common example being the frequent name Meall, meaning a lumpy round hill. It is pronounced Myal in one syllable, with the same 'my' sound as at the beginning of the English word 'mule'.

Language

The climber can understand and enjoy a piece of hill country better if he knows something of the people who live there and appreciates something of their speech, life and history. Gaelic was the language of all but the coastal strip and Aberdeen till the 13th century. It survived as a living tongue W of Ballater till the early 20th century, and in Strath Spey, Atholl and Inverey well into our century. The people of Spey and Atholl now speak English with a Highland intonation, and occasional words of Gaelic or Scots origin. The language of the folk of Dee, Don and Deveronside now is the North-East Scots dialect, strongly influenced by the farming people of lower Aberdeenshire. It contains many words of Gaelic origin but a large number of Norse origin, many of them like modern Norwegian. If you are a visitor, remember that this North-East Scots, and not English, is the language the people are at home with. The folk of the Angus glens speak a different variety of Scots, less rich in dialect words and more influenced by the intonation of Dundee, Perth and Strath More.

History

The history of the people in this hill country is a vast subject with much literature. The text gives some brief pieces of historical information which relate mainly to the hills rather than to the region as a whole, but there was not space for much of this. References are given below for the reader who wishes to know more. In addition, the various village guide booklets describe many historical events down in the inhabited valleys.

'Glenmore' 1859 *Highland Legends*. Includes old legends and Gaelic poetry from Spey, Avon and Dee.

J. Grant 1861 *Legends of the Braes o' Mar*. A racy account on old legends in the previous three centuries. Selective but good story-telling.

J. G. Michie 1872 *Deeside Tales*. Local history since the 17th century, and 19th century way of life. Selective but good story-telling.

W. Scrope 1883 *Days of Deer-Stalking in the Scottish Highlands*. Descriptions and historical material about Atholl.

A. MacBain late 1800s. *Badenoch: Its History, Clans and Place Names*. A good, careful collection; much on the Cairngorms massif.

J. G. Michie (ed) 1901 *The Records of Invercauld*. New Spalding Club. Collections of old Invercauld Estate records, with detailed documentation.

W. M. Smith 1904 *The Romance of Poaching in the Highlands*. Accounts of some well known poachers of Mar and Atholl.

T. Sinton 1906 *The Poetry of Badenoch*. An excellent collection of the Gaelic poetry not just of Badenoch but also Braemar and Atholl.

T. D. Miller 1925 *Tales of a Highland Parish: Glen Shee*. Local story-telling.

W. D. Simpson 1943 *The Province of Mar*. A good account of local history, emphasising castles.

Seton Gordon 1948, reprinted 1972 *Highways and Byways in the Central Highlands*. A useful book which collates and repeats many of the old legends and descriptions of historical events in Atholl,

Spey and Dee, including many long quotations, which are otherwise available only in scarce old books.

V. Gaffney 1960 *The Lordship of Strathavon.* 3rd Spalding Club. A detailed documentation of the shieling system in Strath Avon.

I. F. Grant 1961 *Highland Folk Ways.* Authoritative and detailed account on old ways of life, much of it from Strath Spey, by the originator of Am Fasgadh Museum at Kingussie.

F. Wyness 1968 *Royal Valley.* Useful book on Deeside history, drawing on a wide literature.

S. Piggott & W. D. Simpson 1970 *Illustrated Guide to Ancient Monuments.* Vol 6, Scotland. A general booklet with detailed summaries of all the sites and a good list of further reading.

Articles in *CCJ* are worth reading in Vol 2 'The Braemar Highlands after the '45', 6 'Tales told in Rothiemurchus', 'The Cairngorm parishes and the (old) Statistical Account of Scotland' and 'Rights of Way in Braemar and Glen Tilt in 1840–50', 10 'The Canadian lumber camps in the Cairngorms', 12 'James Downie, Guide' and 'The Glen Doll Right of Way Case', and 14 'Braemar of old: extracts from a Highland diary'. V. Gaffney wrote a short but interesting and detailed account on 'Shielings of the Drumochter' in *Scott. Stud.* 11, 91, with two fine old maps.

The article by I. H. Adams on 'The historical geography of Glenfernate 1460–1968' in *Ann. Rep. Scott. Fld Stud. Ass.* 1969, 17, is a good short study of the old clachans and their depopulation.

Estates and land use
Each chapter gives an approximate idea of the boundaries of the estates and of the main land uses on the hill there. When you are planning a trip, it may help to know this in case deer stalking is in progress. It will also help you to know which estate office to contact for permission to camp, visit a particular hill, or ask for a key so that you can open a locked gate and motor on a private road. The telephone directory shows many of the estates' phone numbers under the estate names. As a rule, most estates will not allow motoring on these private roads, but some estates allow it on one or two of their many roads, and other estates may give you a key if you have some special reason or if it is a season when you cannot do much harm. Private, locked roads where estates sometimes allow motoring are not listed here as things too often change; on the whole, these permissions

are gradually being withdrawn as the pressure from more and more motorists steadily increases.

Man's land use greatly affects your ease of walking and also the appearance of the hills. Foresters have made dense jungles on many lower slopes, but forest roads usually give some access to the hill above. On the higher and western deer forests the stalkers burn the heather to give the deer a young bite, often in great fires of up to 40 ha or more; this makes for easy walking but less wildlife. On the grouse moors – such as in Strath Don and near Lumsden – the fires are usually small, often in long narrow strips, giving a unique appearance to this kind of landscape, which you see dramatically when a light dusting of snow shows up the contrasting chess-board pattern. On some of the lower northern and eastern moors where the keepers have burned little in recent years, the heather now grows very rank and many young trees are taking over.

Clubs

Cairngorm Club, Aberdeen, formed 1887. Secretary R. C. Shirreffs, 18 Bon-Accord Square, Aberdeen AB1 2DJ. Good Club library, long-established Journal.

Carn Dearg Mountaineering Club, Dundee. Secretary A. C. Ingram, 12 Bruce Road, Downfield, Dundee DD3 8LL.

Deeside Field Club, Aberdeen. Secretary J. T. C. Gillan, 40 Union Street, Aberdeen AB1 1BD. All aspects of the Deeside countryside.

Etchachan Club, Aberdeen. Secretary G. S. Strange, 402 King Street, Aberdeen. Library, journal, produces coast rock climbing Guide.

Grampian Club, Dundee. Secretary A. C. Gardner, 30 Marlee Road, Broughty Ferry, Dundee DD5 3EX.

Inverness Mountaineering Club. Secretary Mrs D. C. Carroll, 255 Mackintosh Road, Raigmore, Inverness IV2 3UB.

Junior Mountaineering Club of Scotland, Perth Section. Secretary D. Wares, 2 Rowan-bank, Scone, Perth.

Moray Mountaineering Club. Secretary J. Burns, Braemoray Cottage, Grantown.

Scottish Rights of Way Society, 6 Abercromby Place, Edinburgh, EH3 6JX.

Strathspey Mountain Club. Chairman Mrs P. Scarbrough, Tigh Guish, Inverdruie, Aviemore.

Accommodation, transport and local guide books

There are now specialist guides on accommodation and transport, issued by the following organisations:

The Scottish Tourist Board, 23 Ravelston Terrace, Edinburgh EH4 3UE. Also guide booklets on various outdoor sports for the non-specialist.

The Grampian Tourist Association, 17 High Street, Elgin IV30 1 EG. Publishes an annual *Accommodation Guide* called *Touring in the Five Counties*; this includes farmhouse and cottage accommodation as well as hotels, and caravan and camp sites.

The Highlands and Islands Development Board, Bridge House, Bank Street, Inverness IV1 1QR. Also publishes guides on downhill skiing and fishing.

Alexanders (Northern) Timetable, published annually, gives full details of most bus services in the area covered by this District Guide.

Most towns and larger villages in the hill country, such as Braemar, Ballater and Grantown, produce their own local guide books which give details of local accommodation, tourist facilities and many short walking routes in or near the valley.

You will find a bicycle useful – more so here than in most parts of the Highlands – to reach many now very inaccessible hills which nevertheless have glen roads leading to the foot of them. Almost all 'private' glen roads that were open to cars 30 years ago now have locked gates, but you can still cycle on these very long approaches to the hills and the main passes. Indeed, cycling is a public right on the many long glen roads which are rights of way. These are 'private' only against cars, and this is always the reason for locking the gates.

Remote occupied houses, bothies and camping

Remote inhabited houses are described in case of emergency. Often you may get some kind of accommodation there if you politely ask permission, usually a nearby barn or shed where you can cook and stretch out your sleeping bag. Uninhabited bothies and refuges are mentioned in detail in the higher hills. On the lower hills and grouse moors you will see many stables, shooters' lunch huts, outhouses and boathouses, most of which have no locks; these have not been described individually as they are far too numerous to mention and as they lie in country that hill walkers use mainly for day-trips rather than for longer stays. Above all, they are not traditional bothies long used by many walkers. Hence the quickest way to have them locked or demolished by the estates would be to publicise them in this or any other guide book. In the area there have been several forcible break-ins of unoccupied houses and lodges by hill walkers, and in one case this led to immediate destruction of an excellent bothy which had been used by the culprits.

Various semi-natural shelters or 'howffs' in caves or under boulders in the glens are also not mentioned. They offer no value as emergency shelters as they are so hard to find except with detailed local knowledge, and in any case they occur well down in the lower glens where emergencies would seldom happen. They are places found and used by some local climbers, and it might spoil things for them to mention these howffs here. The keepers turn a blind eye to their use, but could not do so if a few people well known to them were to grow too many.

For camping, most of the area lies wide open and free. No camping is allowed in most woodland areas because of fire, and no camping or fires anywhere in the Cairngorms National Nature Reserve. In such places and in the lower valleys you should go to the organised camp sites or camp at the many crofts and farms which allow this.

Maps

1 inch to 1 mile (1:63360). The Ordnance Survey's 1972 Tourist Map of the Cairngorms covers all the Cairngorms massif, Lochnagar and much of the Mounth, ranging from Grantown to Spittal of Glenshee, and from Loch Insh to the Lecht. This map has hill shading and different – sometimes rather dark – colours indicating different altitudes. On the editions in the 1960s these made it less easy to see the contour lines in poor light, but the 1972 edition has become much better. Fourteen sheets from the OS 7th Series cover the entire area right to the coast – 28 to 31, 37 to 43, and 48 to 50. All the 1 inch maps show contours every 50 ft, many of which are drawn by eye and thus sometimes inaccurate. All have the national 1 km grid superimposed for map references. The main text of this Guide does not mention the various sheet numbers of this old series, as the OS decided in 1973 to withdraw them.

Metric 1:50000. The OS decided in 1973 to replace the 1 inch to the mile maps with a new metric series at 1:50000 or approximately

27

1·27 inches to the mile. At the time of writing, full details of the new series are not yet available. See also note on page 79.

1:25000. The OS have for some years published maps on this scale at about 2½ inches to the mile, with km grid superimposed. Contours are every 25 ft.*

Metric 1:10000. New metric OS maps at 1:10000 are now available for most of the area. Made from vertical aerial photographs, they look extremely detailed and accurate for topographical features; contours occur every 10 m, but confusingly 8 m in some maps. Names of many rock-climbing features are inaccurately located, and a few of the innumerable deer and sheep tracks appear as if proper human paths. However, all cliffs are shown, not just the somewhat random ones chosen selectively and without standardisation on the 1 inch maps. For areas not yet covered, the old 6 inch to the mile maps may still be available, with spot heights but no contours. They give a good idea of what this hill country was like before the massive depopulation of the glens and before the coming of bulldozer and chair lift. The OS photographs are very interesting for anyone visiting the area in some detail, and can be bought from the OS headquarters.

½ *inch to 1 mile.* Bartholomew's maps on this scale, though on too small a scale for navigation in mist, are useful for getting a general idea of large tracts of countryside.

Heights
In this Guide, altitudinal heights of places are given in the following two standard ways throughout. 1. These are estimates based on the reading of contours, and have usually been rounded to the nearest 5 or 10 metres or sometimes the nearest 20 if taken from the OS 7th Series, but occasionally have been estimated to the nearest metre if they happened to lie beside one of the 7½ or 8 metre contour lines from the new 1:10000 maps. All these estimated heights in the Guide are preceded by the words 'about' or 'approximately'. 2. These are precise heights to the nearest metre, as copied from recently surveyed heights on the OS 1:10000 metric maps. Any altitudinal height of a place in this Guide which is not preceded by 'about' or 'approximately' should be taken as a precise height.

In feet. The 1 inch maps show some confusion about heights of the hills. Within the last ten years the Ordnance Survey have kept most of their original heights in feet but have changed several. Unfortu-

*In 1974 they issued a new 1:25000 map, *High Tops of the Cairngorms*, from Aviemore S. to Geldie and Feshie E. to Derry.

nately they have changed the height once again to a different figure in at least two cases; Beinn a' Ghlo has gone from 3671 up to 3677 and down to 3673 ft, and Ben Macdui from 4296 up to 4300 and back to 4296 again. Most heights have not changed on the latest 1 inch maps. Nevertheless, if one converts to feet from the figures in metres on the brand new 1:10000 metric maps, the result does not always agree with the figure from the latest 1 inch map. One reason for this in at least four cases – Beinn a' Ghlo, An Socach, Fafernie and Clachnaben is that the latest survey has discovered another bump on the hill top, which rises higher than what was previously considered the highest point. However, as it would be confusing to print figures in feet that differ from those in the latest 1 inch map, the writer has given the figures in feet from the latest 1 inch map, even though they do not always agree with the 1:10000 metric figures. Carn a' Mhaim is an exception where no height on the 1 inch map has ever appeared in feet for the higher of the two tops; here the figure in feet for this Guide has been calculated by converting from the metric height on the 1:10000 map. Craigendarroch is another case of this.

In metres. Precise metric heights for nearly all the hills and cols described in this Guide have been taken directly from the printed heights in metres on the new OS 1:10000 maps. Two exceptions are Cairn Toul and Tom Buidhe where the new metric maps give no heights and the OS could offer no further information; these two metric heights in the Guide have been calculated by converting from the figures in feet on the latest 1 inch map. On ground not yet covered by the new metric maps, sixteen metric heights of hills were kindly supplied by the OS from their unpublished data, but they could not give metric heights for the Hill of Fare, Bennachie and Mormond; for these three, this Guide shows the figures in feet from the latest 1 inch maps, and the metric heights as calculated by conversion.

Times

A few times based on notes from the writer's earlier diaries have been given for some of the more popular hill walks, but these are very approximate; you should make your own calculations based on knowledge of your own capabilities. Naismith's formula (*SMCJ* 2, 136) is very useful, one hour for every 3 miles or roughly 5 km, plus ½ an hour for every 1000 ft or 300 m of climbing. It includes short halts for food, but not delays because of bad weather, any rock climbing, fording streams in spate, etc. The formula works out fairly accurately in practice on recorded times in the Cairngorms (*CCJ* 8, 19). A special note of warning is that in bad weather with mist, gales or heavy rain, on icy frozen slopes, and above all in deep snow with or without drifting snow and mist, you should forget about Naismith's formula. In bad conditions one level mile can easily take one hour, and in extreme cases can be impossible. Big packs also slow a party.

Long hill walks

The six main Cairngorms have attracted many hill walkers keen on breaking records. Though this sport does not appeal to the writer, a few details are given here as it involves some historical interest and provides as worthwhile an experience to its devotees as any other sport. In June 1908 H. J. Butchart and four others from Aberdeen, who started from Loch Builg at midnight, covered a 45 km or 28 mile, 2700 m or 9000 ft 'round' of the six tops of Ben Avon, Beinn a' Bhuird, Cairn Gorm, Ben Macdui, Cairn Toul and Braeriach, to the now non-existent Lower Bothy of Einich. J. Beattie, W. D. Hutcheon and G. Shand did the same round during June 1932 in 16¼ hours. Then, in July 1932, R. P. Yunnie and party completed the alternative easier route from Ben Macdui by Braeriach to Cairn Toul and Corrour Bothy in 14 hours 45 minutes (*CCJ* 13, 99). In the summer of 1933, W. D. Hutcheon and G. Shand next cut the time for this easier alternative to 13 hours 25 minutes (*CCJ* 13, 191). E. F. Johnston greatly reduced it to 11 hours 10 minutes on 31 July 1960 (*CCJ* 17, 210). This was then beaten by V. C. Wynne-Edwards who, in his sixties, covered the same route in 9 hours 34 minutes in September 1968 (*CCJ* 17, 273).

Eric Beard or 'Beardie' did some very fast hill walks. On 12 June 1967 he climbed Braeriach, Cairn Toul, Ben Macdui, Cairn Gorm and Beinn a' Bhuird from Glenmore Lodge back to Glenmore in 15 hours, a considerably longer route than the others. In 1963 he went round the four highest Cairngorms in 4 hours 41 minutes from and back to Glenmore Lodge, travelling by the gap at Creag a' Chalamain to Braeriach, Cairn Toul, Ben Macdui and Cairn Gorm. Many have climbed these same four tops from Rothiemurchus and from the Derry. For a good walker, 12 hours will give plenty of time to stop and enjoy the scenery, but anything less than 10 is a race.

The longest walk continuously into new country was done very leisurely with a tent, by J. Duff. When a policeman at Braemar, he decided to get to know his enormous 'beat' better by walking round its perimeter. The route covered just over 160 km or 100 miles, for 7½ days walking round the main watershed of the Cairngorms and the Mounth from Carn an Fhidhleir to Lochnagar, and then along the subsidiary watershed by the Crathie-Gairn hills. P. D. Baird once leisurely walked 121 km or 75 miles round all the 22 Munros – i.e. separate hills over 3000 ft – in the Cairngorms during 2½ days, camping and studying snow patches en route and also claiming a new record of having smoked his pipe on top of each Munro (*CCJ* 17, 75)!

One of the greatest of walkers was Lord Kennedy. *The Times* of 31 August 1822 tells how he, as shooting tenant of Fealar near Glen Tilt, wagered 2000 guineas that he would, in one day, shoot 40 brace of grouse at Fealar, and then ride 140 miles on a horse to Dunnottar near Stonehaven and back to Fealar. He won the bet on 12 August. Starting to shoot at 04.15, he completed the 40 brace by 08.56, changed his clothes and ate, mounted his horse at 09.30 and rode the 70 miles to Dunnottar by 14.00. After resting an hour, he reached Fealar again at 19.56. Later that evening he even rode to Braemar, arriving at 22.00, thus adding another 14 miles. Perhaps even greater was the wager he made one night at Blackhall near Banchory, when Sir A. L. Hay bet Lord Kennedy £2500 that he would get to Inverness before him. 'Off they started at nine o'clock at night in their evening costume, thin shoes and silk stockings. Sir Andrew Leith Hay went by the coach road via Huntly and Elgin. Lord Kennedy, with Captain Ross as umpire, struck straight across the Grampians. Amid pouring rain they walked all night, next day, and the next night, reaching Inverness at 6 a.m. on the third day. Sir Andrew Leith Hay, who had chosen the longer but far more comfortable route, did not arrive till four hours later.' If, as is likely, Lord Kennedy went by the Lairig Ghru, Aviemore and Tomatin, the distance was 100 miles in 35 hours; he would have had a road from Banchory to the Linn of Dee and again from Aviemore to Inverness (*CCJ* 3, 312).

Rock, snow and ice climbs
For climbing routes on rock, ice and snow, the region is now covered by seven special Climbers' Guides, already available in the shops, or in press, which describe and illustrate all the many hundreds of routes that have now been done. Five are by the SMC, one on the coastal routes has been published by the Etchachan Club and one by G. Tiso covers the accessible *Creag Dubh and the Eastern Outcrops*.

There would therefore be no point in trying to duplicate any of this material here. Instead, the intention is merely to give a brief sketch of the chief features of each main cliff and to note only a few of its routes and their history, concentrating on the classics. This will help the serious hill walker who does not climb rocks, to appreciate better these grand cliffs. Sporting routes to the plateaux are also noted.

During the preparation of the first edition of *Climbers' Guide to the Cairngorms Area* the writer climbed most of the routes with T. W. Patey while helping him to check them. For recent new routes, very useful comments were given by D. Pyper, and particularly by W. J. March and G. S. Strange who edited the new 1973 edition of the Cairngorms *Climbers' Guide* (Vols 1 & 2). The grading of routes is as in the *SMC Journal*: E easy, M moderate, D difficult, VD very difficult, MS mild severe, S severe, HS hard severe, VS very severe, and Grades I to V increasing in severity for climbs in winter conditions. The SMC Climbers' Guides give full details of these gradings, as well as of the usual system (A1–A3, increasing in difficulty) for routes where pegs and other artificial aids are used much for direct ascent and not just for safe fixed and running belays. Tom Patey's article 'Cairngorm commentary' (*SMCJ* 27, 207) is recommended for its well written factual and witty history of the great surge of exploration which began on the crags after 1945 and led to publication of the first edition of the SMC Climbers' Guides.

The reader will see that the sections on rock, snow and ice climbing in this District Guide strongly emphasise summer rock. This will help the average hill walker, who is usually a summer visitor to the Cairngorms and not a winter walker or climber, to identify some of the more interesting or popular climbs. Most winter hill walkers are also snow and rock climbers to some extent and well aware of the Climbers' Guides. Thus, although a few notes have been given here on some of the finer winter routes, it would be outside the function of this book to give much space to these; the reader who wishes more should refer to the appropriate Climbers' Guide. However, in passing it is important to emphasise that this lesser space does not mean lesser interest. The very opposite applies, as the Cairngorms and Lochnagar form the most dependable hills for snow and ice climbing in Britain.

Hill walkers may be interested to learn that, unlike summer rock climbs which do not differ very greatly whether wet or dry, the same routes in winter vary enormously from one day to another, depending on the current conditions. Gullies with rock pitches can be smoothed out into easy snow climbs, or in early winters or mild winters can be a series of difficult giant ribbons of ice. Routes that are wet, grimy and vegetated in summer, and thus not recommended then – as in many gullies, chimneys, and on faces with green mossy ledges – become very fine climbs in winter. The hard lower pitches of some ridges and buttresses may be buried so much under deep snow that you can step across on to the rocks high up the route. Easy rock may become ensheathed in a slippery film of icy verglas, or a few days later may turn into dry rock with powdery snow filling the cracks and ledges. The snow can be firm and reliable, or a great variety of unstable types; hardly any two days are the same, and you frequently encounter marked changes in snow type and reliability within even one day. The cornices on these hills are often massive, giving formidable problems of tunnelling or other means of escape to the plateau for a party that has completed all the difficulties of the actual route on the cliff. There are scores of different kinds of snow and ice, and only experience enables you to assess and know their qualities and dependabilities. Some of the big gullies like the Black Spout on Lochnagar and the spouts of Coire Sputan Dearg can give marvellous, fairly safe glissades for experienced winter mountaineers, but in other conditions these gullies become dangerous avalanche slides of unstable powder, heavy wet snow, or wind slab, and next day can change to beautifully tough reliable hard snow for step-cutting.

H. A. Alexander 1928 *The Cairngorms.* SMC District Guide. The original fat classic, later editions 1938, 1950, 1968.

W. H. Murray 1947 *Mountaineering in Scotland.* Two chapters in this beautifully written classic describe Lochnagar and the Cairngorms.

J. H. B. Bell 1950 *A Progress in Mountaineering.* Good pioneering chapters on the Cairngorms, Cairngorm granite and climbing on Lochnagar.

E. Langmuir 1969 *Mountain Leadership.* Official Handbook of the Mountain Leadership Training Boards of Great Britain. Detailed, comprehensive account, for hill walkers and mountaineers a good summary handbook on techniques of mountaineering and hill walking in Scotland, including equipment.

Tom Patey 1971 *One Man's Mountains.* Some brilliantly written chapters by the North East's greatest climber, published posthumously.

Climbers' Guide to the Cairngorms Area. Current S.M.T. series commenced 1971 and published in five volumes by various authors. Original series, now out of print, issued in two volumes 1961–62, by Malcolm Smith. The series is comprehensive over all summer and winter climbing routes.

J. Cunningham 1972 *Winter Climbs in the Cairngorms and Creag Meagaidh.* A wide selection to the best winter climbs in the region in booklet form.

General articles in *ECJ* 3 that you will find worth reading are M. Smith's 'Twenty-one years on. A history of the Club' and H. R. Spencer's 'The Cairngorms for mountaineering'.

Corries and plateaux

The corries and the high arctic-like plateaux excel as two of the most wonderful features of the Cairngorms country. Some previous books on the area tended not to do justice to the wealth of corrie scenery, and wrote of featureless or dull plateaux. This Guide puts more emphasis on the richness of corries and on the attractions of the many plateaux which are unique in Britain. A particularly interesting point is that, on the plateaux of the high Cairngorms, the general appearance of the landscape, the landforms, the soils, weather, vegetation, invertebrates and birds are all much more akin to stony hill ground in high-arctic Canada, Iceland, or the arctic tip of Norway than they are to the Alps, the Caucasus or the Rockies. Sir H. Alexander, author of the first edition of this Guide, wrote of the high plateaux, 'Not less impressive than the corries, the cliffs, and the dark lochs are the great wastes of shattered stone and sand which form the summit plateaux and ridges of these mountains, and on which only a few of the hardiest Alpine plants maintain a footing. Here are the largest areas of lofty ground in these islands where the forces of nature – frost and heat, snow and rain, wind and tempest – work with a power and a violence undreamed of at lower heights. The very bareness of these mountain-tops is on a majestic scale, and it forms one of the elements in the massive grandeur and repose which are the distinguishing characteristics of the Cairngorms. The first fleeting impression made by these mountains may be one of disappointment, for their appeal is not of the picturesque or obvious kind; but, as one explores them and wanders among them, the magnitude of everything begins to reveal itself, and one realises the immensity of the scale upon which the scene is set, and the greatness and dignity and calm of the Cairngorms cast their spell over the spirit.'

The Mounth Roads

The many long-distance paths across the Mounth and other hills were once much used for travelling and cattle droving, and most of them are now rights of way. For hillmen they form one of the area's finest assets. Some have become very popular today but most are seldom visited. This book emphasises their qualities, as many of them offer fine ways of exploring the remote, secluded and less well known of our areas of wilderness country.

G. M. Fraser 1921 *The Old Deeside Road: Aberdeen to Braemar: Including the Mounth Passes over the Grampians.* The best detailed account of these old roads in Deeside.

A. R. B. Haldane 1952 *The Drove Roads of Scotland.* The best account on the droving, its economics and history, and way of life, including much material from NE Scotland.

G. M. Fraser's article on 'The "Mounth" Passes over the Grampians' *Scott. Geog. Mag.* 36, is also useful, and W. M. Alexander's 'The Mounth Roads' in *Scott. Gael. Stud.* 5, 154.

Ski touring

The region covered by this book, the snowiest in Britain, offers the best skiing. Some fine ski tours were done here in the early years of the sport (*SMCJ* 10, 345; 12, 253; and 16, 196). For instance, in March 1913 a party crossed Cairn Gorm and Ben Macdui on skis, on their way from Aviemore to the Derry, returning to Spey over Carn Ban Mor and Sgoran Dubh. H. MacRobert described Scottish snow for skiing and suitable skiing places in the Cairngorms (*SMCJ* 21, 379). One of the pioneers, H. J. Butchart, wrote an accurate and remarkably far sighted description for the early editions of this Guide. An early attempt in the 1930s to make Braemar a ski centre failed because of a lack of snow in very mild winters. More people took up skiing after 1945, and the sport grew rapidly in the late 1950s. This led to the new road, chair lifts and cafés being built at Cairn Gorm and the Cairnwell in the early 1960s. As the main runs are well known and described fully in tourist publications, there is no need for further mention here. However, the new tows and other facilities have been noted briefly in Chapters 2 and 10, as some may find them useful starting points for walks or ski tours.

Very few of the new downhill skiers have taken to climbing on skis or to ski touring. Walking on skis offers a different way of exploring the hills, corries and glens in winter, and the following section describes some of the area's potential for it. During severe winters with heavy snow you may get good ski touring from November till May, and exceptionally from October till June. In most years, however, good heavy snowfalls in November and December are often followed by great thaws and even January snowfalls may be unreliable. Indeed, in the mildest years such as 1964 and 1973, there may be far less snow on the hill in January or February than in June of other years. In mild years a continual succession of snowfalls, thaws and freeze-ups may last most of the winter, producing temporary stretches of skiing only on some weekends, often on poor sticky or crusty snow, or on dangerously icy snow with a surface almost like rough concrete. However, in most years from February to April there is plenty of snow on the higher hills and corries.

If you are skiing wholly on the lower hills and glens up to 750 m (2500 ft), or if you wish to start in the glens, climb over the hills and keep your skis on all day, you can do so never or very rarely in mild years like 1964 or 1973. However, in the hard winters like 1955 and 1963, excellent conditions for skiing occur on the lower slopes and glens from December to March. In 1951, which was the longest winter in the Cairngorms since 1943, you could ski on the glens from late November till late April. If you are content to carry your skis up snowfree glens or lower slopes, there will usually be good skiing higher up from February to May every year, except in the mildest winters. However, as this merely forms a variant of hill walking up snowfree ground combined with downhill running on narrow drifts, it is not further described here.

During heavy snow, especially in long hard winters like 1963, you can get fine touring on the lower hills such as Kerloch, Mount Battock, Geallaig and the hills of Cromdale and Glen Esk, but you cannot depend on it for long if the winter is average or mild. The Ladder Hills, Morven, Mount Keen, Drumochter and the Clova hills offer good conditions frequently in January to March of most winters. The lower hills in the Cairngorms massif, such as Sgor Mor and Beinn Bhreac, likewise give good ski touring then, and in deep snow the pine woods of Ballochbuie, the Derry, Dubh Ghleann and

Rothiemurchus are magnificent when visited on ski. These lower grounds become attractive on short mid-winter days as they are so accessible.

On the higher hills of Glen Feshie and the Mounth between Glen Ey and Glen Doll, good ski touring usually lasts into the spring, and on the even higher Cairngorms above 1100 m or 3500 ft you will then get a great variety of excellent touring. After climbing to the summit, you should make for certain places where the snow drifts in and usually gives a good downhill run. Such places are the stream N of Carn an Tuirc, the Ballochbuie side of the White Mounth, several streams off the Glas Maol, Allt Fhearnagan on Carn Ban Mor, and Allt a' Mharcaidh on Sgoran Dubh. In the higher Cairngorms, some of the best such places are N of Sron na Lairige, W of Coire an Lochain of Braeriach, down the corrie S from the cliff edge of Garbh Choire Mor to the Moine Mhor, Allt Clais an t-Sabhail, from the S top of Cairn Toul towards the Devil's Point, Garbh Uisge Mor of Ben Macdui, the Macdui slopes to Loch Etchachan and to Allt Carn a' Mhaim, Allt Creag an Leth-choin, Coire Ruairidh to the W of the N top of Beinn a' Bhuird and Feith Ghiubhasachain N of it, Coire Gorm, Alltan na Beinne and Ear Choire an t-Sneachda of Beinn a' Bhuird, Cnap a' Chleirich (sometimes dangerous) to Clach a' Chleirich, and the slopes of Ben Avon to Allt Phouple and Feith Laoigh.

From November to early February the days are so short and the weather so often stormy that ski tourers or hill walkers who head for the highest summits should leave early in the morning and be prepared for very severe weather. Beautiful weather can, however, come at any time in winter, with frost, blue skies and much calmer air than in summer; then you can feel too hot skiing in your shirt sleeves. At these times, ski touring from powdery white glens up through snow-laden pines to the highest ground shows the Cairngorms at their finest: waves of frozen hills stretching for many miles and great cliffs plastered white or creamy in thick ice, snow and hoar frost. In April and May the storms can be as bad as in December, but with long hours of daylight and usually more reliable weather, you often have days when it is like a scene in the high Arctic, with strong sun, deep blue skies, bright colours on thawed patches of vegetation, a beautifully uniform snow surface, and the odd ptarmigan croaking lustily on its chosen snowfree patch.

Unless you are to ski only on the lower hills, it is safer to use

Vibram-type soles on skiing-cum-climbing boots rather than down-hill ski boots or ski-touring boots with flat soles; these give a far better grip on steep slopes if you have to take your skis off. You should carry an ice axe and crampons on any route where even a small part of the tour lies on steep slopes or places that are often icy, such as climbing down into or up out of Lairig Ghru and Coire Dhondail. Try to avoid steep slopes in any case because of the risk of avalanches, a risk which is heightened when you have the skis on your feet.

Timing and difficulty are often much worse than in summer, but sometimes can be much easier; it all depends on the snow conditions you meet. There exist at least 40 recognisably different kinds of surface, varying from exhausting plodding in deep powdery or thawing snow, to hard ice. Which ones you meet, and the extent of them, will entirely govern how well and fast you can ski and thus how long you will take. Danger is always greater than in summer. During the winter, the risk of a fall on skis when you are moving much faster than walking speed is obviously far greater than a fall when walking on foot. This risk becomes heightened by the fact that the skis enable you to penetrate into country far from roads and houses and thus far from safety, in conditions when anyone plunging in on foot could never get half as far out. Forget, therefore, about fine skilled technique, and ski downhill not as if you are beside the thronged Coire Cas ski grounds, but as if you stand in the middle of the Greenland ice cap.

There is no point in listing here all the routes of ascent or descent on cross-country ski tours; most of the walking routes described later in the book are suitable, the only difference being that the skier on his descent should if possible include one of the better downhill runs mentioned above. One way of giving a brief sketch of the possibilities is to describe some of the more notable tours done in the area since 1945. Many have crossed Cairn Gorm and Ben Macdui from Spey to Dee and vice versa. Such cross-country tours from point A to point B are recommended, as it is finer to start in one valley and finish in another without going over the same ground twice. The next best alternative involves a return to your starting point, but on a different round tour all into new ground. Special precautions, how-ever, need to be taken for such tours right across or around a massif (p 44).

Fewer have come on skis over Cairn Toul and Braeriach from Spey to Dee or vice versa, though this makes one of the finest tours in the Cairngorms. Ben Avon and Beinn a' Bhuird have been crossed several times. The four highest tops of Cairn Toul, Braeriach, Cairn Gorm and Ben Macdui were traversed on skis in a day by N. D. Clark in January 1953 from Glen More back to Glen More, by the writer in April 1958 from Luibeg back to Luibeg, and in March 1972 by W. D. Brooker, D. Grieve and J. M. Taylor from the top of the Cairn Gorm chair lift to Glen Feshie. In April 1962 the six highest tops, including these plus Beinn a' Bhuird and Ben Avon, totalling 61 km or 38 miles, with 55 km on skis, were crossed in a long day without any hurrying from Allt Dourie at Invercauld to Derry Lodge (A. Watson, *SMCJ* 27, 348).

The Lairig Ghru can be a tough journey on skis as the snow there often lies very deep and powdery. However, after a long hard winter it can be much faster than in summer; in April 1951 the writer crossed in only four hours from Aviemore to Luibeg without any hurrying, on perfect hard-packed snow that covered every boulder, stream and hollow under a uniform, smooth sheet. The longest day tour from W to E in the region, for 48 km, started at Gaick Lodge and ended at the Derry, again in that exceptional April (A. Watson, *ECJ* 2, 186). The longest continuous tour so far recorded, lasting $4\frac{1}{2}$ days, was accomplished by M. and J. Slesser in March 1970; starting at Glen Clova, they crossed to Drumochter on a tough tour in bad weather and poor snow (*SMCJ* 29, 322). Many fine but shorter tours have been done elsewhere in the area, for instance from Drumochter to Gaick, the Cairnwell over to Inverey, Luibeg to Kingussie by Glen Feshie, Glen Clova to Lochnagar, and the Cairnwell to Lochnagar and Ballochbuie.

Most touring in the Cairngorms has been done with light wooden skis or with the heavier modern downhill skis whose bindings allow heel-lifting. An innovation a few years ago was a short, light, plastic ski, easy to carry uphill, and fast and easily turned on the descent. Though not giving the satisfaction that comes from touring on longer skis, these short skis are useful when snow cover is patchy.

Immediately after heavy falls of powder snow that have not been accompanied by gales to pack it down, even on skis you can sink in up to the calf or the knee, which is very tiring. Snow shoes then become the answer, allowing you to go on top of the snow. They are particularly handy for walking in the forests and lower glens after deep snow. On the high tops, they are useful when there is

39

deep powder but not a uniform-enough cover to make skiing easy. Traditional Canadian-type snow shoes and the new plastic ones have both been used successfully in the Cairngorms. The plastic ones withstand rough wear from granite boulders sticking through the snow better than does the gut of the traditional type, but you will find the old-time shoes better after deep snowfalls in the glens.

V. A. Firsoff 1965 *On Ski in the Cairngorms*. A lot of information on the developed ski grounds and especially on ski touring.

M. Slesser 1970 *Scottish Mountains on Ski*. Describes in detail some routes in the area covered by this District Guide.

W. D. Brooker 1972 The other side of the hill. *Aberdeen Ski CJ* 1972–73, 20. A good summary mainly on the Cairngorms, particularly useful for its detailed information on equipment.

Mountain safety

There are many basic lessons of common sense, good judgement and safety which every hill walker, climber and ski tourer should learn before venturing into any kind of mountainous or upland country anywhere. As these lessons have been described in detail in E. Langmuir's *Mountain Leadership*, in many other handbooks on technique, in the Police Mountain Codes, and in the Donald Duff exhibition on mountain safety, there is no need to mention them here. The point of this section is wholly to mention features which occur in the Cairngorms but which do not necessarily apply and often do not apply elsewhere. Most of these lessons stem from the special peculiarities or characteristics of the Cairngorms. So, paradoxically, the features which make these hills so special, attractive and enjoyable are the very same features which can in other circumstances make them a place where people easily become lost, injured, or can die.

One feature which the high Cairngorms share with Ben Nevis is that the tops rise higher than elsewhere in Scotland. This means more likelihood of mist, stronger gales, heavier falls of rain and snow, and colder temperatures than on lower hills. Often a drop of only 150 m or 500 ft from the summit at over 1200 m takes you into conditions that, though still stormy, become so dramatically better than where you have just been that it is like entering another world. The greater height of these 4000 footers (1200 m) and the huge tracts above 1100 m or 3500 ft also mean that you are more likely here to encounter a greater variety of snow or ice conditions on a single outing than on other hills. This means in turn a greater risk of meeting icy snow or deep powder on the higher ground, on days when all the lower hills below may be largely free of snow. You will find it not uncommon in mild winters to see little or no snow low down, and yet with the gentle slopes of the highest plateaux under snow so icy that crampons are the only safe way of progressing even on almost 'flat ground. There comes also a greater risk of being soaked in rain or sleet on the lower slopes (which dangerously reduces the insulation of clothing) and then later that day freezing higher up.

One of the area's main characteristics is the long distances to the higher hills and their cliffs, with consequent feelings of great space, complex country and fine remoteness. In most British hills, you are usually only a short distance from a road or a house, and so can usually get down to safety quickly by plunging downhill. In the Cairngorms you may be up to 16 km or 10 miles from an inhabited house or a road, separated from it by miles of plateaux and slopes that may involve travelling uphill as well as down. These great distances and the lack of shelter are reasons why bad weather is more dangerous here than in more dissected steeper hill country. Even in the lower but fairly unsheltered long open glens, winds with sleet or cold rain have killed some people with inadequate protective clothing, by wetting them to the skin and destroying the insulation of their clothing; this has happened even as early as September. Even once you are down off a higher hill into a glen, you usually have many miles to go along uninhabited glens, moors and lower hills before you reach a house or road.

Very few of these glens and lower hills support scrub or trees, so you cannot quickly warm up or dry out, as in the Rockies and many other mountain ranges, by dropping quickly to the tree line and then lighting a fire. Another feature is that the plateaux, slopes and glens are so smooth-sided and vast that you can seldom get quickly into good shelter behind a ridge, corrie or steep stream-side, as you can commonly do in the more dissected hills of western Scotland and most mountain ranges elsewhere.

Because of these vast smooth slopes, the wind has free play during storms, whirling the loose snow off huge areas of exposed open plateau or moor into a dense storm of drift within a few metres of ground level, even when no snow is actually falling. Equally, if you are in any slightly sheltered place on these plateaux or moors, the snow coming off square miles of ground will start to rest instead of continuing to blow above the ground. You can watch it visibly piling up at a fantastic rate, quickly covering your skis or your boots as you look. At the edges of steep slopes it also quickly builds bigger cornices than on most Highland hills, which form an extra risk. Another danger of the huge snow depths that pile up on steep slopes is the greater likelihood of avalanche.

For the same reason about the ground being so open, visibility tends to be worse than in most other hills during a storm. A characteristic of smooth slopes and wide plateaux is that they contain fewer landmarks. In the dissected western hills and the Alps you seldom travel far without coming to ridges or other obvious features. Visibility in a blizzard or thick mist is mainly a matter of having some object, even the odd stone, for the eye to latch on to. With a general snow cover and mist on the high plateaux of the Cairngorms, particularly bad 'white-outs' develop where you find it hard to know if you are going uphill or downhill. As soon as you reach bouldery ridges, even if snow largely covers them, the visibility and your speed and confidence rapidly improve.

One of the main dangers on the plateaux is the wind. These tops are often swept by gales and winds of hurricane force, especially in winter. The writer has often seen small gravel blowing in the wind and plants torn out by the roots, and the strongest man can be blown right over and thrown on the ground, or reduced to crawling on all fours. Of course this happens equally on other Scottish high hills, but in the Cairngorms the consequences are more vital as you may have to travel so much further to get safely out of that wind.

When a gale is accompanied by thick storms of ground drift, or worse, by heavy falling blizzards plus ground drift, or worse still by mist as well, conditions can be extremely serious on the plateaux, making it suffocating and difficult to breathe, hard to open your eyes, impossible to see anything beyond your own feet, and unable to communicate with your party except one at a time by cupping an ear and shouting into it. In these respects the blizzards of the Cairngorms can be as bad as anywhere in the world (see also 'Shelter', by P. D. Baird *CCJ* 17, 184). They can be severe not only on the high plateaux but also on the lower plateaux and moors which, in deep snow, are often even more lacking in landmarks than the high Cairngorms. For these reasons, to travel in parties bigger than three to four people must be unwise and more than five very foolish.

The important rule here is to learn to assess the weather throughout every day, even if you are just on a summer stroll, until the habit becomes second nature. There can be nothing ghoulish in doing this. An experienced hillman does it not remotely with possible death or injury in mind, but the better to understand and become part of his environment and so enjoy his days on the hill more. It is useful to learn the meaning of the radio or TV low-ground forecasts, to use them, to know how they relate to the weather at higher altitude in the Cairngorms, to telephone the RAF stations for local and more accurate forecasts, and to learn your own weather lore by reading and local experience. Also, a board at the top end of the car park at Coire Cas gives the latest local forecast of weather for the upper part of Cairn Gorm, including wind direction and speed. Unless you are in mist all day, you will see signs of bad weather coming hours before it actually hits you, and can take commonsense action accordingly. For instance, in the Cairngorms a rapid greying of the blue sky is a sign of impending bad weather, and a wide ring round the sun is a fairly sure sign of heavy rain or snow in the Highlands within 12 to 24 hours, though fortunately it often hits only the western hills and does not get through as far E as the Cairngorms. A sudden and sustained change of wind from S, SW or W to any other direction will quickly bring much colder air to the Cairngorms in winter, apart from a few rare exceptions that you should not rely on; within two hours, easy wet snow can turn into frozen icy sheets. There are many other useful tips about weather in the area, but of course most of these apply elsewhere in Scotland as well.

In a Cairngorms storm the most important aim should be to reach sheltered lower ground as quickly as you can. Above all, do not battle into a gale, especially a snow-laden gale. It exhausts, numbs the mind, and can easily kill. In any case, there is here a simple practical point. Given a storm or hurricane on the plateau, which is not an uncommon event in winter, the strongest and fittest man may be unable to walk even a single metre into the wind, just because of its force. The best plan should therefore be to get the wind flat on your back or at least at one side of your back, and use it to help you along. Even though buffeted uncomfortably, you will travel fast, breathe far more easily, see better, and soon be taking an escape route off the hill. There are always a number of options and escape routes from any place in the Cairngorms. The best one will be different on different occasions; it all depends on wind direction and various other conditions of the moment. The important thing is not to be influenced by having arranged to be back at some scheduled place or time because you have booked a youth hostel or train ticket, a mistake that has led to a few deaths in the area.

One feature which the Cairngorms share with oceanic hills and subarctic hills near coasts is the big fall in temperature with increasing altitude, which becomes far greater than in continental mountains. Especially in April to May, it may be a pleasant sunny breezy day at Loch Morlich, warm enough to bask or sleep in the sun. At 1200 m or 4000 ft, out of the 'rain shadow' in the wide valley below, it can be a roaring gale, snowstorm and dense fog, 9°C (15°F) colder or worse.

To assess snow conditions underfoot is not easy. The penalties for failure are worse in the Cairngorms than elsewhere in Scotland. Many have become exhausted by ploughing to the knees or even to the waist in powdery snow, while carrying heavy packs. Here again the long distances and the flat or uphill stretches of these hills tell heavily; on steep slopes you can soon plunge downhill even in deep snow. Few things are more tiring than floundering for miles in deep snow; the speed of the strongest man on flat ground can be reduced to only $1\frac{1}{2}$ km or about 1 mile in one hour, even with skis on, and without skis can be so dreadfully slow and exhausting that any long journey becomes impossible.

Cross-country routes in snow, starting on Spey and going right over the hills to finish on Dee, or vice versa, or crossing the higher parts of the Mounth, are the most dangerous walking routes in the Cairngorms region. Elsewhere, and on any individual hill in the Cairngorms, all you usually have to do if bad weather hits you is turn and walk quickly down the way you came up. But on cross-country treks you are always heading into new conditions which may as easily get worse as better, and your route to safety may well involve having to climb uphill on ground not yet seen. You cannot assess this by looking from your morning base; after snowfalls there will often be light hard-packed snow on one side of the Cairngorms but deep heavy powder on the other side. This is something you cannot see until you get to the other side, by which time you may be in trouble. An early start in winter should be common sense on a long trek; it is crucial to be off the exposed plateaux and the steep hillsides below them by mid afternoon and at the very least well down a sheltered lower glen by dusk. In bad weather you should aim to be at your bothy, car or on a good road while daylight lasts.

For rock and ice climbers the dangers are far greater than in other British hills. If a climber has an accident, he will have a very long wait for help as it is so far for a fit member of the party to go to the nearest house or telephone. If you start a hard climb late in the day and finish in fading light or darkness, you take a big risk as the weather may have become much worse during the climb. Once you are off the cliff and on to the plateau, tired and perhaps relaxing mentally at getting safely off the climb, you may have to fight a storm in the dark. Here the early start and sensible anticipation of weather become imperative.

Another special feature of the Cairngorms is that the hill burns roar down in dangerous flood during heat waves at the end of a long wintry spell. Then, the vast accumulation of snow on the plateaux and corries melts rapidly and funnels into narrow burns. High streams that are gentle, shallow and meandering during the rest of the year – or even earlier that day in the morning's hard frost – turn into deep, fast, roaring torrents. The snow bridges over these streams become rotten and dangerous, needing careful testing. You should avoid the snow-covered ice over the high tarns in early summer; be particularly careful here, as you can often walk on to one of these tarns without realising it exists, so uniform is the cover of rotting spring snow.

The fact that many streams in the area funnel into narrow glens draining vast areas of plateau higher up adds another danger in summer and autumn. After torrential downpours, huge quantities of rain over the great plateaux concentrate into tiny burns, which rise in spate more quickly than most burns in other parts of Scotland. Good examples are the Gaick burns, Tarf, Eidart, Caiplich, Allt an Dubb Ghlinne, Mark and Lee.

There has been much talk of improving hill safety by erecting lines of cairns over the plateaux of the Cairngorms (for a rebuttal, see B. H. Humble, SMCJ 28, 286), by building strings of huts over the plateaux with flashing lights and sounding devices, and by issuing radios and full survival gear to parties. If accepted, these and other such innovations may well make inexperienced people who would not otherwise climb the more remote hills, take the risk of venturing far out. They might well go with a feeling of security that would be false and could be fatal. It would then take only one human error or technical failure for an irreversible chain of serious troubles to set in. The Feith Buidhe disaster in 1971 is a type case. No doubt the

Cairngorms could be made much safer for inexperienced folk, but only by destroying the beauty and wild appeal of these hills. No rural place can be completely safe; some have died during blizzards even on lowland Aberdeenshire farmland beside public roads. People can continue to enjoy the special character of the Cairngorms, in reasonable safety, providing they are made safe for the hills.

H. R. Spencer 1961 Storm on Macdhui. *CCJ* 17, 214. Describes a summer day when it stayed very hot and sunny on low ground but when a storm came very rapidly to the high plateau, with dense mist, torrential rain and violent gales. These demoralised and put in danger a party which wandered lost and was lucky to get off the hill safely.

G. Tiso 1968 First footin'. A New Year avalanche. *SMCJ* 29, 34. A graphic personal account of a serious avalanche accident at Loch Avon.

E. Langmuir 1969 *Mountain Leadership*. This gives a good detailed summary of the problems of safety in the Scottish hills.

A. Watson & J. Duff 1973 Lessons to youth parties from the Feith Buidhe disaster. *Climber & Rambler* 12, 282.

Accidents and mountain rescue by *John E. M. Duff*, BEM

Accidents. The first recorded mountain accident was the 'Loss of Gaick' in early January 1800, when Captain John MacPherson of Ballachroan ('The Black Officer') and four others were overwhelmed in bed in a hut near Gaick Lodge by a snow avalanche. All died. A selection of other noteworthy accidents is given below.

Xmas 1804. Five soldiers out of a party of seven died of exposure in the Lairig an Laoigh in a snowstorm, while walking from Edinburgh to their homes in Abernethy for Christmas leave.

January 1928. Thomas Baird and Hugh Barrie died of exposure in Gleann Einich after being overtaken on Braeriach by a snowstorm. January 1933. Alistair Mackenzie and Duncan Ferrier died of exposure on Cairn Gorm in a storm.

February 1940. While glissading on Lochnagar, Miss Ray Fyfe lost her ice-axe and slid about 120 m. Her companion failed to find her, and rescuers did not discover her till $23\frac{1}{2}$ hours later. Although badly gashed and bruised, she was still conscious in spite of very cold weather and snow during the night, and was able to walk off the hill with assistance.

September 1940. Henry Ogilvy and Lucy Robson were both killed while climbing on Sgoran Dubh. A search party found the bodies still roped together at the foot of the cliffs.

January 1948. Six climbers were avalanched on Sgor Mor of Glen Clunie and four suffered multiple injuries.

September 1950. James Mackay drowned while crossing the water of Dee in spate at Corrour. One of his companions, William Pinkerton, died of exposure later that day near the Pools of Dee.

March 1951. Donald McConnach was killed when he walked over a cornice on Beinn a' Bhuird in a 'white-out'.

April 1952. John Harvey, David Stead and Margot Weaving were avalanched in Coire an Lochain near the top of a climb, Harvey and Stead being killed and Weaving suffering a compound leg fracture.

January 1959. Five men who had set out from Braemar to Glen Doll by Jock's Road on New Year's Day died of exposure in a snow-storm.

April 1960. Nigel Milne and Jean McBain became overtaken by a sudden snowstorm on Cairn Gorm and died of exposure. One body was found near the Lairig an Laoigh path and the other near the Castle rock on the Ailnack.

May 1960. Dr Fischer, an elderly South African, set off from the Linn of Dee to walk to Kingussie by Geldie and Feshie. He was not reported missing till July, and his body has never been found.

March 1962. William Garland became lost while skiing on Cairn Gorm in bad weather. Two nights and almost three days later he was found alive near Loch Avon, although meanwhile the weather had been cold with a N wind and bad visibility. On one of the days he had climbed uphill but slipped and then rolled and fell a long way without injuring himself. After being found and having been given hot drinks, he was able to climb up Coire Raibeirt in deep snow without help.

April 1962. Oliver Roughton, who was a teenage member of a school party, died of exposure on Ben Macdui.

December 1964. Alexander Mackenzie, Alexander MacLeod and Robert Burnett were buried by a wet snow avalanche on Beinn a'

Bhuird, Mackenzie and MacLeod being killed. Burnett was dug out, still conscious but badly frostbitten, after 22 hours.

March 1965. Robert Clark was struck by a falling cornice while climbing in the Black Spout of Lochnagar, and died just after the rescue party reached an ambulance at Balmoral.

April 1965. Stewart Turnell and Kenneth Macdonald, who were teenage members of a party of Army Cadets, died of exposure in Glen Derry after the group had been overtaken by bad weather on Beinn a' Bhuird. Several other members of the party were near to death when found, but recovered.

July 1967. John Birss fell on Braeriach and suffered a compound fracture of the leg. He improvised a makeshift splint and crawled for 12 hours to the Lairig Ghru, where he was found next day, 18 hours after the accident.

February 1969. John Dempster and James Wallace died of exposure on Lochnagar after trying to complete a climb on Eagle Buttress at night in a snowstorm.

February 1969. A large avalanche in Coire Cas carried down a party of nine. Some were seriously injured, but none died.

May 1970. Janie Cameron was drowned while trying to cross Eidart Water in spate.

August 1971. David Driffield survived in perfect weather for nine days and nights without any supplies, in the Gleann Einich-Sgoran Dubh area, after becoming separated from a youth party.

November 1971. Five teenage schoolchildren and an 18 year old trainee instructress died of exposure at an emergency bivouac in a blizzard 500 paces E of Lochan Buidhe on the Cairn Gorm-Ben Macdui plateau. A 15 year old schoolboy and a 20 year old instructress survived, although both were badly exposed and frost bitten.

Although the Cairngorms have their share of rock climbing and snow and ice climbing accidents, the word 'exposure' crops up again and again, especially with young people; in fact, 22 out of 48 deaths between 1950 and 1972 occurred from exposure. Very often this kind of accident starts off when a party leaves base with insufficient or inadequate clothing, subsequently is overtaken by bad weather (not necessarily snow) and gets lost because of inefficient navigation. This leads to the classic exposure syndrome of demoralisation, ex-

Table of incidents for the 10-year period 1963 to 1973 in the area covered by this Guide

		1963	1964	1965	1966	1967	1968	1969	1970	1971	1972	10-year total	% of total
Number of deaths	Exposure	0	0	3	0	1	0	2	0	6	1	13	42%
	Accidental injury*	0	1	1	1	2	0	0	2	3	1	11	36%
	Other causes*	0	2a	0	0	0	0	1n	3n, d, c	0	1n	7	23%
	Total	0	3	4	1	3	0	3	5	9	3	31	100%
Number of incidents	Exposure	0	1	4	4	4	2	0	1	2	3	21	11%
	Accidental injury including frostbite	2	7	4	5	6	8	6	2	7	9	56	30%
	People missing or overdue	8	10	9	6	9	14	6	9	9	14	94	51%
	Total including other causes	12	18	17	15	21	24	16	15	20	28	186	100%
Number of false alarms		1	1	3	3	1	2	2	2	5	3	23	12%

* a avalanche, d drowning, n natural causes, c aircraft crash

NOTE: An incident is taken to mean an occurrence in mountainous terrain where all or part of a rescue team left base to deal with it. The statistics have been compiled from material provided by the Chief Constables concerned. As comprehensive records were lacking before 1969, some minor incidents in the earlier years may have been overlooked.

haustion and hypothermia, which can kill very rapidly, and especially quickly with children or young people.

The decision to modify a route or to turn back, although often difficult, is of crucial importance. The writer has information on 37 exposure deaths since the year 1800 in the Cairngorms area. Of these, 28, or almost 76%, are attributable to the party failing to turn back when they met bad weather, because they were determined to stick to a previously planned route.

Long trips can be dangerous, especially in winter conditions. This is partly because the heavy load necessary for such an undertaking becomes so tiring. Also, people outside may not realise that a party has landed in difficulties until it is overdue at the end of the trip, after perhaps several days have already passed. Aberdeenshire Education Authority wisely impose the following restraint on leaders of parties using their Centres for Outdoor Activities: 'No party including young people of under eighteen years of age will undertake in winter conditions any cross country expedition involving an overnight bivouac or a traverse of a mountain range, e.g. from Deeside to Speyside or Angus'.

Avalanches are more common than has generally been supposed. There is some evidence to suggest that airborne avalanches occasionally occur, for example on the steep slopes on the N side of Loch Muick, where a reliable observer has reported extremely fast-moving avalanches. After the Loss of Gaick in 1800, contemporary accounts relate that the bodies of the victims were found mangled and widely scattered, and some of the debris of the hut lay 500 yards away, again suggesting something much more destructive than the usually fairly slow-moving ground avalanche; indeed so terrible was the destruction that local people believed it to have been the work of the Devil. Cornices feature quite often in accidents, and many gully-climbing parties in thaw conditions have become avalanched by a collapsing cornice. Some gullies such as Raeburn's Gully on Lochnagar have been the scene of several accidents like this. Several people have died or injured themselves by walking over cornices, usually in bad visibility. Slopes of hard snow are especially inviting and dangerous to the inexperienced, and many serious injuries have occurred when individuals lost control while glissading and were dashed headlong into boulder fields below.

In addition to the fairly straightforward if perhaps technically difficult rescues such as known accidents on cliffs, the vast area of

the Cairngorms occasionally gives rise to extremely large and prolonged searches for people who have completely disappeared. Some
of these last for months and at their peak they involve hundreds of
searchers. Notable examples are: Hugh Barrie in 1928 – 3 months;
the Glen Doll tragedy in 1959 – 10 weeks; Nigel Milne and Jean
MacBain in 1960 – 8 weeks; Dr Fischer in 1960 – many weeks, not
found; Brian Goring in 1967 – 8 weeks.

Occasionally, bodies have been found but never identified. The
most bizarre of these incidents occurred on the S face of Ben Avon
on Tuesday 20 September 1938. A stalker on the beat which includes
the remote Allt an Eas Mhoir was searching for a wounded stag,
when in the stream he found a badly decomposed human head. A
short distance upstream lay the remains of a man, dressed in what
appeared to have been a dark suit with a light check. On the bank a
plain walking-stick was found, and then a brown leather attaché case
containing a pair of pyjama trousers, two collars, a toilet roll, a pair of
scissors, a box of safety matches and a handbill referring to Simpson's
Two-Day Tours. On a ledge of rock sat a razor, shaving brush, soap,
comb, toothpaste and toothbrush, with a bowler hat nearby. It was
estimated that the man had been dead for at least six months. No
clue to his identity could be found apart from the fact that the two
collars bore the name of an Aberdeen firm. Despite intensive police
enquiries, the man's identity has never been established.

Mountain rescue. The Police are responsible for mountain rescue,
and Chief Constables bear the responsibility for their own areas.
The four constabularies in the region covered by this Guide are
Angus, Inverness, Perth and Kinross, and Scottish North-Eastern
Counties. The five civilian teams in the area are usually called out
by the Police, with whom they work closely, and have their bases
at Aberdeen, Aviemore, Braemar, Glenmore Lodge and Gordon-
stoun School. The two RAF teams, based at Kinloss and Leuchars,
carry a prime responsibility towards Services aircraft, but are always
made available for civilian rescues and play a big part in mountain
searches and rescues over the whole of Scotland.

MOUNTAIN RESCUE POSTS IN THE AREA

Place	*Telephone*	*Supervisor*
Aviemore Police Station	Aviemore 222 or 380	Officer in Charge
Ballater Police Station	Ballater 222 or 348	Officer in Charge
Braemar Police Station	Braemar 222	Officer in Charge

Place	Telephone	Supervisor
Derry Lodge (Nature Conservancy Hut)		Mr. D. Rose (phone Braemar 678)
Dundee Central Police Office, Bell Street, (Mobile Kit)	Dundee 23200	Officer in Charge
Glendoll Lodge		The Warden
Glenmore Lodge	Cairngorm 256	The Principal
Gordonstoun School, Elgin	Hopeman 445	Mr. J. Rawlings
Spittal of Glenmuick, Ballater	Ballater 530	Mr. J. Robertson
White Lady Shieling, Cairngorm	Cairngorm 230	The Principal Glenmore Lodge

NOTE: There is a first-aid box on Lochnagar at 253856, on top of the mound rising from the SE corner of the Loch towards the main left-hand wall of cliff.

The equipment at these posts is maintained by the Scottish Home and Health Department through the Mountain Rescue Committee of Scotland. Each post holds a mountain stretcher and two rucksacks which contain medical supplies including morphine. At some posts extra equipment has been provided, depending on local needs. The Mountain Rescue Committee issues a national handbook that gives details of all Rescue Posts and Teams, and includes advice on Mountain Safety and First Aid. This inexpensive booklet is available on request from the Secretary of the Committee.

If an accident occurs, the quickest way of starting a rescue is usually to go either to the nearest Rescue Post or to the nearest telephone, and dial '999'. Very few climbing and walking parties have either the numbers or experience necessary to carry out an efficient rescue by themselves. Almost invariably it will be best to call in the local rescue organisation, which has the manpower, the equipment and a full knowledge of local medical services and evacuation techniques. If an injured person must of necessity be left alone while you summon help, it is vitally important before leaving to write down a six-figure map reference of his location for the information of the rescue team, and to mark his position well, for instance by a rope spread out over boulders or by some other means. The casualty should also be left with a torch or whistle to attract attention, otherwise the rescue party may well have difficulty in finding him; indeed in winter he may become covered by drifting snow.

After an accident the Mountain Rescue Committee of Scotland requests that the party involved should send an accurate summary of what happened to the Accident Statistician, who prepares an

INTRODUCTION

annual analysis of all mountain accidents. If you do not know his address, the local Police will have up to date information. No charge is made for rescue services, but local teams have to find the bulk of their own finance and contributions will invariably be welcome, as the annual expenditure of a rescue team may quite easily average out in excess of £100 per call-out (1972). Donations should generally be in cash to the team, not gifts to individual team members.

The mountain rescue service should not be confused with the ski rescue services which work during the winter and spring at Cairnwell and Cairngorm, usually only on the heavily used piste areas.

Weather

The prevailing wind is SW, bringing moist and usually mild air from the Atlantic. As the Cairngorms lie far to the E, they get half or less of the precipitation received by hills just in from the mainland's Atlantic seaboard. The average precipitation on the lower ground in Deeside and the Spey Valley reaches only 75 to 87 cm or 30 to 35 inches, hardly any more than on the E coast at Aberdeen. These wide main valleys lie in a 'rain shadow' and often bask in sunshine when it is raining and cloudy on the hills on either side, but the narrower valleys like Glen Esk get little of a 'rain shadow'. On the tops of the high Cairngorms, the total precipitation becomes much heavier, roughly 225 cm or 90 inches a year according to a recent figure based on readings from the weather station on Cairn Gorm.

The Cairngorms stand exposed to winds from N around to SE, which are the main snow-bearing cold winds in Scotland. This is the reason why coastal Aberdeenshire gets far more snow and frost than Skye, and also why the Cairngorms in most years become the snowiest hills in Scotland. As they lie in the centre of Scotland their climate tends to be more 'continental', with warmer summers and colder winters than on the coasts round about. This again means more frost and snow in winter, which makes the Cairngorms so attractive for snow and ice climbing and for skiing. You can see this continental effect even very locally as you move in from the E coast. Even with snowfalls coming from the E, the snow line drops lower in altitude as you go inland; the decrease is particularly rapid from E to W along the Hill of Fare and on the hills between Cairn Mon Earn and Glen Dye. You will see the same effect as you go inland up Glen Esk or in the Moray hills.

In the bottoms of deep basins the dense colder air flows downwards on very still nights, producing much harder frosts than on the hill-tops. These 'frost pockets' often feature in the news because of their low temperatures, and the area covered by this book has most of Britain's frostiest places: Glen Livet, Grantown, Glenmore Lodge, Dalwhinnie, Braemar, Glen Shee, Tarfside, Balmoral and Strachan. Early-morning winter temperatures below −18°C or 0°F are not uncommon there, and temperatures of −29°C or −20°F have been recorded. You will frequently hear the snow squeak under your boots or feel your hands sticking slightly to metal; both happen below −5°C. During windless sunny days in winter, the cold air stays in the valley bottoms, sometimes producing a frosty fog, while up on the tops it feels much warmer. If you see deer right up on the high ridges in deep snow, this is a good sign of these special conditions.

Usually, however, it becomes much colder as you climb; this is virtually always the case if any wind blows, even with a light wind. P. D. Baird's observations from 4120 ft or 1250 m on Ben Macdui, 900 m above Braemar, showed average temperatures that usually sank about 12°F (7°C) lower, or 4°F (2·2°C) per 1000 ft (300 m) of altitude. In any one month, however, especially in April–June, they could be 15°F lower. The hills are far windier than lower down, and Baird found that wind speeds on Ben Macdui were usually double and sometimes treble those in the valley. Weather instruments since they were put up near the Ptarmigan Restaurant on Cairn Gorm have proved this to be one of the most windy places in the British records, along with some exposed places on coastal islands. The top gust recorded in Britain – 125 knots – occurred here on 6 March 1967.

The weather varies a great deal locally. During spring and early summer, and sometimes at other seasons, it may be fairly calm in the valley and yet with a very strong, dry, warm, Föhn-like wind blowing down the lee slopes of the moors and higher hills. Subsidences of dry air on to the summits during anticyclones, and cold winds that are katabatic (due to convection when air drops in altitude as it flows down hillsides) sometimes produce locally violent winds on fine sunny days. Exceptionally these reach hurricane force and may cause a blizzard of ground drift, when there is virtually a calm day only 2 km away on ground only 100 m in altitude lower down. These severe conditions sometimes occur even in the glens, and can arise suddenly and with little or no warning.

The likelihood of snow increases rapidly as you climb. The average number of days per year with snow falling amounts to about 10 at Dartmoor, 20 in Skye, 50 near Aviemore and about 100 at the top of the chair lift on Cairn Gorm. The average number of mornings with snow lying also increases as you go up, 20 in Skye, 30 near Aberdeen, 60 at Braemar, 100 at 460 m or 1500 ft at the Derry, and over 150 above 600 m at the Derry. Like other Scottish hills, the Cairngorms can have tremendous thaws in winter with warm Atlantic winds, but less than in the far west. In summer you are more likely to get snowfalls here than on any other British range. Snowfalls occur during most years in June and September, during some years in July, and rarely in August; these may involve heavy falls of a foot or more, usually with drifting and frost. In May, blizzards can be frequent and very severe. In some years the maximum snow depth above 1100 m or 3500 ft occurs in mid or late May, but in most years in April. With May storms the glens and lower hills below 600 m or 2000 ft usually stay clear, but occasionally, as in 1973, the glens receive a fall of 30 cm or one foot, with drifting. In 1971 a June snowfall lasted a week on the high Cairngorms.

Much precipitation on the higher hills comes in mist, which condenses on to stones, cliffs, or the existing snow surface as frozen rime. This builds into fantastic frost feathers, and in long snowy winters into a plating several feet thick. Mist or hill fog also become far more frequent as you climb, but these hills are much less misty than at the same altitude in western Scotland.

In the Cairngorms region you can often use weather information and local experience of it to your advantage. When a wind is dumping heavy rain on Drumochter or Cairn Toul, bright sun often shines on Beinn a' Bhuird, Ben Avon and Mount Keen. These changes can be very local; for instance, when heavy rain and mist from the SW enshrouds the Cairnwell, you may enjoy bright sun as near as at Morven. But the east is not always best. The heavy low mists and sweeping rain or snow over lower Deeside and Lochnagar, with winds from NE to SE, will often give you beautiful weather in the upper Spey and Glen Feshie, or even at Derry Lodge. In summer anticyclones, prepare for the weather becoming far hotter than at the coastal strip which may even be enshrouded in cold fog; shade temperatures of 27°C or 80°F are not uncommon. Because of these higher temperatures, thunderstorms occur more frequently in such weather than nearer the E coast.

The importance of weather for mountain safety is described under that heading. The frequent and rapid worsening of weather, as well as being a risk to the incompetent or unobservant, form part of the ever-varying character of our hills that is one of their great attractions. Also, the weather can change equally as fast for the better and indeed faster if you are already in the cloud and cannot see the change coming. If you stand in cloud or snowstorm which suddenly clears up to show blue sky and sun and unearthly bright colours on vegetation and stones, it is far more exciting than any day of blue sky from morning to night.

P. D. Baird 1967 Weather and snow on Ben Macdhui. *CCJ* 17, 147. A brief but fascinating account of his observations at a weather station near the top of Ben Macdui.

One chapter in E. Langmuir's *Mountain Leadership* makes a good summary of meteorology and weather for the hillman anywhere in Britain, including topics such as understanding forecasts, lightning, etc. A fairly detailed account on the particular climate of the Cairngorms is contained in a chapter by F. H. W. Green, in *The Cairngorms* by D. Nethersole-Thompson & A. Watson (1974).

Geology

The main rock of these hills, as indeed of a vast area to the W and NW, is schist; it covers nearly all the Morayshire hills, and with only a few interruptions much of the Strath Don hills and the great block of hill country on the Mounth from Drumochter to Glen Esk. Once having been sediments of limestones, sandstones and shales lying on the gneiss underneath, they became metamorphosed or greatly changed by heat and pressure when great movements of the earth 500 million years ago folded them into huge schist mountains. Vast masses of granite formed either from molten rock coming up from far below or from melting of the bottom of the hot folds themselves. These granites make up the high Cairngorms massif, Lochnagar and Broad Cairn, the Mounth from Mount Keen to Cairn Mon Earn, a big mass at the Hill of Fare and Bennachie, and smaller patches at Geallaig, Ben Rinnes and other hills.

Millions of years later, weather and water wore down these huge peaks to their foundations, more sediments were laid down in layers, and in turn erosion wore these down selectively. The result that you now see is a mere remnant, composed of much of the schist foundation of the folded mountain range plus the masses of once-molten granite that are included in the foundation. Less commonly you also see some smaller intrusions of other rock, that have been emplaced

1. Climbing the 'crack for thin fingers' of The Needle, on the magnificent Sticil crag.

2.   W. March on the first ascent of Window Gully, Creag an Leth-choin.

3. Beside the top of Aladdin's Couloir, Coire an t-Sneachda.

4. Ski touring along the Bad Chrasgaigh between Cromar and Don, with Morven behind.

5.   On Cairn Lochan, at the edge of Coire an Lochain.

6 and 7.   Two famous Cairngorms characters. Bob Scott with 'Punchie' in Glen Luibeg, ready to sledge down to Inverey, and Tom Patey at Luibeg bothy.

8. Ruthven Barracks near Kingussie.

9. Lochan Deo of Rothiemurchus, beside the Gleann Einich gate, looking up to Carn Eilrig (right), the snow-splashed Creag an Leth-choin, and Cairn Gorm (far left).

10. Southwards from Loch Pityoulish to Cairn Lochan (left), the 'V' of Lairig Ghru, Braeriach with the conical Carn Eilrig below it, and Gleann Einich to the right.

11. Looking down the Coire Cas ski tow in May.

12. Loch Avon from the plateau edge at the top of the Feith Buidhe waterfall.

13. The Shelter Stone from its E end, looking W to Hell's Lum Crag.

into the granite and schist. Some of the intrusions, earlier than the granites, have been metamorphosed to form epidiorite, whereas others which were later than the granites form narrow 'dykes' and 'sheets'. The metamorphic rocks make up fairly continuous narrow bands, such as those formed by the limestone and epidiorite stretching from Blair Atholl past Ballater to Portsoy. The later sedimentary cover has remnants which you can now see in the sandstones of the Hopeman and Pennan sea cliffs and the conglomerates of Fowlsheugh.

The geologist is like a detective. He goes to the few places on cliffs, lumps or slabs where the bedrock outcrops on the surface. He then classifies this bedrock by its crystal size, gross appearance and chemical composition. He cannot see most of the bedrock, so has to infer what probably lies under the ground between one cliff or rock outcrop and another. By comparing with many places elsewhere in the world where the layering and the folds can be seen more clearly, he reconstructs the layering and folding that probably went on here. He has to think in terms of three dimensions of rock, based on scattered outcrops on the two-dimensional surface. It is easier to grasp the geological story if you can try to visualise the Cairngorms in three dimensions too, when you come to look at a geological map or read a detailed article or book on the geology.

The massif of the high Cairngorms is a very large foundation mass of granite, which accounts for the infertility of that hill range. The Lochnagar granite consists of a much smaller circular lump, surrounded by rings of schist and some diorite; this makes it a more fertile massif for vegetation and animals than the Cairngorms. Other big masses of granite occur from Mount Keen to Cairn Mon Earn and from Aberdeen through the Hill of Fare to Dinnet and Bennachie. Geologists classify the schists into two kinds. The Moinian or Central Highland granulites were sandstones which have been metamorphosed by heat and pressure into a fairly uniformly-coloured, layered rock with even-sized grains; it covers the Morayshire and Drumochter-Atholl hills. The Dalradian schists further E are far more varied and have given rise to the fertile black and calcareous schists, and the sparkling mica schists.

The local rock greatly affects the appearance and scenery of an area. Granite weathers fairly uniformly as it varies little in its make-up and hardness; one result is the even weathering and typically massive, smoothed slopes so characteristic of the Cairngorms. The scenery in

Glen Clova and just E of Braemar, with its more variable schists, diorites and gneisses, looks quite different and more 'western', showing many rocky bluffs as well as a more grassy vegetation. The schists, diorites and gneisses form cliffs with many small, stable holds for climbing, whereas the granite tends to wear uniformly into smooth slabs and faces where the few holds are rounded. Climbing on granite is therefore partly a matter of guile where you use any kind of friction to work up chimneys, cracks and slabs, whereas on the schist it involves delicate footwork on the many small holds and a greater choice from the many face routes available. On the coastal cliffs, the contrast appears again with the granite of Longhaven and the small holds on the Dalradian schists E of Macduff. Granite is not always uniform in a corrie, however, as it does not wear uniformly beside fractures and joints. You will find a good place to see this variable weathering and rock appearance near the Mitre Ridge in the Garbh Choire of Beinn a' Bhuird. Some of the granite there looks pale, worn, smooth and sandy-looking, from top to bottom of the cliff. Nearby, masses of darker, harder rock with many cracks also continue from top to bottom of the cliff, and project outwards from the plateau at the Mitre Ridge and Squareface.

The hill Cairn Gorm has given us the name of the smoky quartz crystals which occur there and on many other granite mountains. These 'cairngorms' are usually brown, but blue varieties exist. In the 19th century, many made a living by searching for these gems in the gravel in the streams of the Cairngorms, or breaking up veins of white quartz on the open hill with hammers. In recent years the bulldozers at Coire Cas have dug up a few fine specimens, but the veins on the open hill are largely worked out, and the big trade in 'cairngorms' for Scottish jewellery now depends a lot on stones imported from Brazil. One of the biggest-ever 'cairngorms' is the 5 lb one at Invercauld House. You can read interesting articles on stones in No. 2 of *The Deeside Field* in 1925 by A. W. Gibb on 'Cairngorms and other local gemstones', and W. M. Alexander's 'The stones of our district' in *CCJ* 12.

G. S. Johnstone 1966 *British Regional Geology: the Grampian Highlands.* 3rd ed. The best summary for those with a little knowledge of geology. Summarises previous literature. 1974 The Geology of the Cairngorms. In *The Cairngorms*, by D. Nethersole-Thompson & A. Watson. A chapter on the geology of the Cairngorms,

Lochnagar and much of the Mounth, fairly detailed but technical terms are simply explained in the text.

The detailed Geological Survey Memoirs on this region were published from 1896 to the 1910s, and you can see them in the bigger libraries. They are: The Geology of Upper Strathspey, Gaick and the Forest of Atholl (explains sheet 64 of the geological map), The Geology of the Districts of Braemar, Ballater and Glen Clova (sheet 65), The Geology of Mid Strathspey and Strathdearn (sheet 74), and The Geology of West Aberdeenshire, Banffshire, etc (sheet 75).

Landforms
One of the characteristics of the region is the vast areas of plateau. The highest level just below 1200 m includes all the grand high plateaux of the Cairngorms massif, but the lower plateaux around 800–900 m at Drumochter, Gaick, E of the Glas Maol, and Clova-Glen Esk, and at 600–750 m at Caiplich, NW of Tarfside, the Ladder Hills, and Cromdale Hills are far more extensive. Before the Ice Age, rivers had cut into these plateaux, producing many smooth steep valleys like upper Glen Gairn. Apart from Spey and Deveron which run NE along similar lines in the underlying rocks, the main rivers cut across the lines of the rocks, going SE off the Angus hills and E at Dee and Don. The Cairngorms are the best place in Britain for seeing a great variety of tors. These tors and the many patches of deeply rotted rock at the surface are thought to have developed in a warmer and wetter climate than today.

The glaciers later cut into the gentle rolling hills and valleys, producing many steep, rocky hillsides and great cliffed trenches as at Loch Avon, Gleann Einich, upper Glen Clova, Caenlochan and Glen Geusachan. Other ice-cut trenches broke right through a hill mass, as at the Lairig Ghru and at Gaick-Sronphadruig, and several others diverted rivers like Avon, Feshie and Tarf to flow in completely new directions and add to a different river system in a different county. The ice wore over many lower hills, which became eroded rocky lumps with ice-smoothed sheets of rock on the side next to the oncoming ice; Craigendarroch and the tiny hills S of the Burn o' Vat are good examples of these 'roches moutonnées'. The great ice sheet, which probably covered the highest summits, generally moved eastwards, a fact confirmed by the finding of 'erratic' boulders of rock originating from bedrock far to the SW. Meanwhile, small corrie glaciers went on cutting and formed the grand corries and corrie cliffs that we see today.

Many of the landforms which now make the scenery so varied were formed by rivers flowing beneath and roaring off the huge melting ice sheet as it began to retreat and thin with the milder climate. These rivers cut the dry cliffed gullies so common in the region; many are small, like the one between Clachnaben and Mount Shade, or even smaller, but some are big, such as Clais Fhearnaig, the Burn o' Vat, and several between Lairig Ghru and the Eag Mhor of Dorback. Other rivers dumped great masses of gravelly ridges and hillocks along the sides of the wasting lumps of ice. A smaller number of gravelly ridges were once moraines dumped by the ice itself, sometimes forming a low wall across a glen as at the Derry Dam and Glen Callater.

After the ice sheet disappeared 10000 years ago, a few corrie glaciers continued to form moraines. In the early 1960s D. Sugden tried to date these moraines in the corrie floors by measuring the diameter – and by assumption the growth rate – of patches of the common yellowish-green lichen, *Rhizocarpon geographicum*, on the boulders. (Geomorphologists have used the growth of this lichen in the Arctic and in the Alps to estimate when the stones were last free of ice.) From this evidence Sugden concluded that the moraine in Garbh Choire Mor of Braeriach may have held glacier ice as recently as 1810. His evidence also suggested that seven other corries probably held corrie glaciers up to about 1740: Coire an Lochain and Coire an t-Sneachda of Cairn Gorm, Coire an Lochain and Coire Bhrochain of Braeriach, Coire an t-Saighdeir of Cairn Toul, Coire an Lochain Uaine of Ben Macdui, and of course Garbh Choire Mor whose presumed '1740' moraine lies 1 km further downhill than its presumed '1810' moraine. The hill walker should look at these corries to see if he can find these moraine ridges of boulders. These conclusions, of course, involve partly speculative assumptions about the growth rate of the lichen here as compared with other countries with different climates; nevertheless, they are of great interest to anyone who knows the Cairngorms.

These dates of presumed recent glaciation tally with known advances of the glaciers in Scandinavia and Iceland, and with known periods of worse climate, hard winters, poor harvests and sometimes famines in Scotland itself. Travellers in the Cairngorms at these times gave the impression of seeing large snow fields or snow-capped hills in summer, terms we would scarcely use today. However, in a few summers today, when the snow does lie very extensively, as in 1951, or in 1967 when scores of small patches survived through to the next winter, one can easily see how near the Cairngorms are to having permanent snow caps or glaciers. Probably a drop of only 2°C in mean temperature would be needed for this to happen again.

Since the ice sheet melted 10000 years ago, we have had warmer climates but nevertheless cold enough to form great stone polygons on flat ground, like those in the Arctic. Stone-banked lobes and stone stripes are common on slopes. Another relic of colder times is the huge boulder fields on the plateaux and high ridges, torn by frost and thaw from the ice-smoothed bedrock. However, you can still see where small stone polygons and miniature stone stripes are forming in gravel. Usually the finer soil lies in the middle of the polygon, whereas in the tiny stripes running straight downhill in gravel, the dark soil forms a pattern with a long line of fine gravel next to each line of soil. You will often see these in spring when movements of stones and gravel due to alternate freezing and thawing are so common. Another type on well-vegetated flat high ground, which is very common on lowland in north Iceland, occurs in parts of the Cairngorms as a regular pattern of hummocks about 30 cm across, with hollows between them. Alternate freezing and thawing continue to eat away the cliffs, causing rockfalls, new screes and new exposures of virgin pink granite for the weather to work on.

You will also see other forms of recent erosion in the Cairngorms. One is the blowing of gravel during gales, another the hagging of peat, and a third you can watch being caused by deer or people moving soil or tearing off vegetation under their feet as they walk along. A commoner kind is erosion by water. In heavy rain storms, you may have the alarming experience of watching the ground around you visibly disappearing downhill, especially on the sparsely-vegetated high tops. Water action by massive thawing of big snow fields in early summer often washes out gravel which piles up further down as cones and ridges, often on top of the snow. During the heaviest rain storms, as in 1956, water roars down some hillsides, gouging out a trench up to 3 m deep and throwing great masses of gravel and boulders hundreds of metres downhill. You can see some of these trenches well in Glen Geusachan. River floods cause other great deposits of washed-out gravel and boulders, as in Glen Luibeg and beside Allt Mor by the bridge carrying the ski road to Cairn Gorm.

A. Bremner 1912 *The Physical Geology of the Dee Valley.* 1921 *The Physical Geology of the Don Basin.* Good semi-popular writing on local landforms with many examples, some of it now slightly out of date.

J. B. Sissons 1967 *The Evolution of Scotland's Scenery.* The best whole book on landforms for those with a little knowledge of geomorphology. Covers all Scotland but some information on the Cairngorms region.

D. Sugden 1974 Landforms. In *The Cairngorms*, by D. Nethersole-Thompson & A. Watson. An up to date chapter on the landforms of the region, fairly detailed but written for the lay reader.

There are also good articles in the *Scott. Geog. Mag.* by D. L. Linton on river captures (Vols 65, 67, 70) and 'Problems of Scottish Scenery' (67), and by P. D. Baird & W. V. Lewis on the Cairngorm floods in 1956 (73). In 1935, A. Bremner published detailed notes on the lochs of the Dee basin in *The Deeside Field* (No. 6).

Soils

Soil is a part-living, part inorganic medium which supports most terrestrial plants and animals. Different rocks break down into soil of very different fertility, depending on the rock's lime content but also on the size of the weathered rock grains. However this can be modified by very local fertile patches or strips of lime-rich rock even on the poorest masses of granite. It has also often been modified by glacial drift. For instance, some ground over granite includes many boulders and gravel deposits which have been dumped there by ice flowing from schist, limestone or diorite hills nearby. An example occurs N of Crathie, where the hill is much richer than ground in the middle of a vast tract of pure granite, such as in upper Glen Dee. Deposits of deep acidic peat may also keep the roots of plants far from the fertile mineral soil which may be lying above lime-rich rocks underneath. Nevertheless, the soils usually reflect the fertility of the underlying rocks. The soils on the granites of the Cairngorms, Lochnagar and Mount Keen are thinner, more acid, more gravelly and thus more infertile than on the schists of the Mounth. On the schists you will also see far less bare unvegetated gravel than at the same altitude on the granite. The lime-rich patches of limestone near Braemar and Tomintoul, of diorite near Crathie, Glen Tilt and the Moine Bhealaidh, and of epidiorite in Glen Muick and on Morven, are even more fertile. You will see spectacular changes from heather to grass where rich and poor rocks make contact, as in Glen Builg near Inchrory, on the slopes N of Craig Derry towards the Glas Allt Mor and on the grassy nose at the foot of Glen Baddoch.

The farmland on the granite generally looks poorer and stops lower down the hillside than over the richer rocks; this is why the farms of Strath Don are higher and better than on the granite N of Lochnagar. On the granite of Balmoral, the Cairngorms and Glen Tanar, sheep have never done well and no sheep are now run there. Sheep occur on nearly all other hills and moors except in winter; on the most fertile ones such as around the Glas Maol, upper Glen Callater and Glen Fearnaid, the place is renowned for its hill sheep. Hares, voles, moles, red grouse and ptarmigan in most years live at much higher numbers on hills with rich rocks, as around the Cairnwell, than on the granite. So do dunlins, golden plover and meadow pipits.

In the Cairngorms you will see a great variety of soil types. Soils have formed there since the last ice left the ground below as a plantless desert without life, 10000 years ago, but mostly since 7500 years ago. At one extreme, the boulders and screes have been colonised so far only by bacteria and a few lichens which are the first steps in soil formation. On the highest ground about 1200 m, severe winds, frost, the short growing season, and in dry periods the lack of water in the well-drained grit, depress plant growth. Tiny pockets of soil here and there support a few sparse mosses and flowering plants, but most of the ground is like a desert, covered with stones, bare gravel or sand. In some places, woolly fringe moss and crowberry have begun to blanket the rocks and form a sparse soil. The bare gravelly plateaux and ridges are covered by a well-drained granite grit, with a thin infertile soil below in which soil organisms and organic matter occur sparsely because plants are so few. A similar type has developed at altitudes below 1070 m, with a thicker layer of organic matter lying underneath it. This organic layer often becomes more complete in the more sheltered hollows where snow lies long and where mat grass forms a continuous cover of vegetation. All these hill soils are very acid and infertile, except where lime-rich 'flushes' or springs pour out water rich in calcium and other minerals; you can often spot these places by their bright green appearance and luxuriant vegetation.

On the moors and lower hills the plant cover is usually complete and the organic layer underneath has grown much thicker. The acidity and the washing out of minerals by water reduce the ability of 'decomposer' soil organisms to break down the material from dead plants. The resulting accumulation produces a build-up of peat. On well-drained ground it is called a 'peaty podzol', with a thin layer of black peat and a reddish hard iron pan below which forms a barrier to roots and water and often causes waterlogging. Deep peat builds up in the poorly drained hollows, in places up to 3 m thick. These thick blankets cover vast tracts from 450–750 m and some flat ground up to 900 m. Deposits even as little as 30 cm thick are rare much above 900 m but small patches occur up to 1000 m. A similar but less peaty kind of podzol has developed under the pine woods, and less acid, browner soils without peat under birch woods. Good places for you to get to know more about local soils are now common-place in the gravel quarries, bulldozed hill roads, new cuttings on public roads, and gravel slips on river banks. There you will see the different layers or 'horizons' that the soil consists of, clearly exposed in vertical section.

An up to date, more detailed but readable account on the soils of the hill country of the Cairngorms is R. Heslop's chapter in *The Cairngorms* by D. Nethersole-Thompson & A. Watson (1974).

Vegetation

One of the most outstanding features of the region is the variety of its arctic-alpine vegetation. In the Cairngorms massif the special snow-patch vegetation is richer in its extent and number of species than anywhere else in Britain. It also has a remarkable variety, depending on the length of snow cover. Under the longest-lying patches as at Garbh Choire Mor, a sparse brownish or blackish-looking vegetation of tiny mosses and liverworts grows on largely bare soil, with the granite bedrock showing its virgin colour, mostly uncolonised by lichens. Under the less prolonged cover in the snow hollows on the Ben Macdui plateau, where snow usually lies till August, some flowering plants grow such as dwarf cudweed as well as the mosses. In many hollows of the Cairngorms, snow lies into June and July; here you will find a vegetation dominated by mat grass, and other grasses in some places where patches of fertile soil occur.

The high Cairngorms and Lochnagar are unique in Britain for the size and variety of their great plateaux and ridges of wind-swept granite grit where the snow usually blows off, sparsely dotted with the three-pointed rush which also grows commonly in the high Arctic.

Where the snow lies longer on slightly less exposed ground on the plateaux and open high slopes, the circumpolar dwarf willow commonly creeps low over the ground. Over the schists, where soils are more fertile than over granite, the plateaux tend to be covered with a complete coat of vegetation, mainly composed of the arctic sedge *Carex bigelowii* mixed with woolly fringe moss. The drier eastern plateaux, such as on the Glas Maol, have more lichen and less woolly fringe moss. Boggy streams with very wide, braided, shallow channels dotted with mosses are a special characteristic of the highest plateaux in the Cairngorms above 1100 m, and occasionally occur down to 850 m.

On the lower slopes from 600 to 750 m, where snow cover is decreasing, blaeberry dominates the small deep hollows that hold the snow longer; the top of the Cairnwell road is a good place to see this. On the windswept gravelly ridges up to 900 m a prostrate mat of heather forms the main vegetation. The bouldery or stony slopes from 600 to 1100 m, where snow usually blows off, support a sparse heath of blaeberry and crowberry, with pure crowberry on some exposed dry boulder fields.

The arctic-alpine vegetation of the crags is outstanding, especially on the fertile lime-rich crags of Glen Doll, Glen Callater, Caenlochan and the head of Gleann Einich. On a single hill, only Ben Lawers is better in Britain, but as a whole hill range, the Lawers range lacks the great variety of the Cairngorms or especially that of the Mounth between the Glas Maol and Glen Clova where rare arctic willows and many other uncommon species grow in fair abundance locally.

For both plants and animals, you will often see a big change around 750 m or 2500 ft, where you pass from an obvious arctic-alpine zone with many screes and much blaeberry and crowberry, down into a less stony moorland zone dominated by long heather. The point of transition varies from 600 to 900 m, depending on snow cover, exposure, and kind of ground; you see it well in Glen Clunie at the foot of Meall Odhar or on a shelf on the Cairnwell uphill from the top car park. The transition also involves a change from ptarmigan to red grouse.

On the moorland zone below, there is again a varied flora on lime-rich crags near Tomintoul and elsewhere. On patches of well drained fertile soil in the glens, you see bright green turfy grasslands, Glen Lui being a good example. Many were once farmed or used for summer cattle grazings, but now are grazed mainly by deer and hill sheep; they make excellent walking. On the poorer, more peaty soils in some of the flat glens like the middle part of Glen Derry, and on the peaty tops of some flat low hills, you will also see grassland but of a poorer sort with a lot of purple moor grass, deer's hair grass and cotton grass. The walking becomes much heavier on the softer, hummocky surface, except by the well drained burn-sides where you often come upon short turf again.

By far the main vegetation on the moorland slopes consists of heather. Mixed through it grows much sedge, rush, bog asphodel, cotton grass, purple moor grass and cross-leaved heath on the wetter western hillsides and on poorly drained bogs in the drier east. On blanket bog, where the peat is a metre or more deep, the abundant cotton grass gives a special greyish-brown colour to the hills. You will find this blanket bog on very shallow slopes. In places it has eroded into peat hags with some of the most difficult walking in the region as well as some of the hardest navigation in bad weather. You see this country well on the Glen Dye side of the Cairn o' Mount, on the low hills between Tarfside and Glen Muick, the Ladder Hills, and some of the Atholl-Gaick upper moors.

Much of the drier moorland, as in Morayshire, Cromdale, Donside, lower Deeside and the lower Braes o' Angus, is dominated by a fairly uniform sward of heather, which colours whole hillsides a warm pink in August and September. On well drained fairly fertile dry ground, such as in lower Glen Clova and at the Muir of Dinnet, bell heather, bearberry and petty whin are mixed through the heather, along with various other flowering plants. When you visit the higher fertile moors, such as N of Crathie, you will see that more blaeberry, cowberry, bearberry and scrub juniper are the signs of greater fertility. On the less fertile moorland slopes you will find a much more uniform sward of heather. Places to watch out for are the bright green mossy flushes of *Sphagnum* on all these moors; a step into them can land you up to your chest or deeper in a quagmire.

Much of the moorland is artificial, maintained as open heath by burning, grazing, and tree-pulling. This produces economic benefit in grouse and deer for the estates and in sheep and cattle for the hill farmer. There are a few patches of forest left up to 600 m or 2000 ft, with scattered small trees up to 670 m or 2200 ft. In the peat bogs you will see plenty of roots up to these heights on now-treeless moors. Forests and scrub would spread over all this ground again if burning and stock grazing were stopped; you can see the process at work on the

NW corner of Kerloch and on Geallaig W of Ballater. Burning and grazing have wiped out most of the forests, but have completely obliterated hill scrub as a common type of vegetation, apart from a few scattered good stands of juniper on many moors, such as at Morven Lodge. In subarctic and arctic countries a dense scrub of dwarf birch and willow, $\frac{1}{4}$ to 1 m high, spreads above the tree line and sometimes in tongues or patches uphill, occupying the land between the trees and the prostrate ground vegetation of the arctic-alpine zone. In Scotland it has gone on the open hill, but the Cairngorms region retains the best relict patches of it in Britain, on craggy ledges in the Glen Doll hills away from the mouths of sheep and deer. It also has a few good though very small patches of dwarf birch and willow in other glens.

The boreal forests of pine and birch give this region much of its outstanding character. Especially in Strath Spey, the great natural forests of Abernethy, Rothiemurchus, Glen Feshie, Glen More and Dulnain together make up the biggest area in Britain that is largely timbered, mostly with natural forest. The junipers grow tall in these woods, and they and the plants under the trees add to the boreal character; examples are the abundant chickweed wintergreen and creeping ladies' tresses, and the rarer St Olaf's candlesticks and twinflower.

The literature on vegetation and wild animals is now extensive, particularly in the last ten years when much ecological research has been done in the region. Only general reviews or else semi-popular yet authoritative treatments are mentioned below; however, these give references to the many definitive papers with the original data, for anyone who wishes to read further.

J. G. Roger 1954 The flora of Caenlochan. *Trans. bot. Soc. Edinb.* 36, 189. 1956 Flowering plants of the Cairngorms. *CCJ* 17, 57. Full species lists with brief notes, by the acknowledged Scottish expert on the flora of the region.

J. Raven & M. Walters 1956 *Mountain Flowers*. New Naturalist. A good semi-popular description with many photographs. Two chapters on the Cairngorms and a third on the early pioneering botanists.

H. M. Steven & A. Carlisle 1959 *The Native Pinewoods of Scotland*. The best book on the old woods, with two chapters on the Cairngorms.

D. A. Ratcliffe 1974 The Vegetation. A long chapter in *The Cairngorms* by D. Nethersole-Thompson & A Watson. Gives a fairly detailed description of the vegetation in all parts of the region, including also some hills to the W, such as Creag Meagaidh, Am Monadh Liath and the Ben Alder range.

Wild animals

The region is unique in Britain for the richness of wild animals in its relict boreal forest and on the arctic-alpine tops. On the high ground of the Cairngorms massif lies a fairly large area of natural habitat largely untouched by man. Many species of insects, spiders, and other invertebrates on that high ground also thrive on lowland, good examples being the big harvestman *Mitopus morio* and the shiny dark beetle *Carabus problematicus*, let alone the house fly, the cleg and the midge! However, many of the hill invertebrates have a largely arctic distribution. Some species are rare, such as the high-arctic sawfly *Amauronematus abnormis* which has been found in Britain only on the Braeriach plateau, feeds on least willow and has flightless females. The arctic weevil *Otiorrhynchus arcticus* is more common, as are the dung beetle *Aphodius lapponum*, the water beetles *Agabus arcticus* and *Dytiscus lapponicus*, and the ground beetles *Amara alpina* and *Miscodera arctica*. *Zygaena exulans* the mountain burnet, a moth common in Lapland, has been found in Britain only on high ground S of Ben Avon. These examples show that for insects the Cairngorms form a piece of the Arctic in the middle of Scotland, remaining as a relic from colder, glacial times.

The arctic affinities are rich for birds also. The ptarmigan, most arctic of birds, has its main Scottish centre in the hills of the Cairngorms region, where its populations live at a higher density than anything recorded in the Arctic. Only a few pairs of the arctic snow buntings nest on the higher Cairngorms, among boulder fields near big snow wreaths and mossy flushes, and rarely anywhere else in Scotland. They belong to no permanent Scottish race; instead, birds on their way home to the far north stop here and breed. The dotterel nests on the vast arctic tundras of northern Siberia and Lapland, and also here; most dotterels nesting in Britain are on the Cairngorms and the Mounth. You may see this beautifully-coloured little plover, so tame that the old folk used to call it An t-amadan mòinteach – the fool of peat mosses – on the high bare grasslands and gravelly tracts of the highest plateaux. Since 1950, many bird watchers have seen a snowy owl on the Ben Macdui – Cairn Gorm plateau in several years. Although dunlins and golden plovers also nest on low moors in Britain, their world distribution is mainly arctic, and so it comes as no surprise to find that they breed over much of the arctic-alpine zone in the Cairngorms; in some years they are particularly abundant on the Mounth. In autumn and spring the high passes and valleys become good places for seeing migrating northern birds, especially wild geese, redwings, fieldfares, some wild duck and a variety of small birds.

The lower hills and moors below the arctic-alpine zone in the Cairngorms are now of some international importance for the conservation of peregrine falcons. Almost everywhere in its vast world range the peregrine has declined dangerously because of contamination with insecticides and other pollutants; in fact this poses a serious warning to man himself. In many places like the Arctic where these chemicals are not used, the peregrines pick them up by having to migrate S in winter to where they are widely applied. Our peregrines in the North-East Highlands can stay at home in winter, as their prey is so abundant on these less contaminated hills. The golden eagles here have also continued to do better than in western Scotland where for some years they picked up poisons from eating dead sheep treated with chemical dips. A few scattered pairs of greenshanks nest on the bare lonely glens and forest bogs. On some of the lower moors, red grouse and mountain hares reach higher populations than anywhere else in Scotland, and you will find a big variety of other moorland birds nesting here. Particular features are the good stocks of black grouse, snipe, curlews, golden plover and other waders, the nesting hen harriers on many lower moors, and the many goosanders up the high open or wooded glens. Wild cats now breed fairly commonly on moors and in woods over the whole region except on farmland and on the highest tops, and foxes occur throughout. Red deer also live throughout the area except on farmland, some woods, and some eastern moors, at a higher density than elsewhere in Scotland. A special feature is the many roe deer that live on the open lower hill or moor all the year round, even up to nearly 600 m.

In the natural pine woods, the area excels in Scotland for its many crested tits in Spey and Moray, and its nesting Scottish crossbills of Spey, Moray and Deeside. For siskins, lesser redpolls, capercaillies, and red squirrels, it contains some very good habitats with high densities. Other interesting species, which are typical of the northern boreal forest of Scandinavia and Russia, do not breed regularly or commonly. However, their occurrence in the Cairngorms in spring, with records of nesting for most of them, shows that the remnants of boreal forest here do attract them. Examples are the redwing, fieldfare, brambling, waxwing, green and wood sandpiper, Temminck's stint, whimbrel, spotted redshank, red-spotted bluethroat, goldeneye, whooper swan and Slavonian grebe. Some of these occur at boreal forest bogs and forest lakes, where again the area is unique for Britain in its richness.

The variety of the forest shows again in the fact that, here also, many typically southern or central European summer migrants occur or breed near or at their northern Scottish limit. They do so in pine and birch woods as in their Scandinavian boreal-forest habitats, not in habitats more like England; the wryneck, garden warbler, chiffchaff, blackcap and pied flycatcher are a few examples. You also see southern marsh-birds here near their northern limit for Britain, namely the grasshopper warbler, spotted crake and marsh harrier. For variety of forest and loch birds, Spey is slightly richer than Dee, but for moorland and arctic-alpine slightly the other way round. The Spey ospreys have become a great tourist draw like the Cairn Gorm chairlift. On the rivers, ringed plovers, common terns and oyster-catchers nest right to the centre of Scotland.

To entomologists, the Strath Spey woodland zone is one of the most exciting places in Britain. Here, in the boreal forests of pine and birch and on the nearby moorlands, they have found a rich group of boreal species, with many rare insects and some species new to science. Others are common and characteristic of the old forests, like the wood ants, which have not yet colonised and formed their great mounds in the new pine woods in lower Deeside near Banchory, but which live abundantly in new plantations next to the old forests, as at Culbin.

In 1954, domestic reindeer from Swedish Lapland were introduced to a low forest bog in Glen More. They did not thrive, but a later introduction to a fenced area that included some windswept hill on Airgiod-meall was successful; now there are over 100 Scottish-born reindeer. You also see them often on the ski grounds around Coire Cas and grazing on the high plateau towards Ben Macdui.

A fairly detailed review describing the wild animals of the region is in *The Cairngorms* by D. Nethersole-Thompson & A. Watson (1974), with separate chapters on insects, fish, birds and mammals.

A. Watson's 'Hill birds of the Cairngorms' in *Scott. Birds* 4, 179, summarises information on the birds from tree line upwards. Semi-popular summaries occur in Seton Gordon's chapter on 'The wild-life of Glen More', in *Glen More* (National Forest Part Guide) and in other publications mentioned in the main Bibliography (p 77).

Nature conservation and nature reserves
The region of the Cairngorms, Lochnagar and the Mounth is outstanding for its very large continuous areas of high country resembling the high Arctic, its great tracts of natural pine and birch forest and forest bogs, and the wildlife of soils, plants and animals that go with them. For these things it is certainly unique in these islands. Of course you can see relict pine forest and arctic-like summits in other parts of Scotland, but nowhere else in Britain does there exist any other region which contains such a variety and extent of these habitats and their associated wildlife. It is also unique in Scotland for the great extent and variety of its lochs, lime-rich crags and vast tracts of moorland and glen. Many naturalists have come here for generations, and the area's value for scientific research also ranks very high. It has now become essential to plan so that the most outstanding or easily damaged features of this hill country are safeguarded, and so that interested folk who go there in future will enjoy them as much as we do. If there are to come big new developments for large numbers of people who simply want open-air recreation but not necessarily the special kinds of it available in the Cairngorms, they should be put in parts of the country that are not outstanding or fragile.

It was for these reasons that the Nature Conservancy declared its large National Nature Reserve in the Cairngorms massif, another at Caenlochan-Clova, and smaller ones in the birch woods at Craigellachie near Aviemore and at Morrone near Braemar. The boundaries are shown in green on the Cairngorms OS Tourist Map. Apart from Invereshie and Inshriach which the Conservancy Council owns, these Reserves entail agreements with the landowners, which have to be periodically renewed. The Conservancy Council has to be consulted and its agreement secured before any developments on these National Nature Reserves are allowed; therefore it has power to prevent developments which threaten the integrity of the Reserve, such as new roads or ski lifts. It also gives advice to the Secretary of State for Scotland when planning applications for developments relevant to nature conservation are sent to him.

The Reserves are much used for scientific research by the Institute of Terrestrial Ecology and others, mainly in ecology. Most of this is aimed at getting a better understanding of wildlife and its environment; as new problems keep cropping up which may possibly threaten the area, the Nature Conservancy Council will thus be in a stronger postion to take good decisions about them and thus to manage the whole area better. The Universities also use these National Nature Reserves a lot, for pure and applied research.

One good reason for keeping a close watch on new roads and other developments in an outstanding area like the Cairngorms is that no one can say now what important information the researchers may turn up in the future. For instance, the very interesting work by D. Sugden leading to fascinating conclusions about possible glaciation in the Cairngorms only 160 years ago (see p 60) could not have been attempted if the necessary research material – in this case the small corrie moraines – had been disturbed by bulldozers for roads or other developments. Sometimes it is not enough just to maintain things as they are, and active management of habitats or wildlife may be needed. For example, some forests have decayed so far that the lack of regeneration led the Conservancy to fence off plots and plant trees from local seed. Deer stalking by the owners still goes on, and indeed the shooting of deer is necessary to prevent marauding of deer to other people's ground where they are a pest to farmers and foresters.

The Nature Conservancy Council welcomes people, provided they do not abuse the rights of future generations by picking or digging plants, leaving litter, allowing dogs which are untrained to wildlife to roam free, and lighting fires in dry weather. On the Cairngorms Reserve, the Conservancy paid for the four footbridges at Corrour, Glas Allt Mor, the Derry Dam and Derry Lodge, for visitors to cross safely in flood. The Reserve wardens live at Lilybank at the edge of Braemar on the Inverey road ('phone Braemar 678), the chief warden at Kinakyle just out of Aviemore on the A9 (Aviemore 250), and at Achnagoichan (Aviemore 287), with a part-time warden at Luibeg (Braemar 232). The wardens will gladly give you advice and information, including leaflets on the Cairngorms Reserve, and you should tell them if you see any damaging behaviour or hear of any proposal likely to threaten the area. Other small nature reserves with access to the public are owned by the Royal Society for the Protection of Birds at the osprey nest near Loch Garten and at the fen-marshes of Loch Insh, and by the Scottish Wildlife Trust at the Loch of the Lowes near Dunkeld.

Conservation of wilderness and landscape

The natural beauty, scenery and wilderness of the Cairngorms are a great attraction for tourists, and to many city dwellers form a source of priceless physical enjoyment, mental renewal and peace. However, some parts of the area have been much changed by new roads, chair lifts, hotels and other developments, many plans exist for further developments, and the huge increase of countryside recreation threatens the beauty that people come to see.

Conservationists have no desire to halt all development or to prevent skiers or any other recreational group from enjoying their sport. What they suggest is that every group such as downhill skiers can have most of that they want, without entailing the free-for-all of development which would completely spoil the sport or interest of some other group such as climbers and lovers of wilderness. This is the point of planning. To achieve this aim, each group will have to give up something of what it would ideally want, but this agreed compromise offers the only hope. With the increase of pressures on the hills, future hillmen cannot have the same freedom as in the past. People can motor, camp, boat, fish or walk anywhere they like and still have nature and wilderness and no conflicts with the interests of others, but only if a very few of them are doing it. As a few grew to a great many after 1945, so did locked gates in the Cairngorms region become the rule, low-ground bothies become demolished by the owners because of vandalism, theft and litter, and camping become restricted.

The Countryside Commission for Scotland, which was set up in 1968, works with local authorities to plan for recreation in the countryside and to advise the Government on the payment of grants for recreation projects. These grant-aided schemes provide suitable facilities and access to the countryside, and also protect the resource itself – such as beautiful scenery, natural forest or litter-free loch sides – from damage by overuse or thoughtlessness. The Commission soon realised that problems had arisen in the Spey Valley because of the demands of intensive recreation on sensitive terrain, and this was why the Commission began its first development project in this district. It involves 'project officers' or countryside rangers who educate and inform visitors, while at the same time helping to protect the more delicate areas from hazards such as fire, litter and wild camping. The Commission hopes to show the value of this method of receiving visitors, as a demonstration to all the landowners and organisations in the area. It also hopes to improve the visitor's experience and to protect the scenic and other resources which attract so many visitors in the first place. The Commission has been making a study of landscape and it may be expected that they will be producing ideas on the conservation of outstanding Scottish landscapes and wilderness in the years ahead.

W. H. Murray 1962 *Highland Landscape, A Survey*. A far-sighted book describing areas of outstanding landscape, including two chapters on the Cairngorms and Balmoral Forest.

A. Watson 1967 Public pressures on soils, plants and animals near ski lifts in the Cairngorms. In *The Biotic Effects of Public Pressures on the Environment*, p. 38. Natural Environment Res. Council, London. Describes development threats to the Cairngorms.

The 1972 and 1973 reports by the project officer of the Countryside Commission for Scotland are interesting, especially the surveys of people on Cairn Gorm and its plateau.

A. Watson & N. Bayfield 1973 The need for a conservation code for the hills. *Recreation News Suppl.* 10, 7. Describes some of the conservation problems due to more people on the hills, and gives a simple code for visitors. Based on experience in the Cairngorms.

A. Watson 1974 The vanishing wilderness. *Mountain Life* 11, 18. Article and maps on new bulldozed roads in the Cairngorms.

N. Keir 1974 How does the law stand? *Mountain Life* 11, 19. Describes the planning laws on the subject of new bulldozed roads and on other conservation matters.

Selected bibliography
There exists such a vast literature on this district that only a brief sketch can be given here. An early record of a visit to the Cairngorms is from 1618, in *The Pennyless Pilgrimage* of John Taylor the 'Water Poet'. Travelling from Glen Esk over the Mounth at Mount Keen, he came to Braemar, saw 'Mount Benawne' and watched the Earl of Mar's hunt. Carrying on to 'Ruthen' in 'Bagenoch' presumably by Glen Feshie, and to Darnaway, he then headed S by 'Stroboggi' and the 'Carny Mount to Breekin'. P. H. Brown reproduced his tour, in *Early Travellers in Scotland*, an interesting book reprinted again in

1973. Blaeu's *Atlas Novus*, published at Amsterdam in 1654, contains maps by Scottish geographer Robert Gordon of Straloch. They were based on work by Timothy Pont, including a notably accurate description of the region in Latin, which was translated centuries later by C. G. Cash (*CCJ* 5, 196; and 6, 18). Gordon's map mentions Carn-gorum, Bini bourd, Bin-Avin, Bini vroden, L. Avin and L. Garr.

The next general traveller was Pennant in 1769. In his *Tour of Scotland* (1774) he wrote of the 'naked summits, many of them topped with perpetual snow'. The *Statistical Account* (1791–99) describes all the parishes, each written by the parish minister, and gives much information on the district, especially on the local people and their life. Around 1786, Col T. Thornton, game shooter, in his *Sporting Tour* (1804) visited Strath Spey, climbed Sgoran Dubh (p 157), and first used the term 'Cairngorms', referring to the 'Aurora peeping over the immense Cairngorms'. In 1796 the Hon Mrs Murray Aust crossed the Drumochter to Aviemore, and during 1801, in her *Companion and Useful Guide to the Beauties of Scotland* (1810), she writes how she returned to Rothiemurchus, 'that most enchanting place', climbed Cairn Gorm, and visited Loch Einich. She then rode through Lairig an Laoigh and advises 'all travellers, in search of uncommonly fine scenery, not to omit visiting every part of the district called Braemar, the charms of which have hitherto been unheard of, and unseen, except by the very few'.

Some pioneering scientific descriptions of the Cairngorms appear in the *General View of the Agriculture of Aberdeenshire* (1811) by the Rev G. S. Keith, who in 1810 climbed some of the hills with a barometer to measure their height (p 102); his account was reprinted in 1968 in *CCJ* 17, 238. In 1814, G. F. Robson published his *Scenery of the Grampian Mountains*, a book with 40 etchings, descriptive notes and a map, on the hills from Ben Lomond to the Cairngorms, including 11 on 'Lochan-y-Gar' and the Cairngorms, and later he published an edition with coloured plates in 1819. Artists in those days often exaggerated the steepness of the hills, but most of his etchings look fairly reasonable, all catch the mystery of these hills, and the descriptive notes show an observant eye. Lord Cockburn's *Circuit Journeys* (1837–54) speaks enthusiastically of the view from the Inverness road W of Carrbridge, 'the approach to Aviemore becomes interesting soon after the waters begin to flow Speyward, till at last the full prospect of these glorious Cairngorms, with their forests and peaks and valleys, exhibits one of the finest pieces of mountain scenery in Britain'. From her base at Balmoral, Queen Victoria climbed Ben Macdui, Lochnagar and other hills, and wrote lovingly and in observant detail about some of this country in her *Leaves from the Journal of Our Life in the Highlands*, published in 1868.

Walking from Aberdeen to the hill, and thinking nothing of striding out across Scotland from Aberdeen to his home in the far west, Prof W. MacGillivray did much exploration of the Cairngorms and Deeside hills. His *Natural History of Deeside and Braemar*, published in 1855, is a fascinating account by this all rounder, covering geology, plants, animals, pioneering ecological descriptions, the hill folk and their way of life. The *Guide to the Highlands of Deeside*, appearing in 1831, and again in 1869 as the *New Deeside Guide* by J. Robertson, was the first guide book in our area, but did not describe the hills in any detail. Of more interest to walkers is *The Cairngorm Mountains*, published in 1864 by historian J. H. Burton; it gives some description of these hills and appreciates the value of fine scenery in Scotland.

Many later books and publications are listed below. In addition, since 1893 the Cairngorm Club in Aberdeen has published a *Journal* which contains a great amount of material about our region, that is indispensable to anyone with a serious and wide interest in the area. From the late 1940s till 1964, the Etchachan Club in Aberdeen has also printed or duplicated a *Journal* with much information on the area, especially on the post-war exploration for rock and ice climbing. The Deeside Field Club has published issues of *The Deeside Field* with interesting papers on topography and a great variety of subjects for Deeside. Only general literature is described below; other more specialist papers are given under the separate sub-headings of this Introduction and in the Further Reading at the end of each chapter. Only books that the author considers authoritative and worth reading have been mentioned, so as to save space; much of the huge literature available is largely repetitive.

A. I. McConnochie 1885 *Ben Muich Dhui and His Neighbours*. 1890 *Bennachie*. 1891 *Lochnagar*. 1893 *Deeside*. Prob. 1897 *Queen Victoria's Highland Home and Vicinity*. 1898 *The Royal Dee*. 1900 *Donside*. 1902 *Strathspey*. 1902 *Guide to Aviemore and Vicinity*. A remarkable series which includes some good descriptions of the hills, glens and local history.

Eliz. Grant 1899 *Memoirs of a Highland Lady*. Observant personal account of local life in Rothiemurchus in the early 19th century.

W. Forsyth 1900 *In the Shadow of Cairngorm*. A good general book on life and traditions in Abernethy and Strath Spey.

G. M. Fraser 1921 *The Old Deeside Road*. Good descriptions of the Dee valley, the old roads, bridges and villages.

Seton Gordon 1925 *The Cairngorm Hills of Scotland*. A 20th century classic, one of the best books for fine descriptions of the Cairngorms massif, with much information on traditions and wildlife.

W. A. Poucher 1947 *A Camera in the Cairngorms*. Ninety-three photographs of the area.

R. Perry 1948 *In the High Cairngorms*. A personal account of wildlife and trips in the Glen Feshie hills.

Seton Gordon 1948, reprinted 1972 *Highways and Byways in the Central Highlands*. 1951 *Highlands of Scotland*. Some good descriptions of the hills and local history in the Cairngorms.

V. A. Firsoff 1949 *The Cairngorms on Foot and Ski*. A mainly personal account of the author's journeys in the Cairngorms massif.

J. R. Allan 1952 *North-East Lowlands of Scotland*. Good, readable book on farmland, town, people and way of life.

C. Gibson 1958 *Highland Deerstalker*. Memories of a deer stalker from upper Glen Clova and Glen Muick, written by a friend.

J. Walton (ed) 1960 *Glen More*. National Forest Park Guide. Excellent booklet on the Glen More Park and nearby ground, with good bibliography.

H. L. Edlin (ed) 1963 *Forests of North-East Scotland*. Brief chapters describing scenery, geology, vegetation, wildlife, landscape, history, and other aspects of the entire region, not just of the forests.

British Association 1963 *The North-East of Scotland*. A survey of the natural features of the whole area including the hills, climate, rocks, soils, plants and animal life, in addition to human history, population changes, local dialects and other aspects of human culture. Although the chapters are brief, this is the best general introduction to the region, its main features, and its people. Mostly a semi-technical style and content.

D. Fraser   1966   *Discovering Angus and Mearns*. Includes information on topography and local history.

Technical Planning Group   1967   *Cairngorm Area*. A survey of skiing potential and possible tourist development. Urged many new roads through Tilt, Feshie and other glens and on to a few hills, plus new ski lifts on various hills. Largely ignored the conservation-wilderness case and made proposals for huts and paths, without consulting mountain rescue organisations, which are dangerous for hill safety.

T. Weir   1970, 1972   *The Scottish Lochs*. Vols 1 & 2. Fine photos of many lochs in the Cairngorms, plus brief descriptions of them and of the surrounding country and its history.

A. Gray   1970   *The Big Grey Man of Ben Macdhui*. A book giving detailed case histories.

D. Nethersole-Thompson & A. Watson   1974   *The Cairngorms*. Collins. A 'new naturalist'-type book on the history, physical background, natural history, sport, conservation and future of most of the area covered by this District Guide, but omitting Moray and Nairn and the North-East lowlands and coast. Mostly natural history, with a semi-popular style and content.

Metric 1: 50 000 maps

The OS intend to publish this scale of map for Scotland in spring 1976. See pages 27, 28. The sheet numbers of this map relative to chapters in this book are as follows:

Chapter 1— 27, 28, 35, 36
           2— 36, 43
           3— 35, 36, 43
           4— 36, 43
           5— 36, 43
           6— 35, 42, 43
           7— 43
           8— 36, 43
           9— 36, 37, 43
         10— 43, 44
         11— 37, 44
         12— 43, 44
         13— 44
         14— 37, 38, 44, 45
         15— 28, 29, 30, 36, 37, 38

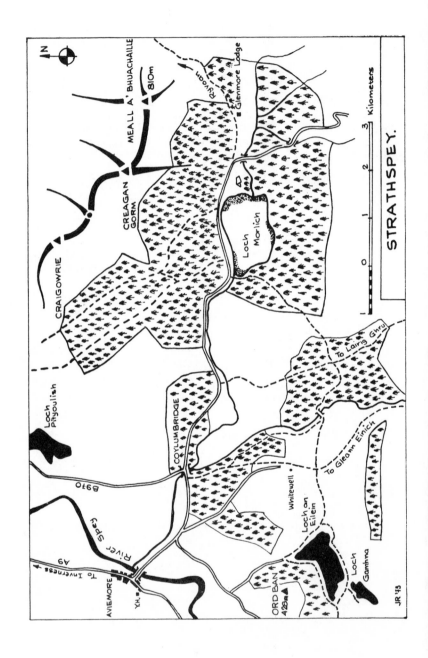

STRATHSPEY.

0 1 2 3 Kilometers

N

CRAIGOWRIE

CREAGAN GORM

MEALL A' BHUACHAILLE
810m

Ryvoan

Glenmore Lodge

Loch Morlich

Loch Pityoulish

B970

COYLUMBRIDGE

To Lairig Ghru

River Spey

To Inverness
A9

AVIEMORE

Y.H.

Whitewell

Loch an Eilein

To Gleann Einich

ORD BAN
428m

Loch Gamhna

JR'43

1

Strath Spey and Moray

Ord Ban	428 m, 892085
Meall a' Bhuachaille	810 m, 991115
Sgor Gaoithe	628 m, 076219
Ben Rinnes	840 m, 255354
Carn Glas-choire	659 m, 891291
The Knock of Braemoray	455 m, 011417

Access

Plane and rail to Inverness, rail to Aviemore, Elgin and Forres, buses in Speyside and in lower Moray and Nairn.

Accommodation and other facilities

In Speyside there are many hotels, boarding houses and bed and breakfasts, as well as pubs and restaurants in all villages. Aviemore has many facilities, including shops for outdoor clothing and a mountain rescue centre at the police station. Fish and chip shops and automatic petrol machines occur there and at Grantown. Glenmore Lodge is the Scottish Sports Council's outdoor centre and mountain rescue centre. A youth hostel stands at the S end of Aviemore, another in East Terrace at Kingussie and a third at Glen More. The Ladies' Scottish Climbing Club hut of Milehouse at 839044 has nine places; its custodian is Mrs A. R. Rae, 3 Tannoch Drive, Milngavie, Dunbartonshire. You will see many shooters' huts on the Moray and Nairn moors and on the Inverness-shire ones N of Carrbridge and around Dorback, but this is not 'bothying' country (see p 26).

General description

With one of Scotland's most varied and beautiful valleys, the country of Speyside has now become a boom area for tourism. This chapter emphasises the finest part, Strath Spey – the wide valley in the middle reaches of Spey – but includes the hills of the lower reaches and the counties of Moray and Nairn. The Central Highlands District

Guide covers the range of Am Monadh Liath to the W, the hills around the Upper Spey W of Newtonmore, and the hills W of the Pass of Drumochter.

Geology and landforms

The Moine granulites or schists dominate the Monadh Liath, the moors and hills of Moray and Nairn, and the hills of Cromdale. Patches of limestone occur near Ord Ban and in Strath Avon, and granite at Ben Rinnes. The district contains some of the best examples of cliff-sided glacial meltwater channels in Scotland, as at the Eag Mhór (Aik *Vore*) or big notch near Dorback and at Stac na h-Iolaire S of Mam Suim. Loch Morlich and most of the other lochs in the area occur because the glaciers dumped gravel and boulders which dammed up the water coming from the hills after the ice had all melted. The great conical hillocks SW of Loch Morlich, called the Sìthean (*Sheean*) or fairy knoll, are fine examples of one type of glacial landform. At the tree line near the road to Cairn Gorm, the broad back from Allt Mor to Airgiod-meall (*Er*ikit Myal) or silver lump is one of the largest glacially-formed ridges in Scotland; the burn of Allt Mor has cut through it, and a couple of big landslides which were caused during a spate in 1962 show well the kind of sandy material making up the ridge. Floods dumped much of the gravel from this landslide near where the road to Cairn Gorm crosses the bridge over Allt Mor.

Natural history

For natural history, Strath Spey is a place for superlatives. The natural pine forests are bigger and more varied than anywhere else in Britain and generally in better regeneration, so the flora and fauna that go with the boreal pine forest are also richer here than elsewhere. Strath Spey has the best set of forest lochs and forest bogs in Britain. Loch Insh (Innse, Eensh) or meadow lake and its neighbouring marsh are now a reserve run by the Royal Society for the Protection of Birds. The marsh is an outstanding example of a northern fen, which supports a very rich bird life (D. Weir, 1973. Insh marshes. *Birds* 4, 274). The loch also contains many char, a northern fish relict of colder climates. The other RSPB reserve at Loch Garten is famous for its ospreys.

Estates

There are many small ones. Rothiemurchus Estate owns the ground from Loch an Eilein to just W of Loch Morlich, and the Forestry

Commission has Glen More. The road W of Forest Lodge divides Forest Lodge Estate, which goes S to Ryvoan and Meall a' Bhuachaille, from Seafield Estate which stretches N to Grantown and includes most of the Cromdale Hills.

History

The upper Spey by Newtonmore was the country of Clan MacPherson, and Badenoch was also part of the ground occupied by the confederation of the 'super-clan' Chattan (*Chatan*). There is a clan museum at Newtonmore. For those interested in learning about the life and history of the folk of Badenoch and Strath Spey, an outstanding place to visit is the Highland Folk Museum of Am Fasgadh (Um *Faska* or the shelter) at Kingussie, which was founded by Dr I. F. Grant, the expert on Highland folk tradition and social organisation. A more pictorial presentation with less detail is offered at the Landmark Exhibit at Carrbridge, which also has a 20-minute nature trail, films and an excellent selection of books on all Highland topics. It was at Ruthven near Kingussie in 1736 that James MacPherson was born, later to become well known as the man who gave us the book *Ossian* with its fine Celtic poetry.

Up in the rocks on the face of Kennapole Hill near Loch Gamhna is a cave called the Cat's Den. Here 'black Sandy' Grant who had attacked and badly injured a Speyside drover, lay hidden for a while, but later had to emigrate to America and is said to have become the ancestor of President Grant. Near there, the little parish church of Rothiemurchus nestles among trees below the road from Insh to Inverdruie. In the graveyard lies a flat stone on which rest five cylindrical stones. The inscription commemorates Farquhar, who led the Shaws in combat on the North Insh at Perth in 1396, and tradition has it that anyone moving the five stones will be cursed. Once some reckless youths risked the curse by moving the stones, and before the year was out they were all dead. On the flat ground nearer the river stands the Doune, old home of Elizabeth Grant, who wrote *Memoirs of a Highland Lady*; first published in 1899, it gives a fascinating account of Highland life at the beginning of the 19th century.

In 1728, much of the woodland of Abernethy was sold to the York Buildings Company for iron smelting. The Company went bankrupt but introduced modern methods of tree extraction, sawmilling and timber floating to the area. Since then, Abernethy, Glen More and

Rothiemurchus have all been continually exploited for timber. The timber floating, which lasted until the mid 19th century, was a special feature of life in Strath Spey in the old days, and is well described by Elizabeth Grant in her *Memoirs*. Where the River Luineag (*Loo*eenak) leaves Loch Morlich you can see the site of the old sluice gates that were used in the days of timber floating. After the cut logs had been dragged to the river side, the sluice gates were opened and the flood swept the logs down to the sawmills at Inverdruie or into Spey. There the timber floaters made rafts with the logs and guided them down to the shipbuilding yards at Kingston on the Moray Firth.

In Glen More an old legend spoke of the glen being haunted by a giant spectre, the Làmh Dhearg (Laav *Yerr*eg) or red hand, who offered battle to belated travellers through the woods. At the far end of the glen, the Pass of Ryvoan forms part of the old Rathad nam Mèirleach (*Ra*-at na *Myer*lach) or road of the thieves. The reivers from the traditional marauding clans of Cameron and MacGregor from the W Highlands used this track when they were heading for the lowland farms and returning with their spoil. Leaving Feshie-bridge, the caterans struck along the S side of Loch an Eilein through Rothiemurchus, and next along the S side of Loch Morlich to Ryvoan. From here the thieves' road – now a very fine walking route – went through the top of the Nethy woods at Loch a' Chnuic to the Eag Mhor, and then by the Braes of Abernethy and Dorback to Tomintoul (12 km Ryvoan to Dorback). A glance at the map will show that Rathad nam Meirleach was not just the most direct route but also avoided the populated Spey Valley where the caterans would have been resisted.

At Lynachork near Tomintoul, where Rathad nam Meirleach comes over the hills from Nethy, a great feat of eating occurred in the early 19th century. A wandering preacher called Nicol ate a whole sheep at Abergeldie on Deeside about 1840. At Lynachork he ate a peck (two gallons) of raw meal and cream. When the meal began to swell inside him he was in great pain and cried 'Raip me an' row me or I'll rive!' (Rope me and roll me or I'll burst!) So they bound him with straw ropes, the safeguard that had to be taken in these contests! Just up from Lynachork the rocky gorge of Ailnack comes out at Delnabo. A cave in the gorge is called after Seumas an Tuim or James of the hill, who was the subject of a quaint old Gaelic poem, reproduced in the book *Highland Legends*.

Walking ascents

By Spey, from Newtonmore – Nethy Bridge. Aviemore (An Agaidh Mhór or the big gap) is one of the best centres for exploring Strath Spey, but the climber may prefer one of the smaller villages less affected by the tourist boom. From this whole district the Monadh Ruadh or Cairngorms show their N side as a single great front, so there are innumerable places in the flattish valley below where you can have magnificent and detailed views of these hills. The great dark green carpet of Rothiemurchus Forest forms a fine foreground. Some especially good viewpoints from the low ground are from the railway station or high in the tall hotels at Aviemore, from the Nairn road between Lochindorb and Duthil, from the Inverness road W of Carrbridge, and best of all the nearer view from the end of the public road at Whitewell, where the great forest of Rothiemurchus makes a wonderful setting.

The upper stretches of Spey from Newtonmore to Kincraig are prone to flooding, giving rise to the district's name of Badenoch (Bàideanach) or drowned land. To the SW of Loch Insh lies a big area which was once drained for farming but has now become a marsh again; here the river drops only 15 m in a distance of 20 km. The name of Newtonmore is a corruption of the English translation of Baile Ur an t-Sléibh or new town of the moor, the nearby Kingussie being Cinn a' Ghiuthsaich (Keen*yoo*see) or head of the pine wood. South of Aviemore on the A9 road you will see the old inn of Lynwilg, overlooking Loch Alvie with its fine old church. Near Lynwilg, between Spey and Loch Alvie (Ailamhaigh, at a rock plain), rises the wooded 358 m hill of Torr Alvie, which bears a tower commemorating the 5th and last Duke of Gordon. As the hill stands alone in the centre of the valley, it gives fine views both up and down Strath Spey, especially of the lower Monadh Liath. At its base lies Kinrara, home and burial place of Jean Maxwell the Duchess of Gordon, who helped to raise the Gordon Highlanders.

For seeing the Cairngorms, one of the best viewpoints from any hill in the district is N of Kinrara, at the top of Craigellachie (Creag Eileachaidh, *Ail*achie) or rock of the stony place, the rocky birch-clad spur that rises immediately behind the new Aviemore 'Centre' with its hotels and shops. This was the origin of the war cry of Clan Grant, 'Stad, Creag Eileachaidh!' or 'Stand fast, Craigellachie!' It makes a pleasant walk to go from the Centre past the quiet Loch Pulladdern and into the Craigellachie birch wood, which is so outstanding for its richness of plants and rare insects that it became a small National Nature Reserve. In 1967 a nature trail was laid out there for visitors (40 minutes walk).

The valley widens at Aviemore, with Rothiemurchus stretching away far to the E, and spreads even more at Boat of Garten and Nethy (Naythie) Bridge. Here the huge sweep of flat forest, moorland and low hills rolling out to Dorback in the E and to Am Monadh Liath in the W gives a feeling of great space, more like a valley in Sweden or Canada than one in Scotland. Boat of Garten, Nethy Bridge and Grantown, all at about 200 m, lie further from the Cairngorms than Aviemore, but make very good centres for visiting Abernethy and the other forests, lochs, and lower hills and moors of Strath Spey. These are seldom visited by climbers, but to the curious walker who likes exploring new upland country which still retains a strong link with its past despite the big influx of outsiders, this countryside offers one of the most varied and interesting tracts of any in Scotland.

The Strath Spey pine forests. Rothiemurchus (probably from Ràta-mhurchuis or fort of Muircus) is the gem of Spey forests, giving a magnificent contrast of high hills, lochs and rich natural woodland. One of the finest tracts of forest in Britain, it stretches from Loch an Eilein to Loch Morlich. Near Coylumbridge (Cuing Leum or narrow leap) many birches grow but the bulk of Rothiemurchus Forest consists of naturally-seeded pine, with many junipers underneath. Regeneration is excellent in the lower forest but poor in the higher parts where deer are abundant in winter.

Around Loch Morlich, just E of Rothiemurchus, lies Glen More (Gleann Mór) or big valley. Here also stood a great natural forest, but after the 1914–18 War it was one of the first areas to be bought by the Forestry Commission, which felled much of the natural woodland and replaced it with densely planted pine and spruce. Later the Commission turned this 'Queen's Forest' into the Glen More National Forest Park. You will see an interesting contrast between the natural forest of Rothiemurchus and the artificial forest of Glen More as you drive up the Glen More road and enter the Park at the cattle grid and fence just short of Loch Morlich. Nearby, to the S of Luineag, the great forest bog and adjacent hillocks W of Loch Morlich on Rothiemurchus were ploughed up and planted with exotic spruce and lodgepole pine as recently as 1970. The Forestry Commission caters a lot for visitors to the Park, including a forest exhibit in a building above the camp site, and specially prepared walks for $\frac{1}{2}$–$2\frac{1}{2}$ hours through the woods.

North of Glen More, Abernethy Forest extends far as the largest tract of natural pine forest in Britain. Here you can drive for miles along public roads through the forest, and wander in pine woods so big that you can easily imagine yourself to be in Scandinavia or Russia. It is a magnificent place for wildlife, and, although it has been under continual exploitation for timber for centuries, it is still thriving well. For decades, until recently when some clear-felling has been done, the foresters had cut individual trees here and there and did not clear-fell big areas, so the place stayed good to look at as well as remaining a continuous forest full of wildlife.

Loch an Eilein and Ord Ban. Apart from Loch Morlich, Loch an Eilein is the most beautiful loch in Strath Spey, a sheltered sunny loch at 256 m, nestling among high wooded slopes. It reaches only 19 m in depth. Loch an Eilein (*Ail*in), or lake of the island was named after an islet bearing a 14th century ruined castle, where one of the last ospreys in Scotland nested before the old Scottish stock became extinct early this century. Where the road ends at the N end of the loch, the Nature Conservancy opened a small exhibit in 1972, and has had a nature trail ($2\frac{1}{2}$ hours walk) round the loch for some years. The pressure of visitors has risen too high at the N end of the loch, where motorists driving cars to the loch edge have scarred the ground. Òrd Bàn (Baan) or fair round hill, rising W of the loch, is well worth the 170 m of ascent for its grand views of Spey and hill. Its slopes are thickly clothed with birch, and under them lies a carpet of lush green vegetation due to the rich limestone. To the SW of Loch an Eilein, a track runs round below Kennapole Hill, and at about 270 m comes to Loch Gamhna (Gawn) or lake of stirks, a beautiful little loch with water lilies.

Loch Morlich. This name may come from Loch Mór Leac (*More*-lich) or lake of a great slope. Lying at about 320 m in a great forested basin below Cairn Gorm, Loch Morlich has one of the finest settings of any lake in Britain. The view over pine-clad ridges to the snowy corries of Cairn Gorm seems like a scene from subarctic Lapland, as does the view from the golden strand at the loch's E end looking far over the spacious sweep of Strath Spey to the distant rolling hills of Am Monadh Liath. The loch is shallow – only 15 m at its deepest – but covers 120 ha, and thus form the biggest sheet of water in the Cairngorms massif. It supports a great variety of habitats for wildlife, and the Forestry Commission has left some of the best of the old pines around the loch as well as patches of alder and some scrub. The pressure of countless human feet has eroded the sand dunes near the western strand and caused windblows, but the Commission has fenced off the worst damaged ground, which is beginning to recover. A private Forestry Commission road comes to Loch Morlich from the N by the pass of An Slugan (*Sloog*an) or the gullet. The Slugan is part of an old right of way and now leads to the public road N of Loch Pityoulish. Just N of there you will see the fine old church of Kincardine with its narrow 'Leper's Window' where in the old days the diseased people stood outside and peered in during the church service.

Glenmore Lodge. The old Glenmore Lodge is now a youth hostel, and past here on the left you can visit the Forestry Commission's exhibit. Just beyond stands Reindeer House where Mr M. Utsi lives; he owns the reindeer and takes visitors to see them on Cairn Gorm. About 1 km from the camp site, up the road towards Ryvoan and beyond the Commission's 'Norwegian House' for youth parties, lies the new Glenmore Lodge, a modern cedar and glass building. In the late 1940s, the Scottish Council for Physical Recreation set up their outdoor centre at the old lodge, starting courses in skiing, mountaineering, canoeing, sailing and other outdoor sports. To cater for the great increase of people taking these courses, the Council, which is now called the Scottish Sports Council, then built the larger new lodge; enquiries should be made to the Principal, Mr F. Harper. On the staff are some well known climbers who stand in the forefront of rock and ice climbing and mountain rescue techniques in Scotland.

Lochan Uaine and Ryvoan. A gravel road leads from Glenmore Lodge through the Pass of Ryvoan to Abernethy. The pass is narrow, with broken rocks and tree-studded screes on Creag Loisgte (Craik *Loishk*) or burnt rock on the W side, and on Creag nan Gall (Craik na *Gaal*) or rock of the lowlanders, on the E side. In the middle of the pass, at about 358 m, lies An Lochan Uaine (*Oo*an) or the green tarn. one of the chief wonders of the Cairngorms. The water has an extraordinary pale greenish-blue colour, the old legend being that this resulted from the fairies washing their clothes in it; it looks so brilliantly translucent that you can easily see the fallen logs and stones on the bottom. The echo here sound very fine, reflected back from the screes of Creag nan Gall. Beyond the tarn, the track climbs out of the scattered trees to the grand viewpoint on the moorland top at Ryvoan (Ruighe a' Bhothain, Ree *Voe*-an) meaning the shiel of the cottage. Formerly a farm, it is now an open bothy for public use, 4 km from the Glen More camp site and at about 400 m in altitude. About ½ km before you reach Ryvoan, another rough road forks right and leads for about 2 km ESE, past Loch a' Gharbh-choire to the open bothy beside the River Nethy at Pit Fyannich (*Fyann*ich).

Meall a' Bhuachaille and Abernethy. From Ryvoan you can keep on down the road for 4 km N to the beautiful old croft at Rynettin, then N to the public road at 012162, and back by the road W through the crofts of Tulloch. The higher crofts are empty and ruined, but this still looks a varied and pleasant landscape with patches of arable farmland, wood and scrub, offering fine views over Abernethy Forest. An alternative (1½ km, 400 m ascent) from Ryvoan, via a path from the bothy that goes up to about 560 m, is to climb the conical Meall a' Bhuachaille (Myal a *Voo*achil) or lump of the herdsman. Rising to 810 m or 2654 ft, it blocks much of the Cairngorms in the view from Grantown. The broad ridge continues for 3½ km to the NW of the summit, commanding a series of glorious views of the Cairngorms across the foreground of Glen More, and a fine outlook far up and down Strath Spey. From Meall a' Bhuachaille you can drop W to a 624 m col and then climb to reach Creagan Gorm (Craikan *Gor*om) or blue little rock, at 732 m. Beyond, to the NW, rises the rough rocky 686 m hill of Craiggowrie (Creag Gaibhre) or goat's rock. You can go downhill W from there to the Slugan or S towards Loch Morlich to the Forestry Commission cottages at Badaguish (Bad a' Ghiuthais, Bad*yoo*ish) which means the clump of the pine.

Nethy and Dorback to Tomintoul by Bridge of Brown. Some fine tracks lead E from the basin of Nethy (Néithich or pure stream) to Tomintoul. In the old days, wooden utensils which had been made in the forests of Strath Spey were carried over the hill to Tomintoul and on by the Steplar Road to the Cabrach and Aberdeenshire. The present Grantown–Tomintoul road, which is joined by a branch from Nethy Bridge, goes by the picturesque little wooded gorge beside Bridge of Brown (*Broo*in). It forms part of the military road from Crathie to Grantown that was built in 1754 by the Army to make it easier for them to enforce the subjugation of the Highlands. From this road or from the public road to Dorback you have a grand view over the great expanse of the Nethy valley up Strath

Nethy to Bynack More and Cairn Gorm, with a glimpse of Beinn Mheadhoin behind. Through the great gap of the Pass of Ryvoan you can see beyond Glen More to the rocky gash into Lairig Ghru at Creag a' Chalamain. Below Dorback Lodge the glacial deposits are of fine sand, which has formed exotic-looking small dunes in the midst of the heather moorland.

Nethy to Tomintoul by Glen Brown. Distance: from Dorback Lodge via Lynachork to Tomintoul 10 km, ascent 200 m, time 2½ hours. The direct track from the Braes of Abernethy to Tomintoul starts along the N side of Dorback Lodge. It passes through a grassy hollow by Fae and Letteraitten to Glen Brown, whose name comes from Bruthainn (*Broo*in) or sultry warmth, 'Brown' being an absurd anglicised attempt. This route passes many deserted ruinous crofts, and Glen Brown, although once well populated, is now almost empty. The track then strikes across another grassy col by Strona-chavie to the gaunt ruin of Lynachork, where you wade the water of Avon across to Tomintoul, or you can take another path from Strona-chavie past Torran to the picturesque Bridge of Avon at the ivy-clad Kylnadrochit Lodge. Here, where Avon or Aan hurries swiftly over grey rocks and stones among birch, willow and trembling aspen, you can appreciate the old saying

The watter o Aan it rins sae clear

Twad beguile a man o a hundred year

Nearer Tomintoul the road passes a limestone quarry and goes round a hillside which looks lush green from the fertility of the rock. Here you can see interesting lime-loving hill plants such as viviparous bistort growing at the roadside.

Nethy to Avon by Ailnack. Distance: from Dorback Lodge to Avon bridge at Dalestie 12 km, ascent 350 m. This route from Dor-back to Tomintoul was the recognised way in the old days for travel-lers going direct from Abernethy to Strath Don. Here you take the bulldozed road which runs 5 km up Dorback Burn SE of the lodge to end at the col leading to Ailnack. The route continues as an old path S of Carn Ruadh-bhreac, and crosses Ailnack at a ford at 132124, lying just below the junction of streams to the W of Carn na Rua-braich. The path now goes S of Carn an t-Sleibhe and Geal Charn, and drops to Avon at 160103 S of the bridge at Dalestie. Beyond, the old route continues 4 km S to Inchrory and then E for 9 km down Féith Bhàit (Fay *Vaatsh*) to the Cock Bridge by Don, or E for 12 km over the Eag to the Cock Bridge. Opposite Dalestie, another path climbs past Clach Bhan on to the moor towards Ailnack, by a route called the Pass of Alltanarach (Alltan Nathrach).

An interesting walk takes you from the road end at the top of the Dorback burn for 7½ km to the Ca-du Ford and down Ailnack to Delnabo (total 12 km, total ascent from Dorback about 200 m). Indeed, it makes a fascinating day to explore the whole course of the water of Ailnack. This word comes from Ailneag (*Al*nach) or little stony one, which makes a good name as it has two remarkable gorges or canyons, an upper one at the Castle and another above Delnabo by the River Avon. Near the upper end of the ravine on the W bank, the Castle rises as a striking pinnacle of rock whose summit you can easily reach from the neck connecting it to the steep hillside behind. It is always a surprise when you come upon this winding ravine through which the water of Ailnack forces its way, as the surrounding countryside looks so peaty, gently undulating, and devoid of crags. You can walk along rather precarious sheep and deer tracks 60 m above the river, but in places can descend down screes to the water's edge. Rocks on either side bar easy progress along the actual stream but for climbers it makes an interesting trip to go down by the stream itself. After the upper canyon, which stretches for over 1 km, the steam comes into open moorland again down to the Ca-du Ford. Below here it plunges again into another remarkable gorge which extends for 4 km down to Delnabo (Dail nam Bo) or the haugh of the cows. From Tomintoul you can easily see the rocks at the lowest end of this gorge. A new bulldozed road now runs from Delnabo almost two thirds of the way to Ca-du, above the N bank of Ailnack.

Upstream from the Castle, Ailnack becomes Uisge Caiplich or the Water of Caiplich (*Caap*lich), meaning place of horses. This district stretching from the Dorback hills to Glen Avon consists of vast expanses of peaty moors and rolling bare hills, with winding shallow glens stretching for miles. To some, it may seem desolate and even dreary or boring. However, it is a place that gives a feeling of tremendous space and grand wilderness. Far beyond to the S, you look up to the fantastic rocky warts of Ben Avon and the rolling bulk and fine corries of Beinn a' Bhuird. The low hills and high moors carry an interesting vegetation on the peaty flats and bare dry tops, and support a few dunlin, greenshank and other uncommon moorland birds. They make difficult navigation on a misty day in winter. The two chief hills that rise out of these moors are the 821 m Geal

Charn (locally An Geal Chàrn, Ung *Yel* Charn) or the white hill, and further S the slightly lower Carn Bheadhair (Vair) at 803 m. Both sweep up from the E end of the pine forest at Abernethy, and are lonely hills that carry snow patches far into the summer. A bulldozed road runs towards them up the Faesheallach Burn to an altitude of about 620 m, NW of Bile Buidhe. Stretching from Eag Mhor over the Geal Charn, a fence continues S of the Castle and then goes E to Glen Avon.

The Hills of Cromdale form a distinct line between Spey and Avon, and are prominent in the view from near Dulnain Bridge and Grantown. The best viewpoint is the 628 m Sgòr Gaoithe (Skor *Goo*ee) or peak of wind, the shapely little top 1 km above the road from Grantown to Bridge of Brown. You reach a magnificent roadside viewpoint where the road to Nethy Bridge branches off, looking above the great peat bogs of Revack (*Ray* Vach) and the pine carpet of Abernethy to the Cairngorms and Monadh Liath; indeed, it forms one of the best views from any road in Scotland. To the NE of Sgor Gaoithe the ridge of hills continues for $4\frac{1}{2}$ km at over 600 m to the highest 722 m (2368 ft) top at Creagan a' Chaise (Craikan a *Chash*ie), where the big cairn was erected in 1887 to commemorate Queen Victoria's jubilee. From here the broad back of the ridge stretches for 9 km further NE to the slightly separate northern end of the ridge at Creag an Tàrmachain (Craikan *Taar*machan) or rock of the ptarmigan. The Hills of Cromdale have crisp walking on lichen and moss on the highest points but blanket peat on the flattish ground high up, and heathery well drained moors lower down. To the W, the hills slope to the Haughs of Cromdale, a name with a tautology, as Crom Dhail means curved haugh. On the bottom edge of the hill, back in 1690, the Battle of Cromdale was fought between a force of Highlanders and the troops of King William who routed them. Nearby lies Clach nam Pìobair or the stone of the pipers, a big boulder where pipers took their stand to urge on the Highlanders.

Strath Avon. The name Tomintoul comes from Tom an t-Sabhail (Tam in *Tow*el) or hillock of the barn. One of the highest villages in Scotland, it stands at about 345 m among open high moors and low rounded hills 13 km from the base of Ben Avon, which is the nearest of the high Cairngorms. It makes a useful stopping place on several cross-country walks, and a base for exploring Glen Avon and Ailnack. The finest way out of Tomintoul goes by the road that runs down the E side of Strath Avon. For variety of river and hill scenery, Avon cannot be bettered in Scotland. There is no dull stretch in the whole 70 km of its course, from the arctic stony snowy wilderness of the Ben Macdui plateau, over the wild dark cliffs to Loch Avon, down to the luxuriant sheltered beeches of Dalnasaugh where it flows deep and dark to enter the swift water of Spey. Strath Avon is one of the best parts, where groves of silver birches soften the valley side and where oystercatchers and sandpipers sweep over the water and call loudly by the shingles. The old church of Kirkmichael (Kerk *Mi*chil, 'e' as in her), near where green Glen Lochy comes in from the Cromdale Hills, is a particularly lovely spot.

Ben Rinnes. Beinn Rinneis, probably meaning headland hill. Although reaching only 840 m or 2755 ft, this is a grand and beautiful individually-shaped conical hill, gradual on Spey side, steep on Glen Rinnes side. Being isolated, it commands a glorious view over the Laich o' Moray and across the Moray Firth to the hills of Ross, Sutherland and Caithness. The actual summit, which is called the Scurran (Sgòran) of Lochterlandoch consists of a typical granite tor, and two others occur on the NW side towards Aberlour. The easiest way to climb Ben Rinnes is to walk from the Dufftown–Tomintoul road to beside the house at Glack. From here, a rough road goes at about 380 m altitude through the steep-sided Glack Harnes, often locally called the Glac o' the Beatshach. An easy climb then follows W to the top over Roy's Hill (4 km from Glack to summit, 570 m ascent). Another way goes S of Aberlour from the distillery near Milltown of Edinvillie, from which an old track goes uphill to about 470 m; many years of peat digging to fire the whisky stills have removed a big patch of deep peat here.

Around Dufftown, Little Conval (Con-mheall or combination of lumps) has an interesting old fort on its top, and its higher neighbour Meikle or big Conval (*Mick*il *Con*val) gives its name to the local distillery of Convalmore. Ben Aigan (Éiginn or difficulty) rises commandingly over the steep richly wooded banks of lower Spey. This part of the valley from Craigellachie up to Cromdale forms one of the finest though lesser-known parts of Spey, where the river winds among green haughs below steep slopes clad in birch and pine, rising further back to the bare, vast brown moors of Knockando (Nock*an*doe) and Tulchan. There is a particularly interesting view near Archiestown where you can see right into the Slochd Mor of Beinn a' Bhuird.

Moray and Nairn. Previous District Guides all ignored this area, and also that nearby fine countryside around Loch Duntelchaig just S of Inverness, with its many lochs and rich wildlife, scrubby copses, and innumerable small hills with little crags that offer very short but sporting scrambles and climbs. This omission is typical, as most people think of the back of Inverness town and of Moray and Nairn as fine farmland, prosperous towns and interesting coast, and not as hill country. Yet these two counties contain a higher proportion of woodland than any others in Scotland, and a very high proportion of wild moor and hill. You can walk for many miles through vast tracts of Scots pine like a forest in northern Finland, rich in capercaillies, red squirrels, crossbills, crested tits, red wood ants and other boreal forest animals. The high hills and moors on their N side give wonderful views far out over the low coast to the peaks across the Moray Firth from Ben Wyvis to the beautiful cone of Morven in Caithness.

You can explore a multitude of shallow, lonely glens, once populated by many farmers and crofters but now sadly empty in most places. These moors and hills are rich in wildlife. It is a country of vast space, with huge gentle slopes rolling into the distance. Despite the very low rainfall, the shallow gradients and thus poorer drainage have encouraged peat to build up thickly, and infertile wet bogs cover some of the flatter ground. The contrast in climate and scenery between the lush, warm Laich (lowland) o' Moray and the cold bare hill country of Bràigh Moireibh (brae or upland of Moray) comes as suddenly as anywhere in Scotland. Here you will find a good district for cross-country walks along old tracks, and in hard winters a fine place for ski touring. It is a complex tract of country, difficult to get to know, apparently featureless and uniform at first sight, but really all different and full of interest on closer acquaintance. In mist, dark or storm it becomes quite a difficult place for navigation.

In Nairnshire, a recommended trip is to walk down that fine wild stretch of Findhorn (Fionn Eireann or white Ireland) which starts at the A9 Inverness–Aviemore road just N of the Freeburn Hotel at Tomatin (Tom Aitinn, Tome-*at*in) or hillock of juniper. A path or road runs all the way down the NW bank of the river. Findhorn races down past great shingle beds into a narrow, twisting, steep-sided valley. Once you are into Nairnshire, you will see that the steep glens which cut into the hills on either side show many gravel scars from erosion. Beyond Drynachan (from Draighneachan or place of thorns), the Findhorn valley becomes wooded, especially below Dulsie Bridge and Glen Ferness (distance from A9 road to

Drynachan 12 km, to Dulsie Bridge 20 km). The glens above Drynachan lead up to extensive bare plateaux rising to 600 m where there is an unusual tundra-like vegetation rich in *Cladonia*, the 'reindeer moss' lichen. One of the biggest of these plateaux lies on the 659 m Carn Glas-choire, 5 km in walking WSW of the summit of the B9007 Forres-Duthil road, and also accessible (6 km) by a bulldozed road from 914281 up to the flat ground E of the top. Better still is the plateau on the remote Càrn nan Trì-tighearnan (Caarn nan *Tree* Tyeearnan) or hill of the three lairds, NE of Loch Moy. Distance: from 777335 on the A9, up the E side of Loch Moy and then by path, 10½ km. From Drynachan 4½ km.

The B9007 road from Nairn to Carrbridge runs into Invernessshire at a fine steep gap called Beum a' Chlaidheimh (Baim a *Chligh*) or gash of the sword, which shows up well in the northward view from Rothiemurchus. East of here the hills are much rockier with many small crags. These rocky hills stretch N to Lochindorb and E almost to the Forres road N of Grantown, and resemble the little rocky hills of Strath Nairn, though somewhat less varied, barer, higher, and less wooded. Lochindorb itself, with its old ruined castle on an islet, lies hidden behind a low hill. The moor of Dava (Damhàth, *Daa*va or ox ford) near here stretches far out as a rolling wide heather tract dotted with clumps of juniper and pine, and with many lochans and flat peat bogs. One of the best hills, well worth climbing, is the Knock of Braemoray (455 m or 1493 ft) overlooking the vast Dunphail and Altyre moors by the River Divie (Duibhidh, *Div*ee or black one). You can easily climb up for 1 km from the A940 just N of Dava and it gives an outstanding view. An old road across the moors here, which makes a fine cross-country walk, goes 13 km from the A940 at 020465 beside the viaduct at Dunphail, E past the farm of Johnstripe and over to 121500. This takes you across the rolling gentle slopes of the huge sweep of boggy moorland above Dallas (Dalais or meadow place), beside the head waters of the River Lossie. It becomes particularly good after the spring thaw, when the moors here resound with the songs of returning skylarks, curlews and golden plovers. The old railway line, now disused, also offers a secluded walking route. Another good way goes for 15 km from the viaduct to 047338, up Divie side and over the top to the S by Badahad to the woods of Castle Grant.

On the lower ground, the banks of Findhorn from Dulsie Bridge down past Sluie to the Forres–Inverness road make one of the finest walks in lowland Scotland, through magnificent river and woodland scenery along the edge of historic Darnaway Forest (distance from Dulsie Bridge to Ferness bridge 9 km, to A96 28 km). To the SE of Forres, the extensive pine woods of Altyre and Romach Loch in its steep defile are interesting features, as is the steep stony escarpment near Pluscarden. The tidal flats of Findhorn's estuary you will find to be one of the best places for wading birds in E Scotland. Nearby, Culbin Forest extends far on flattish ground as a vast tract of pine which, although new and planted on sand dunes, has already become a stronghold of the wood ant, crested tit and capercaillie.

Climbing routes

Although it lies just outside the region of this book, any climber in Strath Spey should visit Creag Dhubh. Here soars a remarkable 140 m steep wall of smooth schist close above the Fort William road about 5 km W of Newtonmore. You can now buy a special climbers' guide book for this crag, by G. Tiso (see Further Reading). There are many small crags in Strath Spey, such as at Eag Mhor and Ailnack. Two that are more accessible lie just outside the area for this book, but will be obvious to anyone staying long in the Spey Valley on a visit to the Cairngorms. One is Creag Bheag at Kingussie, which overlooks the town beside the golf course; here, at 749015, a crag of schist from 20–50 m high offers some fine slab climbing. Another you will find immediately behind the hotels of the Aviemore Centre, where the steep 60 m wall of Craigellachie has three or four VS climbs. A third low crag, this time on the E side of Spey, is the 30 m cliff at 826031, S of the B970 road beside Loch Insh, with several routes varying from S to VS. The best of these more accessible crags lies at Huntly's Cave in a gorge about 5 km N of Grantown beside the A939 road to Forres, at 024327. Park your car in the lay-by on the right, walk through the wood for 50 m to cross the disused railway by a stile, and then descend into the valley to the cliff, which forms a very steep 10–15 m outcrop with a line of overhangs. About a dozen routes have been made, all severe or harder, one of the best being a splendid girdle traverse across the crag (VS and A1). A second small crag lower down the valley on the other side gives a few good routes of about 20 m in height. W. March and others at Glenmore Lodge have done most of the exploration on these lower Strath Spey crags. The hills between the Nairn–Carrbridge road and the Forres–Grantown road contain many small less accessible crags of schist which offer plenty of scrambling and in places give good though very short climbs. On Ben Rinnes, the largest Scurran or tor makes a short climb about VD in standard on dry rough granite.

On the coast between Burghead and Lossiemouth, an unusual stretch of sea cliff which consists of Triassic sandstone of a beautiful warm creamy-brown colour, faces the wide Moray Firth. The rock is rather friable in places and very steep, the majority of the routes being above severe in standard. Although only 12–20 m high, these cliffs make a very good training ground, but you should not go at high tide when many of the routes become inaccessible from below. One of the best climbing areas, at 125692 just E of Burghead, has been much used by the Moray Sea School and you will see belay stakes on the cliff top. Another good stretch begins at 179708 beside Gows Castle E of Hopeman and extends W of there for about 2 km. Gows Castle itself is a stack nearly 20 m high, with one route (S) on its landward side. The climbs along the coast here are mainly severe or harder. Just W of Elgin in the Quarry Wood beside the A96 road to Inverness, the Old Quarry at 188628 forms another accessible training ground which is also much used by the Moray Sea School, with 20–25 m routes on quarried sandstone.

Further reading

W. Forsyth   1900   *In the Shadow of Cairngorm*. A native of Abernethy and minister of the parish, he wrote a good account of the district, its history and bygone life.

J. Walton (ed)   *Glen More*. National Forest Park Guide. A booklet with much useful information. Very short but good articles on old way of life, geology, vegetation, wildlife and particularly on forests and plantations. Useful bibliography of books on Strath Spey.

G. Tiso   1967   *Creag Dubh and the Eastern Outcrops*. Climbers' Guide. On sale G. Tiso, 44 Rodney Street, Edinburgh 7.
The following are of historical interest:

R. Anderson   Ben Aigan. *CCJ* 2, 150.

C. G. Cash   The Rothiemurchus Forest fire. *CCJ* 3, 96.

A. I. McConnochie Loch an Eilein and its Castle. *CCJ* 3, 104.

C. G. Cash. The Loch an Eilein ospreys. *CCJ* 4, 125, and 5, 270.

C. G. Cash. Timber floating at Rothiemurchus. *CCJ* 4, 301.

E. P. Buchanan. Through Rothiemurchus to Rebhoan. *SMCJ* 13, 251.

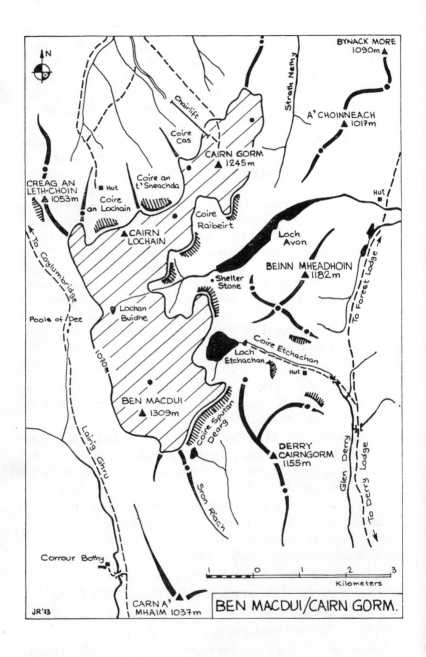

BEN MACDUI/CAIRN GORM.

2

Cairn Gorm and Ben Macdui

*Cairn Gorm	1245 m, 005041
*Ben Macdui	1309 m, 989989
Cairn Lochan	1215 m, 986026
*Bynack More	1090 m, 042063
*A' Choinneach	1017 m, 032048
Creag an Leth-choin	1053 m, 969033
*Beinn Mheadhoin	1182 m, 025017
*Derry Cairngorm	1155 m, 016981
*Carn a' Mhaim	1037 m, 995953

Access

Public roads go to Linn of Dee, and on Spey to Coire Cas and Whitewell. A bus runs from Aviemore to Coire Cas.

Accommodation and other facilities

As in Chapters 1 and 8. A board at the top end of the car park at Coire Cas gives the latest forecast of weather for the upper part of Cairn Gorm, including wind direction and speed.

Remote occupied houses

Glenmore Lodge 987094, Rothiemurchus Hut 951067, Achnagoichan 914083, Luibeg 036933.

Bothies and shelters (see also Chapter 3)

All these are open throughout the year except for the Hutchison Hut which is closed during the stalking season. In addition, a locked hut stands E of the White Lady Shieling at Coire Cas, perched on the hillside; apply to the Scottish Ski Club. *Jean's Hut* stands at 981034, at 892 m altitude in Coire an Lochain. From the path slanting slightly uphill from the Coire Cas car park to Allt Creag an Leth-choin, a path branches off to Jean's Hut, going up the W side of Allt Coire an Lochain towards the hut on the E side (3 km from the car park, 240 m ascent). The hut has an entry corridor with storage space, and a big inner room with fitted bunks and window. *Clach Dhion or the Shelter Stone* 003016, lies at about 755 m. *El Alamein refuge* 015054, at about 975 m, is a tiny storm refuge. Cairns mark the route from the col to the NW. *St Valery refuge* 001022, at about 1060 m, is a tiny storm refuge measuring $8 \times 5 \times 5$ ft, among rocks at the E end of a small flat grassy shelf, E of where the broad ridge from the top of the Coire an t-Sneachda cliffs ends at Stag Rocks, and immediately to the W of a tiny tor. *Curran Bothy* 983010, stands at about 1125 m, immediately S of Lochan Buidhe, and holds 5 to 6. Caution: Curran, St Valery and El Alamein are often snow-filled inside or buried by snow outside. *Hutchison Memorial Hut* 023998, lies at about 700 m in Coire Etchachan in the centre of the flattish corrie basin, on the S side of the path. Built in 1954, it is run by the Etchachan Club. *Jamie Murray's Cave* 023055 on the W side of Garbh Allt, 2 km N of The Saddle, makes a comfortable shelter for 3, under a big stone. *The Sappers' Bothy* 991988 is a roofless ruin but still provides a little summer shelter.

General description

Ben Macdui and Cairn Gorm form a rampart of high hills E of the Lairig Ghru, lying in the centre of the Cairngorms massif. At 1309 m, Ben Macdui is the highest hill in the Cairngorms and only Ben Nevis rises higher in Britain. The plateau between Ben Macdui and Cairn Gorm is unique in Scotland as a large tract of varied arctic terrain; there exists nowhere else in Britain a place where you can feel so much that you are in Greenland or high-arctic Canada. Streams from both hills plunge in waterfalls into the great trench of Loch Avon, unsurpassed by any Scottish loch in its grandeur and its wild, remote setting, and in this sense it is one of the wildest places in Europe outside Norway. Reaching about 240 m high, the cliffs at Loch Avon make a magnificent climbing ground.

Geology and landforms

The rock is virtually all granite. At Coire an Lochain a huge slab of granite keeps in its virgin pink colour because of the snow avalanches and water that pour down it every summer. There are many varieties of crag, varying from broken rocks disintegrating into scree in the Lairig Ghru to the sheer smooth wall of the Sticil (Styeechkeel) or the Shelter Stone Crag. In the early 1960s, a hugh rockfall on Carn Etchachan's W side exposed a big new face of fresh pink granite. Arctic-like braided streams, stone stripes and polygons are common on·flat ground on the plateau, and mud flows occasionally occur on Cairn Lochan during the big summer thaw.

Natural history

With the biggest and most varied area of arctic-like terrain in Britain, the plateau and shoulders between Cairn Gorm and Ben Macdui are of very great interest to naturalists. Many big snow patches occur higher and longer here than anywhere in Britain, so the special snow-patch vegetation is very rich and shows obvious transition zones that depend on how long the snow lies. The great whaleback of Cairn Lochan is especially interesting for the extensive gravelly barrens of three-pointed rush on its summit, gradually merging lower down into an unusually large area with a continuous turf of alpine grassland along Feith Buidhe and the smaller stretch of this in Coire Domhain. Along the flat top of Miadan Creag an Leth-choin, on the gentle slopes E of Coire na Ciste and on A' Choinneach, woolly hair moss dominates the vegetation, mixed with three-leaved rush and heaths. The wide mossy flushes and streams are a special feature at the higher altitudes, and in summer become attractive feeding places for the insect-eating birds. You will see huge boulder fields SE of Lochan Buidhe, NW of Derry Cairngorm, NW of Ben Macdui and over much of the ground from Lochan Buidhe towards Loch Etchachan. The many corrie cliffs also have an interesting arctic-like vegetation ungrazed by sheep or deer, and a rich subarctic heath covers the ground at the head of Loch Avon. The ptarmigan is the commonest bird. Special features are that these hills form a breeding haunt of the snow bunting and dotterel, and excel as one of the best places in Britain for insects of arctic origin. In some summers a snowy owl lives on the plateau. Domestic reindeer from the herd at Glen More often live on the plateau in summer, as do domestic sheep, but the numerous red deer stags, hinds and calves which used to summer there have gone. There have long been many good trout in Loch Avon. A new feature is that crows and seagulls now hunt the plateau, attracted by scraps of food from tourists. Fortunately, recent research has shown no evidence so far that this invasion has harmed the unique wildlife of the high tops.

Estates

The Aberdeenshire part belongs to Mar Lodge, the Banffshire part to Inchrory, Creag an Leth-choin to Rothiemurchus, the N side of Cairn Gorm and its corries to the Highlands and Islands Development Board, and Strath Nethy to Forest Lodge.

History

Johan Blaeu's *Atlas Novus* of 1654 shows 'Carn-gorum', and not far to the SW also 'Corintrack' which is probably Coire an t-Sneachda (pronounced Cor an Tre'achk). In her *Guide to the Beauties of Scotland* (3rd edition 1810) the Hon Mrs Murray Aust describes an ascent of Cairn Gorm in 1801. Further back in time comes the story of Fuaran a' Mharcuis (*Foo*aran a *Var*kish) or the well of the Marquis, which is the spring beside the track NE of the summit of Cairn Gorm. It was named after the Marquis of Huntly who chased Mac-Calum Mor, the Marquis of Argyle, westwards after the Battle of Glen Livet in 1594.

The first account of Ben Macdui appears in the *General View of Aberdeenshire* (1811) by the Rev Dr G. S. Keith who, in 1810, surveyed the altitudes of some Deeside hills using a barometer. Keith made the height of Ben Macdui to be 4300 ft, and although the Ordnance Survey subsequently gave it as 4296 ft, they changed it in the 1960s to agree exactly with Keith's 4300, but have since gone back to the 4296 again in the latest maps! In the 19th century, many thought Ben Macdui was the highest hill of Scotland, but when Dr Keith sent his son with the barometer to Fort William, he reported that Ben Nevis was 50 ft higher. The argument was not finally settled till the Ordnance Survey set up their trigonometrical station on Ben Macdui in 1847; the ruined remains of the surveyors' stone hut, which local people still call the Sappers' Bothy, still lie just E of the summit. As a result, Ben Macdui was recorded as 4296 ft and Ben Nevis as 4406 ft. The story is that John Hill Burton, an 'old adherent' of Ben Macdui, would 'fain have gone down on his knees and begged the surveyors not to depose his beloved mountain'!

The 19th century was the great period for lairds building memorials for themselves on Scottish hilltops, dominating the surrounding countryside. Fortunately, what would have been the worst of these outrages in Scotland was not actually carried out. This was the Earl of Fife's plan, described in 1819 in *The Caledonian Itinerary*, to build a sepulchral pyramid 100 ft high on the summit of Ben Macdui, with a burial vault inside. On their pioneering explorations of natural history, Prof W. MacGillivray and other naturalists of the early 19th century climbed Ben Macdui. In October 1859, Queen Victoria went up to the top on a pony by Glen Derry, and later wrote '*Never* shall I forget this day or the impression this very grand scene made upon me; truly sublime and impressive; such solitude'.

Dr Keith wrote of a story that grass growing on the high hills became poisonous to horses. The local legend was that the grass was poisoned by a glutinous matter ejected by the Famh (Faav), a mythical monster which appeared only at the head of Loch Avon, only at daybreak and only on the highest verge of the hill! Another old local legend is that a giant spectre called Am Fear Liath Mór (Um *Fer* Lee-a *More*) or the big grey man, haunts Ben Macdui. When Prof N. J. Collie the well known Victorian mountaineer stood alone on the summit, he heard footsteps in the snow like somebody accompanying him, and was so scared that he ran fleeing from the top (*CCJ* 11, 214). Many others have had strange experiences there (Further Reading). Perhaps the best story is of one Aberdeen climber, on leave in the mid 1940s, who emptied his army revolver into one particularly menacing shape of mist!

During the 1939–45 War, commandos and mountain troops trained in the Cairngorms, and you can still see their many stone bivouacs NE of Ben Macdui. You will also come across pieces of aluminium here and there; in the early 1940s a British services plane crashed at the top of Allt a' Choire Mhoir NW of the summit. Others crashed on Stob an t-Sluichd, in Coire na Lairige of Braeriach, on the Little Pap and near Moulzie.

Views from the summits

From the hill ridge between the Ptarmigan Restaurant and Cairn Lochan, the view is one of the finest in all Scotland. The N face of Cairn Gorm drops 900 m to Strath Spey with no intervening ranges of foothills, so you have the effect of walking on a great uplifted terrace, on the roof of Scotland. Below, the pine forests of Glen More and Rothiemurchus spread like huge green carpets towards the upper Spey and Creag Meagaidh, the Monadh Liath and the Moray-shire moors. On fine days Loch Morlich turns into a mirror reflecting the pines on its N bank. You look across the blue Moray Firth to the cone of Morven in Caithness, and in clear weather you can see to the hills of W Sutherland, Torridon, Kintail and Knoydart, up to 160 km away.

In 1897–98, A. Copland, first chairman of the Cairngorm Club, surveyed the panorama of hills to be seen from Ben Macdui, and published it (*CCJ* 2, 73, 243, 314, 391; and 3, 119). Later, J. A. Parker checked and revised it, and in 1925 the Club built his indicator on the summit. The furthest hills on it are: to the SSE the Lammermuirs at 150 km, and to the N Ben a' Chielt of Caithness at 140 km. In fact, on the clearest days you can see many further distant hills that are not shown on the indicator, including peaks in Knoydart, Torridon and NW Sutherland.

Cairn Gorm 1245 m (4084 ft)

The name Cairn Gorm comes from Càrn Gorm or blue hill, pronounced Cairn *Gor*om. Cairn Gorm dominates Strath Spey and looks a beautiful peak especially from around Nethy Bridge and Dulnain Bridge. From Loch Morlich, it and its corries form one of the best views in Scotland. It has become well known as a ski ground and also for walking, rock climbing and other outdoor pursuits.

Ski developments

Since 1961 when a new road and chair lift were built, the easiest access to Cairn Gorm has been by Glen More. From E of Loch Morlich, a wide public road passes beyond the Glen More camp site and heads through the woods up into Coire Cas to a car park at 650 m, with toilets, telephone kiosk and snack bar. From here a chair lift goes up to the middle chair lift station beside the White Lady Shieling at about 760 m or 2500 ft, where there is a large café and toilet. The upper part of the chair lift leads from there to the top station and Ptarmigan Restaurant at about 1080 m or 3600 ft. Just above the tree line on the road to Coire Cas, you will see a spur road going E to a car park at the foot of Coire na Ciste. A chair lift and ski tow were built in autumn 1973 up this corrie to the basin and ski tow E of the Ptarmigan Restaurant. All these facilities and several more T-bar ski tows are owned by Cairngorm Sports Development Ltd. Construction work has scarred some of the hillsides and led to soil erosion, but this has decreased a lot since 1970 due to better roads, new drains and reseeding of the damaged ground with grasses. The odd-looking black rocks and soil that you see in places are coloured by bitumen which is sprayed on to the grass seeds and fertilizers so that the germinating seeds do not dry out. If you are not using the chair lift, do not wander about and thus damage the reseeded patches, but stay on the prepared roads. A rough road zig-zags from the car park all the way to the Ptarmigan Restaurant.

Walking ascents to Cairn Gorm

From Coire Cas. From the Ptarmigan Restaurant a short walk of 1 km with a 150 m ascent, along a broad path with marking posts,

14. The granite tors of the Barns of Bynack.

15. John Cunningham climbing the left fork of Y Gully in Coire an Lochain.

16. Winter frost on the remarkable rock architecture of West Buttress in Coire an Lochain, with the fissure of Savage Slit.

17. Climbing steep ice on Hell's Lum Crag in March. Carn Etchachan is the pointed crag, with the Sticil jutting out to the right.

18. *Opposite*. The Sticil or Shelter Stone Crag, with Forefinger Pinnacle above the horizon (right) and Carn Etchachan (left).

19.   *Opposite*. Forefinger Pinnacle and the west wall of the Sticil.

20.   Climbing Thor, beside the beautiful sheet of smooth granite on the
Central Slabs of the Sticil.

21. *Opposite*. Climbers on Djibangi in July, on the Crimson Slabs of Creagan a' Choire Etchachan.

22. *Above*. The largest of the Pools of Dee in Lairig Ghru during October. Cairn Toul (right), and the Devil's Point (centre).

23. From Braeriach, looking S down Lairig Ghru.

24. Bringing down a stag from the pine-studded flats of upper Glen Derry.

25. From Ben Mac-dui, looking across the Lairig Ghru to Sgor an Lochain Uaine (left), Garbh Choire Mor to its right, then Garbh Choire Dhaidh.

takes you in a long curve past Fuaran a' Mharcuis and through patches of moss, dwarf willow, gravel and stones to the summit of Cairn Gorm. The cairn stands on an outcrop of granite near a locked mountain rescue hut. Routes from the White Lady Shieling are to take the winding road up to Ptarmigan Restaurant, or to break off the lower part of that road beside the Fiacaill tow and walk on to Fiacaill a' Choire Chais (*Fee*achkill a Chorrie *Chash*) or the tooth of the steep corrie. You follow this prominent broad stony ridge on the W side of the corrie to its top at 1141 m and then go E to the summit of Cairn Gorm.

By the path from Glen More. Distance: about 7 km or 4½ miles from the camp site, 920 m ascent, 3 hours up. The walker who wishes to avoid these developed slopes can go up the old path to Cairn Gorm. Although it was unfortunately obliterated by the road in the lower forest, you will still find it alongside the stream of Allt Mor, just after the road crosses the bridge half way up the forest; it then climbs among some fine old pines. Later it crosses the road on the hill beside the big bends, and slants uphill near the huge boulder of Clach Bharraig (*Varr*ig) to the ridge at An t-Aonach (Un *Tain*ach) or the height. The track now leads straight up the long ridge of Sròn an Aonaich (Stron an *Ain*ich) or nose of the height, past the granite tor of Caisteal Dubh (*Castyal Doo*) or black castle to the Ptarmigan Restaurant.

Descent by Cairn Lochan. Distance: 5 km from Cairn Gorm to Creag an Leth-choin. A good route for descent is round to Cairn Lochan, which should be spelled Càrn Lochain (Caarn *Locha*n) meaning tarn hill, and then to Creag an Leth-choin. You drop down the dome of Cairn Gorm W to Fiacaill a' Choire Chais at 1141 m and then follow the path, at first down to a col at 1099 m and then gradually rising along the cliff edge of the wide Coire an t-Sneachda or corrie of the snow to the highest top at 1176 m. Beyond, you stroll along the path near the cliff edge and down to the 1111 m col at the top of the long green Coire Domhain (Cor *Daw*-in) or deep corrie. An easy climb follows over short turf and gravel to Cairn Lochan at 1215 m, where the cairn stands at the cliff edge (3 km from Cairn Gorm, 180 m ascent). Here you look down the steep crags of Coire an Lochain (Cor an *Locha*n) or corrie of the tarn, one of the most impressive corries of the Cairngorms.

The granite of the Cairngorms weathers in horizontal and vertical lines, often producing an effect like huge masonry. This is particularly striking in Coire an Lochain, where some of the rocks look as if built in gigantic towers, deeply cut by gullies. From Cairn Lochan, easy walking follows along the broad whaleback which stretches SW for over 1 km towards the Lairig Ghru. A cairn at the end of the flat part marks the junction of Inverness, Banff and Aberdeen counties; it is Càrn nan Trì Crìoch (*Tree Cree*-uch), the cairn of the three boundaries. From it you drop down the stony slope towards Creag an Leth-choin on to a wide green flat, which rises slightly on to stony ground to a cairn at 1083 m at its SW end; the name of this green is Miadan Creag an Leth-choin (*Mee*-adan or meadow). From the Miadan a path goes downhill to the NNE, beside the stream and then slanting across the steep grassy slope W of Coire an Lochain. If snow lies here, even in summer, avoid this path as the slope is steep and prone to avalanches. A safer way off goes straight down the wide ridge which starts at the N end of the green from the cairn on Fiacaill an Leth-choin, or else NW towards Creag an Leth-choin and then downhill. Both ways take you to the path leading to the Coire Cas car park, or to another path to Glen More by a footbridge over Allt Mor just S of the trees. Distance: from Creag an Leth-choin to car park 4 km, from Cairn Lochan via Fiacaill an Leth-choin to car park 5 km.

Descent by Ryvoan. An interesting way down or up goes by the long N ridge past Cnap Coire na Spréidhe at 1151 m (*Crap* Cor na *Spray*) or knob of the cattle corrie. You will find it delightful walking over the mossy and gravelly ground, and by skirting the cliffs you can look into the great dark gulf of Strath Nethy. A pleasant walk follows past a 1028 m top and N of it down the long nose of Sron a' Cha-no, past a fenced experimental forestry plot, to Lochan na Beinne (*Peen*) and down Allt Ban by a path on its N side to Glenmore Lodge, 8 km from Cairn Gorm. An alternative route is to climb the 742 m Stac na h-Iolaire and drop N down Màm Suim (Maam *Soo*eem) and Creag nan Gall on the way to Ryvoan, 9 km from Cairn Gorm; you will then see An Lochan Uaine on the walk back. This will show you several crags and valleys, now almost dry, which were cut by great rivers flowing out when the huge Glen More glacier was hemmed in here by Cairn Gorm and Meall a' Bhuachaille. Particularly striking among these are Stac na h-Iolaire (Stachk na H*yoo*lar) or eagle's precipice, and Eag a' Gharbh Choire.

Walking in Cairn Gorm's corries

The corries of Cairn Gorm are rough, bouldery and fairly unfrequented, despite their accessibility from the car park at Coire Cas. At the N end, Coire Laogh Mór (Cor Lay *More*) or big corrie of calves, forms a small steep bowl fringed with broken rock. Coire na Ciste (Cor na *Keesht*) or corrie of the chest, a steep narrow corrie, holds the best ski run on Cairn Gorm. Coire Cas (Corrie *Cas*) or steep corrie, carries a conspicuous steep snow wreath at its top, which lasts far into the summer; its name is Cuidhe Crom (Coo-ee *Crome*) or crooked wreath. Avalanches occur here and the snow often turns dangerously icy even in summer. The beautiful Coire an t-Sneachda is well worth exploring. Take the track that leads W from the car park, and after 1 km, head up the next stream. A great mound of glacial debris lies high in the E side of the corrie, and further up are several small tarns. Here you stand among great boulder fields and scanty vegetation, looking up at a long and varied set of crags. Coire an Lochain forms Cairn Gorm's most striking corrie, with a steep wall of dark cliffs, long-lying snow patches and two small tarns far below. A very unusual feature is the great curtain of bare granite which slopes from the base of the cliffs towards the tiny loch. From near Grantown, it glistens in the sun and in certain lights has a pink colour. Separating Coire an Lochain from Coire an t-Sneachda rises a long stony ridge climbing to a little peak called Fiacaill Coire an t-Sneachda. The rocky ridge above it is the Fiacaill Ridge. One of the few narrow rock arêtes in the Cairngorms, it makes an interesting summer ascent involving easy scrambling, but can be difficult in winter.

On the S side of Cairn Gorm, Coire Domhain plunges, after its long, green upper section, into a narrow stream bed running steeply to Loch Avon. The next corrie to the E is Coire Raibeirt (Cor *Rabe*rt, 'a' as in tab) or Robert's corrie. A very wide, green corrie with many boggy flushes, it opens out on the S side of the ridge at the top of Coire Cas. To the E of Coire Raibeirt and beyond a rocky tor at 1082 m lies a shallow, nameless green corrie drained by a Feith Buidhe much tinier than the one out of Lochan Buidhe. Still further round the corner higher up and due E of Cairn Gorm, an unusual small sandy pocket faces E on the hillside. Snow often lies in it throughout the year, as also in the hollow to the N nearer Cnap Coire na Spreidhe where a stream furrow running E into Garbh Allt has the name Ciste Mearaid (Keesht *Mair*ad) or Margaret's coffin. Ski races are sometimes held on this hillside when Coire Cas lacks snow.

Ben Macdui 1309 m (4296 ft)

Local folk call this Pain Mach*doo*ee, and the name probably comes from Beinn Mhic Dhuibh, Macduff's hill, or else Beinn Mac Duibh, hill of the sons of Duff; the Macduffs or Earls of Fife for long held the lands of Mar which include this hill. Ben Macdui lies so much in the centre of the Cairngorms that you do not see it well from most places further out, but at Inverey you will get a fine distant view of it. It is the most arctic-like place in these islands. Of all the hills in the Cairngorms, it also has the finest set of high tarns and lakes; and with the Sticil, Carn Etchachan and Coire Sputan Dearg it easily excels with its grand precipices.

Walking ascents to Ben Macdui

From the top of Cairn Gorm. Distance: 6½ km or 4 miles, 275 m or 900 ft ascent, 1¾ hours. Because the ski road and chair lift reach so high on the hill, most people now climb Ben Macdui from the N, and the easier access has led to inexperienced and inadequately equipped tourists wandering over the plateau in summer. Routes as far as the col E of Cairn Lochan are described on p 105. From that col at 1111 m, at the edge of the cliffs of Coire an t-Sneachda, a narrow track slants uphill to the SSW along the W side of Coire Domhain; it then passes over a low neck and runs horizontally SW to Lochan Buidhe. The second-lowest point on this marvellous high-level walk lies at 1125 m beside this tiny tarn, called Lochan Féith Buidhe (Fay *Poo*ee) or tarn of Feith Buidhe by the older local folk. At just over 1120 m it is the highest named tarn in Britain. Here the water flows into Banffshire, but only 100 m to the W across flat turf the ground drains into Allt na Criche (Creech), the burn of the boundary or 'March Burn', at first passing through a stretch of wet boggy ground verging on being another tarn.

From Lochan Buidhe the track, marked by cairns, leads S up a gentle slope, then SE for 90 m of a climb more steeply up the gravelly and bouldery front of the North Top to 1295 m, and finally SSW on the level to the summit at 1309 m. Evidence of the great increase of people on these hills comes from the fact that no tracks existed here in the late 1940s.

By Glen Derry. Distance: 12 km or 7½ miles, 880 m or 2900 ft climb, time up 4 hours. This excellent varied route offers a gradual ascent with a good path. Starting at 420 m, the first 6½ km up Glen Derry are the same as the Lairig an Laoigh route (p 133). At a sign-post at 035992 the Ben Macdui path forks left to the NW, off the Lairig track, crosses the Etchachan burn by a footbridge, and heads into Coire Etchachan (Cor *Ait*shachan) past the Hutchison Hut at about 700 m. This corrie is a vast bowl with steep craggy sides. On the S and W sides rise the rocks of Creagan a' Choire Etchachan (*Craik*an Chor *Ait*shachan) or the precipices of Coire Etchachan, which are especially striking on the sheer W wall. Further back from that wall, you will see a nameless stony cone which rises to 1108 m or 3629 ft behind the corrie.

After climbing steeply up the roaring burn, the path eventually comes out suddenly beside Loch Etchachan at just over 922 m, the highest big loch of this size in Britain. At its E end lies the beautiful grass and thrift-margined Loch Etchachan Beag (*Pick*). The scene is arctic. Towards Ben Macdui, beyond a fine subarctic heath above the S shore of the loch, stretches a complex terrain of broken crags, bulging shoulders and vast boulder fields, with many hollows where snow lingers far into the summer. Usually, the loch has some ice for more than half the year. To the N, a flat col leads through towards the gulf of Loch Avon, with Cairn Gorm rising beyond and the rocky Carn Etchachan sweeping up to the W of the flat. Slanting up the slope on the S side of the loch, the path to Ben Macdui then climbs below the great bulging spur of Sròn an Daimh (Stron an *Digh-f*) or promontory of the stag, and comes out of the Loch Etchachan basin beside a cliff top on the left. The cliff drops abruptly into Coire Sputan Dearg (Cor *Spoot*an D*yerr*eg) or the corrie with red little spouts, so called from the red scree in the main gullies. From the big spout here, the view down Glen Luibeg is magnificent. After a further climb near the cliff edge, the path reaches the plateau and goes W over gravelly ground to the ruined Sappers' Bothy and 200 m further to the summit cairn.

By Glen Luibeg. Distance: 9 km or 5½ miles, 880 m or 2900 ft climb, 3¼ hours up. This is the shortest way from Derry Lodge. The first 3 km are the same as for the Lairig Ghru (p 131). Then, about 300 m in distance before the Lairig path crosses the Luibeg Burn, your path slants up to the right. About 2 km further up, the burn forks at 560 m, the long ridge between the forks being the Sròn Riach or really Riabhach (Stron *Ree*-ach) or brindled nose. The path climbs steadily up short grass and heather to a tor and then becomes indistinct, but the way ahead is obvious over sparse vegetation, gravel and stones, with fine views over to Cairn Toul and Derry Cairngorm. At about 1100 m you come suddenly to a cliff edge where you will enjoy an impressive view down to Lochan Uaine at about 955 m. Here in Coire an Lochain Uaine snow lies in a couple of pockets far into the summer, beside the 300 m of wet avalanche-prone slabs rising to the nameless pyramid peak above (the name Stob Coire Sputan Dearg was an invention for Munro's Tables). The best route now heads up the boulders by the cliff rim to the marvellous viewpoint of this peak at 1249 m, but you can avoid the boulders by slanting left up a grassy slope to the plateau SE of the ruined Sappers' Bothy.

By Allt Clach nan Taillear. To or from Corrour Bothy, a good route goes by the long broad ridge S of Allt Clach nan Taillear (4½ km, 760 m climb). When you are coming off Ben Macdui it is safest to descend to 996984 before turning down the S bank of the stream. The direct route from the summit cairn to the lower part of Allt Clach nan Tàillear (*Taal*yer) has to cross Coire nan Taillear by a frieze of broken slabby rock which stretches along the plateau edge S of the summit and leads on to a very steep slope below. Huge cornices build up here and avalanches occur even in July.

By the Pools of Dee. The easiest route here leads up Allt na Crìche (the 'March Burn') to Lochan Buidhe and then S to Ben Macdui. From the summit of Lairig Ghru at about 835 m, you have 3 km to go and a 480 m ascent to Ben Macdui, first by a steep climb up scree and boulders for 240 m, where the loose scree can be dangerous for a beginner. In fact there are better ways up on either side; look for one of the deer tracks that slant uphill at an angle, as this makes an easier and safer ascent. Remember that icy snow at a high angle lies in a snow bridge at the top of Allt na Criche far into the summer, but you can usually bypass the snow on either side at that season. In winter, it frequently becomes a dangerous route, often icy and other times avalanche-prone; indeed the same is true of the entire W face from Creag an Leth-choin to Allt Clach nan Taillear. The ridge SW of the Ben Macdui cairn, bounding Coire nan Taillear on its W side, you will find a possible exception; as it is heavily boulder-strewn, winds often blow it clear of snow but you should not depend on this.

From Loch Avon. Distance: 3½ km or 2¼ miles, 580 m climb, 1¾ hours up; add 1½ hours to the usual route from Glen Derry if you diverge this way. Loch Avon (routes to the loch on p 112) lies at the start of the finest way up Ben Macdui. You slant up by the side of Garbh Uisge (*Gaar* Ooshk) or rough water, a good name for this roaring cascading stream, which in places dashes over smooth beds of bare granite. For 250 m of height it makes a steep but easy enough way as the slope is well broken by boulders and ledges of vegetation. On the steepest narrow part at about 900 m, you can easily scramble up and around the boulders, but in winter this place can be dangerously icy. Above this point you come into a gently rising basin full of boulder fields and dotted with snow wreaths, where Garbh Uisge divides in two. The main stream is Garbh Uisge Mór or big rough water, which leads up through a magnificent piece of arctic terrain beside some high tarns. It rises in an upper basin called the Snowy Corrie where huge drifts last into the summer; the skyline facing you as you walk up the basin turns out to be the plateau E of the ruined Sappers' Bothy.

Walking in Ben Macdui's corries

For the hill walker the corries of Ben Macdui are magnificent to explore. Coire Etchachan, Garbh Uisge and the Snowy Corrie have already been described. A fine route is to go up Glen Luibeg to where the burn forks below Sron Riach, and then climb by an indistinct path up the E bank of the eastern stream far up into the wilds of Coire Sputan Dearg. A sunny, sheltered corrie, it has a beautiful setting. On the way, it is well worth climbing up the side stream to Lochan Uaine and then dropping N into Coire Sputan Dearg. From the NE end of the cliffs in Coire Sputan Dearg, you will find it a short easy walk up to the 1053 m neck W of the conical, gravelly, 1108 m point at 010996 (there are no cliffs at this neck as shown on the OS 7th Series map), and then down to the path above Loch Etchachan. The 1108 m (3629 ft) point has often been called Creagan a' Choire Etchachan erroneously, but in fact its name seems to have become lost and the Creagan really refers to the rock faces away to the E in Coire Etchachan.

North of Ben Macdui on its W side, Allt a' Choire Mhoir drains the uppermost gentle gravelly hollow towards the North Top, next runs through a green patch among boulder fields – often deeply snow covered in late summer – and then hurries steeply into the Lairig Ghru. Another bouldery corrie lies S of Coire Mor, fringed with a frieze of broken remains of crags; unnamed and with no evidence on the OS 7th Series maps that a steep bowl exists here, it falls off steeply, due W of the Ben Macdui cairn.

Loch Avon and the Shelter Stone

Loch Avon lies at about 724 m in a deep cliff-ringed trench between Cairn Gorm and Ben Macdui on their E sides. Anyone descending to it from either of these hills, especially in winter, should remember that he is going to one of the most inaccessible places in the Cairngorms, and that to escape he will either have to climb out again or else walk miles down the uninhabited Glen Avon. The loch stretches 2½ km long, up to 300 m wide, and only about 35 m at its deepest, with several beautiful beaches of fine golden and white sands. To get the best view of it, you should approach from the lower end by the Lairig an Laoigh or The Saddle, and then go up the loch side. The long line of this grand sheet of water leads the eye up to the dark head-wall of cliffs beyond the top of the loch, and to the hurrying streams that come foaming like white ribbons over the slabs and rocks. These all join into a big stream running into the W end of the loch; it passes through a little green of turf and flowers on the N side, called Meur na Banaraiche (Mair na *Ban*arich) or finger of the dairymaid.

Walking routes to Loch Avon. Leaving the Ben Macdui path at Loch Etchachan, you cross the flat ground N of the loch and then drop down a steep path for 150 m in altitude to the Shelter Stone (2 km). The first sudden view of blue Loch Avon is breathtaking, and the path then goes below the great craggy pyramid on the N spur of Carn Etchachan, down to the Shelter Stone. Distance: 11 km and 500 m climb from Derry Lodge. Another way from the Derry, which is 4 km further but involves 180 m less climbing, goes by the Lairig an Laoigh, breaking off by a path round the W side of the Dubh Lochan and then continuing by a path up the S side of Loch Avon.

From the N, a much-used way, now a path, approaches from Strath Nethy (10 km from the Pit Fyannich bothy E of Ryvoan to the Shelter Stone) by The Saddle at 807 m, and then along the N side of the loch. From Cairn Gorm you can come down Allt Coire Raibeirt by a track down the easier E side of the steeper part of the burn (4½ km from Ptarmigan Restaurant to Shelter Stone), but take care as the steepest part of the path has eroded badly and is loose. The next burn to the W, Allt Coire Domhain, offers another way down, again by a track on its E side. Both routes are steep, and avalanches have occurred there in winter; The Saddle is then a safe route.

Féith Buidhe (Fay *Poo*ee) or yellow bog-stream, after meandering through a beautiful green basin on the high plateau, suddenly crashes over the steep rocks of Creag na Feithe Buidhe in a waterfall, but you can find an easy sporting route to the tops up here in late summer by zig-zagging through the wet granite slabs. Finding a good way down becomes less easy, and this route cannot be recommended for hill walkers in winter or early summer because it is so often heavily corniced with snow. When descending from Lochan Buidhe, you will find it much safer and easier to go SE just before the stream steepens at the waterfall, next traverse a stony shelf to the N of a broken slabby cliff towards Garbh Uisge Beag, and then drop easily into the main basin of Garbh Uisge and so to Loch Avon by that stream. In misty summer weather, hill walkers who have no experience of rock scrambling and little experience of navigating in complex terrain should avoid the routes from Coire Domhain round to Garbh Uisge inclusive.

The Shelter Stone. Clach Dhion (Clach *Yeen*) or stone of the shelter, lies at the head of Loch Avon on the S side. It is the largest of the many big boulders – a relic of some colossal past rock fall – lying below the Sticil or Shelter Stone Crag. Clach Dhion fell on smaller blocks leaving a natural chamber underneath. The sides have been packed with stones and sods, so that the inside feels dry and fairly wind tight. In winter the entrance often becomes snowed up and snow may remain in the shaded interior long after it has gone from outside the stone. Nearby stands a smaller shelter stone, also improved by draught-sealing, which visitors sometimes use when Clach Dhion has no room left. In bad weather it may be hard to find Clach Dhion. If so, its characteristic shape and colour are a help. From below it looks roughly rectangular, but its W end rises 2 to 3 m higher than the E end and carries a cairn. The lowest part of the side facing the loch has a pale appearance, in a zig-zag pattern that reaches higher at the E end, with darker rock above (plate 13). You must stoop when entering, but the roof (formed by the under surface of the huge block) slopes upwards and at the far side you can almost stand upright. At first it seems dark inside but as your eye becomes used to the poorer light you can get a fair idea of what the shelter looks like. On the heather strewn on the floor, 8 to 10 can sleep, but there is comfortable room for only 5 to 6 to sleep, cook meals and hold rucksacks.

A. I. McConnochie measured Clach Dhion as 44 × 21 × 22 ft high, 'which, allowing 12 cubic ft to the ton, would make its weight nearly 1700 tons'. In August 1926, Dr W. Bulloch measured it as 43 × 20 × 22 ft. A sample of Clach Dhion, later examined in London, weighed 2·58 g per cc, which would give 1361 tons as the weight.

Clach Dhion was described in 1794 in *The Statistical Account* (12, 429) which referred to it as a retreat for freebooters holding 'eighteen armed men'. Later it became a famous place for visitors to the Cairngorms. One of the longest visits by a climbing party, lasting 10 days, was described in the *Aberdeen Free Press* in September 1886, in articles that contain historical and topographical information about the Cairngorms. In 1924 a tin box containing a visitors' book was placed inside Clach Dhion, and completed volumes lie in the Cairngorm Club's library in Aberdeen. Over the 14 years from 1931–43, an average of 525 people visited the Stone annually, and about one-fourth of them stayed at least one night. In 1933, which had a very fine summer, 523 visited in July, with 129 on one day alone, and 1018 came during the year. From 1931–43 the monthly averages were: 5 in January, 0·5 in February, 3 in March, 9 in April, 35 in May, 100 in June, 212 in July, 131 in August, 56 in September, 7 in October, 1 in November and 2 in December (see *CCJ* 11, 212; and especially 17, 212).

The Cairngorm Club originated at Clach Dhion. The first climbing club in Scotland, it was founded there on the morning after the night of Queen Victoria's Golden Jubilee, on 24 June 1887. In 1965 the Lord Lyon King of Arms of Scotland granted the Club a coat of arms with the motto Clac-dian (*CCJ* 17, 225). In fact, 'dian' means violent or vehement, the very opposite sense to 'dion' or shelter!

Creag an Leth-choin (Craik an *Laich*in) or the rock of the half-dog or lurcher, 1053 m (3448 ft). An old legend was that a deer chase ended here and in the fury of the hunt one of the dogs went over the cliff. One of the most spectacular hills in the Cairngorms, Creag an Leth-choin is the fine, forbidding rocky peak dominating the E side of Lairig Ghru. A track, skirting along the E side of the furthest N rocks, goes up to about 1000 m altitude on the N slope of the peak. Lower down, this path climbs from the head of the stream N of the Sinclair Hut, after running in from the Glen More direction. The best route is to reach this track after you have climbed up through Rothiemurchus on the Lairig path (10 km from Coylumbridge to summit, 820 m of ascent, 3½ hours up). The easiest though dullest way goes from the Coire Cas car park by the track that runs up Allt Creag an Leth-choin and so westwards to the top. The southern of the two tops at 1053 m carries a cairn right on the cliff edge in a wonderful setting looking along the huge trench of the Lairig Ghru. The northern top at 1026 m overlooks Glen More.

Bynack More 1090 m (3574 ft). Locally Beinn Beithneag, pronounced Pain *Bei*nack. Distance: 5 km from the Pit Fyannich bothy E of Ryvoan, 640 m climb, 2 hours up. Bynack rises high out of Strath Nethy and the flattish range of lower hills towards Tomintoul. A beautiful conical peak when seen from the N, it dominates Abernethy Forest. The easiest way up goes by the Lairig an Laoigh path to the long plateau 2 km N of the summit. Leaving that path at 792 m where it begins to drop down Coire Odhar, you walk along flat ground and then climb S up the prominent northern nose of Bynack. For 300 m in height it rises attractively in front of you, past some interesting rocky knobs. The prominent niche in the summit, which you see so well from Strath Nethy, turns out to be a grassy hollow between two lumps of rock. Here there opens out a fine view of the northern spurs of Ben Avon and Beinn a' Bhuird and of the great wilderness of the Caiplich moors. Bynack Beg stretches out as a lower top ⅘ km to the NW of the summit, reaching about 970 m. The most interesting place on the hill is at Sabhalan Beithneag (*Sowl*an) or barns of Bynack, which lie SE of the summit of Bynack More and 120 m below it, but almost invisible from it (the OS 7th Series map shows them nearly 50 m in altitude below where they really are). The Sabhalan are an extraordinary group of granite tors rising from the bare hillside, bigger and steeper than the many other tors in the Cairngorms. Do not mistake them for the much smaller tors of Sabhalan Beaga Beithneag or little barns of Bynack on the S slope, which you can see easily from the summit. You can vary the return journey by descending to Nethy by Allt a' Choire Dheirg, so called from its fine little corrie with reddish rocks and scree. The grassy haughs by Nethy side are a pleasant way back to the Lairig track.

The hill mass continues SW of Bynack More for 4 km to The Saddle at 807 m, a col that leads on to Cairn Gorm. On the way to The Saddle, you pass over the 1017 m A' Chòinneach (A *Chawin*-yach) or the moss, an interesting medium-level plateau where the walking is excellent on a carpet with much woolly hair moss. To the E of here rise the 895 m Creag Mhor and the 848 m Dagrum (from

Dà Dhruim, *Daa*grum) or two ridges, a pair of remote seldom-visited hills lying N of Avon. Creag Mhor has granite tors, and both hills show unusually big expanses of bare granite gravel and sand for such low altitudes, an indication of great exposure combined with very poor soil fertility.

Càrn a' Mhàim (Caarn a *Veim*) or hill of the pass, 1037 m (3402 ft). Distance: 5½ km from Derry Lodge, 630 m ascent. You can easily climb this hill from the Lairig Ghru track 1 km W of where it crosses the Luibeg Burn, but by far the best approach comes from the long NNW ridge that connects it to Ben Macdui, called Ceann Caol (Kyown *Kail*) or thin head. The ridge is fringed with rocks and offers wonderful views across Glen Dee to Devil's Point. The S top, so obvious from the Derry, stands slightly lower at 1014 m; it rises above the green Coire na Poite (Cor na *Poe*tsh) or corrie of the pot, facing Glen Luibeg.

Derry Cairngorm 1155 m (3788 ft). Distance: 5 km from Derry Lodge, 750 m ascent, 2¼ hours up. Local people used to call it simply Càrn Gorm or blue hill, and later it became Cairn Gorm of Derry to distinguish it from the Cairn Gorm at Glen More. A beautiful high cone, from Inverey or Glen Lui it seems to tower above Ben Macdui. Climbing it is a good way to vary your return journey to Derry Lodge from Ben Macdui. The top consists of a boulder field, which you can skirt on the E side by cutting immediately above the highest rocks of Coire an Lochain Uaine. It is well worth diverging to look down into that beautiful corrie with its waterfall, sheltered tarn at about 755 m, and sunny rocks, immortalised by William Smith's lovely poem. The rocky top N of the tarn has the name Sgor an Lochain Uaine. On the way S to the Derry, you pass the subsidiary, rounded, boulder strewn dome of Càrn Gorm Beag or little Cairn Gorm at 1040 m and then drop to the fine viewpoint of Càrn Crom (Caarn *Crome*) or curved hill at 890 m. Just before you climb the last short rise up to Carn Crom, go left to the edge to get a grand view into Glen Derry. Here you look into Coire na Saobhaidhe (Cor na *Say*vee) or corrie of the fox's den, a wild place with wet slabby rocks, far down to Derry winding sinuously through its green flats dotted with ancient pines.

Beinn Mheadhoin 1182 m (3883 ft). Distance: 9 km from Derry Lodge, 760 m climb. In local speech this was Beinn Meadhon (Pain *Main*) or middle hill. Beinn Mheadhoin blocks the N end of Glen Derry, a great mass of a hill with a prominent tor on its summit.

You will get a grand view of it above the old pines if you climb the knoll immediately behind Derry Lodge. From upper Glen Derry, it rises in a spectacular, triangle-shaped broken crag to a fine point at 1082 m. The easiest way up goes from Loch Etchachan, or from the 740 m col beside the highest part of the Lairig an Laoigh path at the top of Glen Derry. Several great tors or 'barns' rise from the whaleback of Beinn Mheadhoin, called Sabhalan (barns) Beinn Mheadhoin.

The summit itself consists of a big tor with a cairn perched on top, but you can easily scramble up the N or shorter side for about 6 m. You will enjoy fine views if you descend a little to the W to look down over Loch Avon. Be careful in mist as Beinn Mheadhoin has many crags and slabs around it, including some small ones not shown on the 1 inch map. The N shoulder above the Dubh Lochan carries an interesting sharp little point that shows up strikingly from near Nethy Bridge.

Climbing routes

Coire an t-Sneachda. The accessible northern corries of Cairn Gorm were explored fairly early. In 1904 an SMC party led by Harold Raeburn climbed Pygmy Ridge (M) of Coire an t-Sneachda, and in the 1930s the Moray Mountaineering Club were active in Coire an Lochain. In Coire an t-Sneachda, the main crag below the highest top on the plateau above is Aladdin Buttress, leading to the pinnacle of Aladdin's Seat (M) which ends well down the wide gully of Aladdin's Couloir. On Aladdin Buttress the original route which was climbed in 1936 has only one short VD piece and is otherwise much easier. Recent routes on the right part of the buttress are much harder and on more direct lines, the 150 m VS Damnation being the best. The top of Aladdin Buttress ends in the easy upper part of Aladdin's Couloir which leads out by conspicuous slopes of red grit stretching right to the plateau edge. However, a better finish (S) goes up the separate mass of high-lying rock forming the upper couloir's right edge, which looks a spectacular pointed pinnacle from the plateau. Pygmy Ridge is the other separate triangular mass of rock lying slightly further along from Aladdin's Couloir, making a delightful short climb although unfortunately with a rather dirty loose approach. To the right, nearer the col towards Cairn Lochan, stretches the long Fluted Buttress with its many straight ribs of rock, its tiny pinnacles called The Fingers up near the plateau edge, and its many gullies which have good ice climbs in winter. Away to the W and hidden from Glen More stands the fine, steep, bulging Fiacaill Buttress, which has been climbed by a VS route right up the middle of the face by G. Shields. The Fiacaill Buttress is separated from the nearby Fiacaill Ridge by a steep shallow couloir, the Fiacaill Couloir, which gives a good Grade II-III winter climb. The Fiacaill Ridge itself, on the very edge that separates the corrie from the nearby Coire an Lochain, makes an easy but good sporting route to the tops (p 107).

Coire an Lochain. Here a compact set of high projecting buttresses rises above the reddish Great Slab. One of the best climbs in the Cairngorms is Savage Slit (VD) on the large western or No 4 buttress. Well seen from the cliff top to the E, this remarkable crack goes straight up the E wall of the projecting buttress on beautiful rough granite. Some of the other, easier routes in this corrie, have patches of grimy gravel, vegetation and shattered rock, but when gripped by winter frost and snow these N-facing crags at such a high altitude – finishing at nearly 1200 m – give very fine climbing. These remarks about dirty rock are true, for instance, of Central Crack Route (M) on No 2 Buttress (following on above the Great Slab below), and of much of the original route on No 3 Buttress and Western Route on No 4 Buttress. However, the steep rock on No 1 Buttress, to the left of the good winter gully of The Vent, in 1969 gave a couple of VS routes – Daddy Long Legs and Ventricle – on fine rock. The obvious gully between No 3 or Ewen Buttress and No 4 Buttress is Y gully, with left and right branches that give grand 110 m winter ascents. The pillar between them, a piece of fine steep rock which was an obvious problem for long, was climbed in August 1969 by W. March and J. Cunningham (Never Mind, VS). Another good route making a direct line is the VS Fall-out Corner, up the obvious 'dièdre' (i.e. crack or groove up an inset rock corner) lying about 10 m to the right of Savage Slit.

Smaller crags near Glen More. A practice ground with short pitches on dry granite lies on Creagan Dubh (*Crai*kan *Doo*) or black little rock, the little slabby black outcrop near the foot of Coire na Ciste. However, much of the rock and stones nearby are loose, and accidents have occurred from falling stones. A better place is on the short but steep crag to the SE of Creag a' Chalamain, in the gap of Eag Coire a' Chòmhlaich (*Aik* Cor a *Chaw*lich) or notch of the corrie of the interception. Creag an Leth-choin has several obvious ridges of dark granite up to nearly 100 m high on sound clean dry rock, offering good practice climbs only Moderate in standard, which give sporting ways of reaching the plateau from the Lairig Ghru. The wet gullies between the ridges make fine ice climbs, several of which run up to 200 to 250 m and one to nearly 300 m.

Stac an Fharaidh. The finest climbing ground of Cairn Gorm and Ben Macdui, shared with both, lies around Loch Avon. Immediately S of Cairn Gorm you drop into a shallow corrie E of Coire Raibeirt, with a tor at one side. Below here, a grand wall of slabs drops 150 m to Loch Avon; it is Stac an Fhàraidh (Stachkan *A*arie) or the precipice of the ladder, standing to the W of The Saddle. These slabs of fine clean granite were ignored during the earlier explorations which concentrated more on the better-defined ridges, buttresses and face routes. The first climb there was done only in 1952 and none for 17 more years, but in 1969 and 1970 nine new routes were recorded (*SMCJ* 29, 413), giving climbing rather like that on the slabs of Beinn Trilleachan of Etive but easier because of the roughness of the granite. W. Cunningham from Glenmore Lodge has been the main pioneer.

Stag Rocks. On the W side of Coire Raibeirt, these rocks present a long face of black rough granite above Loch Avon. A highly recommended route is the popular, 140 m Afterthought Arête, going up the long sharp edge at the left end of the cliffs, to the right of a wide scree gully; although only Moderate in difficulty, it makes a fine climb. The V-shaped buttress in the centre of Stag Rocks is Pine Tree Buttress, offering the good climb of Pine Tree Route (D). Further to the right, the imposing steep 180 m wall of the Longbow Crag forms the northern part of Stag Rocks. The earliest route on it was the fine Relay Climb – climbed in three different sections in three years from 1953–55 – up the Longbow Crag's obvious left edge beside Amphitheatre Gully. The best route, however, is Longbow Direct (VS) whose first ascent came in August 1962 by D. Pyper and J. McArtney. Starting at the pink water-worn fault at the centre of the Longbow face, it leads up and over the 'Longbow' or overhang in the middle of the face, and makes a good climb on clean rough granite.

Hell's Lum Crag. The next section of cliff between Coire Raibeirt and Feith Buidhe forms the smooth, polished, Hell's Lum Crag. Most of the routes run wet even in fairly dry weather, but the rock is clean and sound, and in winter the water turns the climbs into grand ice pitches. The best of these winter routes is the winter ascent of Devil's Delight in 1973 by J. Cunningham and W. March, a Grade V climb which forms one of the finest and hardest winter routes in the northern Cairngorms. Devil's Delight, a 140 m line near the centre of the crag, also makes an excellent summer rock climb whose first ascent came in August 1957 by R. H. Sellers and G. Annand. The Clean Sweep (S) makes one of the best summer routes, running for 150 m up the greenish whale-backed buttress that lies in the centre of the crag just to the left of Hellfire Corner. On the left part of the crag, the long dark slit of Deep-Cut Chimney (VD) offers a fine climb, giving spectacular scenery in its upper reaches where the chimney cuts far back into the cliff. Round the corner to the left, the great black recess going for 110 m from top to bottom of the crag is Hell's Lum itself. Running water drenches this dark fierce gully in summer, but in winter it becomes a fine ice climb until deep snow smoothes out the ice pitches.

The Sticil. The rock of An Sticil (Un St*yee*chkeel, the kiln-rafter or beam), later called the Shelter Stone Crag, a 240 m N-facing wall of slabby granite, is undoubtedly one of the finest crags in Britain. Harold Raeburn climbed the beautiful feature of Raeburn's Buttress by a dangerously vegetated pioneer route on the Sticil's left flank as early as 1907, but then the crag remained unexplored until the ascent of Clach Dhian Chimney (VD) on the W flank in 1947, and until some fine new routes were made in the 1950s and 1960s. Between Raeburn's Buttress and the huge sweep of central slabs, Sticil Face (HS) in 1953 was an early circuitous route along the left edge of the face, avoiding the main difficulties of the slabs by traversing a long grassy shelf right above the main steep wall; although heavily vegetated in summer, it proved an excellent hard climb (Grade V) in winter 1957. The HS and rather loose Postern, climbed in two parts in 1956 and 1957, was the result of an attempt on the main N face; starting just right of the lowest rocks, it tended rightwards round the corner on to the W face of the Sticil and then up by the upper of the two giant rock steps on this side. The VS finish that was added in August 1969 makes Postern a more direct climb.

In August 1958 came a bigger breakthrough with The Citadel, a VS route by Ronnie Sellars and G. Annand going right up the main face in a direct line, by the chimney at the right side of the central slabs. Then in 1962 came The Needle (VS) by R. Smith and D. Agnew, a magnificent route starting just to the right of Postern and going fairly directly to the top of the crag. Other routes have followed on the Sticil, the big breakthroughs on its once-impregnable main N wall coming in quick succession in 1968. The best of these was Steeple, just to the left of The Needle and between it and The Citadel. Steeple and The Needle form an adjacent pair of excellent direct lines on clean rock of sustained severity, climbed entirely free without artificial aids on a stupendous face; indeed they are possibly the finest climbs of their type in Britain. Steeple, which was pioneered by K. Spence, M. Watson and J. Porteous, is the better of the two and must rank as a particularly outstanding rock climb. Other grand routes, which went up the forbidding smooth central slabs further left, in the very middle of the Sticil's dark N wall, came in quick succession in August and September 1968. These were the remarkable VS ascents of The Pin and Thor (Thor also A2), and in August 1969 the VS Snipers. These three later very fine routes start from the grassy terrace which slants upwards and along the face from the foot of Raeburn's Buttress, and break the great slabs above to reach the grassy ledges on the upper traverse of the Sticil Face route (see in Further Reading the article by W. March in *Climber & Rambler*, the article by J. Renny in *SMCJ* 29, 125, and also the original descriptions of three of these magnificent climbs in *SMCJ* 29, 190). To the right of The Sticil, the Forefinger Pinnacle forms one of the most remarkable rock features in the massif, giving short routes up to 30 m varying from Moderate to Severe. The Sticil's other, left flank ends at Castle Gates Gully, which is an easy scree shoot leading to the plateau.

Carn Etchachan. This great domed crag rises to the E of Castle Gates Gully, again for about 240 m. Although it is one of the biggest cliffs in the Cairngorms, with some excellent crack routes on sound rock, no climbs were done here till a sudden spate of new routes in the early 1950s. The lower part of the cliff is partly vegetated, and a grassy terrace leads across the face from the Loch Etchachan side, giving access to the 90 m of clean, steep upper rocks. Here are some fine routes on excellent granite, requiring jamming, laybacks and friction on steep cracks and ribs rather like Chamonix granite, Boa being particularly good. The excellent Crevasse Route (MS) with a window high up, is a popular climb up the first buttress along the terrace. To the right of this upper face, a couple of much longer routes form magnificent winter climbs, the best being Route Major (Grade IV) from the lowest rocks below Castle Gates Gully right to the summit cairn at 1113 m. The nearby Scorpion (VD), starting slightly higher up Castle Gates Gully below the protruding rock mass of The Sentinel, gave a fine Grade V climb on its first winter ascent, graphically told in a racy article by T. W. Patey (Further Reading).

Next to Carn Etchachan, on the Beinn Mheadhoin side of Loch Avon, an imposing set of steep bulging crags called Stacan Dubha (Stachkan *Dooa*) or black precipices, offers a few routes up to 140 m. Although they look impressive at first sight, the climbs do not reach a high quality as many of the ribs are disconnected by broken rock.

Coire Sputan Dearg. Sheltered from the prevailing wind, the crags here are sunny, dry and warm, yet it looks an alpine corrie with deep snow fields till midsummer, and the main wide scree gullies give good glissades till June. The rock is sound, rough granite. Remarkably, therefore, climbers ignored it for long, till a wave of new routes came in 1948–49. The corrie provides many good ascents of all standards and has for long been a popular climbing ground.

One of the fine routes, though short (80 m), is Crystal Ridge – only Difficult and Grade III - which goes up the edge of a rough slab well supplied with holds, alongside a steep left wall. To its right rises the 120 m steep Grey Man's Crag which forms the main face of rock in the corrie. On Grey Man's Crag, Hanging Dyke (VD) gives a particularly good ascent; starting just to the right of the lowest rocks, at a cairn below a slab, the climb goes up a geological dyke where the rock has the superficial appearance of ancient dark brickwork. On Grey Man's Crag, Grey Slab makes another excellent route, first climbed in September 1963 by M. Higgins, J. C. Innes and B. T. Lawrie. It goes up a prominent dièdre just to the left of Hanging Dyke, tending to lead leftwards to finish by the tops of a couple of routes done earlier (Lucifer Route and then Pilgrim's Groove).

To the right of Narrow Gully, which is the middle one of the three main spouts, three parallel buttresses of steep black granite soar to the plateau. The middle one, called The Black Tower, makes a fine though short (80 m) climb (S). The route starts on the left, about 15 m above the lowest rocks, and finishes by a broken arête leading from the top of the tower to the plateau. Flake Buttress to its right rises into a fine pointed ridge; although steep, it is only Moderate and Grade II, and has good clean rock. The upper part becomes somewhat contrived in that you can easily diverge off the route on to more broken rock and grass, but the climb makes an interesting sporting route to the top, recommended for novices on granite.

The big bulging slabs in the S part of the corrie – called The Red Slabs – were climbed in June 1970 by several routes varying from S to VS and up to nearly 120 m high (*SMCJ* 29, 410). Further S, starting at the side of Lochan Uaine, you can have a good long winter route up to the pyramid peak on the plateau edge 300 m above; it lies mostly on steep snow, but has some broken rock except after deep snow when the whole face becomes a beautiful smooth slope of steep snow.

Coire Etchachan. Sporting climbs occur on dry, rough black granite on the broken buttresses on the Beinn Mheadhoin side of Coire Etchachan. On this big triangular face, many ribs of broken rock offer long sporting ways to the top with easy climbing and scrambling, and in winter the face gives plenty of easy carefree climbing with escape possible at many points.

The best cliff in Coire Etchachan is the grand 120 m E-facing wall which forms part of the line of crags making up Creagan a' Choire Etchachan. On its left side, the dark, wide, recessed gully of The Corridor splits the cliff. The Bastion projects out as the fine convex bulge to its left, wider at the foot than at the tapering top. Outstanding here is the 90 m climb The Talisman (HS) which goes up The Bastion's right edge, next to The Corridor. It starts about 6 m up The Corridor between two huge blocks, and then follows on or beside The Bastion's right edge, up clean granite, steep and sustained. It also makes a grand winter climb (Grade IV). Quartzvein Edge (M), at the left edge of The Bastion, offers a good climb for a novice on granite. Many other fine and mostly harder routes have been done, the best being on the 110 m high sweep of smooth slabs called The Crimson Slabs. These look particularly impressive from the path going up the higher part of the corrie, especially when the water trickling down parts of the slabs glistens in the sun. The two obvious crack corners piercing these slabs have both become classic VS routes, Djibangi on the left and The Dagger (first climbed in September 1955 by T. W. Patey and J. Y. L. Hay) on the right. Although less hard than The Dagger, Djibangi is now the more popular, and has also become one of the best of the hard modern-type winter routes in the Cairngorms since its first winter ascent in January 1965 (Grade V). Two other grand VS lines up The Crimson Slabs are the excellent Scabbard and the impressive Stiletto up a thin crack between Djibangi and The Dagger; Stiletto is at present the hardest climb in Coire Etchachan.

Further reading

Edinburgh Psychic College 1949 *The Grey Man of Ben Macdhui.* A few anecdotes.

A. Gray 1970 *The Big Grey Man of Ben Macdhui.* A full, detailed account.

A. I. McConnochie. The central Cairngorms. *CCJ* 1, 309, 366.

W. Garden The central Cairngorms (Guide Book article). *SMCJ* 7, 323.

G. Barlow On the possibility of seeing the Cuillin from the Cairngorms. *SMCJ* 26, 16.

T. W. Patey Appointment with Scorpion. *ECJ* 2, 145.

W. Barclay Djibangi en hiver. *ECJ* 4, 18.

J. Renny The Shelter Stone Crag. *SMCJ* 29, 125.

R. Carrington The Pin. *SMCJ* 29, 128.

W. March Selected new routes in the northern Cairngorms. *Climber & Rambler* 9, 160.

A. Watson, N. Bayfield & S. M. Moyes Research on human pressures on Scottish mountain tundra, soils and animals. In *Productivity and Conservation in Northern Circumpolar Lands* (ed by W. A. Fuller & P. G. Kevan), p 256. Int. Un. for Conserv. of Nature.

W. March Citadel in winter. *SMCJ* 29, 364.

N. Bayfield & A. Watson The impact of ski-ing developments on plants and animals. *Aberdeen Ski CJ* 1972–73, 34.

Note (July 1974)

Reference *Bothies and shelters* (page 99), it is quite possible thal El Alamein may be moved to 023060 in Strath Nethy, St. Valery to 047075 on the Lairig an Laoigh path, and Curran inside Geldie Lodge near the path to Feshie.

3

Lairig Ghru, Glen Feshie and Lairig an Laoigh

Access
Public roads go to the Linn of Dee, Tolvah and Achlean in Feshie, and Glenmore Lodge.

Accommodation
As in Chapters 1 and 8.

Remote occupied houses
As in Chapter 2, also Carnachuin 847939.

Bothies (see also Chapter 2), all open all the year round. *Lairig Ghru*. Corrour 982958, Luibeg 036933, An Garbh Choire 959986 on S bank of stream 1½ km W of Lairig path, Sinclair Memorial Hut 640 m 959036. *Glen Feshie*. Ruigh Ealasaid 003869 (partly ruined), Geldie Lodge 954866 (mostly ruined), Eidart bothy 510 m 906885, Ruigh-aiteachain 846927, 'Drakes' bothy near Lochan Gorm 885056. *Lairig an Laoigh*. Ryvoan 006115, Pit Fyannich 020104 by Nethy side E of Ryvoan, Ath nam Fiann 042031 (bivouac hut on N bank of Avon at 690 m). See also note on page 124.

General description
Through the great rampart of the high Cairngorms go three of Scotland's finest hill passes. Once much used by Highland folk for cattle droving and other trade, which went on through Lairig Ghru up till the early years of this century, all three are now rights of way. Where you leave the public roads to get on to these tracks, locked gates bar the way for cars, but an open part at the side is wide enough for walkers, bicycles, motor cycles and ponies to pass.

Geology, landforms and natural history
See the chapters covering the different areas of hill country through

which these three passes run: Lairig Ghru, Chapters 1 and 8, Glen Feshie 5 and 7, Lairig an Laoigh 1, 2 and 8.

Estates

The Aberdeenshire parts of all three routes are on Mar Lodge Estate. The Inverness-shire parts of Glen Feshie and Lairig Ghru lie on Glen Feshie and Rothiemurchus Estates respectively. Inchrory Estate has the Banffshire part of Lairig an Laoigh, and Forest Lodge the Abernethy end. This is all deer-forest country. Although all three routes pass through fine natural forest, you will see in Glen Feshie and Mar, and in the upper parts of Rothiemurchus and Abernethy, that there are no young trees; too many red deer eat them. In Glen Luibeg and Glen Derry the Nature Conservancy have fenced off two plots which show that seedlings will thrive if the deer are kept out.

History

Above the Lairig Ghru path in Glen Luibeg an ancient solitary pine grows high on Carn Crom, called Craobh an Òir (Croo an *Orr*) or the tree of the gold. An old legend tells how a Mackenzie of Dalmore had buried a stolen crock of gold here, and later moved it to near the top of Cairn Geldie, NE of Geldie Lodge. Beside the Lairig path in upper Glen Dee, half way between Corrour and Allt Clach nan Taillear, stands the group of weathered, ribbed stones called Clach nan Tàillear (*Taal*yer) or the stone of the tailors. Here three tailors once perished while sheltering in the snow one New Year's Eve. They had wagered that they would dance a reel on the same night in Rothiemurchus and Braemar. Having danced in Speyside, they set out through the Lairig, only to succumb – as usual in these exposure cases – when the worst of the crossing was behind them.

General Wade surveyed the route for a road from the Linn of Dee to Kingussie through Glen Feshie, but never built it. The idea of the road keeps cropping up in county and district councils; climbers and others have recently objected to it as it would spoil one of the best wilderness areas left in Britain. The beauty of Glen Feshie appealed to the hearts of its old folk. The Rev Thomas Sinton, in *The Poetry of Badenoch* (1906), gave this fine verse which he says was repeated to him 'with great depth of feeling' by an aged woman (fairly direct translation by the present writer).

Gleann Féisidh nan siantan!	Glen Feshie of the storms!
Leam bu mhiann bhi'n ad fhasgath,	I had the longing to be in thy shelter,

Far am faighinn a' bhroighleag,	Where I could find the blaeberry,
An oighreag, 's am dearcag,	The cloudberry and the little berry,
Cnothan cruinn air a' challduinn,	Round nuts on the hazel,
'S iasg dearg air na h-easan	And red fish on the waterfalls

Beside the footbridge in Glen Derry 2½ km N of Derry Lodge, at a place still called the Derry Dam, there once stood a sluice for floating cut trees down the glen. It was built in the early 19th century by Alexander Davidson, a noted Deeside character who turned to poaching after the timber floating, and whose racy life story you can read in Michie's *Deeside Tales*. The Lairig an Laoigh track up Glen Derry passes below Derry Cairngorm and its hanging corrie of Coire an Lochain Uaine. It was at the side of the burn from the lochan that William Smith or Gow, often called Uilleam Rynuie, built the little shelter commemorated in his poem 'Allt an Lochain Uaine'. Smith, whose home lay at Rynuie on the Abernethy side of the Cairngorms, still has descendants in Strath Spey today, of whom Carrie Nethersole-Thompson at Whitewell is one of the best known. A famous deer stalker in the late 18th century, Smith used to make poaching raids into Mar Forest with a gun presented to him by the laird of Rothiemurchus. His favourite resort was Lochan Uaine with its fine view down to the Derry, where he could be on guard against the Earl of Fife's foresters, the 'red foxes', as he called them, coming up the glen to catch him. The first verse is given below, along with a fairly direct translation by the present writer as the English translation in previous editions of the Guide grossly distorted Smith's actual words.

Aig Allt an Lochain Uaine,	At the burn of the green tarn,
Gu'n robh mi uair a' tàmh,	I was staying a time,
S'ged bha'n t-àite fuar	And though the place was cold
Bha'n fhàrdach fuathasach blàth,	The dwelling was wonderfully warm,
Ged thigeadh gaoth 'o thuath orm	Though wind from the north would come on me
'Us cathadh luath o'n àird	And fast drifting snow from the height
Bhiodh Allt an Lochain Uaine	The burn of the green tarn would be

Le 'fhuaim ga m'chuir gu pràmh   Putting me to slumber with its
                                        sound

This poem, sung to the beautiful melody found in the collections
called 'Gu ma slan a chi mi' or 'Good health be with you', was for
several generations the most popular song in Braemar and Strath
Spey. As the old language has gone, only a very few older local
people now know it, but it should surely rank as the finest song of the
Cairngorms.

Lairig Ghru

Name: Làirig Dhrù (*Laa*rig *Groo*), pass of Dhru or Druie, probably
from Drùdhadh meaning oozing. Distance: from Whitewell to the
locked gate at the foot of Glen Lui 28 km, from Coylumbridge 30 km
or 19 miles, total ascent 670 m or 2200 ft (see also distances and times
on p 129). You can shorten this by cycling the 5 km up the private
road from the locked Lui gate to Derry Lodge and then for 1½ km
of smooth path up Glen Luibeg, or at the Rothiemurchus end as far
as the place where the four paths meet E of the Cairngorm Club
footbridge and 3 km from Whitewell. On the rest of the route, which
becomes very rough, you will have to wheel it much of the way.

    The Lairig Ghru is the finest and best known pass in Scotland.
From Strath Spey, its huge dark cleft carves a deep 'V' in the great
masses of Braeriach and Ben Macdui, and its red screes glow red in
the evening sun. From Rothiemurchus, the Lairig has an air of
mystery, dark and somehow more challenging than the often more
dangerous high tops around it. It takes you into the very heart of the
Cairngorms and through a very rich variety of hill and natural woodland scenery. The Lairig Ghru should always remain the finest
cross-country path in the country, and a grand challenge to the hill
walker who is not a mountaineer. We must guard its priceless value
from the modern super-vandals, for – unbelievably – there have
been serious demands by developers and district councils to put a
tarmac road right through it with ski lifts on either side.

    The best approach is to start in Rothiemurchus and finish on
Deeside; the climb up into the great 'V' of the Lairig by the pine
forest offers one of the most magnificent walks of Scotland. From
915106 near Coylumbridge a rough road goes up Rothiemurchus.
You take the signposted path that breaks off at 917100 to the left
of this road and leads to the Cairngorm Club footbridge. An easier
though less fine way is to drive up the public road from Inverdruie to

Whitewell, walk down to the little tarn of Lochan Deo and then E along a rough road to the footbridge erected by the Cairngorm Club in 1912 (*CCJ* 7, 235). The bridge stands not far below where Allt Druidh from Lairig Ghru joins the larger Am Beanaidh from Gleann Einich. It is miscalled the 'Allt na Beinne Mhoir' footbridge, from the old map error for Beanaidh (*Benn*ie). On the parapet, a tablet gives approximate distances and times:

	Hours	*Miles*
To Aviemore	1½	4
„ Coylum Bridge	¾	2
„ Lairig Ghru summit (2733 ft)	3	5½
„ Derry Lodge	6½	14
„ Linn of Dee	8	18
„ Braemar	10	24½

Beyond here you pass a beautiful grassy clearing, once cultivated as the croft of Allt Dhru, and then come into the forest to the junction of the four paths at a signpost. To your left a track leads to the old Medicine Well and over Luineag by a bridge up from Allt nan Caber (Alt na *Gap*er); ahead lies the way to Loch Morlich, with a spur road coming off it further on which leads up to the army's Rothiemurchus Hut. Your path to the Lairig turns sharply and then climbs more steeply through small pines and heather high above Allt Druidh, with wonderful views back over Rothiemurchus. For 2½ km, you now pass along open peaty moorland, where in 1973 the badly eroding path has been repaired in places. Just before you reach the Sinclair Hut, which stands 8 km from Whitewell and 8 km from the W end of Loch Morlich, an alternative path to this spot comes in on the left from Glen More. It leads through a rocky gap SE of Creag a' Chala-main, called Eag Coire a' Chomhlaich. Beyond the gap it goes down the moor to cross Allt Mor by a footbridge above the forest edge, a crossing which is 4½ km from the Lairig path and 3 km from the Glen More camp site.

Before entering the narrow pass, you reach the Sinclair Memorial Hut at about 640 m, built in 1957. From here on, the screes and crags of Creag an Leth-choin hem in the pass on the E, and those of Sron na Lairige on the W. Violent winds often funnel through this narrow part of the pass even when the rest of the Lairig is fairly calm. The path rises up the long narrow trough along increasingly stony ground, until near the summit at about 835 m or 2733 ft, the floor of the pass becomes rough with boulders, which local people no longer clear from the path as they did annually last century. Nevertheless, a good Highland pony can still go through the Lairig Ghru; the other two passes, of course, are easy for horses. You will find the summit a very good place for ptarmigan, which nest there regularly; indeed, this is the only one of the three passes where you can depend on seeing them. Just past the summit, Allt na Crìche or the 'March Burn' plunges down from the plateau, only to disappear underground below the boulder fields. However, the water comes out on the Dee side of the summit as a series of one large and three smaller beautiful pools in hollows of the boulder field, where you can watch trout swimming in the clear water above the stony bottom. The old name was Lochan Dubh na Làirige or black tarn of the Lairig, which anglicisation has turned into the erroneous and less poetic Pools of Dee.

The path soon comes to easier ground and drops gradually into Glen Dee, giving magnificent views up to An Garbh Choire and the soaring peak of Cairn Toul. After 3 km downhill, the rough track goes on the level till you are past Corrour. It crosses Allt Clach nan Taillear (9 km and 2 hours from the Derry) and shortly afterwards you come upon the group of curiously ribbed stones called Clach nan Taillear on the E side of the path. Above, the slope of Carn a' Mhaim has been rent by furrows gouged out by torrential rains; old Charles Robertson, once a deer watcher at Corrour, witnessed one such torrent in 1901 (*CCJ* 3, 370).

To the S of here a footbridge crosses Dee over to Corrour Bothy below the Devil's Point. The views are very fine; above on the E side, the slabby rock faces of Carn a' Mhaim lead N to the enormous screes of Ben Macdui. As you go S, the views of the Devil's Point and then the grand opening of wild Glen Geusachan with its green floor hemmed in by rocky hillsides, look especially impressive. Just past Corrour, the Lairig track divides at a signpost. The right branch goes 9 km down the E side of the narrowing Glen Dee to the White Bridge and then another 5 km to the Linn of Dee. Before reaching the White Bridge you pass Ciste Dhé (Keesht *Yay*) or Chest of Dee, a place of beautiful wide dark pools and rapids set among square-topped masses of rock.

The more interesting left branch climbs gently to 610 m to curve round Sron Carn a' Mhaim, and then heads E for Derry Lodge. Near here you pass the lonely peaty tarn of Lochan Féith nan Sgòr

(Faina *Skor*), and then gradually drop into Glen Luibeg. Now comes a grand viewpoint down to the first pine trees which always look a welcome sight, to Lochnagar far beyond, and N up to the fine cliffs of Coire Sputan Dearg on Ben Macdui. You can usually cross easily where the path reaches the Luibeg Burn, but in high water you should go 400 m upstream to the safe crossing by a bridge built by the Cairngorm Club. The first copse of trees below here, which has for long been a favourite camp spot, is Preas nam Mèirleach (Praiss na *Myer*lach) or the copse of the robbers. After the ford, the path crosses the Sands of Lui, a stretch of gravel washed down by floods in 1829 and 1956, and then comes through the beautiful winding Glen Luibeg with its scattered old pines to the keeper's house at Luibeg, at about 420 m near the Derry.

Glen Feshie

Name: Gleann Féithisidh (Glan *Fay*shee) or boggy-haugh valley.
Distance: from Linn of Dee to Ruigh Ealasaid 7 km, to beside Geldie Lodge 12, to county boundary 16, to Eidart bothy 18, to Ruigh-aiteachain $26\frac{1}{2}$, to Carnachuin 28 km or $17\frac{1}{2}$ miles ($6\frac{1}{2}$ hours), another 4 and 6 km to public roads at Achlean and Tolvah respectively; total ascent 180 m or 550 ft. From the Linn of Dee at 370 m, a private rough road beyond a locked gate goes W through pine woods and then along the bare open Glen Dee with its old ruined crofts to a signpost at the White Bridge at nearly 410 m. Now you turn SW up Geldie (*Gail*dee), getting fine spacious views up to Beinn Bhrotain and Beinn a' Ghlo. The road soon passes a small new plantation and then the gaunt ruined house of Ruigh nan Clach (Roo-ee na *Glach*) or shiel of the stones. You continue to a signpost W of where Bynack Burn meets Geldie below the partly-ruined stable at Ruigh Ealasaid (Roo-ee *Yal*asitsh) or Elizabeth's shiel. From here, the rough road turns W to beside the ruined Geldie Lodge. On the way you cross Allt Dhaidh Beag and Mor, two fast burns coming off Beinn Bhrotain; these are map errors for Daimhidh (*Daa*vee) meaning stag. At about 520 m altitude, a signpost that stands 300 m in distance before the road crosses Geldie, marks where the path to Glen Feshie continues westwards along the N bank of the stream. The footbridge over Geldie Burn here, giving access to Geldie Lodge, has been swept away.

Glen Geldie is unique in Scotland for a special character of extraordinary bareness, loneliness and wilderness combined with high arctic-like hills nearby; a wide treeless strath runs up for miles of very gentle slopes on either side to the massive stony high tops and green tundras of Beinn Bhrotain and Monadh Mor in the N and An Sgarsoch and Carn an Fhidhleir in the S. Other places in our region have this spacious character but nowhere will you feel it as strongly as on Geldie. In deep winter snow, this character is enhanced by the pervading whiteness of the smooth slopes, unrelieved by any of the black wind-scoured ridges so common in the steeper Cairngorms. Through this flat landscape the path to Feshie climbs imperceptibly to the summit at about 560 m, at the watershed between Spey and Dee where only a low bank of moorland separates the two. Standing at this spot, you can easily imagine how the E-flowing upper Feshie once ran into Geldie and Dee, and how a very little gravel dumped by glaciers could easily block it and move it in that tremendous bend – locally called the 'turn o' the Feshie' – far round into Glen Feshie and Spey. Below here you can cross the fast Eidart (*Ait*yart) by a footbridge 300 m distant up from Feshie, which was built in 1957 by the Scottish Rights of Way Society. To the N, Eidart runs for about $1\frac{1}{2}$ km in a miniature rocky canyon leading up towards the higher Cairngorms. A small bothy stands 300 m in distance further down Feshie side from Eidart, beside the main path.

Near the rocky little gorge of Allt na Leuma (Alt na *Laim*) or burn of the leap, which is the stream whose upper fork has the name of Allt Coire Bhlair, you come to a bulldozed road down Feshie. The scenery becomes striking as the glen narrows almost to a canyon and bends sharply at the Caigeann, between steep hills with many broken crags, foaming waterfalls, screes, and in places fine clumps of old birches and pines. Lower down, where the glen curves N, it opens out into wide grassy flats where the river wanders among great shingle beds and you pass through lovely glades of ancient pines and junipers. Unfortunately the fine old walking path through the woods has been obliterated by the bulldozed rough road.

Beside the bothy at Ruigh-aiteachain (Roo-ee *Ait*yachan) which probably means juniper flat, you can see the ruins of The Huts where Landseer once painted a fresco above the fireplace, still visible until about 1930. A footbridge crosses Feshie at Carnachuin, from which a private road continues to the locked gate at about 300 m near Tolvah, a name from Toll a' Bhàthaidh (Tole *Vaa*) or hole of the drowning. The footbridge to the E side of Feshie at Tolvah no longer exists. A nearer public road comes to Achlean on the E side, and you can cross Feshie to reach it by a footbridge near Stronetoper. At 847976 N of Stronetoper, an old drove road and right of way runs W across Allt Chomhraig for 11 km to Drumguish. At the very foot of the glen, Feshiebridge is a charming spot where the river winds darkly through a deep pool overhung by trees and spanned by a fine old bridge.

Lairig an Laoigh

Name: This is Làirig Laoigh (*Laa*rig *Loo*ee) or pass of Lui, distinguishing it from Lairig Ghru or Druie pass. Distance: from locked gate at the foot of Glen Lui at 366 m to Derry Lodge 5 km, to the forking of the path in upper Derry 11, to Ath nam Fiann hut at the ford over Avon 15, to Pit Fyannich bothy at Strath Nethy 24, to Glenmore Lodge $28\frac{1}{2}$ km (18 miles and 7 hours), and to public road at 012162 W of Forest Lodge 31 km; total ascent from foot of Lui 490 m or 1600 ft.

Though not quite so grand as Lairig Ghru, Lairig an Laoigh is a very fine walk taking you through the magnificent pine woods of the Derry and Abernethy and into a wild bit of country at the head of Glen Avon and the Caiplich. A good approach starts from Derry Lodge at about 420 m. Crossing Derry by the footbridge just past the lodge, you come on the old path which here leads through one of the finest pieces of ancient pine forest in Scotland. On the left you pass the high knoll of An Toman Dearg (Un Tooman *Dyerr*eg), now fenced in to allow regeneration of the pines. About $1\frac{1}{2}$ km up, the path bends left away from the stream; beyond, hidden from the path, lies a stretch of beautiful falls and smooth shelving rocks. The path now climbs a mound giving a grand view of upper Glen Derry, and crosses a footbridge at about 500 m to the E side, immediately below the site of the old Derry Dam. You can also reach this spot by a road bulldozed up the E side of the Derry woods from Derry Lodge, but it is less attractive than the old path.

From the footbridge at the Dam, the bulldozed road now carries on N along the previous line of the old track, giving fine views over the green, pine-studded flats to the stony corries of Derry Cairngorm. The road ends 2 km N of the Dam below the screes of Craig Derry, but the path continues through a fertile meadow to a footbridge over Glas Allt Mór (*Glass*alt *More*) or big green burn. Beyond here at nearly 600 m altitude it diverges, left to Coire Etchachan, right to

Lairig an Laoigh slanting up to the pass at about 740 m between Beinn Mheadoin and Beinn a' Chaorainn. At the top of the pass, a grand prospect opens N down Allt an t-Seallaidh (Altan *Tyoll*ie) or burn of the view, to the Dubh Lochan and beyond to Avon. You cross Avon at about 690 m at Àth nam Fiann (Aa num *Fee*an) or the ford of the Fianna or Fingalians. A rough bivouac shelter hut stands near here on the N bank.

Ahead, the path runs on the level past the blue waters of Lochan a' Bhainne (Lochan a *Van*yi) or milk tarn, and then climbs gently to over 770 m on the E shoulder of Bynack More. It then drops slightly into the wide green peaty basin of Coire Odhar, crossing the little stream of Uisge Dubh Poll a' Choin (Ooshk *Doo* Pole *Choin*) or black water of the dog's pool. A number of people have died in this area by wandering in winter storm NE down this stream or down the burn of Glasàth (*Glass*-aa) or green ford further S, instead of keeping uphill round Bynack. The gentle walking downhill by these streams takes you on to the vast windswept wilderness of the Caiplich, miles from any house. Indeed, if you are to walk the Lairig an Laoigh in winter, and do not know it well, it is safer for this reason to start at the N end and finish at the Derry, as you then come to this deceptive part while you feel strong at the beginning of the day. On the last section from Avon S to Derry Lodge, the route looks obvious as you merely have to stay in a fairly straight line along the bottom of the valley, hemmed in between the hills.

On the N side of Coire Odhar, you climb again gently to 792 m or about 2600 ft over the N shoulder of Bynack, before beginning the long descent to the footbridge over Nethy at about 442 m, beside the remains of the wooden bothy at Pit Fyannich (*Fyann*ich). A more interesting alternative for a summer walk, and a safer detour on a bad winter day, is to go from Ath nam Fiann up to Loch Avon, climb to 807 m at The Saddle, and then walk by a path down Garbh Allt to Strath Nethy, below the great broken cliffs of Cairn Gorm and Bynack More.

The quickest and very fine way down from the Pit Fyannich bothy in Strath Nethy leads along the rough road to the Ryvoan pass, past Loch a' Gharbh-choire. You then drop past lovely Lochan Uaine into the pines towards Glenmore Lodge (p 88). Another way runs from Ryvoan N past Rynettin, which is a beautiful place overlooking Abernethy pine forest, and then to Forest Lodge, 1 km to the W of which you come to the public road to Nethy Bridge. However, the old Lairig an Laoigh path breaks off to the right at a signpost just before the path from Bynack reaches the footbridge and the Pit Fyannich bothy. Later it goes through fine old pines along the E side of Nethy to Forest Lodge, and from the pine edge onwards has now become a new rough road.

Further reading

R. Anderson   Glen Feshie. *CCJ* 1, 348.

H. Macmillan   The Lairig Ghru. *CCJ* 2, 297.

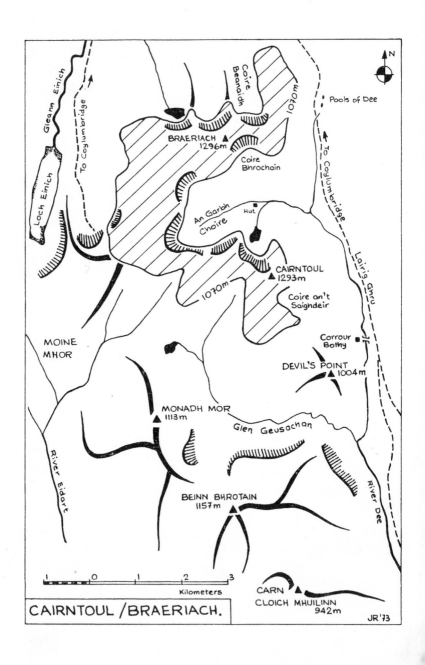

CAIRNTOUL / BRAERIACH.

4

Braeriach and Cairn Toul

*Braeriach	1296 m, 953999
*Cairn Toul	1293 m, 963973
Sgor an Lochain Uaine	1258 m, 954977
*The Devil's Point	1004 m, 976951
*Beinn Bhrotain	1157 m, 954923
*Carn Cloich-mhuilinn	942 m, 968907
*The Monadh Mor	1113 m, 938943

Access, accommodation and remote occupied houses
As in Chapter 3.

Bothies and shelters
As in Chapter 3. The Garbh Choire hut measures $9 \times 7 \times 7$ ft, standing on the S bank of Allt a' Gharbh Choire below the waterfall from Lochan Uaine. In Garbh Choire Dhaidh, a built-up cave lies under the second largest boulder, just above the pools along the course of Dee, NW of the corrie lip at 946987; it holds 2 comfortably.

General description
The Lairig Ghru divides the four 1200 m (4000 ft) hills of the Cairngorms into two parts. Cairn Gorm and Ben Macdui stand to the E, whereas to the W of the Lairig and Glen Dee rises Braeriach, facing Aviemore, and to the S of it Cairn Toul of Mar. For variety of hill and corrie scenery these two hills and their surroundings are equalled in the Cairngorms massif only by Cairn Gorm and Ben Macdui. For their wildness, remoteness, and freedom from the recent effects of man, they are clearly unmatched. Indeed, this is the only large part of the Cairngorms which has escaped the bulldozer and the scars of new roads although these have penetrated the fringes at Gleann Einich and Glen Dee. It is therefore now one of the most precious parts.

Geology and landforms
The rock is nearly all granite. Gleann Einich, An Garbh Choire and Glen Geusachan wore away as long glaciated trenches, with

many small hillocks of glacial debris. The same kind of material dams up several lakes. The long-lying snow patch in Garbh Choire Mor is Scotland's most permanent snow, having melted only twice this century in 1933 and 1959. Unusually extensive boulder screes cover Cairn Toul's summit and the Coire Bhrochain side of Braeriach. Beinn Bhrotain is notable in having a big expanse of sandy gravel, virtually devoid of vegetation, just E of its summit. Glen Geusachan shows many signs of recent and past catastrophic floods which tore huge furrows down the steep slopes on either side, due to heavy rain storms funnelling off expanses of bare slabby rock higher up.

Natural history
The cliffs of Cairn Toul and Braeriach at An Garbh Choire are fairly good places for uncommon arctic-alpine plants. You will see extensive areas of arctic-like barrens with three-pointed rush on the Braeriach plateau, and big stretches of alpine grassland on the S flanks of Cairn Toul and the Monadh Mor. Dotterels and snow buntings breed on these hills. Red deer graze most of the ground in summer but nearly all of them leave for glens much lower down in winter. Spawning salmon go up Geusachan and up the Dee past Corrour, and the char, a northern relict, lives in Loch Einich.

Estates
The Aberdeenshire part is on Mar Lodge. The Inverness-shire part draining to Einich lies on Rothiemurchus, and that draining to Feshie belongs to Glen Feshie estate.

History
Blaeu's *Atlas* in 1654 names only 'Bini vroden' in this group of hills. In 1810, Dr G. S. Keith climbed Braeriach and Cairn Toul, and made one of the earliest recorded Scottish climbs, the ascent of the Dee waterfall in Garbh Choire Dhaidh. He wrote 'It was in flood at the time, from the melting of the snow and the late rains; and what was remarkable, an arch of snow covered the narrow glen from which it tumbled over the rocks. Here our landlord and our guide ascended the mountain by an easier, though more circuitous course; but I was determined not to lose sight of the river. We approached so near to the cataract as to know that there was no other lake or stream; and then we had to climb among huge rocks, varying from one to ten tons, and to catch hold of the stones or fragments that projected, while we ascended in an angle of 70 or 80 degrees.'

In earlier centuries, many folk from Rothiemurchus lived at shielings in upper Gleann Einich during summer. They grazed their black cattle on the fertile grass of the wide Coire Odhar S of the loch, where streams foam over the broken rocks from the Moine Mhor above. Here was born an earlier Grant of Rothiemurchus, John of Coire Odhar, who left money to build Coylumbridge and a house at the head of Loch Einich 'which should always have meal in it'. During the 19th century, a wooden sluice gate at Loch Einich produced a rush of water for floating timber lower down in Rothiemurchus.

In her *Memoirs of a Highland Lady*, Elizabeth Grant described how the man who went up to open the sluice gates once perished in the snow, and how a young shepherd also died in a snowstorm, on Braeriach. In 1974, Carrie Nethersole-Thompson of Whitewell told the present writer how some cattle belonging to her grandfather fell to their deaths over the cliffs of Coire Bhrochain on Braeriach in bad weather after straying from Gleann Einich. Doubtless it was the jawbone of one of them that Seton Gordon found about 1927 below the cliffs (*The Highlands of Scotland*, p 139). Local tradition explains the corrie's odd name – 'Brochan' means porridge – from the smashed cattle.

Last century, people from Mar grazed their cattle at Glen Geusachan and up the Coire Odhar of Glen Dee, but in the late 1800s the area was kept clear for deer. The zig-zag paths of Coire Dhondail and on Cairn Toul's Coire Odhar date from the deer stalking heyday of last century. So does Corrour Bothy which was built in 1877 to house a deer watcher in summer; the last watcher, Frank Scott, left in 1920. Subsequently Corrour (Coro*wer*) became a famous open bothy for climbers. Already in 1928, when a party from the Rucksack Club at University College in Dundee left a visitors' book, hundreds were visiting annually. From June 1928 to April 1931, 1100 came, and from then till July 1933, 1000; over half stayed one night or more. Two thirds came in June and July, and only 60 between October and March during all five years. Later, visitor-vandals tore off the woodwork for firewood until, by 1949, snow sprayed through the roof during hail storms. In 1950 the Cairngorm Club restored the bothy, which is now a fine shelter open all the year round.

Braeriach 1296 m (4248 ft)

Bràigh Riabhach (Brigh *Ree*-ach) means brindled upland. Braeriach, second highest hill of the Cairngorms and third in Britain, is a huge crescent-shaped massive bulk of a hill with bulging convex shoulders, many corries and a vast high-level plateau. From Aviemore it rises high above Rothiemurchus, but unlike Cairn Gorm it lies mysteriously further back, behind an approach that hides under the hills of lower Gleann Einich. The three symmetrical northern corries carved out of its N face are a grand sight from Strath Spey. Other corries overlook Loch Einich, and on the SE face towards Deeside lies the magnificent set of corries, shared with Cairn Toul, making up the huge amphitheatre around the Glen of the Garbh Choire. Braeriach is so big and varied that no one can know it well who has not wandered into every corrie and explored its plateau and flanks without hurry on long summer days.

Walking ascents to Braeriach

From Glen Dee. For routes to Braeriach from Deeside, see pp 142, 148.

From Gleann Einich by Coire an Lochain. Distance: from Whitewell to the summit 12 km or $7\frac{1}{2}$ miles, total ascent 1000 m or 3300 ft, time up $4\frac{1}{4}$ hours. At Inverdruie, just past the road to Loch an Eilein, a public road slants right, going past Blackpark and ending at a car park beside Whitewell. Less than 1 km to the S, beside the tarn of Lochan Deo, you come to the private road up Gleann Einich at a locked gate. From here a rough Land Rover track goes up the glen to just short of Loch Einich, 8 km or 5 miles from the gate.

Gleann Einich should really be spelled Gleann Eanaich (Glan *Enn*ich) or marsh glen. It ranks as one of the grandest of Cairngorms glens, narrow and clothed with beautiful natural pine woodland in the lower part, then bare and open, and finally ending at Loch Einich where it becomes hemmed in by massive crags. Among the upper trees the old road slid away in landslides, so a new road was bulldozed uphill. At the point where the road leaves the last trees, the entry to the glen narrows between Cadha Mor on the W and the stony Càrn Eilrig (Caarn *Ail*rik) or deer-trap hill on the E. This narrow pass is Caigeann Beanaidh (*Kigh*-gan) or rough pass of Beanaidh; here the road bends sharply at Windy Corner, where the wind often strengthens as you turn into the open glen to the S. On the hillside above, the solitary stunted pine called Craobh Thillidh (Kroov *Hyeell*ee) or tree of the return, still stands, now very ancient. In the old days in spring the cattle were driven through the forest as far up as this tree and then found their own way to the shielings at Loch Einich, to which the people all came a few days later. Below Craobh Thillidh, among the stunted outpost pines the river Beanaidh (*Benn*ie) roars down over boulders. It has now been tapped by a pipe to give water for the rapidly growing villages of Strath Spey. Above Craobh Thillidh you come into a long stretch of wide open glen, cross Beanaidh at a bridge, and 7 km from Whitewell you reach Beanaidh Bheag *(Vick)* at about 470 m, where the footbridge 150 m in distance upstream disappeared in 1973. You will find it worth crossing Einich and climbing the knolls beyond to see the hidden loch to the W. This is Loch (locally Lochan) Mhic Ghille-chaoil (Lochan Mig *Eel*ie *Choo*-il) or tarn of the thin young man's son, who was said to have died here in a fight with Lochaber cattle thieves; a rusty dirk was found at the lochside some decades ago.

The easiest way to Braeriach from here goes just past Allt Easan na Bruaich, the next stream up the road, and then uphill to 930010 where a path zig-zags up to 1070 m on the shoulder W of Loch Coire an Lochain. Distance; from Beanaidh Bheag direct to the summit 5 km or 3 miles, time up $2\frac{1}{2}$ hours. However, you will find it well worth diverging to see the loch at about 995 m; Loch Coire an Lochain is one of the highest tarns in the Cairngorms. From it you can climb up either side of the corrie, the ridge between it and Coire Ruadh to the E giving particularly grand views. The final ascent to Braeriach runs along the top of Coire Ruadh.

From Loch Einich. Distance: $6\frac{1}{2}$ km or 4 miles, 780 m ascent, time from road end to summit 3 hours. A better, though longer route than by Coire an Lochain is to walk or cycle the last 3 km of road beyond Beanaidh Bheag to Loch Einich. The loch stretches 2 km long, up to $\frac{1}{2}$ km wide and just over 45 m deep, and lies at 496 m in a hauntingly lonely place amid wild scenery with vast broken crags. Although less dramatic and varied than Loch Avon, Loch Einich gives a stronger feeling of mystery and of the puniness of man, perhaps because the more straight, open and wide U-shape of the glen shows the full sweep of these great hillsides.

The route from Loch Einich to Braeriach climbs by Coire Dhon-dail (Cor *Gown*tal). From the road end an old stalkers' track slants uphill into the corrie. A deep recess surrounded with rocks, Coire Dhondail lies between Braeriach and the rocky spur of Creag an Loch. This spur runs northwards on the E side of the loch, and offers a fine way up to the plateau giving marvellous views and a little scrambling. In Coire Dhondail the path zig-zags over the steep vegetation on the upper part of the corrie, up to 1010 m on the flat ground above. Avoid this place in winter, because of its cornices, icy snow and avalanches; then, a safer and easier route climbs up the broad slope N of the cliffs of Coire Bogha-cloiche. At the top of Coire Dhondail you come out on a wide terrace of turf and gravel at about 1000 m or 3300 ft. An easy climb follows from the terrace to the Wells of Dee or to the 1265 m point (4149 ft) at Carn na Criche at the S end of Braeriach's high plateau. For the rest of the route to the summit of Braeriach, see p 147.

It is easy to contour from the terrace above Coire Dhondail along the 5 km to Cairn Toul, or to go SE to the Monadh Mor. All these SW slopes of Cairn Toul and Braeriach are gentle, rolling down over crisp turf and heath to the Mòine Mhór (Moin *Vore*) or great moss. About 1 km towards Cairn Toul, going SE along the terrace, you come to a stream draining a shallow corrie due S of Carn na Criche, where a big snow wreath lingers far into the summer. The corrie has the grand old name of Clais Féith Inbhir Féithisidh (Clash Fay Heener *Ay*shee) or hollow of the stream at the mouth of the boggy haugh. This burn runs into Allt Luineag – often locally called Allt Luinneach – from the next hollow of Clais Luineag which lies to the E nearer Sgor an Lochain Uaine.

If you are returning to Gleann Einich from Braeriach you can drop down on either side of Loch Coire an Lochain. Alternatively, you can go to 963002 on the col towards Sron na Lairige and then E down the zig-zags of the Duke's Path into Coire na Lairige just S of the Pools of Dee (14 km and $4\frac{3}{4}$ hours ascending by this route from Derry Lodge). An interesting way back is to carry on over the 1184 m Sròn na Làirige (Stronna *Laa*rig) or nose of the Lairig, and then go down its long N nose to the Sinclair Hut in the Lairig Ghru, a route which avoids the rough walking on the Lairig track ($4\frac{1}{2}$ km to the hut, $12\frac{1}{2}$ to Whitewell). From Sron na Lairige the strong walker may prefer to visit the remote Lochan Odhar among its peat hags and then climb the beautiful cone of Carn Eilrig for a magnificent last view before dropping into Rothiemurchus.

Walking in Braeriach's corries

The long, shallow Coire Gorm (Cor *Gor*om) or green corrie goes down the middle of the Aviemore side of Sron na Lairige. A grassy open corrie, it often holds snow till midsummer and in spring gives a fine ski run. The easternmost of Braeriach's set of three northern corries, Coire Beanaidh (Cor *Benn*ie) now contains hardly any rock as its cliffs have long crumbled into great screes. The middle Coire Ruadh (Cor *Roo*a) or red corrie has a beautifully symmetrical circular shape with broken rocks; a grand feature is the pair of narrow stony ridges on either side leading to the rounded top of Braeriach behind. The western Coire an Lochain looks finest, with its very high tarn that carries ice into June or July, and its crescent of broken crags and late snow patches offering sporting easy lines to the plateau. Above Loch Einich, Coire Bogha-cloiche (Cor Baw *Cloich*) or stone-arch corrie has a frieze of broken cliff at its top. Coire Clach lies between it and the fine Coire Dhondail already mentioned, being no more than a shallow indentation in the bulging W slopes of Braeriach.

The most magnificent corrie of the Cairngorms is the vast super-corrie of An Garbh Choire (Un *Gar*a Chorrie) or the rough corrie. In late summer you can descend laboriously into it from Braeriach by the boulder slopes W of Coire Bhrochain. From the W, another good way in drops from the low col W of Sgor an Lochain Uaine, where a wide shoot of boulders runs N into the corrie. By far the most impressive route leads up Allt a' Gharbh Choire from the Lairig Ghru track; from Corrour Bothy it takes $2\frac{1}{2}$ hours to reach the furthest recesses of Garbh Choire. In this lower Glen of the Garbh Choire, Cairn Toul's Coire an Lochain Uaine soars on the left, with the waterfall from its green tarn plunging over slabby rocks. Opposite on the right hangs Coire Bhrochain under the top of Braeriach, a huge boulder-strewn cup facing S, with one of the grandest rock faces in the Cairngorms reaching up to 230 m or 750 ft of steep granite.

Once past these two corries, you look into An Garbh Choire itself which forms an enormous complex sloping bowl between Sgor an Lochain Uaine and Braeriach. In the S, a striking face of dark precipice W of Sgor an Lochain Uaine is gashed by the dark furrow of Chokestone Gully. Further W lies Garbh Choire Mór (*Gar*a Chor *More*) or big rough corrie, with fine 100 m cliffs rearing up out of great snow fields. It almost became a couple of corries; the outer is the whole wide stretch of Garbh Choire Mor, but within it, higher up and in the westernmost corner, a smaller recess holds Scotland's longest-lasting snow field. In this most alpine of Cairngorms corries you can often see small crevasses, bergschrunds, avalanches, enormous cornices, and rock which hides under snow for so much of the year that the grey-green lichens of Garbh Choire Mor have failed to colonise on the virgin granite. A 30 m vertical depth of snow occurs in some springs and some of the lower pitches of the rock climbs are buried till late summer. A group from University College in Dundee has done research on this snow field (*SMCJ* 28, 273). Photographs taken by the writer in late April 1951, after the snowiest winter in the Cairngorms since the early 1940s, show that the snow almost buried the rock climbs S of Sphinx Ridge.

Northwards, a projecting broad nose separates Garbh Choire Mor from Garbh Choire Dhaidh, which is a map error for Dhé, pronounced Yay, meaning rough corrie of Dee. When snowfree, this nose gives an easy way to the plateau, without rock climbing. It is fine to explore Garbh Choire Dhaidh. Although less snowy than Garbh Choire Mor, nevertheless it still looks a very snowy place at mid-summer, and used to be called Fuar Garbh Choire, meaning cold rough corrie. A grand steep wall of granite rises N of the Dee waterfall, with smaller cliffs further N again. As Garbh Choire Dhaidh has more of a gently-sloping floor than Garbh Choire Mor, it is much more grassy. The waterfall plunges not in one great leap, but in a series of cascades down innumerable steps of pink granite, polished smooth by the force of the water and by frequent snow avalanches. Below, the stream runs through a tiny meadow of crisp herbage watered by spray. It then rumbles underground below boulders, and at the foot of the gentle basin opens into wide pools almost like tiny tarns, shortly before rushing more steeply into An Garbh Choire below. Long after rain the black cliffs stream with water. The poet Hogg's lines are appropriate

the grisly cliffs which guard
The infant rills of Highland Dee.

Cairn Toul 1293 m (4241 ft)

Càrn an t-Sabhail (Caarn *Towel*) means hill of the barn. Cairn Toul is by far the sharpest of the high Cairngorms. Although flat-looking and square-shaped when viewed from the W, it rises as a beautiful conical peak when seen from Braemar and Glen Dee, falling steeply for 680 m to Glen Dee and with a tiny hanging corrie nestling just below the summit. On its SW flanks, it slopes gradually into vast open green corries with screes and foaming burns, towards the plateau of the Moine Mhor and the huge trench of Glen Geusachan. The outlying hills of the Devil's Point, the Monadh Mor and Beinn Bhrotain, which almost encircle this finest glen in the Cairngorms, excel in wildness, variety and remoteness.

26. Summit of Braeriach and cliffs of Coire Bhrochain in April.

27. Lochan Uaine and Cairn Toul in late June from the top of Braeriach

28.   In October from the edge of the Coire an Lochain of Braeriach, looking out over the plateau of the Moine Mhor.

29. Garbh Choire Mor in June, from the slope of Sgor an Lochain Uaine: the most long-lying snow bed in Britain.

30.   Coire Bhrochain in October, rising to the top of Braeriach.

Walking ascents to Cairn Toul

From Derry Lodge. Distance 11 km or 7 miles, 1020 m or 3350 ft of ascent, time up 4 hours. The route from the Derry to opposite Corrour comes in by the Lairig Ghru path (p 130). You now cross to Corrour Bothy at about 560 m by the footbridge over Dee, 7½ km or 4½ miles from Derry Lodge. Corrour Bothy was named after the wide Coire Odhar or dun corrie, which stretches behind the bothy from the Devil's Point round to Cairn Toul. A stalkers' path goes up the corrie from the bothy. Although steep, the last part is easily climbed by the path's well-made zig-zags, but it can be a dangerous place in winter, often with a bulging snow drift or cornice which occasionally avalanches. In icy snow or avalanche-prone snow, the ridge at the N end of the corrie makes a safer route, the scree slopes nearer the Devil's Point being sometimes also safer. One of the most delightful spots in the Cairngorms is where the Coire Odhar path comes on to the 915 m flat sandy neck of An Diollaid (Un *Dyee*ulitsh) or the saddle, connecting the Devil's Point to Cairn Toul. The stream of Allt a' Choire Odhair, icy cold and refreshing, hurries on among beautiful mosses. Behind lies the steep gulf of Lairig Ghru; ahead, wide grassy slopes like an arctic tundra stretch towards the Monadh Mor.

From here a short detour of 700 m (100 m in ascent) takes you to the cairn on the Devil's Point at 1004 m or 3303 ft. This perch gives a magnificent aerial view down steep broken cliffs into Glen Dee and Glen Geusachan, with the Geusachan stream winding far below through beautiful green flats. The Gaelic name for Devil's Point was Bod an Deamhain, pronounced Pote an *Dyaw*-in. Every book and reference that the writer has seen skates over this subject by saying the Devil's Point is a 'euphemistic' or a 'literal' translation. It is perhaps time to be accurate and say that Bod an Deamhain means the penis of the Devil. The name seems appropriate if you view this grand hill from the Lairig Ghru path opposite.

From the neck of An Diollaid above Coire Odhar, the way to Cairn Toul lies N along the edge of the corrie to a 1213 m top overlooking the wild Coire an t-Saighdeir (Cor an *Deid*yir) or corrie of the soldier. Still following the cliff edge you drop slightly to 1167 m, and then comes the final rise over boulders to the top of Cairn Toul. From the summit, two ridges, each with a cairn at its top, run towards Glen Dee below, enclosing the high hanging corrie of Coire an t-Sabhail (Cor an *Dow*el). You can make a pleasant descent from the summit by dropping W to the col above Lochan Uaine, and then going down the green boulder-strewn valley of Clais an t-Sabhail (Clashan *Dowe*l) or hollow of the barn, into Glen Geusachan.

Walking in Cairn Toul's corries

Coire an t-Saighdeir is a wild corrie full of boulder fields, broken rock and snow, lying S of the sharp peak of Cairn Toul. An easy way out in late summer goes by the Slichit (*Slichi*t), a wide gravelly shoot in the centre of the corrie, which leads through the cliffs to the 1167 m col above. To the N, Coire an t-Sabhail is the fine hanging corrie immediately under the top of Cairn Toul. Although a continuous mass of boulders covers the corrie, nevertheless in deep winter snow it can offer a quick way off Cairn Toul. In suitable conditions it makes a fine glissade or trot from the top down this corrie and the snow-filled burn below for about 680 m or 2200 ft to the water of Dee in 13 to 20 minutes, and indeed this forms one of the longer glissades of Scotland (see *SMCJ* 15, 225). Be careful at the very top, which is steep and often corniced, but the ridges on either side of Coire an t-Sabhail merely involve easy scrambling on steep boulders.

Lochan Uaine or green tarn in Coire an Lochain Uaine is one of the priceless gems of the Cairngorms, lying at about 910 m on a rocky shelf high on the N slopes of Cairn Toul. From the loch, a small stream tumbles over the rocky lip of the corrie down to Allt a' Gharbh Choire 260 m below. Steep slopes of rock, scree and grass sweep for over 300 m above the loch up to Cairn Toul and to the even more imposing sharp peak of Sgor an Lochain Uaine further W. The ridge running from the loch to the Sgor forms one of the few such arêtes in the Cairngorms, and makes a fine way up which involves easy scrambling up steep boulders, narrowing to a crest near the top.

Cairn Toul to Braeriach

This is perhaps the finest high-level hill walk in Britain. Distance 6 km or 3½ miles, total climbing 320 m, 1¾ hours. After leaving Cairn Toul you drop about 150 m in altitude W to the 1140 m col along the edge of Coire an Lochain Uaine and climb again a short way to Sgòr an Lochain Uaine (Skor an *Loch*an Ooan) or peak of the green tarn. This fine hill, 1258 m in altitude, lies 1 km WNW of Cairn Toul. From Sgor an Lochain Uaine you descend W along the cliff edge to the lowest point of the whole round, at about 1130 m or 3700 ft, at the col between Cairn Toul and Braeriach where you have a magnificent view down to Garbh Choire Mor and its snow fields. An easy slope leads up from the col, along the cliff edge where the biggest cornices in the Cairngorms build up in winter. You can keep following the steep edge all the way to Braeriach, but it is more interesting to diverge on to the plateau, where the small cairn of Càrn na Crìche or cairn of the march stands near the highest point (1265 m or 4149 ft) of a great stretch of stones and gravel. To the N of here on the watershed rises Einich Cairn at 1237 m, near which you will get fine views of the Sgoran Dubh cliffs.

In the centre of the plateau, the infant Dee flows through banks of gravel after rising in a spring at the foot of a bank of grass and moss, which is crowned by a small cairn of white quartz stones. Here at 1220 m or 4000 ft, a powerful stream gushes forth, to be reinforced further down by other springs; these are Fuaran Dhé (*Fooaran Yay*) or Wells of Dee. 'No other river in the country has such a source, at such an elevation, and the whole scene is unique in British hills. This summit plateau of Braeriach in its bigness and bareness exceeds anything in the Cairngorms or in these islands' (Alexander, first edition). Although not so variable as the Ben Macdui plateau, without its huge boulder fields and snow fields, nevertheless here there stretches a far bigger expanse of gravelly flat tundra. You also become aware of a great feeling of vast space and of the attractive quality that some people notice about deserts. After $\frac{2}{3}$ km on the plateau, the infant Dee crashes over the rocky face of Garbh Choire Dhaidh and cascades 150 m to the bed of the corrie below. A large snow bridge often lasts far into the summer at the top of the fall; below, the stream thunders on down to Glen Dee. Many think that Spey is the fastest Scottish river but Dee far exceeds it, dropping from 1200 m to the sea in only 137 km.

About 300 m in distance NE of where Dee falls over, the cliffs, which have been almost continuous right round An Garbh Choire from Cairn Toul, come to an end. Here a wide bouldery slope faces S between Garbh Choire Dhaidh and Coire Bhrochain. It offers an easy though laborious way down in late summer but in winter often carries a big cornice well below the top of the slope; if so, you can usually descend the ridge immediately bounding the W side of Coire Bhrochain. An easy 80 m rise in altitude takes you over stony gravel from the plateau to the edge of Coire Bhrochain (Cor *Vrocha*n) or corrie of the porridge, and for the last 200 m of distance you walk along the top of its magnificent cliffs to the cairn of Braeriach. Immediately below that cairn the cliffs drop 230 m past the prominent

Black Pinnacle. If returning to Deeside you descend to the col between Braeriach and Sron na Lairige. From here the Duke's Path
zig-zags down the steep grass of Coire na Lairige – called Coire
Ruadh by the old folk of Mar – to the Lairig Ghru below. Avoid this
route after deep snow as a cornice often builds out here and avalanches sometimes occur. In deep snow the E ridge of Coire Bhrochain
between it and Coire na Lairige makes a much safer descent,
although rough and laborious because of boulders.

Beinn Bhrotain 1157 m (3795 ft) and the **Monadh Mor** 1113 m
(3651 ft). These are best climbed as a pair. Beinn Bhrotain (Pain
*Vroet*an) or hill of Brodan (who was Fingal's dog), stretches far as a
vast complex granite hill with many bulging shoulders, dominating
Glen Dee and Glen Geldie. The easiest approach is to cycle from the
Linn of Dee for 5 km up to the White Bridge in Glen Dee. From here
a new rough bulldozed road, which you can cycle on, goes 5 km up
the W side of Dee ending at Caochan Ròibidh (*Coch*an *Ropp*ie), a
stream S of Glen Geusachan. Distance: from the road end at 480 m
to Beinn Bhrotain 3½ km, ascent 690 m. Another way is to cycle up
Glen Geldie; you can then climb from the nearest point on the road
there (p 131), past Duke's Chair for 5½ km to the summit. Looking
prominent from the White Bridge, the nearer stony cone of Càrn
Cloich-mhuilinn (Caarn Clach *Vool*in) or millstone hill rises to 942
m or 3087 ft; you can easily climb it on the way up above Duke's
Chair. The upper corrie of Allt Garbh, SE of the summit of Beinn
Bhrotain, has the name Coire an t-Sneachda (Cor an *Drechk*) or
corrie of the snow; here on the W slope of the burn a huge drift lasts
far into the summer, often corniced on its E edge. The slabs (not
shown on the map) in the upper corrie of Caochan Roibidh form
another hazard.

If you go 1 km NW of Beinn Bhrotain and 150 m lower, you come
to the col at 975 m between the two hills. At the col you look N
down the wild Coire Cath nam Fionn (*Cor* Ca na *Vyung*) – into
which you can easily descend from here – and S down Allt Dhaidh
Mor. Ahead, the slope rises to a beautiful green shoulder at 1093 m
called Leac Ghorm (*Leeachk Gor*om) or green slope. From here you
enjoy a delightful stroll on springy mossy turf to the 1113 m cairn
of Am Monadh Mór (Um Monna *More*) or the big hill, which stands
2 km from the col towards Beinn Bhrotain. To the W of the cairn,
gentle slopes fall to the huge grassy and peaty plateau of the Moine
Mhor. The E slopes are at first gentle but soon become steep and

rocky, and you may find it hard to see good ways down. Moreover, 200 m in distance E of the summit, the high Coire Creagach (Cor *Craik*ach) or rocky corrie falls off steeply with shelves of broken rocks and a steep snow field; the snow lasts long into the summer and stands out well even from as far as the Blue Hill at Aberdeen. For the easiest and most interesting way off the Monadh Mor back to Glen Geusachan you should descend for 2 km N to about 865 m at Loch nan Stuirteag (St*yoo*rtach), which is a beautiful tarn in a green basin lying 5 km from where Geusachan enters Dee at 496 m.

The name Glen Geusachan comes from Gleann Giùbhsachain (Glan *Gyoo*sachan) or glen of the little pine wood, and many roots of pines still stick out of the bare peat. Not a single tree now survives in the glen, but you can see plenty of small trees on the lower cliffs of the Devil's Point and Beinn Bhrotain, where they can grow out of the reach of red deer. Here is the most beautiful of the high hill glens in all the area described in this Guide. Wild broken crags rise all around, running into screes and huge slabs of wet smooth granite. Streams foam down over the rocks, in places through hidden miniature upper corries that are almost invisible from the glen floor. In several places, enormous piles of boulders and gravel show where heavy rain has torn up the hillsides. Yet the floor of the glen forms a marvellous contrast, as the Geusachan burn meanders peacefully through a fertile grassy flat over shingles and peaty pools.

If you are heading for the Derry, 6½ km away, a good place for crossing lies about ⅔ km N of the confluence of Geusachan and Dee, where Dee flows in a thin sheet over slabs of pink granite. In higher water, a nearby place is better where you can jump across on big boulders, but you need to be sure-footed as the water surges strongly between the boulders; in flood, go to Corrour footbridge. South of where Geusachan enters Dee you will see a lovely quiet deep pool at a bend, called Poll an Éisg (Pole a *Neeshk*) or pool of the fish, where salmon often lie. One of the finest stretches of Glen Dee lies between here and Caochan Roibidh, where a great slabby crag of Beinn Bhrotain, shining with water, rears up above a moorland studded with little tarns.

Climbing routes

On Cairn Toul, the NE ridge of Sgor an Lochain Uaine gives a good, Grade I winter climb from the shore of Lochan Uaine to the summit cairn of the Sgor. When combined with an ascent of Allt an Lochain Uaine which turns into great cascades of ice in winter (Grade II), the two routes together form a grand winter ascent 500 m in vertical height.

Garbh Choire Mor. West of Sgor an Lochain Uaine a long line of rock extends round to Garbh Choire Mor. Here lies Chokestone Gully, an impressive N-facing dark line which cleaves the cliffs for 150 m. A wet gully, it makes a very fine Grade III climb in winter; after hard frost the pitch high in the gully beside the great chokestone often becomes a thick ribbon of vertical ice, but in times of deep snow the entire gully forms merely a high-angle snow slope with a massive cornice. The nearby long gully to its left is The Shroud, a grand 150 m winter climb which was Grade IV on its first ascent, with fine ice pitches.

The high inner recess of Garbh Choire Mor has many small 100 m buttresses of steep granite tinged greenish with lichens. In spring the cliff top carries a fringe of enormous cornices which make exit to the plateau a difficult problem, and cornices up to 11 m thick have been recorded. The most remarkable feature in the corrie is Sphinx Ridge which rises straight up from Britain's longest-lying snow bed; after a hard winter the steep slab at the bottom becomes completely buried. Sphinx Ridge tapers to a fine crest above the gully to the N, and from this crest you look up to the rocky knob of the Sphinx which projects above you beyond a small pitch. You now go round the Sphinx on the left and then climb slabs to another crest and little pinnacle just below the plateau. To the right of the obvious open gully – Great Gully – at the S end of the inner, upper recess of Garbh Choire Mor rises the fine climb of She-Devil's Buttress (VD, 120 m). Immediately to the right of She-Devil's Buttress, the 140 m VS route of Vulcan is one of the corrie's finest climbs, going up a prominent V-groove. To the right of Sphinx, the prominent Pinnacles Buttress (D) soars above the easy Pinnacle Gully. The next buttress to the right, called Tower of Babel (VS), forms one of the harder climbs of the massif. The name Egyptian Fantasy (D) up the first crest to the left of Solo Gully (the gully left of Sphinx Ridge) has some historical interest. Its originator was M. Smith, author of the first edition of the Climbers' Guide and lover of Cairngorms granite. He gave it this name as a parody after a writer had rather depreciated Cairngorms rock and had called much of it 'Egyptian'!

Garbh Choire Dhaidh. A beautiful 140 m wall of cliffs extends on the N side of the Dee Waterfall. The Great Rift (VD) is the long dark chimney up the middle of the crag, making a grand climb up continuous granite and bringing you to magnificent viewpoints looking across a belt of steep, ribbed slabs over to the Dee waterfall. One of the best and popular climbs of the Cairngorms, the St Andrews Climb (S), lies up the ridge just to the right of The Great Rift. As The Great Rift stays wet long after rain, it becomes heavily iced-up in winter and made a fine Grade IV climb on the first winter ascent in February 1965. The rocks at the far right end of the corrie lie back at a more gentle angle, Pisa (D), the furthest right buttress, being one of the corrie's easier climbs on good rough granite. The dark gully on its left is Chimney Pot, first ascended in 1942. Avoid it in summer unless you wish a bath, as you will get a cold shower while climbing past its big chokestones; it becomes heavily iced in winter. Helicon Rib (D) on its left side is a recommended climb for a novice, on fine sound granite, with the difficulties easing half way up.

Coire Bhrochain. This grand cirque carries a wild semicircle of big cliffs up to 230 m high, in a sheltered and sunny position. It holds a variety of interesting routes of all standards but mainly of medium difficulty, on dry clean granite. The cliffs consist of three main parts, a West Buttress which is separated by the wide West Gully from the Central Buttress below the cairn of Braeriach, and then the East Buttress made up of a set of distinctive small buttresses. High in the middle of Central Buttress, the prominent Black Pinnacle rears up below the summit of Braeriach. A popular climb is Braeriach Direct (MS), which goes for 230 m from the lowest rocks below the Black Pinnacle to the plateau just E of the Braeriach cairn. The nearby climb of Bhrochain Slabs (200 m, VD), lying just to the W of the Black Pinnacle, is a recommended route giving a fine ascent on clean, dry, rough slabs. There are several routes up the Black Pinnacle itself, starting from the broad Slab Terrace which you can easily walk up or down and which slants leftwards up from the E part of the corrie floor. The Black Pinnacle really forms a buttress which is slabby below and tapers to a point protruding above a neck that lies behind it, a neck not far down from the plateau edge. The Ordinary Route (M) was first ascended in 1911 by J. A. Parker, H. Alexander, J. B. Millar and W. A. Reid. They went from the highest part of Slab Terrace up the loose first pitch of Central Buttress Gully straight above, which is the gully separating the Black Pinnacle from the bulging Braeriach Pinnacle (another buttress) to the E. Above this pitch the gully forks; ahead, easy ground leads straight up to the plateau, but the pioneers headed leftwards to the neck of the Black Pinnacle. The 45 m Direct Route (D), which was climbed solo by J. H. B. Bell in 1938, makes a far better route on a fairly direct line from the foot of the Pinnacle to its top. To the E of the Black Pinnacle, the projecting convex buttress of Braeriach Pinnacle takes you out at the plateau E of and slightly below the cairn of Braeriach; its final knob rises level with the plateau behind. The Original Route (D), climbed by P. D. Baird and R. N. Traquair in 1931, goes up the high part of the buttress from near the foot straight to the top; you can wander here and there over much of this section. A recommended, defined line runs up the exposed 90 m West Wall Route (MS), which was climbed by A. Tewnion, W. T. Hendry and G. Lumsden in 1942; it goes on or near the left edge of the buttress on excellent steep rock.

Other crags. The cliffs of the Devil's Point, although impressive, extensive and very high (up to 350 m), generally lack definition and are mostly broken. Various rock climbs have been recorded but none is recommended, although the place offers sporting ascents in winter and plenty of easy scrambling in summer on the way to the tops. Geusachan Cave, lying fairly low down in the middle of the slabs on the Glen Geusachan side, is an interesting place to visit, which you can reach by heathery ledges from the W. Although not seen from far down the glen, it becomes obvious from directly below. Beinn Bhrotain carries an unusual set of short slabs well to the S of Glen Geusachan, and a small buttress of good rock high in Coire Cath nam Fionn. On Sron na Lairige, the 140 m Lairig Ridge (only D) offers a grand sporting route up on to Braeriach on sound rock, by the most obvious long ridge in the northern half of the line of broken rocks facing into the Lairig Ghru; broad at first, it tapers higher up into a fine crest.

To sum up, the main feature of Braeriach and Cairn Toul for climbing routes centres on the very long and varied crags around the Glen of the Garbh Choire, which in the Cairngorms massif are equalled only by that other grand set around Loch Avon. The Garbh Choire looks markedly different, however, as the cliffs lie at a higher altitude and also carry far more blown snow than the Loch Avon cliffs. The winter potential of the Garbh Choire cliffs is therefore outstanding. They are so snowy and icy that they give excellent alpine-like winter routes on the long days and in the fine weather of April and even May, when most other crags in the massif have thawed and become largely free of snow.

Further reading

A. I. McConnochie   The western Cairngorms. *CCJ* 2, 38.

D. McDougall Loch Mhic Ghille-Chaoile: a tradition of the Cairngorms. *CCJ* 2, 294.

A. I. McConnochie Across Braeriach and Cairn Toul on New Year's Day, 1891. *SMCJ* 1, 195.

W. A. Smith The western Cairngorms (Guide Book article). *SMCJ* 7, 254.

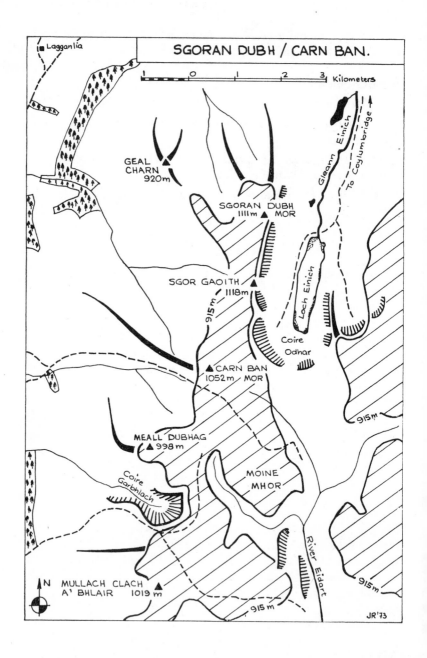

SGORAN DUBH / CARN BAN.

Lagganlia

Kilometers

GEAL CHARN 920m

SGORAN DUBH 1111m ▲ MOR

SGOR GAOITH ▲ 1118m

915m

Gleann Einich

To Coylumbridge

Loch Einich

Coire Odhar

▲ CARN BAN 1052m MOR

915m

MEALL DUBHAG ▲ 998m

Coire Garbhlach

MOINE MHOR

River Eidart

N MULLACH CLACH A' BHLAIR 1019m

915m

915m

JR '73

5

Sgoran Dubh and Carn Ban

Sgoran Dubh Mor	1111 m, 906003
***Sgor Gaoith**	1118 m, 902989
***Geal Charn**	920 m, 884014
***Carn Ban Mor**	1052 m, 893972
***Meall Dubhag**	998 m, 881955
***Mullach Clach a' Bhlair**	1019 m, 883927

Access, accommodation, remote houses and bothies
As in Chapter 1. Public roads go to Whitewell at 916085 below
Einich, and to Achlean at 853975 up the E side of Feshie from Feshie-
bridge. A roofless stone shelter stands at the rock outcrop of Clach a'
Bhlair at 885927, 200 m E of the cairn on Mullach Clach a' Bhlair.
Lagganlia near Feshiebridge is Edinburgh Corporation's outdoor
centre. For remote houses and bothies, see Chapter 3 (Glen Feshie
section).

General description
Rising from Glen Feshie, this 15 km line of tops, connected by a high
plateau, forms a great rampart along the W end of Am Monadh
Ruadh or the Cairngorms. From between Loch Alvie and Kingussie
you can see this particularly well; the wall of steep lower hillsides,
some with broken rocks, rears out of pine forests and up to broad
summits, in places cut by wild narrow upper glens. Up there on the
top, a tableland of springy turf rolls on for miles. The deep craggy
glens of Einich and Eidart away to the E almost cut off these hills,
but in the middle they are connected to the loftier Braeriach, Cairn
Toul and the Monadh Mor still further to the E by a flattish broad
belt of high peaty country called the Mòine Mhór (Moin *Vore*) or
the great moss, a grand subarctic wilderness with a habitat unique
in Scotland. It makes an easy trip to traverse all these tops in series,
as they all form mere bumps in a high-level whaleback ridge. However, the best way to appreciate the full grandeur of the group is to

come in from Gleann Einich and see the contrast between the wild crags of Sgoran Dubh on that side and the smooth western slopes. On the W side of the group, you will find the great rocky trench of Coire Garbhlach above Glenfeshie Lodge especially worth visiting.

Geology and landforms
Most of the rock is granite, including the great wall of cliffs W of Loch Einich. However, the floor of Glen Feshie itself lies over part of the huge Central Highland granulite formation of schist. This also makes up the SW and S parts of the hill groups, for example at Coire Garbhlach (also has some granite on its N side) and at Coire Mharconaich. The schist occurs again under the Moine Mhor through to Coire Odhar, in the Eidart glen and at Mullach Clach a' Bhlair. Coire Garbhlach has a remarkable, long, cliff-sided glacial trench, and Feshie an unusual braided stream and great shingle beds. The Moine Mhor is notable for its extensive high peat bogs and for the innumerable subarctic-like tiny hummocks, caused by alternating frost and thaw, on better drained ground.

Natural history
On Creag Fhiaclach you can see one of the best examples of a natural tree line still left in Scotland. All this ground is deer forest; in winter the deer crowd into Glen Feshie which they overgraze, but in summer they range far out on to the Moine Mhor and higher. Dotterel and dunlin nest on the tops and on the Moine Mhor. Many uncommon willows and other rare arctic-alpine plants grow on the fertile lime-rich rocks around the head of Coire Odhar above Loch Einich and at Coire Garbhlach. A nature trail leads from Achlean into the old pine wood (1 hour walk).

Estates
The ground draining into Einich is on Rothiemurchus, and that draining into Feshie lies on Glen Feshie Estate, except that the Nature Conservancy Council owns Invereshie and Inshriach with a boundary from Creag Fhiaclach to Creag Dhubh to Carn Ban Mor to Glac Ghiubhsachan.

History
Clach Mhic Cailein, the Argyll Stone on Creag Dhubh, was named after the Earl of Argyll who passed here when fleeing home from the battle of Glen Livet in 1594, where he had been defeated by the Earl of Huntly. At Muileann Dubh near Feshiebridge, later translated

to Blackmill, one of the party was said to have composed the popular Highland song and dance tune of 'Muileann Dubh'. Ciste Mearaid or Margaret's coffin on Carn Ban Mor was called after a Margaret, who, jilted by Mackintosh of Moy, cursed sterility on his family and died here on her mad wanderings.

In his *Tour of Scotland* in 1794, Pennant was the first to mention any of these hills, writing of 'Sgorgave in Rothiemurchus', presumably meaning Sgor Gaoith. Later, Colonel Thornton in his *Sporting Tour*, published in 1804 (account in *CCJ* 2, 55), climbed Sgoran Dubh. High up, he 'deposited our champaign, lime, shrub, porter etc in one of the large snow-drifts, beneath an arch from which ran a charming spring' (probably Fuaran Diotach). '. . . It is impossible to describe the astonishment of the whole party when they perceived themselves on the brink of that frightful precipice, which separated them from the lake below . . . Let the reader imagine a mountain at least eighteen thousand feet above him' (probably Braeriach) 'and a steep precipice of thirteen thousand feet below'. Imagine the SMC Rock Guide he might have written! His hilltop lunch also far surpassed the modest sandwich of today's climber. 'The chief dish consisted of two brace and a half of ptarmigants and a moorcock, a quarter of a pound of butter, some slices of Yorkshire ham and reindeer's tongue with some sweet herbs. . . . These with a due proportion of water made each of us a plate of very strong soup, which was relished with a keenness of appetite that none but those that have been at Glen Ennoch can experience. We now drank in a bumper of champaign . . . and with the addition of a tumbler of sherbet and a cordial, were enabled to pack up our apparatus and proceed.' Could one have a better invitation to visit Gleann Einich?

Walking ascents

Sgoran Dubh Mor 1111 m (3635 ft) and **Sgor Gaoith** 1118 m (3658 ft). The finest approach comes from Gleann Einich (for the route up the glen, see p 140). The easiest way up is to cross the flat ground just N of Loch (locally Lochan) Mhic Ghille-chaoil, climb to the neck at 776 m and then S up to the top of Sgoran Dubh (4 km, 640 m ascent, 2 hours). But the better approach goes to Loch Einich, and up the W side of the loch by Ross's Path which climbs to 710 m below the high corrie of A' Phòcaid (A *Fochk*itsh) or the pocket. Distance: from the road end to Sgor Gaoith 5 km, 620 m ascent. Broken rocks ring the top of A' Phocaid and the wider Coire Odhar

(Cor *Ow*er) to the E, but you can easily zig-zag between them on to the plateau, to where Fuaran Diotach (Fooaran D*yee*tach) or dinner well flows from a beautiful spring in a grassy hollow. A gentle walk follows from there along to Sgòr Gaoith (Skor *Goo*ee) or peak of wind at 1118 m, where the summit cairn perches on the edge of the precipitous 600 m drop to Loch Einich. Although these big crags are mostly broken, some of the buttresses consist of steep rock. On one of the buttresses (No 5, see p 162) below Sgor Gaoith stands the sharp pinnacle called A' Chailleach (A' *Chal*yach) or the old woman, her counterpart being a rocky pillar named Am Bodach (Um *Pot*ach) or the old man near the top of the Creag an Loch spur of Braeriach opposite.

From Sgor Gaoith you drop about 50 m in altitude and then climb the grassy slope leading to the cone of Sgòran Dubh Mór (Skorran Doo *More*) or big black peaklet. Unlike Sgor Gaoith, its cairn stands well back from the cliff edge so the view is less fine. Many local people call the whole hill group The Sgoran. (In the maps of the last three decades, there has been no confusion, as incorrectly stated in the previous four editions of the District Guide and in the first edition of the Climbers' Guide, about the local names of these hills.) From Sgoran Dubh Mor, the broad northern ridge makes an easy descent offering splendid views over to Braeriach on the right and down into Spey on the left. On the way you pass the fine rocky 996 m point of Sgoran Dubh Beag at the cliff edge, and further down-hill a path takes you to the col at 760 m, just W of Coire Creagach nam Bo and lonely Lochan Beanaidh. During the gentle rise from that col to the bare flat 848 m top of Creag Dhubh, you will see two small tors. The first is Clach Choutsaich or Coutts' stone, the second being Clach Mhic Cailein or Argyll stone, which stands out prominently from Strath Spey. From here the easiest way down lies over Cadha Mor (Ca *More*) and then NE to the Gleann Einich road, or N by the tree-girt Cadha Beag below it towards Whitewell. A more interesting way goes NW towards Creag Fhiaclach (Craig *Ee*achklach) or toothed rock which has a fine natural tree line, then to a path at 900046 beside Allt Coire Follais, and finally down it through long heather and pine trees to the rough road S of Loch an Eilein.

For another way off Sgoran Dubh you can walk out along the long nose to the 976 m Meall Buidhe and beyond to the shapely 920 m (3019 ft) hill of Geal Charn. Geal Chàrn (*Yal* Charn) or white hill is the shapely top which stands out prominently in the view from Strath

Spey, being the furthest W hill of the Cairngorms massif. Below Geal Charn, Creag Mhigeachaidh (Craik *Veg*echie) shows a fine rugged face of broken rocks and pine trees towards Feshie. Here, in 1896 and 1900, avalanches swept hundreds of trees and masses of rock and boulders into the valley below (*CCJ* 3, 192).

A third way down from Sgoran Dubh drops by the path which zig-zags from Creag Follais down to Allt a' Mharcaidh. A second path goes straight down the E side of that burn, from the neck between Meall Buidhe and Geal Charn, while a third path branches off the second path at 890014 to contour round the N side of Geal Charn and so to the lower Allt a' Mharcaidh. To the S of Creag Mhigeach-aidh, you can approach by a bulldozed road that runs up the N side of Allt Ruadh to 460 m and then by a path to 600 m at 883994. Both Allt Ruadh and Allt a' Mharcaidh flow down lovely glens which are bare, wide and open higher up, but lower down become narrow, steep and finely wooded with old pines, where both streams rush through rocky ravines (wooden footbridge over Allt Ruadh at 871004). The glen of Allt a' Mharcaidh is called Glen *Mark*ie, and leads down to the swampy Lochan Gorm on the valley flats beside the big pine woods of Inshriach Forest.

Carn Ban Mor 1052 m (3443 ft). Càrn Bàn Mór (Caarn Baan *More*) means big fair hill. The easiest approach is to take the public road from Feshiebridge up the E side of Feshie to Achlean (Ach*lain*). Distance to top: 5 km, ascent 720 m, 2½ hours. From Achlean a bulldozed road goes a short way uphill, changing to the Foxhunters' Path up the N side of Allt Fhearnagan (Alt *Yar*nagan) or burn of the little alder place. The path continues up Coire Fhearnagan to 1030 m on the plateau just S of the summit. The hollow at the source of this burn, called Ciste Mearaid or Margaret's coffin, holds snow late in the year. Not far to the N of the path here, the hill slopes N into the wide Coire Ruadh and down to Allt Ruadh.

Meall Dubhag 998 m (3268 ft). Called Myal *Doo*ich, this hill forms a mere bump rising from a big flat plateau, about 2 km SW of Carn Ban Mor. To the S of Meall Dubhag the craggy Coire Garbhlach bites far into the hills. An easy way up to the plateau now starts at Carnachuin, to the E of which the fine old path up Allt Choire Chaoil has been obliterated into a bulldozed Land Rover road. It climbs the nose S of Coire Garbhlach, giving grand views into that fine corrie, and comes right on to the plateau.

Mullach Clach a' Bhlàir 1019 m (3338 ft). From the plateau, one branch of the road leads S and then E, passing this top which one pronounces *Moo*lach Clach *Vlaa*-ir, or summit stone of the plain. This name comes from Clach a' Bhlair, a nearby rock outcrop, whereas the hill itself is really Meall Tionail (Myal *Tyaini*l) or lump of meeting. At this point you stand 6 km from Carnachuin by the Land Rover road, ascent 670 m. From the summit a long nose runs SW to the rocky point of Druim nam Bo at 918 m, then beyond it to the tarn of Lochan nam Bo in a tiny recess, and further still to end at Creag na Gaibhre. Creag na Gaibhre is a spectacular viewpoint above an Alpine-like face of shattered rocks, screes and small trees, dropping 300 m to the flats of Feshie below. A zig-zag track leads from the 737 m top behind it NW to Ruigh-aiteachain.

Beyond Mullach Clach a' Bhlair the bulldozed road from Coire Garbhlach goes 3 km E. It ends at a point $\frac{1}{2}$ km SE of the nameless 971 m plateau bump that rises E of the 958 m col of Diollaid Coire Eindart (*Dyee*ulitsh Cor *Ain*dyart) or saddle of Coire Eindart. (The 1 inch map is erroneous here in naming the hill top as Diollaid Coire Eindart.) Here you stand near the cliffs of remote Coire Mharconaich, and look over the River Eidart to the great green bulges of the Monadh Mor. Unfortunately, stalkers' Land Rovers now roam freely over these dry plateaux off the prepared roads, causing marks that take years to heal.

The Moine Mhor. Another branch of the bulldozed road system runs N around the head of Coire Garbhlach and then E almost to Allt Sgairnich (*Skar*nich) just W of Loch nan Cnapan. The collector of remote tops will visit the 918 m Tom Dubh (Tome *Doo*) or dark hillock between Allt Luineag and Allt Sgairnich, about 4 km from Carn Ban Mor by the track. In a secluded little basin N of Tom Dubh lies Loch nan Cnapan (*Craa*pan) or lake of knolls, which sends its water N to the cascades of Coire Odhar and Loch Einich, but most of the burns on the Moine Mhor drain into Eidart. Although the bulldozed roads have badly spoiled the feeling of wilderness on the Moine Mhor, the eastern parts of this great moss around Loch nan Cnapan and Allt Luineag are still wonderful places with unscarred green hollows of turf and moss, sparkling clear burns, and stony ridges. Bare green slopes rise gently to the snows and higher hills to the E.

For a more varied way to climb these hills, you can walk up Glen Feshie and take the path to the hut just W of where Eidart enters Feshie. From there a path goes NE, not far from the edge of a minia-

31. A view in June from the slope of Cairn Toul across Glen Dee and Carn a' Mhaim to Lochnagar, and Mount Keen (left).

32. April on the wide plateau of the Moine Mhor, looking from the top of Coire Garbhlach over to Braeriach (centre), Sgor an Lochain Uaine further right, and Ben Macdui peeping over to the left of Cairn Toul.

33. The bare flats beside Gaick Lodge in mid April, looking S to Sron Bhuirich, A' Chaoirnich (right), and the Gaick Pass (far right).

34.   From Ben Vrackie north across Glen Girnaig to Beinn a' Ghlo, with Carn Liath (left), Braigh Coire Chruinn-bhalgain (centre), Airgiod Bheinn (cone at right), and the summit at Carn nan Gabhar (far right).

35.   Beyond the Old Bridge of Dee in April, Ballochbuie pine forest sweeps up to the snowy White Mounth.

ture rocky canyon with waterfalls, in which Eidart flows for $1\frac{1}{2}$ km here. Above this the river runs through open shingle and grassy haughs where the path goes up the E bank. In the upper part of the glen on its W side rises a fine line of broken crags which finish at their N end on the E ridge of Coire Mharconaich. Further up still, the stream divides into branches which plunge steeply down rugged little ravines from the Moine Mhor above; this fork lies $6\frac{1}{2}$ km from the Eidart hut and 15 km from Ruigh-aiteachain via Eidart. These steeper slopes hem in the grassy hollow of Coire Mharconaich (Cor *Vark*onich). The main part of the corrie doubles back SW in an inner recess, bounded on the E by a ridge which gives a fine walking route up to the plateau and Diollaid Coire Eindart.

Walking in the corries

Coire Garbhlach (Cor *Gar*lach) or rugged corrie is worth exploring on the way down from these tops. As the crags are rotted and broken in many places, in the late summer you can scramble fairly easily down the screes near where the waterfall comes over from the Moine Mhor. At the subsidiary Fionnar Choire (*Fyunn*ar Chorrie) or cool corrie, which lies high on the N side of Coire Garbhlach and due S of Meall Dubhag, you can descend slopes of steep grass without rock. One of the main attractions of being right inside Coire Garbhlach is that much of the wide upper corrie keeps hidden from Glen Feshie by the narrow and curving entrance. The type of the corrie looks unique for the Cairngorms, as it forms not a typical corrie basin but a $2\frac{1}{2}$ km-long narrow, V-shaped glen, with cliffs rising on either side and at its top, and with the bottom of the corrie leading steeply downhill beside a roaring stream. It still has some steep rock buttresses which support a rich alpine vegetation.

Climbing routes

On Sgoran Dubh the SMC were early pioneers with several routes in March 1902. The face runs for 3 km and up to 370 m high, with cliffs of dark, rough, dry granite. As the crags consist mainly of broken rock, few fine summer routes exist, although in winter the place gives grand climbing in alpine surroundings. Climbers have numbered the buttresses from N to S, starting with No 1 under Sgoran Dubh Beag, Nos 2 and 3 under Sgoran Dubh Mor, No 4 below Sgor Gaoith, and No 5 further S including the pinnacle of A' Chailleach. The hollow between Nos 1 and 2 is Coire Sgoran Dubh Beag, that between Nos 2 and 3 being Coire Olc (Cor *Olk*) or evil corrie, later miscalled fan corrie. The one between Nos 3 and 4 is Coire Meadhon (Cor *May*-in) or middle corrie, and that between Nos 4 and 5 is Coire na Cailliche (Cor na *Cal*yich), the corrie of the Cailleach or old woman.

The best climb by far runs up the 140 m Roberts' Ridge (MS) on No 1 Buttress. The gully of Spùt Seilich (Spoot *Shail*ich) or willow spout divides this buttress into two parts, directly below Sgoran Dubh Beag. To the left of Sput Seilich the southern part of the buttress rises from the lower, less defined rocks up to the tapering steep upper section of the Northern Rampart. The Rampart forms a set of four steep bulging small buttresses in a row, 50 m high, of fairly holdless smooth granite. Although this crag looks impressive the climbing cannot be recommended. Much finer is the northern part of No 1 Buttress to the right of Sput Seilich, where Roberts' Ridge goes up the immediate edge by a variety of interesting pitches to a protruding rocky lump called The Anvil, above which the ridge narrows to a knife edge. Sput Seilich itself makes a long, fairly easy, Grade I winter climb amongst fine alpine scenery. Rose Ridge (VD), first climbed in 1904, makes another good route up the narrow, defined, fairly straight ridge on the northern part of No 2 Buttress. Diamond Buttress (VD), which you will notice as the obvious lobe of rock high in the upper part of Coire Olc, is another recommended route, by a ridge edge with a steeper wall in the middle section (see Further Reading, J. H. B. Bell's articles).

No 5 Buttress or Pinnacle Ridge (M) offers an interesting easy way to the plateau up the right edge of the buttress, passing close by the remarkable pinnacle of A' Chailleach or the old woman. Three routes go up A' Chailleach herself, all of them Difficult. Pinnacle Ridge is notable in being the highest continuous climb in the Cairngorms with a total vertical ascent of 370 m, and in giving a grand, classic, long alpine-type route in winter (Grade II). The obvious No 5 Buttress Gully to the right of it makes a Grade II winter climb, a nearby much harder one being The Slash (VS) which goes up the obvious steep gash in the lower slabs of the buttress. Away to the S and higher up, A' Phocaid is an interesting wide corrie with plenty of easy winter lines and much attractive ice. Coire Garbhlach round in Glen Feshie also offers fairly easy, interesting climbing in winter, when snow and ice cover the vegetated ledges.

Further reading

R. Anderson Glen Feshie. *CCJ* 1, 348.

H. T. Munro Loch Eunach, Sgoran Dubh, and the western Cairngorms. *SMCJ* 2, 296.

W. A. Smith The western Cairngorms (Guide Book article). *SMCJ* 7, 254.

J. H. B. Bell Fan Corrie and Diamond Buttress of Sgoran Dubh. *SMCJ* 22, 135. Sgoran Dubh No 2 Buttress. *SMCJ* 23, 47.

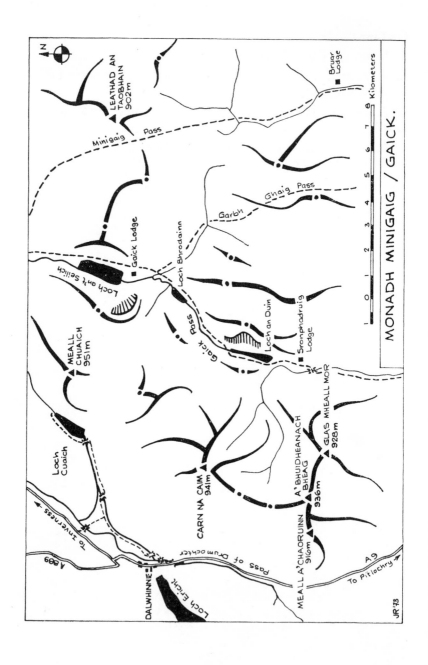

MONADH MINIGAIG / GAICK.

6

Monadh Minigaig and Gaick

*Carn na Caim	941 m, 677822
*A' Bhuidheanach Bheag	936 m, 660776
*Meall Chuaich	951 m, 717879

Access
The rail trains from Perth to Inverness stop at Blair Atholl and Kingussie, and some at smaller stations. The A9 public road takes a similar route; where it crosses the top of Drumochter Pass makes a good starting point.

Accommodation and other facilities
Hotels, bed and breakfasts and pubs are at Blair Atholl, Dalwhinnie, Newtonmore and Kingussie. Kingussie has a caravan site, youth hostel, and fish and chip shop. There is a restaurant and museum at Blair Castle, Blair Atholl.

Remote occupied houses (all inhabited by gamekeepers)
Drumochter Lodge 631796, Glentromie Lodge 777967, Gaick Lodge 757848 in summer and autumn only, Sronphadruig Lodge 717783 in summer and autumn only, Bruar Lodge 832761, Dalnaspidal 645733, Dalnacardoch 721702, Dail na Mine 753696.

Bothies
Glas Choire Lodge 752725, ruined outhouse still gives shelter. Bhran Cottage 753913, ruin with a little shelter. Unroofed stone shelters 720868.

General description
The Pass of Drumochter (Drimochter, 'o' as in hope) separates the more distinctive and higher hills on its W side, which used to be called Druim Uachdair or ridge of upper ground, from the smoother high ground to the E. This chapter describes this eastern hill country stretching across to Bruar and Feshie, part of the range whose old

name was Monadh Minigaig (Monna *Meen*ee Gaa-ick). Some Celtic scholars have thought it comes from Mion Gaig or little cleft, but it may well be derived from Mìne Ghaig or smooth Gaick, in contrast to the nearby Garbh Ghàig or rough Gaick to the W. An old document gave the name as the 'wild Month and hills of Myny-gegg'.

Monadh Minigaig begins just E of Dalwhinnie and Drumochter, where a crescent of rounded hills, flat on top, rises to 900 m. Many walkers visit them as they are so near the road. Apart from this inhabited corner, the huge district stretching E from here to Glen Bruar, and NE to Glen Feshie and Glen Tromie, spreads far as a vast remote wilderness. The boundary between Perth and Inverness runs along an enormous medium-level plateau, with many rounded undulating bumps rising above 750 m but none above 914 m or 3000 ft. Innumerable streams meander down gentle peaty slopes and hollows into lonely glens, with many peaty tarns high up. There also come pieces of spectacular country where the plateaux suddenly end in wild steep slopes, often with broken rocks, hidden corries and foaming burns. The ground around Gaick Lodge and southwards to Sronphadruig Lodge has this wild character, and also some very fine lochs down in the glen bottoms. The three important cross-country routes offer more interest to hill walkers than many of the rounded hills themselves. However, the other less spectacular glens and tops are worth wandering into, unhurriedly. Here you will still find wilderness and peace, although in the last decade the bulldozers have scarred some of the remote glens and hills. In winter mist, storm and snow, Monadh Minigaig becomes one of the most difficult parts of the Highlands.

Geology and landforms

A vast extent of the Central Highland granulites or schists dominates the area. The smooth plateau far around shows how uniform a level this part of the Highlands reaches; from the tops you tend to see not low valleys but mostly other rolling whalebacks and plateaux rising to about the same height as the level you stand at. The deep trenches at Gaick are a good example of erosion by glaciers, and glacially-dumped gravel holds up the 31 m deep Loch an Dùin (*Doo*in) at its N end. The largest of the Gaick lochs, Loch an t-Seilich (Loch an *Tyail*ich) or the loch of the willow copse, extends for 2 km long, 30 m deep in its pre-hydro-electric state, and 100 ha in area.

Natural history

This is an infertile high peaty country, much of which has little variety of wildlife. However the mossy tundras on the Dalwhinnie hills are quite exciting places for naturalists, with interesting vegetation, soil features and birds. A similar vegetation grows on the bare hill-tops further E around Gaick. The main plants on the area as a whole are the mixture of wet cotton grass, heather and deer grass so common in the Highlands, but lime-rich patches on a few crags away from grazing sheep support a much greater variety of flowers.

Fine old birch woods grow by Loch an t-Seilich of Gaick and down Glen Tromie, but otherwise the deer and sheep have put an end to most trees and scrub. Dotterel nest on the high tops and dunlin in the high peat mosses. Ptarmigan are common, the odd eagle hunts over the tops, and a few greenshanks nest in the lonely treeless glens.

History

Loch Bhrodainn of Gaick had an old legend that Brodan, the hound of Celtic myth, chased the White Stag of Ben Alder into the loch, where both sank for ever. Gaick is well known for the story of Call Ghàig or the Loss of Gaick (*SMCJ* 14, 181). In early January 1800, Capt John MacPherson of Ballachroan – known as the 'Black Officer' – and four companions had gone up to Gaick to shoot and were spending the night in a hut, when an avalanche from the steep hill above overwhelmed and killed them. MacPherson was a vicious recruiting officer, so folk looked on his end as a kind of judgement. Standing on the S side of the path immediately S of Gaick Lodge, a rough block with a Gaelic inscription commemorates the 'loss'.

The Pass of Drumochter lies on the route of the great Highland road which General Wade built from Perthshire to Fort Augustus so as to help his army control the Highlanders. The work finished in September 1729, and was celebrated with a feast – four oxen roasted whole and four kegs of brandy – held beside Dalnacardoch. The pass used to be called 'Strath Downaig' on the N side and Srath Dubhaig (*Doo*ack) on the S side. Until Wade built the Drumochter road to connect more easily with his Corrieyairack road to Fort Augustus, the Minigaig road over the Mounth to the E was far more important for travellers. Many used it for driving hill cattle (*CCJ* 7, 4) and indeed a few still did so until the end of last century. A 16th century document (MacFarlane's *Geographical Collections* 2, 598) mentions 'a way from the yate of Blair in Athoil to Ruffen in Badenoch maid be David

Cuming Earle of Athoil for carts to pass with wyne, and the way is called Rad na pheny'. W. C. Smith (*CCJ* 7, 4) thought that this referred to the Minigaig. In 1974 the present writer heard the old road from Bac na Creige over Sron a' Chleirich – that is the Garbh Ghaig route – still called Comyn's or Cumming's Road by folk in Atholl.

The Gaick area was the site of one of Scotland's first hydro-electric schemes. The engineers took S-flowing water from Edendon through a tunnel to Loch an Duin, and raised Loch an t-Seilich 3 m by a dam built in 1940 at its N end. From here, a 7 km tunnel goes under the hills to Loch Cuaich and then E of Dalwhinnie by an aqueduct to Loch Ericht.

Estates

Apart from the separate estate on the Dalnacardoch–Sronphadruig drainage, the Perthshire part all belongs to Atholl Estate at Blair Castle. Glen Feshie Estate owns the ground NE of the Inverness-shire part of the Minigaig path. Gaick and Glen Tromie form one estate, and the ground stretching W to Dalwhinnie lies on Phoines. Deer and sheep are the main land use, with grouse shooting on the lower slopes.

Walking ascents

A' Bhuidheanach Bheag 936 m (3064 ft) and **Carn na Caim** 941 m (3087 ft). These make up part of the high crescent of hills along the E side of Drumochter Pass between Dalnaspidal and Dalwhinnie. The convex side faces Dalwhinnie, whereas the concave side encloses the wild Cama Choire or curved corrie above the head waters of Edendon. All these tops are merely slight rises from a great high plateau, and thus not easy to find in mist. Although looking massive and rather dull from Drumochter as compared with the sharper more individual hills W of the pass, from their summits they give grand spacious views as you have come right to the centre of Scotland here.

Near Dalnaspidal, the 928 m (3037 ft) Glas Mheall Mór (*Glass* Vyal *More*) or big green lump rises 5 km away and 500 m in altitude to the NE, topped by a big cairn. From here you go 2 km WNW to A' Bhuidheanach Bheag (A *Voo*ee-anach *Vick*) or the little yellow place, where a large quartz cairn stands beside a fence running along the county boundary. (The original name for this was not Bheag but Mhor, the old name A' Bhuidheanach Bheag referring to the lower peaty bump at 672772.) Now you can diverge easily to Meall a' Chaorainn (Myal *Choor*in) or lump of the rowan tree, which rises as a mere bump 1½ km to the W at 916 m. The main watershed carries on from A' Bhuidheanach Bheag along the fence N to a peaty col where a fine steep ravine runs into Allt Coire Chuirn. You can easily follow the fence far out N to Càrn na Caim (Caarn a *Keim*) or hill of the twist. Here, 6 km from A' Bhuidheanach Bheag, the fence divides, the left branch going towards Dalwhinnie. There now exists a new, much easier but unattractive way of reaching this fine plateau by a fresh road bulldozed in 1973 almost to the plateau edge, starting from S of the Wade Bridge on the A9 just S of Dalwhinnie. It was built with a view to possible commercial extraction of quartz from a quarry below the plateau edge, and its scar now shows for miles. A finer alternative way to reach these hills comes from the Gaick pass by Cama Choire.

Meall Chuaich   951 m (3120 ft). Meall Chuaich (Myal *Choo*ich) or cup lump sweeps up from Loch Cuaich below it. It stands out as an isolated rounded top which gives a very fine view up and down Strath Spey and up Loch Ericht to the Ben Alder hills. From the A9 N of Dalwhinnie, take the private road just past the cottage of Cuaich and up to the loch at about 400 m, and then walk S of the loch and up the W nose of the hill. Distance: from A9 to loch 5 km, loch to top 3 km, total ascent 600 m. Another approach (5½ km) comes up the tree-lined Allt na Fearna from Bhran Cottage in Glen Tromie, and a third (6 km) from Gaick Lodge by the zig-zag path that climbs steeply up Sgor Dearg to the W on to a wide bare plateau, from which you drop to a 614 m col and then follow the fence to the top.

The Pass of Drumochter. Here, rail and road cross the Mounth at the lowest point between Loch Laggan and the Cairn o' Mount at Banchory. With steep hills on either side, often sporting snow plumes of spindrift in winter, and the long bare glens leading up to the summit, Drumochter Pass makes an impressive gateway to the wilder Highlands lying to the N. It is the highest railway pass in Britain, reaching about 450 m, the nearby road going to about 460 m.

The Gaick pass. The word Gaick comes from Gàig (*Gaa*-ick, at a cleft), a good name for this, one of the most unusual valley trenches in the Highlands. It is an old right of way from Dalnacardoch of Atholl through to Badenoch. In 1774 the Government built the lodge at Dalnacardoch as a public rest-house, as you will see from the

Latin inscription near the door. Distance: from Dalnacardoch to Sronphadruig 9 km, to county boundary 11, to Gaick Lodge 18, to Bhran Cottage 25, to Glentromie Lodge 31½, to Killiehuntly 34, to Tromie Bridge 35 km or 22 miles, total ascent 180 m, time 8 hours. From Dalnacardoch a rough private road goes up Edendon to Sronphadruig Lodge (Stron *Fad*rig) or Patrick's promontory. Above the lodge, the glen of Edendon turns W into Cama Choire, but the path to Gaick goes N along the W side of Loch an Duin which lies in a narrow trench at about 485 m between An Dun and the rocky face of Craig an Loch. You now go gently downhill towards Gaick Lodge, along the flattish grassy floor of a widening glen hemmed in by bold steep hills. Below Loch Bhrodainn (*Vrott*an) you cross a footbridge over the Allt Gharbh Ghaig which runs up a wild glen to the SE, and then come to Gaick Lodge. A rough private road goes from here down to Drumguish at the foot of Glen Tromie. The view from the Lodge, looking back to the S towards Sròn Bhùirich (Stron *Voo*rich) or nose of roarings, is very impressive, as the foreground and hills have an unusual Tibetan-like quality of bareness and steep slopes. Stalkers' paths zig-zag steeply up Sgor Dearg and the slope E of the lodge, to the plateaux on either side. The Gaick hills are notable for their avalanches, which sometimes have even crossed the road along Loch an t-Seilich. In several cases, deer crossing steep slopes have started avalanches that killed them, or sheltering in the valley bottom have been overwhelmed by snow slides from above. The reason for the many avalanches is that drifting clouds of snow blow in across the huge plateaux all around and pile up to great depths when they suddenly come into the shelter of Gaick's steep slopes.

*The Minigaig Road. Meen*ee Gaa-ick. This old track goes from Blair Atholl to Glen Tromie and Kingussie. Although now seldom visited, this interesting right of way over the Mounth takes you into some fine wilderness. Distance: from Old Blair N of Blair Castle by the W side of Glen Banvie to Bruar Lodge 11 km, to fork at top of Bruar 16, to county boundary 21, to Glen Tromie road at Allt Bhran bridge 29, to Bhran Cottage 31, to Killiehuntly 40, to Tromie Bridge 41 km or 25 miles, total ascent 680 m, time 9½ hours.

From Old Blair you can now walk by a road up the W side of Glen Banvie (Banbhaidh or sucking pig) and over a low ridge to Glen Bruar, but this way adds 2 km extra to the journey. The old Minigaig Road goes up the E side of Glen Banvie by the road to Allt an t-Seapail (pronunciation and meaning is chapel), past the cairn of Carn

Mhic Shimidh where a fight once occurred between the Murrays and Simon Lovat. You continue by an old path along Druim Dubh to Bruar Lodge. Great numbers of red deer stags live in Glen Banvie which forms part of the West Hand beat of Atholl, and the vegetation in the lower glen is grazed almost flat by their concentrations in winter here, more so than at any other place in the region described in this book. Another alternative way to Bruar Lodge, 1 km shorter, leaves the A9 at Calvine (Calveen) and takes the road that winds N over Creag Bhagailteach. At Calvine, try to see the fine series of three falls at Falls of Bruar (Brooar or bridge-stream). The Duke of Atholl originally planted the woods here in response to Robert Burns's verse 'The Humble Petition of Bruar Water'.

Beyond Bruar Lodge lies a small artificial loch where the glen narrows below steeper craggy slopes. The rough road ends at about 530 m, above which the main stream divides. Two paths come in here, the Minigaig being the right-hand one. It climbs 230 m to the flat top of Uchd a' Chlàrsair (Oochka Chlaarsir) or brow of the harper. In the next 3 km you pass two little dips and then a long easy rise, marked with quartz cairns, to the summit at about 830 m. You will find it interesting to see how this track was cleverly made over hard ground through a great rolling district of soft moorland and peat.

At the summit you stand high over this hill country, and an easy stroll takes you the short distance NE to the 902 m (2960 ft) Leathad an Taobhain (Lay-at an Tayvin). The top still further to the E, at 912 m or 2991 ft, gives a fine view into the huge basins of the upper Feshie and Geldie. The place of Minigaig is the 766 m col NE of this top, at 826866, and does not lie on the 'Minigaig' path. Just N of here, at the summit of Meall an Uillt Chreagaich, a new bulldozed road runs N on the line of an old stalking footpath to Lochan an t-Sluic and Carnachuin in Glen Feshie. Distance: from county boundary to Carnachuin by this way 11½ km. Another old path leads from Feshie up Allt Lorgaidh (Lorgee) towards the Minigaig col.

From the summit, the Minigaig path drops down the grassy slopes E of Coire Bhran (Cor Vran). It becomes a bulldozed road at the upper weir on Allt Bhran, and after another 1½ km enters Glen Tromie (Tromaidh, Trome-ie or elder tree). Here you join the private road from Gaick Lodge which runs down through fine groves of birch, alder and juniper and under the rocky slopes of Croidh-la – a map error for Chruaidhe Leac – to the public road at Tromie Bridge.

The original Minigaig path takes a short cut from Glen Tromie Lodge over Beinn Bhuidhe to the old ruined barracks of Ruthven (*Ri*win) opposite Kingussie. Built in 1719 to check the Jacobites, the barracks were burned by Bonnie Prince Charlie in 1746.

The Garbh Ghaig pass or Comyn's Road. This old route lying between the Gaick pass and the Minigaig was the shortest Mounth Road from Blair Atholl to Kingussie. A right of way which previous District Guides ignored, it is well worth resurrecting here. Distance: from Clunes (*Cloon*iss) Lodge at 780672 on the A9 to the county boundary at Bac na Creige 14 km, to Gaick Lodge 20 km or 12 miles (5¼ hours), total ascent 700 m but only 450 m if starting from Gaick. From Clunes Lodge a good private road now runs up Allt a' Chrombaidh. You cross a low ridge NW to Allt a' Chireachain where Allt a' Chire Mhoir comes in. The track is indistinct in places, but becomes clear on Sròn a' Chléirich (Stronna *Chlee*reech) or nose of the priest. Beyond, it runs along the plateau, crosses the head of Feith na Mad, and rises gently to the county boundary at Bac na Creige (Bach na *Craik*) or bank of the rocky hill. Here, at about 770 m, you drop into Gaick. The Atholl side has shallow corries and gently sloping hillsides but Allt a' Gharbh Ghaig shows a sudden contrast, a wild glen with broken crags, steep slopes and foaming burns.

An interesting alternative walk starts from the A9 at Dail na Mine (Dal na *Meen*), further W than Clunes. Here you take the private road to the N past the ruined Glas Choire Lodge set on its green hillside, to a hydro-electric dam on Allt Glas Choire (*Glass* Chorrie) near where Allt Dearg comes in. A bulldozed road goes from Druim Ruidh Chail to the top of Bachd Ban, from which a gentle stroll takes you up the broad ridge to the county boundary at Bac na Creige, 11 km from Dail na Mine. You can avoid part of the climb by slanting further W through the col at Carr na Moine at about 660 m, after a 430 m ascent from Dail na Mine, to pick up the more westerly of the two paths down Allt a' Gharbh Ghaig.

Before you reach Glas Choire Lodge, a road branches off to the E and takes you to the stream to the W of Allt a' Chire Mhoir. From here you can pick up the Comyn's Road on Sron a' Chleirich summit, but this route adds 2 km longer than the way going from Dail na Mine by Bachd Ban.

Climbing routes

This is not a district for rock climbers. You will see a few crags and wild corries, but the rocks are broken and ill defined. Nevertheless, in winter you will find on these crags and steeper corries plenty of easy but sporting ways to the summits, sometimes on good hard snow mixed with patches of ice and occasionally broken rock.

Further reading

A. I. McConnochie   The three Gaicks. *CCJ* 9, 71.

'H.W.'   Gaick Forest (Guide Book article)   *SMCJ* 8, 177.

H. Alexander   Gaick.   *SMCJ* 14, 178.

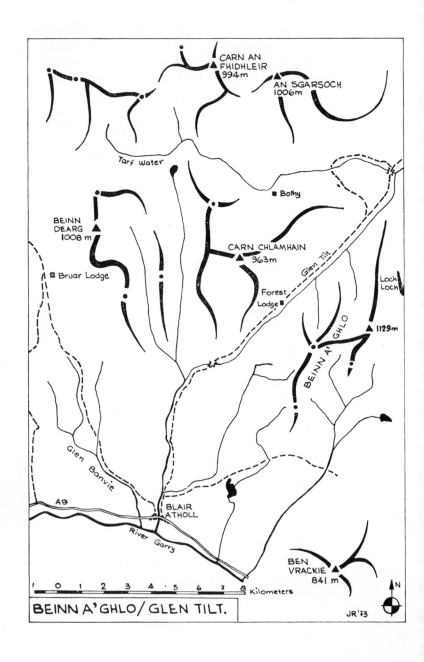

CARN AN
FHIDHLEIR
994m

AN SGARSOCH
1006m

Tarf Water

Bothy

BEINN
DEARG
1008 m

CARN CHLAMHAIN
963m

Bruar Lodge

Forest
Lodge

Glen Tilt

Loch
Loch

1129m

BEINN A' GHLO

Glen Banvie

A9

BLAIR
ATHOLL

River Garry

BEN
VRACKIE
841 m

1 0 1 2 3 4 5 6 7 8 Kilometers

BEINN A' GHLO / GLEN TILT.

JR '73

N

7

Beinn a' Ghlo and Glen Tilt

Ben Vrackie	841 m, 950632
*Beinn a' Ghlo	1129 m, 970732
*Braigh Coire Chruinn-bhalgain	1070 m, 944724
*Carn Liath	975 m, 936698
*Carn Chlamhain	963 m, 916758
*Beinn Dearg	1008 m, 853778
*An Sgarsoch	1006 m, 934837
*Carn an Fhidhleir	994 m, 905842

Access
Rail to Blair Atholl (Inverness–Perth), bus Aberdeen to Braemar.
Public roads to Linn of Dee and to Old Bridge of Tilt at Blair Atholl.
Cars should be left at the car park beside the Linn of Dee at 063897,
and in the village of Blair Atholl.

Accommodation and other facilities
Blair Atholl (about 140 m, hotels) is the best centre, but Inverey
for the Geldie side. A youth hostel stands at the E end of Loch
Tummel. Pitlochry has a big range of accommodation, restaurants,
and a fish and ship shop. For Inverey see p 187. Blair Castle, open
to the public, has a museum and restaurant.

Remote occupied houses
Bruar Lodge 832761, Forest Lodge 932742, Fealar 008800, Linn of
Dee 061895.

Bothies
See also Chapter 3 (Glen Feshie route). Feith Uaine Mhor 926788
of S side of upper Tarf at about 570 m. Bynack Lodge 001855, ruin
with meagre shelter.

General description
Outcrops of limestone, diorite and other rich rocks make this a more
fertile country than the Cairngorms massif. The hills are mostly

rounded and green, well covered with a grassy vegetation which includes much moss and heath. As the lower slopes tend to be very gradual, peat has built up thickly there. These gentle slopes running for miles impart to these wide glens an air of enormous space. Far from being featureless, this gives the district part of its peculiar fascination. A working definition of a wilderness area involves ground more than a few miles from a public road. By this criterion, here we have one of the best wilderness areas in Scotland. In winter snow, it – far more than the rockier Cairngorms – resembles a white polar desert. Along Glen Tilt the hillsides become greener and steeper than in the rest of Atholl, and the valley narrower with broken rocks in places; it looks very unlike most parts of the Cairngorms region, and you can easily imagine yourself to be in W Inverness-shire or the Lake District.

Geology and landforms

Glen Tilt is the site of one of the main geological faults in the region, which passes along the line of the glen, then across by the Clais Fhearnaig near Glen Lui and along the cleft of upper Gairn between Creag an Dail Mhor and Bheag. Most of the area lies over Central Highland schists, with some quartzite, but granite occurs at Beinn Dearg and Beinn a' Ghlo, a large mass of the richer diorite around Carn Chlamhain, and lime-rich rocks along Glen Tilt and near Loch Loch including much limestone. The water of Tarf once ran into Deeside near Bynack, but after the glaciation a low piece of glacial drift turned the water in a very sharp bend into Tilt.

Natural history

Comments apply the same as in the last chapter. However, Glen Tilt and Glen Loch, being much more fertile than most glens in Atholl and Gaick, are interesting places for arctic-alpine and lime-loving plants, including that rare alpine the yellow oxytropis.

Estates

Atholl Estates at Blair Castle own the Perthshire part (except for Glen Fender and the Loch Valigan ground to the S of Beinn a' Ghlo, which are owned by Lude Estate, and the separate estate of Glen Fearnaid). Mar Lodge Estate has the Aberdeenshire side. These are all deer forests, with hill sheep also, and on the lower ground with some grouse shooting.

History
According to an old legend, the Braemar men once tried to cut a
trench through the flat ground at the watershed of Tilt and Bynack
so as to divert the uppermost branch of Tilt into Dee, but were routed
by the men of Atholl; some mounds by Tilt are said to be the graves
of the Atholl men who died in the fight. Atholl has long been a famous
deer forest, and at the base of Beinn a' Ghlo below Forest Lodge
there are the remains of wolf pits. James V in 1529, and Mary Queen
of Scots in 1564 attended deer drives there. In 1844, Queen Victoria
and the Prince Consort saw a deer drive near Forest Lodge, and went
through Glen Tilt to Deeside in 1861. The Duke of Atholl tried to
close the glen in the 1840s but lost this important right of way case.
The Ballad of Glen Tilt, reprinted in *CCJ* 3, 185 (see also *CCJ* 6,
310) told how Prof J. H. Balfour and a party of botanists went there

> Twas a' to poo
>> Some gerse that grew
> On Ben Muich Dhu,
>> That ne'er a coo
> Would care to pit her moo' till'

On their way south they were challenged by the angry Duke:

> The Duke at this put up his birse,
> He vowed in English and in Erse,
>> That Saxon fit
>> Su'd never get
>> Ae single bit
>> Throughout his yet,
> Among the Hielan hills, man.
> Balfour he had a mind as weel
>> As ony duke could hae, man,
> Quo' he, 'There's ne'er a kilted chiel
>> Shall drive us back this day, man.
> It's justice and it's public richt,
> We'll pass Glen Tilt afore the nicht,
>> For dukes shall we
>> Care ae bawbee?
>> The road's as free
>> To you and me
>> As to his Grace himself, man

Between White Bridge and the Linn of Dee you pass the ancient
ruins of the Dubrach (*Doo*brach) on the S side. After the 1745 rising

some English soldiers were stationed here, and one of them, a sergeant, was murdered on a hillside up Allt Cristie. Five years later, two local men were put on trial at the High Court in Edinburgh. The chief witness for the prosecution told how the English soldier's ghost had appeared and told him the murderers' names. When the defence advocate asked what language the ghost of the English sergeant used, and the witness said 'as good Gaelic as myself', the case collapsed in a burst of laughter. The full story was told in a book edited by Sir Walter Scott and published in 1831 for the Bannatyne Club, *Trial of Duncan Terig alias Clerk*, etc. The last tenant of Dubrach, old Peter Grant or 'Aal Dubrach', lived to 110 years; he died in 1824, the last of the Braemar Jacobite fighters for Bonnie Prince Charlie. In 1822, at the age of 108, he went to Edinburgh to meet George IV, descendant of the Hanoverian 'Wee Bit German Lairdie'. Taking him by the hand, the King said 'You are my oldest friend' to which Aal Dubrach instantly replied 'Na na, yer Majestry, I am yer aaldest enemy'. Hundreds attended the funeral of this great Deeside character, headed by pipers playing the tune 'Wha wadna fecht for Chairlie'.

Walking ascents
Ben Vrackie 841 m (2760 ft). The name comes from Gaelic Breac, meaning speckled. This graceful peak stands out as Pitlochry's special hill. A track from Moulin above Pitlochry goes up to Loch a' Choire at about 520 m, just below the upper slopes. Distance: from Moulin main road to summit 5 km, ascent 690 m. An interesting and trackless route starts from about 380 m at the top of the road from Pitlochry to Strath Ardle (5 km to top, 460 m ascent). Ben Vrackie commands a magnificent view up Tummel and across to Moor of Rannoch. A fine way for walking back from Ben Vrackie is to drop W to the magnificent wooded gorge at Killiecrankie and the birches of Loch Faskally. The whole surrounding area looks full of variety, a countryside broken up by many lumpy hills and small crags. In hard winters the ski touring becomes good. On the other side of the A924, a fine old cattle-droving track, now indistinct in places, goes from Kirkmichael W up Glen Derby (*Derr*bee) to Loch Broom and Ballinluig. Distance: from Edelweiss Hotel in Glen Derby to public road at 000525 at Tulliemet 12½ km, 110 m ascent.

Beinn a' Ghlo 1129 m (3673 ft). Pronounced Painna *Gloe*, it means hill of the veil or mist. It used to be Beinn a' Ghlo nan Eag (nan

Yaik, of the clefts), as told in Grant's *Legends of the Braes o' Mar*.
Apart from Lochnagar which projects really as an offshoot to the N
of the main watershed, Beinn a' Ghlo looks the finest hill in the whole
range of the Mounth from Drumochter to Aberdeen. Much steeper
and stonier than the other hills of Tilt or Geldie, it is also a far more
complicated hill, with many tops and corries. An old stalkers' legend
was that it held 19 corries, in any of which a rifle could be fired
without being heard in another. From the Cairngorms, its domed
summit, flanked by subsidiary symmetrical tops on either side and
seen across vast empty bare glens and lower hills, makes Beinn a'
Ghlo one of the most beautiful and mysterious hills of Scotland.

To climb it you will probably go to Blair Atholl (Blar *A*-thole),
whose name comes from the very old Blàr Ath Fhotla or plain of new
Ireland, going back to the time when the Celtic rulers of Scotland
were Irish. North of Blair Castle and its fine old larches and other
trees stands the church at Old Blair, where Claverhouse, Viscount
of Dundee, was buried after the Battle of Killiecrankie.

From Blair Atholl, the usual way to Beinn a' Ghlo goes up Glen
Fender (Fionndobhar or white water) by the road N of Loch Moraig
leading to Glen Girnaig, to about 440 m altitude. You then climb N
fairly steeply up heather and later mossy heath and screes to Càrn
Liath (*Lee*-a) or grey hill at 975 m, which is the conical top so
prominent from Blair Atholl. You can also take a Land Rover
road from Monzie up the N side of the burn to about 560 m, 1 km
due W of the summit. Distance: from Old Bridge of Tilt to Carn
Liath 8 km, ascent 820 m. The next hill ahead, 3 km to the NNE and
beyond a col at about 760 m, sweeps up to the magnificently-named
Bràigh Coire Chruinn-bhalgain (Brigh Cor *Chroo*in *Val*igan) or
upland of the corrie of round little blisters. The route to the summit
from this top, which stands out almost as a separate hill from Beinn a'
Ghlo, lies E down a grassy slope to the 847 m col at Bealach an
Fhiodha (*Byal*-ach an *Ee*icha) or pass of the timber, from which
streams fall S to Glen Girnaig and N to Tilt. From the bealach you
can go SE for less than 1 km to take in the subsidiary 1061 m top of
Airgiod Bheinn (*Erikit* Veen) or silver hill; it forms the end of a long
flattish shoulder running down from the summit of Beinn a' Ghlo 1⅔
km away to the NE. The summit at 1129 m is Càrn nan Gabhar
(Caarn nan *Gower*) or hill of the goats, where you stand 6 km in
distance from Carn Liath by the quickest route (by-passing Airgiod
Bheinn), with an ascent of 550 m. Thus the total distance from Old

Bridge of Tilt to Carn nan Gabhar becomes 14 km or 9 miles, ascent 1370 m or 4500 ft, time up $5\frac{1}{4}$ hours; same way back 4 hours, 400 m of ascent.

The view from the summit cairn is fine, but grows even more striking if you go down to the E a little way, to look down the wild rocky E face to Loch Loch about 680 m below and across to the line of crags on Creag an Loch above the E side of the loch. A good way off Beinn a' Ghlo starts by dropping $2\frac{1}{2}$ km down its N shoulder, then turns W to cross the footbridge over Tilt just below where Allt Fheannach comes in, and so down Glen Tilt. Remember that the River Tilt runs fast and dangerous in flood, and that another bridge stands lower down the glen at Dail an Eas, just up from Forest Lodge.

An interesting route to Beinn a' Ghlo comes in from the E by Gleann Fearnach, a name incorrectly put on the map instead of Fearnaid (*Fer*nit) meaning alder water. From the A924 road 1 km NW of Enochdu (An t-Aonach Dubh) or the dark moor, a private road runs for $7\frac{1}{2}$ km up to the deserted cottage at Daldhu (Dail Dhubh) or black haugh, and continues beyond to Fealar Lodge reaching 660 m on the way. A fine, rich, green glen, with many small outcrops of broken rock, Gleann Fearnaid was home to a big farming community last century, but since then the people have all gone by voluntary emigration. From Daldhu at about 380 m a bulldozed road leads NW up Glen Loch to within 2 km of Loch Loch, and a path carries on to the loch which lies at 450 m, $5\frac{1}{2}$ km from Daldhu. Gleann Fearnaid and this low pass over by Loch Loch to Glen Tilt once used to be a popular route for Highlanders who were driving their cattle to market in the south. Loch Loch lies among meadows in a deep trench with broken crags on either side. A good way to Beinn a' Ghlo goes straight up the wild face of Coire Cas-eagallach (Cas *Aik*alach) or steep fearful corrie W of the loch, where you can have some easy rock scrambling on the way up (2 km Loch Loch to summit, 680 m ascent, $1\frac{1}{2}$ hours).

Carn Chlamhain 963 m (3159 ft). This is not Chlamain as misspelled in the 6 inch map; pronounced Caarn *Chlav*ing, it means the hill of the buzzard or kite. Unnamed on the OS 7th Series maps, this remote secluded hill lies about 2 km NW of Forest Lodge in Glen Tilt, on a plateau behind a steep glen front. The easiest way up goes by the long shoulder that runs E of Allt Craoinidh, starting from the Tilt road above Marble Lodge. Beginning where the road crosses

Allt Craoinidh, a path leads up its W side to 450 m. Then you turn E up the shoulder called Faire Clach Ghlas, eventually coming to the plateau edge at about 850 m on Grianan Mór or big sunny place, where you look down the long steep face to Tilt below; the summit lies across the plateau. Distance from road: $4\frac{1}{2}$ km, ascent 700 m. From 931740 below Forest Lodge, a path zig-zags steeply up to a cairn at 934754, and then turns W to the top. The summit also lies only $3\frac{1}{2}$ km SSW of the lonely bothy which stands just above the place where Féith Uaine Mhór (Fay *Hoo*an *Vore*) or big stream enters Tarf. An interesting route for descending Carn Chlamhain is to walk W for 3 km and then S down the wild, narrow Gleann Mhairc (Mark) or horse valley. Queen Victoria was one of the early tourists to visit Carn Chlamhain, descending by Sron a' Chro.

Beinn Dearg 1008 m (3307 ft). Beinn Dearg (Pain *Dyer*rek) or red hill, takes its name from the reddish-tinged granite boulders on its upper slopes. It lies NE of Bruar Lodge (for route to lodge see p 171). A path from the lodge makes an easy way up the hill's SW ridge right to the top, for 3 km with an ascent of 550 m. A second way starts by an old track just N of the lodge, climbing up Allt Beinn Losgannaich to the higher slopes. Several routes will take you back to Blair Atholl. One, to the S, crosses Allt Sheicheachan and goes down the road by Allt an t-Seapail leading into Glen Banvie, and so to Old Blair. For a second way back, you can walk SSE over the peaty moorland to Beinn a' Chait and Elrig, then take the road down Allt Slanaidh, and so to lower Glen Tilt. A third way is to drop E into Gleann Dìridh (*Dyee*reech) before you reach Beinn a' Chait. This glen becomes deep and narrow, with the burn running eventually into a little ravine. Further on it joins the Allt Mhairc beside a few small crags, beyond which some delightful grassy patches among birches lead down towards Glen Tilt.

An Sgarsoch 1006 m (3300 ft) and **Carn an Fhidhleir** 994 m (3260 ft). An Sgarsoch one pronounces Un *Skar*sach, and Carn an Fhìdhleir is Carn *Eel*er or the hill of the fiddler. These two remote hills look down over the vast peaty moors of Geldie, Feshie and Tarf. The easiest access comes by cycling up to Geldie Lodge (see p 131). Distance: from Geldie Lodge to summit 4 km, ascent 490 m. A new bulldozed track now runs well up An Sgarsoch's N side to about 935862. Longer ways are to come in from Glen Feshie, or to walk or cycle up Glen Tilt past Forest Lodge. From upper Glen Tilt a new bulldozed road leads E of An Sligearnach (Un *Slee*garnach) or the place abounding in shells. It goes on the line of the fine old path to a ford and new hut by the water of Tarf (from Tarbh or bull) at 520 m. An Sgarsoch rises to the NW, 5½ km away by its E shoulder. On both its Geldie and Tilt sides it spreads out as a hill of broad ridges and wide open corries carpeted with short grass, moss and berry plants. In earlier centuries a market for cattle and horses, called Feill Sgarsaich, was held on the summit (see *SMCJ* 14, 104, and Further Reading). An easy descent on the W side of An Sgarsoch takes you to a pass at 710 m. This leads towards Carn an Fhidhleir's summit where the counties of Perth, Inverness and Aberdeen all meet and where you will enjoy a fine view of the bare upper Tarf and of the upper Feshie with its hundreds of small peaty tarns and pools. Distance: 4 km from An Sgarsoch, ascent 270 m. A quick way back goes NNE to the peaty stretch at the Geldie-Feshie watershed and then E down the N side of Geldie by the path. A bulldozed road runs from 925856 ENE down to Geldie Lodge (no footbridge over Geldie there). If you are returning to Blair Atholl, a grand route is to descend into the magnificent wilderness at the head of Tarf, past the remote Loch Mhairc. From here you can go to Braigh Sron Ghorm and back over Carn Chlamhain to Marble Lodge by Tilt, or over Beinn Dearg further W.

The Mounth Roads – Glen Tilt

The name is Gleann Teilt (Glan Telt, 'e' as in her). One of the most popular of the Mounth crossings, Glen Tilt takes you over the lowest point between the Cairn o' Mount at Banchory and the Gaick pass in the W. The best way starts at Blair Atholl and finishes at the Linn of Dee. Distance: from Old Bridge of Tilt at about 150 m to Marble Lodge 6½ km, to Forest Lodge 11, to Tarf 19, county boundary 23, Bynack Lodge 26, the White Bridge 30, the Linn of Dee 35 km or 22 miles; ascent 380 m, but only 160 m if you start at the Linn of Dee. A cycle is handy; although you have to trundle it for parts of the middle section, it cuts the time on the long roads at either end.

From Blair Atholl, the right of way up the glen goes up the E side past the Old Bridge of Tilt, and crosses the side stream of Fender at Fenderbridge. On the N side of Fender you fork right at the road junction, and at 884672 fork left below Kincraigie (cars not allowed N of here). You now walk along the hillside to descend to the river near Croftmore, and so continue to Marble Lodge. This part is a piece of lovely Highland scenery with a mixture of native and planted conifers, and groves of alders and gnarled ancient birches further up. At Marble Lodge you cross to the W bank of Tilt. Now the glen becomes a barer, wilder, and remarkably long straight trench which you look along for miles between the steep slopes of Beinn a' Ghlo on the E and Carn Chlamhain on the W. Beyond Forest Lodge, Tilt narrows into a rocky gorge spanned by a stone bridge at Dail an Eas and 2½ km further up by a suspension bridge beside some fine falls near where Allt Fheannach rushes in from Beinn a' Ghlo. About 2 km beyond the suspension bridge, a new bulldozed track slants uphill on your left side between Dun Mor and An Sligearnach; ignore it. Your track keeps on up Tilt side, crossing Tarf at the Bedford Bridge below Tarf's rocky gorge, near the old ford at Poll Tarbh. Beyond, you climb gently up the slope on the W side of the ravine of Allt Garbh Buidhe (Garra *Boo*ee) or rough yellow burn. Further up this burn, there comes a dramatic change from a steep, green, grassy glen to a flat tract of wide moorland valley.

Out on the open moor the track avoids the wet peat by climbing a little to the W, towards, but not actually in sight of, the secluded Loch Tilt. It then reaches the highest point at just over 500 m or about 1650 ft, and goes down the wide valley to Bynack (*Bei*nack). Standing at about 460 m on a green knoll and surrounded by wind-blown conifers, Bynack Lodge or Shiel has now become a ruin, spoiled by selfish visitors who broke it up for firewood. You next cross Bynack Burn which trickles low in summer heat but sweeps dangerously in high water; in spate, you will find it safer to cross to the E side of the glen and stay on that side all the way down to the house at the Linn of Dee, as the burns on that side are much smaller. On the far side of Bynack Burn, the path leads down a pleasant grassy flat to a rickety footbridge where you can cross the water of Geldie to the partly ruined stables at Ruigh Ealasaid, at the beginning of the rough road down Geldie to the White Bridge over Dee. Lying back from this road, the gaunt ruin of Ruigh nan Clach somehow adds to the bareness and space of the wide flat moor. From Bynack on, a wonderful view opens out up Glen Dee to the crags of the Devil's Point, to the even higher central Cairngorms, and through the Lairig Ghru to a remarkably distant-looking Creag an Leth-choin. The road below the White Bridge then runs down past green flats with ruins of old farms and through pine woods to the locked gate standing at 373 m at the beginning of the public tarmac road beside the Linn of Dee.

Climbing routes

Most crags in the area, although often imposing at a distance, turn out to be broken and lacking in defined lines. However, the district of Strath Ardle, and Glen Brerachan, and the grand stretch of country around Ben Vrackie and Loch Valigan to the NE contain many steep small crags of good rock, which offer numerous good though short summer routes. The area has plenty of easy winter climbing on mixed rock and snow, giving more sporting ways up to the summits.

Craig a Barns (337 m), usually called Craigie Barns, is the finely wooded rocky hill 1½ km NW of Dunkeld (hotels, pubs, youth hostel, fish and chip shop). Its short but steep crags of Dalradian schist provide a great variety of excellent rock climbing which is described fully in a guide by G. Tiso (Further Reading).

Further reading

W. M. Alexander and others   The Sgarsoch market. *CCJ* 8, 166, 215, 262.

H. T. Munro   Notes on Ben-y-Gloe. *SMCJ* 2, 239.

W. Douglas   Beinn a' Ghlo (Guide Book article). *SMCJ* 8, 172.

H. T. Munro   Beinn Dearg, Carn a' Chlamain, An Sgarsoch and Carn an Fhidleir (Guide Book articles). *SMCJ* 8, 174.

G. Tiso   *Creag Dubh and the Eastern Outcrops*. Climbers' Guide. Available Graham Tiso, Edinburgh. Describes routes on Craig a Barns.

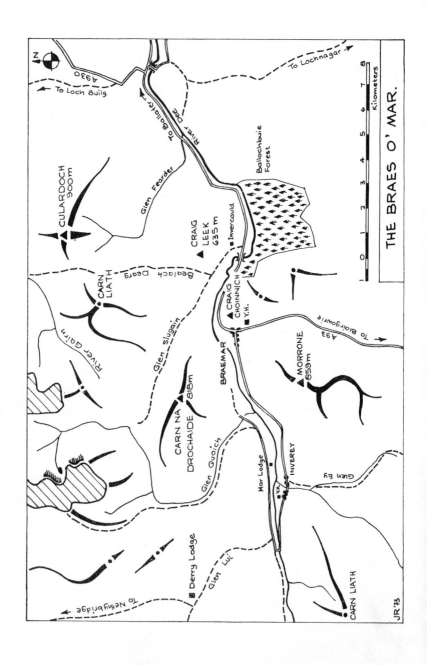

THE BRAES O' MAR.

Kilometers
0 1 2 3 4 5 6 7 8

To Lochnagar
To Ballater
River Dee
A930
To Loch Builg
Glen Fearder
CULARDOCH 900m
Ballochbuie Forest
CRAIG LEEK 635m
Invercauld
Glen Gairn
CARN LIATH
Bealach Dearg
River Gairn
Glen Slugain
CRAIG CHOINNICH
Y.H.
BRAEMAR
To Blairgowrie
A93
MORRONE 859m
CARN NA DROCHAIDE 818m
Glen Quoich
Mar Lodge
INVEREY
Y.H.
Glen Ey
Derry Lodge
Glen Lui
To Nethybridge
CARN LIATH
JR '73

8

The Braes o' Mar

Morrone	859 m, 133885
Creag Choinnich	538 m, 161918
Craig Leek	635 m, 186931
Culardoch	900 m, 194988

Access
Buses from Aberdeen. Grant's garage has taxis.

Accommodation and other facilities
Braemar has hotels, pubs, a youth hostel at 156909, bed and breakfasts, and a mountain rescue centre at the police station, There is a pub and snack bar 6½ km to the W at Mar Lodge Hotel. In Inverey, 8 km W, the furthest W two houses are Muir (Cairngorm Club) at 076897, and a youth hostel at 079896 which closes in winter. The caretaker for both lives at Bellaneye, which is the second house on the right to the W of Ey bridge, but in winter she lives at 3 St Andrews Terrace, Braemar. The first house on the right after the bridge is Aberdeen County Council's outdoor centre. The County Council intend to make a caravan-camp site at Braemar. Unofficial sites without facilities are where Lui enters Dee (site on Canadian lumber camp), at scattered places well up Clunie, and on the grass E of Derry water just upstream from Derry Lodge (for Derry, ask permission at Mar Lodge or Luibeg).

Remote occupied houses
See Chapter 3.

Bothies
Luibeg, at 036933, 16 km from Braemar, was at the centre of post-war climbing history in the Cairngorms massif.

General description
Braemar (Bri*maar*), one of the highest and most attractive villages in the Highlands, nestles at about 340 m among woods and many lower

hills, close to the high Cairngorms, Lochnagar and the Mounth. It makes the best centre for the Aberdeenshire Highlands and most of the Cairngorms massif. The name comes from Bràigh Mharr or upland of Mar, Mar being an old district name, but the actual village consists of two parts with Auchindryne W of Clunie and Castleton on the E bank.

The approach to Braemar from Ballater leads through some of the finest scenery in the Highlands. That part between Gairn and Invercauld, formerly called Strath Dee, is best. Here, big woods of natural pine and birch run down to the banks of Dee, and a multitude of complex small hills and side glens with fine burns leads up to the great bulk of Lochnagar. Shortly after passing over the new Invercauld Bridge which stands upstream from the more beautiful older bridge, you will see the corries of Beinn a' Bhuird coming into view beyond the tree-dotted parkland haughs of Invercauld, framed by steep wooded bluffs on either side. The reverse journey, with golden evening light on the dark green pines, on Lochnagar's plum-coloured W flanks and on the incredibly blue Dee, looks even better, a feast of colour.

The Braemar Highland Society runs the 'Gathering' – locally called the Games – every September, and publishes an annual, *The Book of the Braemar Gathering* which often contains popular-style articles and photographs on the whole Cairngorms region as well as the Braemar district.

Geology and landforms
The very complicated rock structure around Braemar is still much studied by geological researchers. Bands of limestone run along Morrone and NE of Invercauld, but quartzite makes up most of Morrone. However the main rock of the Braemar district, especially around Inverey, Glen Quoich and Slugain, consists of Moine schist, with the richer, dark schist at Creag Clunie and Glen Feardar. These schist rocks account for the steep rocky bluffs near the main valley, which make the Braemar area unusual for the North East, more like country in the SW Highlands of Argyll.

Natural history
The old pine woods, although in scattered smallish blocks, are the finest in Scotland for ancient, uncut and unburned forest, but red deer have for decades prevented young trees from growing. Lower Glen Lui and lower Glen Derry carry particularly impressive old

trees. On the E side of lower Glen Lui towards Mar Lodge, you can see ancient gnarled pines with a girth surpassing anything in Scotland, and also some extremely old birches. On Morrone's N side, where there is a National Nature Reserve, fine old birch groves with juniper climb to 640 m or 2100 ft. This unusual height is also reached by the planted larches on Carn nan Sgliat, which you can see well from Braemar village. Some of the best larches and spruces in Scotland grow on either side of the Mar Brae, by the road down to the Victoria Brig from the grand high waterfall at the bridge of Corriemulzie (Corrie*moolz*ee). Good spots for small flowering plants occur at lime-rich patches on the lower slopes of Morrone, Glen Lui and especially on the rocks of Creag an Dail Bheag to the W of Culardoch. The Braemar district is well known to entomologists as a place for rare arctic-alpine insects; indeed, the subarctic mountain burnet moth occurs nowhere else in Britain. The surrounding district, along with Atholl and Balmoral, supports one of the highest population densities of red deer in the Highlands. So it is a good place for seeing them, but also a poor place for seeing young trees and scrub on the lower slopes and glen bottoms, where the deer crowd in for shelter and food during snow.

Estates

Mar Lodge Estate has the land W of Carn na Drochaide and N of Dee. Mar Estate, a different estate from Mar Lodge, lies S of Dee and W of Morrone. Invercauld (Inver *Kaal*) owns the ground E of Carn na Drochaide and N of Dee, and includes the Clunie and Callater drainages. Balmoral Estate has Ballochbuie Forest.

History

The history of the Braemar district is very rich, but here we have space for only the briefest sketch. Interested readers should refer to Simpson's *The Province of Mar* and Grant's *Legends of the Braes o' Mar*, noting that the later *The Braemar Highlands* by Elizabeth Taylor was a plagiarism of Grant.

The ancient castle of Kindrochit or bridge end, which gave Braemar its original name of Baile Chaisteil or Castleton, stood close to the bridge over Clunie, but only its foundation now remains. Braemar was a Jacobite stronghold, and the Invercauld Arms Hotel now stands on the spot where the Earl of Mar started the 1715 rising; the Jacobite song beginning 'The standard on the Braes o' Mar' commemorates it. After the '45, the new Braemar Castle was re-fortified and used as a base by English occupation troops who stayed here as late as 1831.

The farmers of Glen Lui were forcibly evicted in 1726, but farmers re-occupied the clachans there later on, only to leave once again. The farmers of Glen Ey were cleared out about 1840 to make way for deer (see House of Commons Select Committee on the Game Laws, 1872), and you can still see their many old stone ruins. However, clearances were the exception in the Braes o' Mar, where most glens became empty later on due to folk moving out voluntarily, a process that still continues. Just W of Corriemulzie you will see the ruined croft of Braegarrie. Here was the scene of a lively poem in the now almost extinct Braemar Gaelic, in praise of 'O mo chailin donn Braigh-Gharraidh' or 'O my brown-haired lass of Braegarrie', and later recorded in full by F. C. Diack in his *Inscriptions of Pictland*.

Walking ascents

Morrone (859 m, 2819 ft) Pronounced More-*Rone*, this is the great sprawling mass, brown and heather-covered, which rises SW of Braemar. Its name probably comes from Mór Shròn, meaning big nose. You can motor up Chapel Brae to the flat ground past the reservoir and then walk 1 km up to the croft of Tomintoul, or better still reach there from the 'Princess Royal Park' – locally called the Games Park – by paths which wind up through the birches. The prominent knoll at 472 m near Tomintoul gives a fine view of the Cairngorms, beside an indicator built by the Deeside Field Club. Near here, a path starting at Tomintoul goes for 2 km and 360 m of an ascent to the summit of Morrone, $1\frac{1}{2}$ hours in walking time from the centre of Braemar. The top cairn is an even better viewpoint, beside a radio aerial for mountain rescue teams. You can also ascend from Glen Clunie by a Land Rover track going from the Coldrach opposite Auchallater all the way to the top. North of Morrone grow fine birch-juniper woods, offering interesting ways back off the hill by an upper and a lower track going along the level wide shelf back to Chapel Brae.

Creag Choinnich 538 m (1764 ft). This is pronounced Craig *Chone*-yich and means Kenneth's rock. It makes a $\frac{1}{2}$ hour climb E of Braemar. On the Aberdeen side of Creag Choinnich, the steep rocky bluff now called 'the lion's face' rises boldly above the main road; it used to be named Creag a' Mhurtair (Craik *Voor*ter) or rock of the murderer. The fine path of the Queen's Drive winds below it, after starting from the Glen Clunie road S of the youth hostel and passing below Creag Choinnich to the Aberdeen road.

Hills between Clunie and Ballochbuie. To the SE of Creag Choinnich, Càrn nan Sgliat (Carn *Sklaitsh*) or hill of the slates continues as a long heathery ridge. Its NE shoulder sticks out at Creag Clunie, a remarkably fine viewpoint with a dense growth of natural scrubby pines. About 2 km to the S of Carn nan Sgliat rises Creag nan Leachda with tarns on its 784 m summit – called Creag Leacach (*Lai*kach) locally – and 3 km further on the 849 m Meall an t-Slugain (Myalan *Loo*gin) or lump of the gullet. From Meall an t-Slugain you can return down Ballochbuie Forest or descend by the high, lonely Loch Phadruig (*Faa*rik) or Patrick's loch to Glen Callater. One of the best walks near Braemar goes from Ballochbuie Forest up Gleann Beag and through the gap of An Slugan to Loch Phadruig at 685 m, then over to Loch Callater Lodge (8 km from Invercauld Bridge). You can also continue for 5 km beyond Callater by an old drove path which runs up Allt a' Bhealaich Bhuidhe, and next over the col between Carn Dubh and Creag nan Gabhar. You then drop down to the site of the now-demolished Glen Clunie Lodge, by the good path along the S side of the little steep valley of Allt a' Mhaide (Alt *Vaitsh*) or burn of the stick.

Carn na Drochaide 818 m (2681 ft). Pronounced Caarn *Droch-itsh*, the name means the hill of the bridge. This top is another fine viewpoint, $4\frac{1}{2}$ km from Braemar. When the water runs low you can wade across; go $\frac{1}{2}$ km out the Linn of Dee road to where the river Dee goes close to the road and then turn downstream a short distance to a ford over shingle. Beyond, an extensive marsh stretching almost to Mar Lodge forms an interesting habitat for birds and mammals; a path runs along it going up the bank of Dee and then N along the edge of a birch wood to the foot of Carn na Drochaide. A good route back from the top ($2\frac{1}{2}$ km) is to descend to 333 m at Allanaquoich (Allan *Coo*-ich). From here a public road goes W to Mar Lodge past the boggy Lochan a' Chreagain (Lochana *Chraikan*) or tarn of the little rock. On the way you should first visit the Linn of Quoich where the water has a beautiful blue-green colour, flowing over smooth schist slabs. Above the Linn looms the impressive wild face of Creag Bhalg (*Va*lig), with its broken schist rocks thickly clad in larches.

Craig Leek 635 m (2085 ft). This is the best viewpoint near Braemar, lying behind Invercauld House. The name comes from

Creag Lic or flagstone rock, and indeed the hill throws out a bold bluff of smooth diorite on its E side above the boggy flats of Felagie (Fi-*lai*gee) and Aberarder. You reach it by going to the end of the public road at the Keiloch (*Kee*loch), and then heading for 2 km up a fine old pine wood along the edge of the crags. The view of Ballochbuie, Lochnagar and Braemar is magnificent.

Culardoch 900 m (2953 ft), called Cul*aar*doch. This windswept heathery dome lies to the N of Craig Leek. It rises to the summit at Cùl Àrdach Mór which means the big back high place, Cul Ardach Beag being the spur towards Loch Builg. A recommended cross-country walk is to go from the Keiloch up by Craggan Rour just NW of Craig Leek, where a rough road leads N by the old right of way from Braemar to Tomintoul by the Bealach Dearg (*Byal*ach D*yerr*eg) or red pass, over the W side of Culardoch. Beyond the stable at the pass summit at 590 m, which lies 7½ km from the Keiloch, the old route drops into Glen Gairn and so 5½ km to Loch Builg. One of the most interesting places in the district is the secluded Glen Fearder (Féith Àrdobhair, F*yaard*er) or glen of the bog of high water, which runs S of Culardoch towards Dee at the Inver (8 km from Culardoch via Auchtavan). Once populated by many farmers but now deserted, it has a sad haunting beauty, with old birches and lonely greens where stone rings show the sites of former farms.

Inverey (Inver*ei*), at 350 m, lies 8 km W of Braemar. The last place in Aberdeenshire where Gaelic held out as an everyday speech till about 1930, this pleasant string of houses has now been taken over largely by city dwellers with holiday houses. It is a good starting place for the Cairngorms. From Little Inverey, just W of the old Ey bridge, there opens out a particularly fine view of the Cairngorms rising beyond great pine woods. Ben Macdui and its pointed crag above Lochan Uaine seem lower than the dramatic cone of the nearer Derry Cairngorm, while to the left you can see the top of Braeriach above the great cliff of Coire Bhrochain. West of Inverey the Linn of Dee, formerly called An Eas Dé or the fall of Dee, a spectacular place where the river rushes through a narrow 1 m wide channel cut in the schistose rocks, afterwards opening out into a series of deep circular pools.

Glen Lui and the Derry. To reach Derry Lodge, you cross the bridge at the Linn of Dee and go ¾ km E to the foot of Glen Lui, where a locked gate at 366 m bars all but walkers and those with cycles or motor bicycles. The sluices and concrete banks near here

36.   A frost fog at the Derry in January, looking from Creag Bad an t-Seabhaig.

37. The summit tor of Ben Avon from Stuc Gharbh Mhor in late May.

38. Easy walking in August on the beautiful grasslands of the spacious high plateau of Cnap a' Chleirich, looking over to Ben Avon (prominent tor).

39.   The Mitre Ridge in winter, from the floor of the Garbh Choire of Beinn a' Bhuird.

40.   March among scattered birches in Glen Clunie, with the ruin of Coireyaltie (right) below Creag a' Mhadaidh.

are the remains of the Canadian lumber camp during the 1939–45 war. To the N and hidden from the road, Lui rushes over a series of beautiful falls and pools where the water has a wonderful blue-green colour from the shelves of schist underneath. Lower Glen Lui (Laoigh or calf) is finely wooded with old pine and birch, but beyond the grand viewpoint at the Black Bridge, 2 km up, you enter a more open upper glen with beautiful greens where folk farmed in the early 19th century. On the green above the Black Bridge rise two beautifully symmetrical knolls named Dà Shìthean (*Daa Hee*-an) or two fairy hillocks. About 1 km beyond the Black Bridge, the road crosses a stream called Allt Mhad-allaidh (Vat *Aa*lie, pronounced as in alley) or burn of the wild dog. Immediately before you reach the road crossing, a path strikes uphill to the right. It leads to Glen Quoich by the rocky trench of Clais Fheàrnaig (Clash *Yaar*nak), in whose floor lies an artificial loch for fishing, made by a dam at the Quoich end.

About 2 km beyond Allt Mhad-allaidh you come to Derry Lodge in a gloomy pine plantation. Local people always talk of The Derry, like 'Dairy' pronounced quickly; it comes from An Doire, meaning the grove. Nearby to the W stand the cottage of Luibeg and its bothy at about 420 m. Sgòr Dubh (Skor *Doo*), a 741 m hill immediately behind Luibeg, offers a good way back for 5 km to the Linn of Dee and is a magnificent viewpoint for the Cairngorms. The wind-scoured ridge, gravelly and with crisp heather, goes on 3 km W of Sgor Dubh to the 813 m Sgor Mor above Glen Dee. Local folk call the whole of this hill ridge *Faina Skor*, from Féith nan Sgòr, meaning the bog-stream of the peaks. Sgor Mor has interesting examples of weathered granite tors and pot holes, at an altitude much lower than the better known ones on Ben Avon.

Climbing routes

There are no big crags near Braemar. Various small cliffs of schist, diorite, quartzite and limestone, with small-hold climbing, occur at 'lion's face' and elsewhere but the shortness of the crags has discouraged serious climbing. Try to avoid these medium-height cliffs in Dee, Spey or Angus in any case, as they often harbour birds of prey which may have their breeding ruined by inadvertent disturbance from climbers. However, there are plenty of boulder problems and short sporting routes on much smaller crags, varying from the boulder just W of the Invercauld Bridge, called the Muckle

Steen o' Clunie, to a few quarries and river gorges, and to the practice rocks above Luibeg. There, the fine Creag Bad an t-Seabhaig (*Craik* Patan *Tyoe*-ik) or rock of the hawk's clump, is a bold rocky lump rising out of the pines on the way to Carn Crom. It offers a number of short but sporting climbs on dry rough granite, from M to VS.

Further reading

H. Alexander   Hill excursions from Braemar. *Deeside Fld* 2, 7.

A. E. M. Geddes   The climate of Braemar. *Deeside Fld* 2, 14.

J. Dow   Some road reconnaissances from Braemar. *SMCJ* 19, 96.

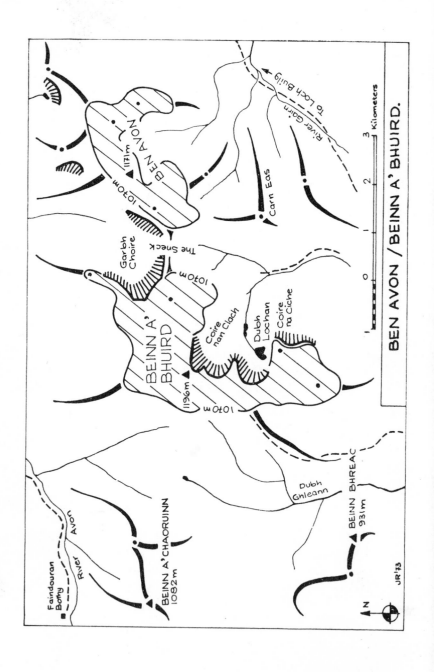

BEN AVON / BEINN A' BHUIRD.

9

Ben Avon and Beinn a' Bhuird

*Ben Avon	1171 m, 132019
*Beinn a' Bhuird N Top	1196 m, 092006
S Top	1177 m, 090978
Beinn a' Chaorainn	1082 m, 045014
*Beinn Bhreac	931 m, 059971
*Revised spelling	

Access
Bus Aberdeen to Braemar. Public roads go to Mar Lodge, Keiloch at Invercauld, upper Glen Gairn, Delnabo near Tomintoul, and Cock Bridge in Strath Don.

Accommodation
See Chapters 1 and 8.

Remote occupied houses
Inchrory 179081, Blairglass 259999, Luibeg 036933, Invercauld 173929, Allanaquoich 120913.

Bothies (open all year)
Faindouran Lodge 081061. Loch Builg Lodge 188028 and Slugain Lodge 119952 both roofless ruins with meagre shelter. Ath nam Fiann 042031, small refuge hut on N side of Avon. Bivouac 097995, a recess underneath one of the bigger boulders below the slabs of Dividing Buttress, holds 3. Gillies' roofless stone shelter 074980, smaller and poorer version 075972.

General description
Ben Avon and Beinn a' Bhuird are among the less-visited of the higher hills in NE Scotland. Both rise close to 1200 m, and, being at the E end of the Cairngorms, both of them – and especially Ben Avon – give magnificent views to the NE and E. You look out over the multitude of low hills and glens of upland Banffshire and Aberdeenshire, far away to Buchan and the North Sea. For the same reasons, Ben Avon appears one of the most prominent hills from the

great sweeps of high farmland in Buchan. Both hills are enormously bulky, with great convex shoulders and slopes bulging steeply into wild unfrequented glens. Both excel in having the biggest stretches of ground over 1000 m on any pair of hills in Britain. Here, on the great tracts of short grass, granite grit and mossy turf, is country where you can stroll easily for miles. But there also come many surprises, for these two hills are in places rent by corries among the wildest in the country.

Geology and landforms

Virtually all the rock is Cairngorms granite. The many tors of Ben Avon form one of the most interesting geomorphological features in the Highlands. You can see very fine examples of dry rocky gaps, which were cut in the distant past by glacial meltwater rivers, in Clais Poll Bhat S of Beinn Bhreac, at Clais Fhearnaig and in the beautiful little gorge at the head of Gleann an t-Slugain. The slopes W of Bruach Mhor are a particularly good place to see stepped terracing of alternate vegetation and gravel, and the Moine Bhealaidh is notable as an extensive high-altitude peat moss.

Natural history

Glen Quoich shows one of the five best stretches of ancient pine wood in Deeside and some fine old birch. As it lies far from houses and people searching for firewood, it has far more dead standing trees – an important part of a natural forest ecosystem – than most Scottish pine woods. Ben Avon and Beinn a' Bhuird support more extensive tracts of windswept high gravelly barrens, studded with that common arctic species the three-pointed rush, than any other two hills in Britain; Carn Eas and the North Top are good examples. In the hollows they also have unusually big expanses of continuous arctic-alpine grassland without bare gravel, as on Cnap a' Chleirich and Allt an Eas Bhig. Tiny lime-rich patches on the high crags of Beinn a' Bhuird and Ben Avon form the micro-habitats for two arctic plants, the rare brook and tufted saxifrages. The limestone of Inchrory supports a fertile green vegetation rich in flowers, including some that grow commonly here at low altitude but elsewhere occur usually as rare mountain species, such as purple saxifrage. Ben Avon and Beinn a' Bhuird are home to great numbers of ptarmigan, and dotterel nest on both hills. Loch Builg is well known for its arctic relict fish, the char.

Estates

The Banffshire part belongs to Inchrory. The Aberdeenshire part lies on Invercauld, except for the area W of a line from N Top to Bruach Mhor to Carn na Drochaide, which Mar Lodge owns. All this country is deer forest.

History

In Blaeu's *Atlas* (1654), Robert Gordon of Straloch refers to the river Avin 'which Timothy Pont, who had surveyed all these parts, told me is the clearest and of the purest waters of all our Kingdom'. Men are said to have gone into the water thinking it was shallow, and been drowned, hence the old rhyme.

The watter o Aan, it rins sae clear

Twad beguile a man o a hundred year

In *The Pennyless Pilgrimage* in 1618, John Taylor describes how he 'saw Mount Benawne, with a furr'd mist upon his snowie head instead of a night-cap: for you must understand that the oldest man alive never saw but the snow on the top of divers of these hills, both in summer as well as in winter'.

In the 18th and 19th centuries Ben Avon became well known as a place for digging out 'cairngorm' crystals, Allt an Eas Mhoir being a favourite spot, and in 1788 a Braemar woman found one of the largest recorded, on the top of Ben Avon. An old tale was that some of the crystal seekers died from drinking the gravelly water of the streams. You can still see the diggers' stone workings on the plateaux and by some of the streams, on several of the hills of the Cairngorms. Another old legend spoke of gold lying below the waters of Lochan Òir (Orr) or tarn of gold, S of Loch Builg; it was said to be guarded by a water kelpie which has more than once driven off rash searchers for the treasure!

There is less early history about Beinn a' Bhuird. Pennant, who visited Deeside in 1769, mentions the hill in his *Tour of Scotland* 'under Ben y Bourd is a small loch, which, I was told, had ice the latter end of July'. Later, about 1820, a herd of cattle which had been driven by bad weather from Glen Avon, fell to their deaths over the cliffs above the loch. On Ben Avon, an old legend which persisted very late was that the lady of Fingal went to Clach Bhan to bathe in one of its rock pools. Pregnant women who were near confinement used to visit Clach Bhan and sit in one of its worn pot holes, in the belief that this ensured an easy labour. In a *New History of Aberdeenshire*,

Smith wrote that in August 1836 he saw the chairing of 12 women who had that morning come over 20 miles from Speyside to sit in the chair, and the custom lingered on as late as the 1860s.

Ben Avon   1171 m (3843 ft)

Locally called Pain *Aan* or *Ah*-in, the name Ben Avon obviously comes from the river below it. Celtic scholars have thought the river to be Ath-fhinn, meaning bright or fair one, after an old legend that tells how Fingal's wife fell on the slippery stones and drowned, whereupon he named the river Ath-fhinn in her memory.

Ben Avon is by far the most complex hill in the entire region described in this book. It is also the biggest, approaching a small hill range in size. From its lower slopes S of Linn of Avon in the NE to its SW corner above Quoich it stretches 12 km in a straight line, and 9 km from N to S between Da Dhruim Lom and Creag an Dail. Ben Avon forms a vast sprawling mass, with bulging convex stony shoulders spreading out in various directions. It has more ground above 900 m than any other hill in Scotland, and an extensive summit plateau which projects out in several huge curves and offshoots. The highest plateaux are gravelly, studded with wiry rushes, but lower down lead to very gentle, stream-watered slopes with wide stretches of grass which make it one of the greenest of hills in the main Cairngorms massif. On the N side, big shoulders project northwards, exposed, scoured by great winds, showing unusually large patches of bare granite grit, and with some fantastic combs of rock. These ridges enclose a few remote wild corries. Ben Avon's chief characteristic, however, is the scores of extraordinary granite tors of varied shape and size which are scattered like plentiful warts over its summit whalebacks and its flanks.

Walking ascents to Ben Avon

From Invercauld. Distance: from the Keiloch to Slugain Lodge 8 km, to summit by the Sneck 16½ km or 10 miles, total ascent 850 m or 2800 ft, time up 4¾ hours. The public road ends at 330 m at the Keiloch, near Invercauld Bridge E of Braemar. A private road leads 3 km from here to Allt Dourie (*Doo*ree). For another 3 km beyond, a rough road runs, at first through pine woods and then ending about half way up Gleann an t-Slugain. Beyond the road end, the path carries on up An Slugan (*Sloog*an) or the gullet, (which consists of a beautiful rocky ravine with sheltered turfy meadows, a lovely winding burn and birches) for 2 km to the ruined Slugain Lodge, about 570 m.

Above here you come to an open moor that slopes W down to Quoich Water and gives grand views of Beinn a' Bhuird.

You now climb very gradually on the path for 5 km N up the glen to 760 m at Clach a' Chléirich (Clach *Hleer*ich) or the stone of the priest, a big boulder on the hillside. Go to 1½ km NNE of here up the grassy glen leading to the saddle at about 970 m or 3200 ft between Cnap a' Chleirich and Ben Avon. This saddle is the Sneck (Sneag, *Snaik*, or notch). Here you suddenly look N down one of the wildest corries in the Cairngorms into An Slochd Mór (Un Slochk *More*) or the great pit. A rugged glen coming up from Glen Avon, the Slochd Mor falls deeply, hemmed in by the craggy and gravelly slopes of Ben Avon on the E side and Stob an t-Sluichd (Stope unt *Loo*ichk) or the point of the Slochd on the NW side. Eventually, Slochd Mor widens into an upper recess called the Garbh Choire or rough corrie, where splendid rock buttresses soar to the green plateau of Cnap a' Chleirich. From the Sneck you can easily walk down scree slopes into the Slochd Mor and so to Avon, along an old right of way between Inverey and Tomintoul by Inchrory.

If going to Ben Avon, however, you walk ½ km E from the Sneck up a slope of loose gravel, turf and stones to the plateau at 1070 m, and then for 1½ km along it NE to the highest point of Ben Avon at 1171 m. The actual summit is a huge black tor whose name appears on the map as Leabaidh an Daimh Bhuidhe meaning the couch of the yellow stag, but local people do not call it this, and the old name was Stob Dubh Easaidh Mór (Stope Doo Essie *More*) or black point of the muckle Essie. You can easily scramble from the neck at the NW side up the rough granite to the cairn, which overlooks a 15 to 20 m drop on the S side.

To vary the return by Slugain to Braemar, a good way in summer and autumn is to head SSW over the green rolling plateau past the 1063 m black tor of Stob Dubh an Eas Bhig (a map error for Stop Dubh Easaidh Beag), so conspicuous from Braemar, to the gravelly flat plateau top (1089 m) NW of the steep slope at Carn Eas (Carn *Yess*) and so to the Slugain. Avoid this steep slope in winter and spring as the steep S face at the plateau rim often carries a giant cornice and occasionally slides down in avalanches. A safer way at that season is to walk SE into the beautiful green bowl of the upper Allt an Eas Mhóir, which is a map error for Easaidh Mór or big cascading one, now often called the muckle Essie. Take care in mist here, as the hillside immediately to the W of the burn at about

900–950 m altitude often carries a vertical snow wall. Lower down you enter a delightful secluded little glen with steep hillsides rising from the cascades of the burn, and then come on an old stalkers' path leading to Gairn.

This upper part of Glen Gairn, lonely, treeless and remote, is one of the wildest glens in the Cairngorms. Up the long glen goes a track from the ruined Loch Buílg Lodge to join the path 1½ km N of Slugain Lodge on the way to the Sneck. In its upper part, Glen Gairn passes through a huge U-shaped gap between steep slopes of broken rock and scree, with Creag an Dail Mhór (Craikan Daal *Vore*) or big rock of the haugh on the NW and Creag an Dail Bheag (Vick) on the SE. Just below where Allt Bad a' Mhonaidh (a map error for the local name of Allt Pit Omie) enters Gairn, a small footbridge gives a safe crossing to a Land Rover track that leads S to the Bealach Dearg pass at the stable below Culardoch (for the rest of the way to Braemar see p 192).

From Loch Buílg. If you wish to visit most of the many tors and tops of Ben Avon, this forms the best route from Deeside. Distance: from public road N of Crathie to Corndavon Lodge 6 km, to Loch Buílg Lodge 11 km, to summit 17 km or 10½ miles. From Loch Buílg Lodge, total ascent 670 m or 2200 ft, time up, 2½ hours. At the public road N of Crathie, at 260981, a private rough road which is often locked at the Crathie end or beyond Blairglass, leads past the largely ruined Corndavon Lodge, named from Coire an Dà Mheann (*Corin Daa* Van) or corrie of the two kids. Beyond, the road goes to the ruined Loch Buílg Lodge. An alternative way to Loch Buílg Lodge starts from the Inver, climbing up the E side of Glen Fearder by an old drove road which goes over Carn Moine an Tighearn, E of Culardoch and down Tom a' Chuir. Lying at about 485 m, with a fine beach at its S end, Loch Buílg (*Boo*lig) or bag loch gives a feeling of great loneliness and open space. Beyond the loch, the water runs N into Glen Buílg, where brilliant green hills contrast with the generally brown, heather-covered landscape around the loch. The path along the loch's E side continues to Inchrory as a bulldozed road, part of the old right of way from Braemar over Bealach Dearg to Tomintoul.

From Loch Buílg Lodge at 488 m, you head uphill to Ben Avon by an old path which ends on the flat moor SW of Carn Dearg. However, just beyond there you can connect with another path (an alternative way from Loch Buílg Lodge), which comes round Carn Drochaide after starting from higher up Gairn. It ends at 890 m beside Allt Phouple (*Foo*pil). Above, you climb easily past some small tors till you reach the pair of large tors on the SE end of the great high crescent enclosing Allt an Eas Mhoir. This pair, so prominent from Braemar, lies at 1120 m on a stony dome called Stùc Gharbh Mhór (*Stooch* Garra *Vore*) or big rough point. About 350 m in distance to the N rises the enormous black wart (1120 m) of Clach a' Chutsaich (Clach *Hootsich*) or Coutts's stone. A stroll follows around the high crescent to the summit of Ben Avon at Leabaidh an Daimh Bhuidhe.

A good way back is to descend the eastern tops by the Tomintoul route towards Inchrory and then come back southwards up Loch Builg side. Avoid the descent of the N branch of Feith Laoigh to the S of Big Brae, a place of broken crags and very steep vegetation, often snow-corniced in winter and spring.

From Tomintoul. Distance: from Delnabo to Inchrory 10 km. From Inchrory to summit 9 km or $5\frac{1}{2}$ miles, total ascent 760 m or 2500 ft, time up $3\frac{1}{4}$ hours. The public road ends at Delnabo, just SW of Tomintoul. A private road beyond a locked gate runs up to Inchrory Lodge going up the side of Avon, a beautiful narrow valley with old birch woods, steep green sides, screes and deserted crofts. You can also reach Inchrory from Cock Bridge in Strath Don, 9 km to the E where the public road ends at 255089 on the valley below Corgarff Castle. A private road runs for 3 km to Delnadamph Lodge, from which a Land Rover track leads up the fertile green bowl of Féith Bhàit (Fay *Vaatsh*) to Inchrory at about 405 m.

The best way from Inchrory to Ben Avon climbs over the 914 m Meall Gaineimh. Take the rough road leading to Glen Builg and cross by the footbridge over Builg Burn, W of which you should diverge to see the fine rocky Linn of Avon. Before you reach the Linn, a path leads S to a little grassy col at 845 m, just W of the top of Meall Gaineimh (Myal *Gaanie*) or sandy lump, a good name for this rounded hill with its extensive patches of bare granite grit. Only 250 m in distance NW of this col stands the fantastic Clach Bhan (Van) or stone of women, which really forms a complex long outcrop of rock. The most extensive of all Ben Avon's tors, though not the highest, it has 'by far the most extraordinary variety of channels, passages, recesses, pot-holes, and other forms of rock weathering to be seen in the Cairngorms' (Alexander, first edition). Many of the pot-holes contain water, others that lay near the edge of the rock have been eroded by drain holes and are now dry, and in others a whole side has worn away to form a large chair. These cavities are symmetrical, either oval or circular, some being deep enough to hold a man standing up to his waist.

The way now lies up the easy broad gravelly whaleback S of Clach Bhan, but you can get some interesting scrambling on its side along the 935 m East Meur Gorm Craig (Mair *Gor*om) or blue finger. This cock's comb of rock runs along the ridge, throwing broken buttresses to the W. After crossing the flat plateau of Big Brae at 937 m, you climb easily to the dome S of West Meur Gorm Craig at 1021 m. It is worth diverging to the W here to look into the beautiful corrie of steep green grass, red gravel and broken slabby black rocks, down to Lochan nan Gabhar (*Gow*er) or tarn of the goats, at about 770 m. A gentle rise now follows to 1122 m at the group of tors SW of Mullach Lochan nan Gabhar (*Moo*lach or summit), and from there along the high crescent running round to the top of Ben Avon.

Across a green hollow NW of the Mullach stands the fine 1076 m spur of Stob Bac an Fhuarain (Stope Bach can *Oo*arin) or point of the bank of the spring. Tucked high up on its W side hides the remote Slochd Beag or little pit, a colourful place where Allt an t-Sluichd Bhig cascades over broken rocks among pink gravel and patches of bright green vegetation. To the N of the Stob, you will see the conspicuous Clach Bun Rudhtair (Clach Boon *Roo*tir), a group of rocks standing up like gigantic rhinoceros horns to 914 m. These and Sabhalan Bynack on Bynack More are the highest and most impressive tors in the Cairngorms. Of the three masses at Clach Bun Rudhtair, the middle one sticks up highest, reaching 25 m, and has a window right through it. North of Clach Bun Rudhtair, a long spur with great patches of bare pink granite grit thrusts out to Da Dhruim Lom (*Daa* Grum Lom) or two bare ridges, above Glen Avon.

The walk from Inchrory to Loch Avon. Distance: from Inchrory to Faindouran Lodge 11½ km, to Ath nam Fiann 17, to Loch Avon 19 km or 12 miles, ascent 320 m, time 4½ hours. This makes a fine walk through some of the least-visited country in the Cairngorms. Glen Avon is a narrow glen, steep-sided and with broken rocks in places. From 600 to 700 m altitude on the N side a huge undulating plateau stretches N over the wilderness of Caiplich, whereas on the S side you look up to the lonely corries and ridges sweeping up to the high Cairngorms.

At the Linn of Avon beside Inchrory the river comes over a series of falls with deep translucent pools of great purity and beauty. A bulldozed road runs up the S side to just W of where Glen Loin breaks off to the N (footbridge over Avon here), and another rough road from Inchrory comes up the N side to about 2 km SW of Faindouran Lodge. A spur of this northern road goes up the E side of Glen Loin to the col S of the Castle rock on Ailnack, whereas a second spur climbs Druim Loin and runs along the top of the rocky escarpment of Creag a' Chadha Dhuibh high above Glen Loin. Glen Loin is a remarkable curving glen, steep and craggy and so impressive that from the plateau of Ben Avon you might easily mistake it for Glen Avon itself.

Between the Linn and the opening of Slochd Mor, the clear water of Avon hurries on over shingle beds among grassy haughs. You will enjoy the fine view up Caol Ghleann (*Kail* Glan) or sma' (i.e. small) glen to the wind-scoured gravelly ridges and corries of Ben Avon and the fantastic horns of Clach Bun Rudhtair. Even more impressive is the outlook up wild Slochd Mor and its many slabby rock faces, some of which do not appear on the 1 inch map. Stob an t-Sluichd and Stob Bac an Fhuarain, which run as level spurs out of the higher hills behind, from below look impressive sharp peaks shielding the entrance to the huge Slochd Mor. Further on up the glen you can look back to Clach Bun Rudhtair and see light through its window.

Beyond Allt an t-Sluichd the road continues to about 2 km past Faindouran Lodge (Féith an Dobhrain, Fay an *Door*an) or stream of the otter, where the cottage and stable at about 590 m have been renovated by the Mountain Bothies Association. In this upper part of Glen Avon you look S past the curious little Spion Rocks (*Speen* or torn out) into the lonely enormous open corries on the N sides of Beinn a' Bhuird and Beinn a' Chaorainn. Eventually, 2 km E of Loch Avon, the path from Faindouran takes you to Àth nam Fiann, the ford of the Fianna or Fingalians, where the Lairig an Laoigh route crosses Avon beside a small refuge hut.

Beinn a' Bhuird   1196 m (3924 ft)

Although spelled Beinn a' Bhùird on maps, probably it should be Beinn Bòrd or table hill; Gaelic speakers on Mar used to call it Paing *Bord*, and older local folk still say Painna *Bord*. Whether you look from Dulnain Bridge, Invercauld or the central Cairngorms, it makes a good name for this great top with its huge flat summit plateau. Beinn a' Bhuird is a hill of contrasts. On its W and N sides, vast heathy slopes fall gently to the peaty wilderness of the

Moine Bhealaidh above Glen Derry and to lonely Glen Avon. On the S it rises commandingly in great steep bulging flanks high above the magnificent old pine forest of Quoich. All along the E side runs a series of wild craggy and snowy corries which you see well from Invercauld. In the NE, the huge plateau rolls on over the green Cnap a' Chleirich and then ends abruptly at the great wall of cliffs above Slochd Mor. The grand high-level walk from the South Top to the North Top gives some of the finest views in NE Scotland. Although the central Cairngorms bar you from seeing the peaks on the Atlantic seaboard, the rest of the view, of innumerable wild hills beyond a vast tract of lonely glens and rolling lower foothills, is unusually impressive.

Walking ascents to Beinn a' Bhuird

From Invercauld. Distance: from Keiloch to Slugain Lodge 8 km, to S Top 13, to N Top 16 km or 10 miles, total ascent 940 m or 3100 ft, time up 5 hours. The first part of this route, up to Slugain Lodge, is the same as to Ben Avon (p 200). Beyond the col above the ruined lodge, a path breaks off to the left, crosses Quoich and then climbs around Càrn Fiaclach (*Fee*achk-lach) or toothed hill to end at 800 m. From there you climb easily on short vegetation and stones straight uphill. Nearby, the shallow hollow at the top of the stream to the W is called Ear Choire an t-Sneachda (*Err* Choran *Drechk*) or east corrie of the snow, where snow lies late into the summer. You will find it worth going to the edge of the cliffs to the E, so as to look into Coire na Ciche and see the huge slabby rock of A' Chìoch (A *Chee*-ich) or the pap, which sticks high up from a tail spur of the plateau and looks so prominent from Invercauld. The 7th Series 1 inch map is seriously incorrect here; the highest point on the cliff edge really falls off much further back on the plateau, at 095983, with A' Chioch at 098987. This error could be dangerous in winter mist when snow masks the obvious cliff-edge; indeed the Aberdeen climber D. McConnach died at this very spot in 1951 by walking over the cornice.

From A' Chioch a stroll along the plateau takes you to the cairn on the South Top at 1177 m, and then along the 3 km of plateau N to the North Top at 1196 m. If you go along the cliff edge, grand views open out into the two huge eastern corries, Coire an Dubh Lochain and Coire nan Clach. You can walk E along the cliff edge from the North Top, but a better way leads further N across the beautiful spacious green hollow at the head of Feith Ghiùbhasachain (Fay *Yoo*asachan) or stream of the little fir wood. From there you stroll easily over the delightful flat plateau to the highest 1172 m point of Cnap a' Chléirich (Cnap Chleerich) or knoll of the priest. You should diverge N of here, passing on the way a very high miniature tarn, to look into Garbh Choire (*Gar*a Chorrie). Alternatives are then to descend to the Sneck and continue to Ben Avon (p 201), or go S to Clach a' Chleirich and Slugain. If you go S, the stream SW of Cnap a' Chleirich makes a good route, but watch out for a deep sandy pocket in the stream bed at about 104003, which often contains a vertical snow bank right through the summer. Remember also that the slope to the E of this stream carries steep broken crags which do not appear on the 1 inch map. Distance: from N Top to Cnap a' Chleirich 1½ km, to the Sneck 2½ km if you avoid detours.

From Cnap a' Chleirich, the walker with plenty of time should not miss the 2 km long spur NE out to Stob an t-Sluichd where a comb of broken rocks and small tors of rough granite leads out along the spur to this fine point overlooking Glen Avon. You can also reach it easily from Glen Avon by going up the road to Allt an t-Sluichd and then taking a path up Cul na Bruaich to a point WSW of Stob an t-Sluichd.

From Dubh Ghleann. This is the finest approach to Beinn a' Bhuird. Distance: from Quoich road bridge (333 m) at Allanaquoich to Allt an Dubh Ghlinne 6 km, to N Top via An Diollaid 13 km or 8 miles, total ascent 800 m or 2850 ft, time up 4 hours. The public road from Mar Lodge and Linn of Dee ends at Allanaquoich, where a footpath runs above the rocky Linn of Quoich to a footbridge beside the now-broken pot hole of the Punch Bowl. To the W of here on the flat above the river, you come on a Land Rover road beyond a locked gate. This road leads up the W side of Glen Quoich (Cuaich, *Coo*-ich or cup) through a beautiful natural forest of mixed old pine and birch, to cross Allt an Dubh Ghlinne at a ford at about 450 m. Here Glen Quoich divides. Dubh Ghleann (*Doo* Glan) or dark valley is the W branch, and Am Beitheachan (Um *Bay*-achan) or the little birch place is the valley to the E. Although local people always call this E part the Beitheachan and not the Quoich, all the maps have omitted it. You can also reach this glen junction by going from the Derry gate at the foot of Glen Lui and taking the path through the rocky Clais Fhearnaig (p 193), a way that is ½ km further than the route from Allanaquoich.

Beyond the junction of the streams, the road also divides. The E branch runs up the Beitheachan to a ford at about 093952, where it loops round and eventually back to Allanaquoich down the E side of Glen Quoich. The W branch goes straight ahead into the pine wood clothing the rounded hill of Carn Alltan na Beinne (not An Diollaid as on the 1 inch map), and then winds round and climbs this hill by a series of spectacular zig-zags before dropping down to An Diollaid at 074967. You will come on an alternative and better walking route if you trace the old stalkers' path which slants uphill below most of the zig-zags. On the opposite steep hillside of Bruach Mhor, the first burn of Allt Tarsuinn (Al*tar*sin) or cross burn rushes down a steep green stripe, while the next one up falls from the wide green upper corrie of Coire Gorm (Cor *Goro*m), a place that has been considered for possible ski developments. The main burn is Alltan na Beinne (Allt'n na *Peeng*) or streamlet of the hill. Cornices often ring the steep lower slopes W of Alltan na Beinne and Allt a' Choire Ghuirm, and an avalanche at Allt Tarsuinn killed two men in 1964. An Dìollaid (Un *Dyee*ulitsh) or the saddle, is an impressive and unusual narrow neck at 744 m where you look down steeply into the wild depths of Dubh Ghleann. Ahead, the bulldozed road climbs to 1080 m, just W of the head springs of Alltan na Beinne. Snow lies late along the shallow upper part of this burn and often builds up into a high vertical wall on its W side. From the road end you can stroll easily to either top of Beinn a' Bhuird.

A finer route is to walk up the deep and narrow Dubh Ghleann to its head, where streams fall tumbling down among steep grass, broken rocks and screes. The eastern burn, Allt Coire Ruairidh, goes up the shallow green Coire Ruairidh (Cor *Oo*arie) or Rory's corrie, to near the North Top.

Beinn a' Chaorainn 1082 m (3553 ft) and **Beinn Bhreac** 931 m (3051 ft). Connecting these two to one another and to Beinn a' Bhuird stretches a vast medium-level plateau, one of the fine wildernesses of the Cairngorms. The map gives it as Mòine Bhealaidh (Moin *Vyall*ie) or broom moss, but local people call it the 'Yalla (? yellow) Moss'. Here, several hills rise in the distance far beyond the great flattish expanses of bog, peat hags and stretches of crisp turf. Looking from Beinn a' Bhuird in the evening you will see its innumerable pools glint like silver, and from the moss itself the views into Coire Etchachan are magnificent.

The quickest way to the shapely cone of Beinn a' Chaorainn (Pain *Hoor*in) or hill of the rowan tree, starts from Derry Lodge by the

41. Ski touring in January through the young pines of Geallaig above Coilacriech, with Glen Muick beyond and Mount Keen (right).

42. The eastern part of Creag an Dubh Loch, with Labyrinth Groove (prominent long icy runnel), the very steep Broad Terrace wall (dark, on left), Central Slabs (right), and Central Gully Slabs (far right).

43. Central Gully Slabs at Creag an Dubh Loch, one of the finest rock walls in Scotland.

44. Climbers on the route of Goliath on Central Gully wall at Creag an Dubh Loch.

Lairig an Laoigh path for $7\frac{1}{2}$ km to the top of the path (p 133). Distance: from top of path at 034004 to summit $1\frac{1}{2}$ km, ascent 330 m. To the E of the summit, $1\frac{1}{4}$ km away, the lower rounded top Beinn a' Chaorainn Bheag stands beyond a set of beautiful tiny tarns along the Avon watershed.

Beinn Bhreac (Pain *Vrech*k) or speckled hill is a dry spur rising at the S end of the Moine Bhealaidh into two tops, the eastern being higher, 5 km from Beinn a' Chaorainn. From here you can stroll NW to Creag Doire (Craig Derry) at 040980, the spur that drops sharply down screes to Glen Derry. It is then an easy walk S to the Derry down the shallow Coire an Fhir Bhogha, which the map makers mistook for Coire Cath an Fhir Bhogha (*Cor* Can Yeer *Voe*) or corrie of the bowman's battle. Another route off Beinn Bhreac goes SSW by the little rocky gully of Clais Poll Bhat (locally called Clash Pole *Vaa*) and the curious hanging tarn of Poll Bhat to Glen Quoich. On the way down in spring, avoid the sudden drop of Coire Gorm to the SSE of the summit, as its steep upper green bank is often heavily snow-corniced. From the Clais, you can also descend easily over the rounded 777 m Meall an Lundain (Myal *Loon*tan) or lump of the grassy marsh, to the pines of the Derry (5 km from Beinn Bhreac to Derry Lodge).

Walking in the corries

Ben Avon shares the magnificent Slochd Mor with Beinn a' Bhuird, and its other corries have already been mentioned. Beinn a' Bhuird carries some grand wild corries where you will see superb cornices and other snow scenery. In the SE the shallow Coire Buidhe (Cor *Boo*ee) N of Carn Fiaclach leads higher up into the much bigger Coire na Ciche. Coire na Ciche (Cor na *Keech*) or corrie of the Cioch, is a sheltered sunny corrie with fine buttresses of rough granite on the W side and the great tor of A' Chioch the pap rising high above its eastern damp slabby rocks. Round the corner to the N spreads the huge Coire an Dubh Lochain – locally called Coire an Loch (Cor'n *Loch*) – a wide corrie with many rocks and screes, and grassy shelves that lead easily but steeply to the plateau above. For its great variety of scenery and its air of remoteness, this corrie is one of the finest in the region described in this book. One of the highest lochs in the Cairngorms, the lovely Dubh Lochan or black tarn lies at about 935 m among the corrie's great screes. To the N, the bold slabby Dividing Buttress separates the corrie from the even larger Coire nan Clach

(Cor na *Glach*) or corrie of the stones, where cornices usually last into July.

Climbing routes

Ben Avon. The crags consist mostly of broken and short rocks. However, the tors give grand sporting scrambling on dry rough granite, which is especially worth while at Clach Bun Rudhtair (*SMCJ* 23, 355). All the climbs below are on Beinn a' Bhuird.

Coire na Ciche. This corrie has two parts which almost form a right angle with the wide South Gully in the corner. To the E of the corner a smooth sheet of slab called Slab Buttress stretches across under the great wart of A' Chioch. A' Chioch itself gives interesting climbing on good black rock but lacking any obvious defined lines. The Slab Buttress below is partly vegetated, often wet, and prone to avalanches in spring, but in summer gives the very good 200 m climb of Quartzvein Route (VD) up a central dyke containing a vein of quartz. To the left of South Gully you will find the best climbs. Here soars a 110 m high crag, so tucked in on the W side of the corrie that much of it hides out of sight from the glen below or from Invercauld; indeed, only when you come right into Coire na Ciche do you fully realise its width. The outstanding routes (both VS) are Hourglass Buttress, which was first climbed in May 1953 by F. Malcolm and A. Thom, and the even better ascent of The Carpet, first climbed in August 1955 by them and G. Malcolm, R. Barclay and G. Adams. Hourglass rises just to the left of South Gully where you will easily recognise it from its hourglass or 'egg-timer' appearance. 'Above the neck of the Hourglass the climbing is exposed and on perfect rock' (Climbers' Guide first edition, Vol 1). The Carpet lies towards the left end of the crags, up an obvious big slab to the right of a huge alcove in the rock. You start from the right corner of a grassy recess below and to the right of the alcove, and climb rightwards up steep slabs to a grand 30 m pitch on the exposed slab. Sustained hard moves follow all the way up the slab to the easier climbing above. The hardest route in Coire na Ciche is Three Step (VS), an excellent climb going up the gigantic steps below and to the right of The Carpet.

Coire an Dubh Lochain. The main features here are the steep bulging wall of Bloodhound Buttress that culminates in a few prominent pinnacles near the plateau edge, the wide easy gully of The Main Rake further N, and N again the slabby Glaucous Buttress. A popular climb is Polypody Groove (VD) on Glaucous Buttress, a fine old classic route climbed first in August 1949 by J. Tewnion and E. L. Smith who went up an obvious, dark, left-slanting line between the smooth slabs on the right side of the buttress and the steeper granite pillars on the left side. At the N end of the corrie, the great bulge of Dividing Buttress projects outward hiding the remote Coire nan Clach further N. Dividing Buttress looks a grand sight and offers mostly indefinite though sporting climbing to the plateau; a more defined way is by the 140 m Slab and Arete up the ridge on the dividing line between the two corries. The gullies further N in Coire nan Clach offer good Grade I snow climbs ending in big cornices.

Garbh Choire. Big continuous crags rise on the S or Cnap a' Chleirich side, with sporting ribs and broken smaller buttresses on the Stob an t-Sluichd side. The finest feature is the Mitre Ridge, a wide, 200 m high black wall projecting as a wedge into an outer ridge, and culminating in a series of fine towers. The Mitre Ridge was the scene of one of the main early breakthroughs in Cairngorms climbing, in July 1933 when two parties climbed two separate routes up the wall; both were exposed face routes that are still among the finest climbs in the Cairngorms. E. A. M. Wedderburn, P. D. Baird and E. J. A. Leslie went up the Direct Route, which has since become one of the classics of the region. The route starts between the lowest rocks and the outer corner of the Mitre wall, and goes up a great slab by a hard groove (S). It takes 33 m of a run-out to reach the first stance just above a strenuous overhang at the top of the slab, a point which you can also reach by an easier variation (M) that starts at the corner of the Mitre wall. The rest of this grand route goes near or on the edge of the ridge, first by chimneys, then up or around two fine towers, and finally over the knife-edged arête and pinnacles of the summit crest. The Mitre Ridge, which faces N at a high altitude, looks a magnificent sight in winter, when the Direct Route becomes a Grade IV winter ascent that is one of the finest in the massif. Round the corner to the W and past the outermost wedge of the Mitre Ridge, the Cumming-Crofton route was also first climbed on that same great day in 1933, by M. S. Cumming and J. W. Crofton. You will recognise it as a dark line running right up the steep face just W of the corner. Although only severe, it is one of the steeper climbs in the Cairngorms, exposed and sustained in difficulty. Its main features are an initial chimney, followed by a delicate zig-zag traversing to the right and then slanting up left, all on fine clean rock, then straight up by a hard embrasure that becomes slightly greasy after wet weather, and finally a crack leading to the arête between the first and second towers. On the remote, steep and spectacular W face of the Mitre Ridge, M. Rennie and G. S. Strange in 1969 climbed Slochd Wall (VS and A2), starting at the foot of North-West Gully, the gully which bounds the W side of the Mitre Ridge. Their route is at present the hardest artificial climb in the central Cairngorms.

The other outstanding feature of the Garbh Choire is Squareface, which projects outwards about half way between the Sneck and the Mitre Ridge. This high-lying black buttress has a largely-hidden W face of dry, rough, clean rock that offers one of the best climbs in the massif. The 100 m route goes up on or near the arête where the N and W faces of this buttress meet in a prominent edge. First climbed in July 1953 by T. W. Patey and J. M. Taylor, this original route (VD) slants off the arête to the right, on to the W face, for the final pitch. A later VS variation to the second pitch goes right up the steep top part of the arête by a delicate and spectacular finish on superb rock. The original summer route was first ascended in winter in January 1972 (Grade IV), by climbing with the front points of crampons on snow crust.

Further reading

A. I. McConnochie   The eastern Cairngorms. *CCJ* 1, 236.

Prof Heddle   Ben Avon. *SMCJ* 2, 225.

L. W. Hinxman   In ptarmigan land. *SMCJ* 4, 214.

The eastern Cairngorms (Guide Book article). *SMCJ* 8, 41.

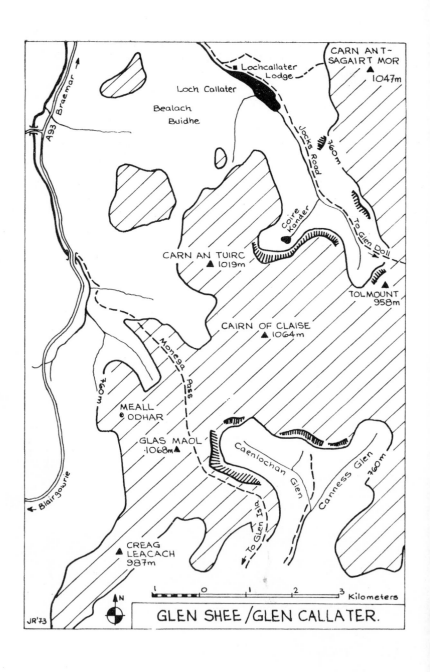

CARN AN T-
SAGAIRT MOR
▲ 1047m

Lochcallater Lodge

Loch Callater

Bealach Buidhe

A93 Braemar

Jocks Road

360m

To Glen Doll

Coire Kander

CARN AN TUIRC
▲ 1019m

TOLMOUNT
958m ▲

CAIRN OF CLAISE
▲ 1064m

Monega Pass

450m

MEALL ODHAR

GLAS MAOL
·1068m▲

Caenlochan Glen

Canness Glen

360m

← Blairgowrie

To Glen Isla

CREAG LEACACH
987m

1 0 1 2 3 Kilometers

N

JR'73

GLEN SHEE / GLEN CALLATER.

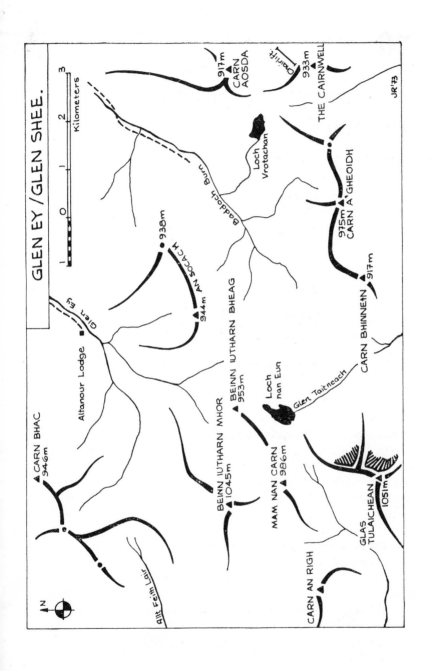

GLEN EY / GLEN SHEE.

10

The Mounth from Callater to Glen Ey

*Carn an Tuirc	1019 m,	174804
*Cairn of Claise	1064 m,	185788
*Tolmount	958 m,	211800
*The Glas Maol	1068 m,	166765
*Creag Leacach	987 m,	155745
Mount Blair	744 m,	167629
*The Cairnwell	933 m,	135773
*Carn Aosda	917 m,	134792
*Carn a' Gheoidh	975 m,	106766
*An Socach	944 m,	081800
*Beinn Iutharn Mhor	1045 m,	045973
Beinn Iutharn Bheag	953 m,	065791
Mam nan Carn	986 m,	050780
*Carn Bhac	946 m,	051833
*Glas Tulaichean	1051 m,	051760
*Carn an Righ	1029 m,	028773

Access

Braemar is the best centre for the N side, Spittal of Glenshee for the S side. Buses run from Aberdeen to Braemar several times daily, and from Pitlochry to Braemar once a week for two months in the summer via Glen Shee and the Cairnwell. Public roads go to Inverey, from Glen Clunie to Glen Shee, and up Glen Isla to Auchavan 191697.

Accommodation and other facilities

See Chapter 8. Hotels and pubs also occur at Kirkton of Glen Isla, at Spittal of Glen Shee and the nearby Dalmunzie, and at Kirkmichael and Glen Derby. There is a youth hostel at the unusual round house of Knockshannoch in Glen Isla, and Kindrogan House at Enochdu offers courses by the Scottish Field Studies Association. You can buy ski equipment and outdoor clothing in a shop at Spittal of Glenshee.

Remote occupied houses

Rhidorroch 128742, Cairnwell chair lift (flat above café). Tulchan 185723, Auchallater 156882, Fealar Lodge 008800. See also Chapter 13.

Bothies and shelters

Coirenalarig at 135835 is a ruin but still gives some shelter, and contains murals of Fraser's Brig and the Clunie hills. Carn an Tuirc 172809 disused ski hut, dangerous because of roof caving in. Locked hut E of Cairnwell café, apply Scottish Ski Club. Open sheds at bottom of Meall Odhar tow, top of Cairnwell lift, Carn Aosda tows. Aberdeen Ski Club open hut 130786 in hollow at 790 m, with first aid kit. Meagre shelter in roofed stone pit at top of Meall Odhar tow and at roofless stone shelters 183811 and 160759.

General description

This chapter describes that grand part of the Mounth from Glen Callater and Glen Isla W to the Glen Ey hills, Fealar Lodge and Glen Shee. Here the Mounth separates upper Deeside from the low ground of Perthshire and W Angus. This makes very good hill walking country on lovely smooth green hills with vast rolling plateaux and broad ridges; even at 1000 to 1050 m you tread on a springy continuous turf of sedge and moss almost like a lawn. The glens have a wild bare beauty, each with a distinctive character all its own. In the centre of the district, the lack of roads, tracks and other signs of man are so few, the wildlife so rich, and the feeling of space so strong, that in some ways this is as good as the Cairngorms massif for a wilderness area.

At the Cairnwell you will find a good centre for developed downhill skiing, and in winter and spring all these hills excel for ski touring. Summer or winter, most of them are unfrequented hills, and if you go more than 1 km from the chair lift or road you seldom see anyone. They offer an infinitely varied set of cross-country walks over the tops, starting in one glen and finishing in another. Although usually easy for hill walking in snow or for ski touring, they can be inaccessible and very snowy hills in some winters. In hard winters with SE winds, as in 1947, 1963 and 1972, they become far more deeply covered than the higher Cairngorms massif to the N. Huge cornices and great convex bulges of snow often build up on otherwise easy slopes, and avalanches are common. Big avalanches have occurred even on gentle slopes like the one E of Sron na Gaoithe on the route of the Monega track to the Glas Maol.

Geology and landforms

The rock consists mostly of schist with some quartzite and big patches of limestone and epidiorite, and with granite on Creag Caorach and Creag an Fhir-shaighde. Glen Callater and Caenlochan are fine examples of glacial trenches with precipitous head walls, the glens of Ey, Clunie, Taitneach and Shee being more typical U-shaped valleys with steep sides. Many of the high corries have beautiful cups or basins with steep slopes but little or no rock. Just N of Blairgowrie, the River Ericht runs through a remarkable beautifully-wooded canyon with cliffs of conglomerate and sandstone.

Natural history

Because of its lime-rich rocks, the district is far more fertile than the Cairngorms massif, with a deeper richer soil, a more fertile and varied vegetation with more grass and blaeberry and less heather, and a more abundant and varied animal life. The lime-rich rocks of Caen-lochan rank with Ben Lawers as one of the two best places in Britain for uncommon arctic-alpine plants. Here you may see snow gentian, blue sow thistle, woolly willow, boreal fleabane and other rarities. Loch Kander is another very good spot for rare arctic-alpines, although less varied than Caenlochan. Over the limestone there occur also a few rich places on open ground where mountain avens, alpine cinquefoil and purple saxifrage grow on the open hillside away from cliffs. The Glas Maol summit plateau has an interesting arctic-alpine grassland that is typical of dry climates, being dominated by stiff sedge with some viviparous fescue, a little woolly hair moss and the brown lichen *Cetraria islandica*. The Glen Ey hills further W, as on Carn an Righ and Carn Bhac, support a more western type of vegetation like that on the Drumochter hills, with more moss and less grass and sedge. A feature of all these fertile hills is that vegetation covers far more of the ground that at the same altitude in the Cairn-gorms, with very little bare gravel or screes. Ptarmigan, red grouse, dunlin, skylarks, and mountain hares reach a greater abundance on some of these hills than anywhere else in the arctic-alpine zone in Scotland, and ptarmigan, grouse and dotterel rear bigger broods here than elsewhere, which again indicates the underlying fertility. Several species of animals live at much higher altitudes than usual on some of these hills. This part of the Mounth is therefore unique in Scotland for its wildlife interest both plant and animal.

Estates
Invercauld has Callater, Clunie and most of the Glen Shee and Glen Taitneach hills. Fealar is a separate deer forest running up to Carn Bhac and Beinn Iutharn. Glen Ey and Glen Connie lie on Mar Estate (i.e. not Mar Lodge), and Glen Lochsie on Dalmunzie (Dal-*mung*ee). Caenlochan and upper Glen Isla belong to Airlie Estate. All the ground is deer forest, with abundant hill sheep in summer.

History
Glen Shee shares with Kinveachy near Aviemore and several other places in Scotland and Ireland an old Celtic legend of Fionn or Fingal who took vengeance on Diarmaid for stealing the love of Grainne, Fingal's queen. After Diarmaid slew the great boar of Beinn Gulbain (in this case Ben Gulabin near the Spittal), Fingal bade him measure the monster from tail to snout with his bare foot, whereupon the poisoned bristles pierced his foot and he died in agony. Grainne in despair flung herself on an arrow, and she and Diarmaid and his white hounds were said to be buried on Tom Diarmaid or Diarmaid's hillock, beside the farm of Tomb (i.e. Tom) across the river from the Spittal (T. D. Miller, *Tales of a Highland Parish, Glen Shee*). Later on, during the period of recorded history, many feuds and minor battles occurred in the Cairnwell district on both sides of the pass, possibly because it was in a boundary area lying between different communities. Grant's *Legends of the Braes o' Mar* is an excellent source for these legends. At Loch Callater, beside the Tolmount path just E of the Lodge, you will see Fuaran an t-Sagairt or the priest's well; legend has it that water flowed freely after a priest prayed here during a spell of severe frost when all wells in the district were frozen over.

In old times people travelling from Tomintoul to Pitlochry walked by the Bealach Dearg and the Cairnwell. Before Gaelic died out here, F. C. Diack noted an ancient verse among Gaelic speakers at Tomintoul, Deeside, and in Strath Ardle. It runs

Cuir is cathadh am Bealach Dearg,
Sneachd is reoth air Chàrna Bhalg,
Cùl ri gaoth air Làirig bhealaich,
Grian gheal am Maoilinn

which means, 'snowing and drifting in Bealach Dearg, snow and frost on the Cairnwell, back to the wind on the Lairig pass, bright sun in Moulin'. The Lairig of the verse is An Lairig or An Lairig Ié, which makes a fine cross-country route that travellers on foot once used a lot as a short cut from Glen Shee to Pitlochry. It climbs up Coire Lairige SW of Spittal of Glenshee and drops gradually down the Allt Doire nan Eun (Der nan *Ai*-in or Dirnanean) to Enochdu (10 km, 320 m ascent).

Walking ascents

Glen Callater. The name comes from Caladair, meaning hard water. Approximately 3½ km S of Braemar at Auchallater, at about 370 m altitude, a private road goes up Glen Callater. At first it runs alongside a fine little rocky gorge and then for 5 km up the treeless glen, twisting around bare stony hills to the locked lodge beside Loch Callater, where a bridge crosses the river and a bulldozed road runs along the S side of the loch. A lake lying just below 500 m and dammed up by glacial drift, Loch Callater stretches 1⅓ km long and 30 ha in area; nearly half of it falls less than 3 m deep but the water reaches 9 m in depth near the SW shore. The loch supports many pike which live unusually high up here. Feral goats lived on some of the nearby crags earlier this century but have not been seen in the last decade.

At the lodge the path to Lochnagar slants up to the left. The Tolmount path goes 1½ km along the E side of the loch, then up the grassy flats beyond, and finally climbs over fairly steep grass and boulders out to the plateau at a dip (883 m) on the E side of the hill of Tolmount (for the continuation to Glen Clova, see p 266). This upper part of the glen beyond the loch becomes gradually hemmed in by crags, steep slopes and corries. It is a wild impressive place, unusual in the Braemar district for being so brilliantly green in summer. About 2 km up from Loch Callater, the burn from Loch Kander comes in on the W side. The main valley continues for another 1½ km until it stops under the steep broken rocks of Tolmount, in the vast green basin of Coire Breac (Cor *Brech*) or speckled corrie.

The hills on the E side of Glen Callater carry a long face of steep slopes and rocks called the devil's kitchen. Forming part of this face, imposing cliffs rise at Creag Leachdach (locally Leacach or *Laik*ach) and particularly on the 100 m granite crags of Creag an Fhir-shaighde. The maps err here also as the local name for Creag an Fhir-shaighde is Creag an Fhleisdeir (Craikan *Laish*ter) or rock of the arrowmaker. On the W side an almost continuous escarpment of cliffs stretches from Tolmount to N of Loch Kander. Just E of Loch Kander on the corner plunges an impressive high waterfall, Eas Allt Briste.Amhaich (Ess Allt *Preesh A*-wich) or the fall of break-neck burn, now often called breakneck falls.

An easy climb of 120 m takes you up beautiful green grass and blaeberry from Glen Callater to Loch Kander (Ceanndobhair, *Kyan*der) or head water at about 670 m. This inky little loch lies in the striking green Coire Ceanndobhair with its fine broken cliffs of schist, including one steep buttress that soars from just above the water line. You can easily climb out of the corrie at its head by a wide gully which leads to the lowest rim on the plateau between Carn an Tuirc and Cairn of Claise.

Carn an Tuirc 1019 m (3340 ft), **Cairn of Claise** 1064 m (3484 ft) and **Tolmount** 958 m (3143 ft). These are the big tops on the W of Glen Callater, forming a vast grassy tableland that is peaty and damp in the hollows but well drained and springy on the ridges. From Glen Callater a bulldozed road now climbs on to them up to an altitude of 940 m on Carn Tuirc Beag which projects out as the spur of dry tundra NW of Loch Kander.

Càrn an Tuirc (Caarn *Toork*) means the hill of the boar. One of the best routes up (3 km to the top, 520 m ascent) starts from the corner of the Cairnwell road at 147799, ⅔ km up from the bridge carrying the main road over the stream of Uisge Bhruididh (Ooshk *Vroo*eetsh). Immediately downhill you will see the old bridge at the site of An Seann Spideal (Un *Shaan* Spital) or the old spital, that carried the first military road. Here you stand in a great amphitheatre which runs from Carn an Tuirc round to the Cairnwell and divides into separate glens or corries further up; it is called Corrie Voo and has long been regarded as an excellent grazing. Across the old bridge, a track winds up the stream along the fine rocky gorge and pools of the Linn of Allt a' Gharbh Choire, and then past some old shielings to the foot of Carn an Tuirc. The upper part of the E burn forms a good ski run where a hut and tow were built and used briefly in the early 1960s. The hollow here has the name Coire na Còinnich (Cor na *Cawi*n-yich) or corrie of the moss.

South of Carn an Tuirc, you pass the top of Coire Ceanndobhair beside an old stone wall and then climb up a gradual green damp slope, where water voles live in the turf over the stream, to Cairn of Claise (2 km from Carn an Tuirc, 110 m ascent). This name comes from Càrn na Claise (Caarn na *Clashi*) or hill of the hollow. A broken wire fence with wooden posts runs for miles along the county boundary here, stretching from Creag Leacach of Glen Shee to Cairn of Claise where a big stone wall replaces it at an unusually high altitude. Cairn of Claise has a southerly top called Druim Mor (961 m) at the end of a long flat grassy spur extending near the Caenlochan cliffs. Below it the cliffs fall abruptly in the prominent triangular face of Creag Caorach (Craik *Herr*ich) or sheep's rock. At its lowest point at about 950 m the main ridge that goes $3\frac{1}{2}$ km round to the Glas Maol passes near the edge of a great steep basin falling to the N, which local people call the Garbh Choire (*Gar* Chorrie).

Tolmount, a conical top 3 km to the E (60 m ascent) of Cairn of Claise, sweeps up from an expanse of high tableland that runs out to the hills W of Glen Clova and round to Lochnagar. The lowest point on the watershed lies at the col E of the top, at 874 m. One of the best routes is to climb all three hills from Loch Callater via Loch Kander and then go down Jock's Road. Two other fine alternatives are to walk from the Seann Spideal bridge up Carn an Tuirc to Tolmount, Cairn of Claise and round the head of Garbh Choire to the Glas Maol ($8\frac{1}{2}$ km) and back 5 km by Sron na Gaoithe, or else to go from Caen-lochan up Glen Canness and then to Tolmount, Cairn of Claise, the Glas Maol and Monega Hill.

The Glas Maol 1068 m (3504 ft) and **Creag Leacach** 987 m (3238 ft). From the road over the Cairnwell, you can see these hills very well from the S end of the highest car park at about 670 m. Creag Leacach (*Laik*ach) looks a fine peak, soaring high out of Gleann Beag up steep slopes of contrasting blue-grey scree, black expanses of peat at an unusually high angle, and bright green grass. However, the best view of the Glas Maol from the Cairnwell road is at the head of Glen Clunie near the new bridge over the stream of Uisge Bhruididh. On this side, Glas Maol presents its northern corrie of Fionn Choire (not Coire Fionn as on the map) as a beautifully symmetrical bowl flanked by the steep Sron na Gaoithe on the left and Meall Odhar on the right.

The easiest way to climb the Glas Maol is to start from the top car park (3 km, 400 m ascent, $1\frac{1}{2}$ hours). The route leads by various churned up paths and vehicle tracks over the heathery hill of Meall Odhar Beag (about 770 m) or up its S side, to the ski grounds in the basin of Coire Odhar beyond. There, a T-bar tow pulls skiers to the 922 m top of Meall Odhar, whose local name is Meall Odhar Mór (Myal *Ower More*) or big dun lump. From here the horseshoe of Fionn

Choire (*Fyan* Chorrie) or cold corrie falls to the E (the new 1 : 10000 map erroneously locates it on Sron na Gaoithe). A curved horseshoe-shaped snow drift lies far into the summer here, and in winter avalanches often occur. A steepish climb straight ahead leads to the plateau, and along the broken remains of a fence you stroll across soft turf to the summit cairn of the Glas Maol (no fence on the last part). Other broken fences which branch off this fence at two different points run out to Cairn of Claise and to Creag Leacach. Aberdeen, Angus and Perth counties meet on the top, where a very fine view opens out, especially towards the S and SW. The name Glas Maol (*Glass* Meel) suggests green bald top, but in local Gaelic speech the old words were An Glas Mheall (Vyal) or the green lump. It makes a pleasant $2\frac{1}{2}$ km walk from the cairn down the stony ridge leading S to Creag Leacach, a fine sharp peak with scree slopes that fall steeply to the W into Coire Bhàthaich (*Vaa*-ich or shelter). The easiest way (3 km) from there to Glen Shee goes down the subsidiary bulge to the SW and then down Meall Gorm to the road above the house of Rhidorroch (Ruighe Dorch) or dark shieling.

The Monega. Crossing from Glen Clunie to Glen Isla, this is the highest of the old rights of way across the Mounth. Distance: from the start at the Cairnwell road to the county boundary 4 km, to summit of the path 5, to Tulchan 10 km or 6 miles, total ascent 520 m, time 3 hours. The Monega (Mon *Aigi*) leaves the Cairnwell road at 145805 on the E side of the bridge over Uisge Bhruididh. The path is indistinct up the N side of the conical 814 m spur of Sròn na Gaoithe (Stron *Gooee*) or nose of the wind, from which you have a fine view of the big horseshoe-shaped Fionn Choire of the Glas Maol. After reaching the county boundary, the indistinct path suddenly becomes a clear Land Rover track which runs from Monega Hill to beyond Cairn of Claise. Just before you reach the highest point at almost 1020 m or about 3320 ft, $\frac{1}{2}$ km E of the Glas Maol summit cairn, the track passes through an interesting stretch of tiny subarctic-like hummocks 15 to 25 cm high, which are caused by alternating frost and thaw. It then skirts the W edge of the corrie of Caenlochan to a small shepherds' hut (often locked) at about 960 m on Glas Maol Beag, and drops down the long dry ridge to Monega Hill and finally to the stalker's house of Tulchan at 426 m in the head of Glen Isla (*Eila*). Further W, another track climbs from Tulchan up to Glas Maol Beag by Glen Brighty and the broad ridge W of Sron Saobhaidhe.

Caenlochan. Glen Isla opens out at the ruined Shielin 4 km above Tulchan, into a wide green basin hemmed in by crags, a place well worth exploring for its wild scenery. At the foot of this basin, N of Bessie's Cairn, the valley divides at about 460 m. The smaller E branch is Glen Canness (Cadha an Eas) or pass of the waterfall, the W branch being Caenlochan (Cadha an Lochain, Ca'n*loch*an) or pass of the tarn. A few straggling larches still remain from the big wood that was once planted and later felled on the lower slopes. A bulldozed road now runs well up Caenlochan. On every side except the way in from the S, you are hemmed in by steep walls of broken rock and scree, which look especially impressive on Monega Hill to the SW and on Creag Caorach to the N. One of the easiest ways to climb out passes near the tarn at the NW corner where a grassy scoop with a zig-zag path leads up to the col between the Glas Maol and Carn of Claise, 3 km from the Shielin. Another goes by a good path which zig-zags steeply right up to the plateau beside Caderg (Cadha Dearg, Ca*derg*) or red pass, which forms the projecting spur between Creag Caorach and Glen Canness. A third way by a steep gully of scree, leads out to the shepherds' hut on the Glas Maol Beag. Glen Canness makes a fine approach to Tom Buidhe, from which you will find the walking very easy across to Glen Doll, or over Tolmount to Callater, of over Cairn of Claise to Glen Shee.

Glen Shee (Sìth or fairy). The longest of the southern glens of Angus or Perth, Glen Shee via Glen Clunie formed the chief route in the old days for travellers walking over the Mounth from upper Deeside to the S. Many used it, and like the Cairn o' Mount it was notable in having a hospice at either side of the high crossing: the Spittal of Glen Shee and the Seann Spideal in Glen Clunie. The road across the Cairnwell is the highest public road in Scotland at about 670 m. For most of its way it follows the line taken by the old military road which was built from Blairgowrie to Grantown in 1750–54. Many people call this a Wade road, but General Wade left Scotland before the 1745 rising. The famous Devil's Elbow, a double bend on the Glen Shee side, has now been bypassed by a wide straight road built in 1972 and 1973.

At the Spittal of Glen Shee the road goes over a fine old stone bridge. The glen divides here, with the steep face of Ben Gulabin (*Goola*-bin) at the division. The E branch, Gleann Beag or little glen, leads towards Glen Clunie, becoming hemmed in by Creag Leacach, the Glas Maol and the hill of the Cairnwell which from here looks a

45. Lochnagar from the birch woods north of Crathie, in high summer.

46. The corrie of Lochnagar, above a fantastic pattern of frozen ice floes on the loch. Black Spout is the gully at upper centre, with Black Spout Pinnacle on its left.

47. *Opposite.* The magnificent cliffs of Creagan Lochnagar in February.

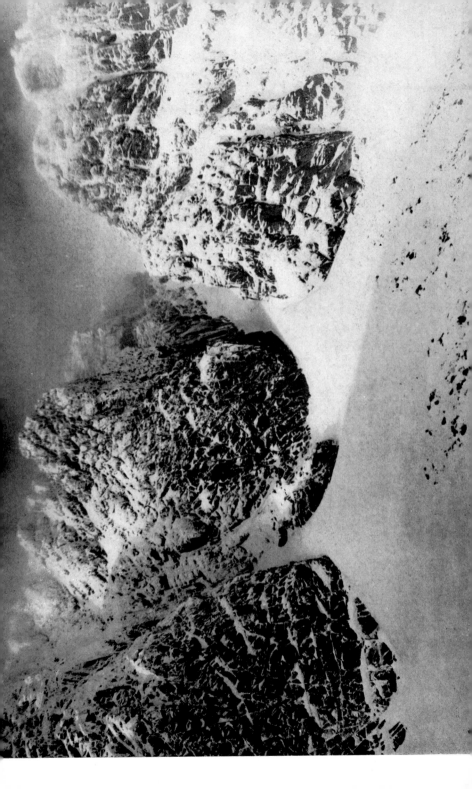

48. Blackface sheep on a hill farm on the bare high moors of upper Glen Esk, looking N to Tampie where the Fir Mounth crosses from Glen Tanar.

fine peak. The W branch, upper Glen Shee, itself divides 2 km up beside the Dalmunzie hotel. Its E sub-branch is green Gleann Tait-neach (Glan *Tat*nyach) or delightful valley, and its W one Glen Lochsie (Lòchsaidh or black river goddess). Gleann Taitneach runs, steep-sided and craggy, for 8 km up to Loch nan Eun, beyond which a pass at about 790 m leads into upper Glen Ey. In Glen Shee and all its side glens, the green hills, the rocky bluffs of varying colour from pink to black, the many fine big burns and the fertile grassy river flats give the scenery a distinctive character and charm.

About 8 km below the Spittal, Mount Blair rises to 744 m or 2441 ft, standing between Glen Shee and Glen Isla and being easily climbed from about 360 m on the road between them at 161646. An isolated hill, it gives very fine views of the lowlands to the S. The Forestry Commission have afforested much of the rolling moorland and smooth low heathery hills between here and Glen Isla and Glen Prosen to the E. Glen Shee you will find much more rocky, like the nearby hill country of Strath Ardle. There are no high hills in this countryside, but a great variety of interesting moorland and low hills, many of which carry small crags.

The ski grounds. The developed ski grounds and car parks lie at the head of Glen Clunie in Aberdeenshire. A chair lift runs in summer and winter from a big café, toilets and shop at 650 m at the roadside, up to about 900 m near the top of the Cairnwell hill. Two T-bar tows pull up skiers in winter further N on the Cairnwell, two more on the S side of Carn Aosda, one on the slope of Meall Odhar Beag opposite the café, and one further E on Meall Odhar Mor. You can also walk up Carn Aosda by a bulldozed road and by other tracks leading to the ski tows. Caterpillar tractors have scarred some hill-sides on these ski grounds and you will see tourists' litter as well as broken snow fencing and metal.

The Cairnwell 933 m (3059 ft), **Carn Aosda** 917 m (3003 ft) and **Carn a' Gheoidh** 975 m (3194 ft). These hills lie W of the Cairnwell road summit and can be easily climbed as they form a series of hill tops. The Cairnwell is pronounced The *Cairn*wal, and comes from An Càrn Bhalg or the hill of blisters. It gives a fine view down Glen Shee to lowland Scotland. To the W the huge basin of Coire Dìreach (Cor *Dyee*rich or perpendicular corrie) slopes steeply, with the broken rocks of Creag a' Choire Dhirich on the far side. From the Cairnwell a broad ridge runs round for 2 km N to the two stony bare summits of Carn Aosda, an erroneous map name as local people pronounce it like Caarn *Naish*. A fine-looking hill from upper Glen Clunie, Carn Aosda sends out a long ridge down the E side of the Baddoch.

Between Carn Aosda and the ridge to the Cairnwell, Loch Vrotachan lies at about 750 m in a fertile basin draining towards the Baddoch Burn, a fine loch for trout. You stroll easily along the broad ridge above Loch Vrotachan past the beautiful tarn of Loch a' Choire Dhirich among its rocky hillocks, and on to the tablelands beyond. Further on rises Carn a' Gheóidh (*Yoe*-ee) or hill of the goose, 3½ km from the top of the chair lift. Beyond again for 2 km is the 917 m peaked Carn Bhinnein (*Veen*in) or hill of the conical top, on whose craggy front of Creag Dallaig (724 m) a small rocky pinnacle sticks out, which you can climb easily from the neck behind it (*SMCJ* 10, 145). Two good routes off these hills are to drop down to the Spittal of Glen Shee by Gleann Taitneach, or down to Braemar by Glen Baddoch (from Badach or clumps). Carn Bhinnein stands 5 km from Dalmunzie hotel, and Carn a' Gheoidh 8 km from the A93 at the foot of Baddoch.

Glen Clunie. The fertile green ridge of the Strone (Sròn or nose) separates Baddoch from the stream of Uisge Bhruididh that runs into Clunie. Below here Glen Clunie opens out into a wide green valley, with heathery slopes on both sides running steeply up to high bare ridges over 750 m; it has something of the same open character as the Pass of Drumochter. In Glen Clunie (Gleann Cluanaidh or valley of a green plain), only one farm survives from what was once a big farming community in the 19th century, and no one now lives in the glen above Auchallater. Well down the glen, the beautifully made Fraser's Brig carries the old road which winds pleasantly down the W side to Braemar.

Glen Ey. Glen Ey (Glan *Ei*) drains a large tract of rolling hills stretching from near the head of Glen Baddoch to the Dee W of Braemar. A good cross-country walk on foot or ski goes from the Cairnwell café for 8 km over to Loch nan Eun (nan *Yain*) or loch of the birds, at about 785 m, where the common gulls nest, and then 5 km down to Altanour in Glen Ey. At Altanour (Alltan Odhar, Altan *Ow*er or dun streamlet), an isolated plantation of larch and spruce conceals a ruined, supposedly haunted shooting lodge at about 500 m. A road runs down Glen Ey from here, passing the weird upright rock of A' Chailleach (A *Chal*yach) or the old woman. Further on, Ey winds sinuously in beautiful dark pools through a grassy flat, and in the lower glen below Auchelie hurries faster through a fine long gorge fringed with trees. A small signpost and track lead off the road downhill to the Colonel's Bed, a rather damp recess by Ey side where John Farquharson of Inverey or the 'Black Colonel', who was a famous figure in the legends of old Deeside, lay hidden after the Battle of Killiecrankie. Further on, the road drops down through scattered birches to where Connie meets Ey, just below the fine Falls of Connie (*Cone*-ie). The road from Inverey up Glen Ey has a locked gate just S of the Knock house at 088888, 8 km below Altanour Lodge.

A number of high tops, described below, ring the head of Glen Ey. It makes a pleasant trip to climb all of them together, as they are connected by high cols where you lose little height; moreover a round trip like this gives you new scenery throughout the day.

An Socach   944 m (3073 ft). Local people call this Un *Sochk*ach, meaning the snout. An Socach is a long bare stony whaleback with two tops, the E one rising to 938 m and the slightly higher W top overlooking Loch nan Eun. A good walk or ski tour starts on Morrone above Braemar and goes 10 km to An Socach along the series of hills between Glen Ey and Glen Clunie, a route that nowhere drops below 700 m. An Socach rises only 4½ km from the top of the Cairnwell chair lift, and a third approach begins from a bulldozed road going up the N side of Baddoch to 103788. An Socach looks its best from Glen Ey where it throws out a bold northern spur at Creag an Fhuathais (Craik *Noo*ish); this towers strikingly above the Ey bridge 3½ km below Altanour.

Beinn Iutharn Mhor   1045 m (3424 ft). Below Altanour in Glen Ey, the wide grassy flats give one of the best views in the district. Beinn Iutharn Mhór (Pain *Yoo*-arn *Vore*) with its great bulging shoulders dominates the top of the glen. The 953 m rocky rounded Beinn Iutharn Bheag (Vick) lies across a corrie to the E, whereas the green 986 m Màm nan Càrn (Maam na *Gaarn*) or round hill of the stony hillsides, standing between the other two, blocks the head of that corrie. A good way to all three tops starts from Gleann Taitneach where a bulldozed road now runs up to the top of the glen below Creag Dallaig, from which you climb up to Loch nan Eun. Another walk goes from Glen Ey by a route that can also be varied to include An Socach, Beinn Iutharn and Carn Bhac. Apart from some peat hags on the cols, the walking is good on crisp heather and alpine mossy grassland with occasional sharp quartzite stones. Distance: from Dalmunzie Hotel to Beinn Iutharn Bheag 8½ km, back to Loch nan Eun via Beinn Iutharn Mhor and Mam nan Carn 13½, back to hotel 21 km or 13 miles, total ascent 880 m, time 6 hours. From Altanour to Beinn Iutharn Mhor 5 km, via Mam nan Carn to Beinn Iutharn Bheag 8½, back to Altanour 12½ km, total ascent 720 m, time 4 hours.

Carn Bhac 946 m (3098 ft). Càrn Bhac (Vachk) or hill of peat banks, is an unfrequented ridge which sends streams into Ey, Connie, Tilt and Bynack. It has three tops in a long line, Càrn a' Bhùtha (*Voo*-a or hill of the anthill shape) at 907 m, which was previously considered a 'top' over 3000 ft but has now been relegated below that height, then Carn Bhac at 920 m, and to the E the unnamed highest top. From the ruined croft that appears erroneously as Auchelie on the map but which local people always call Ach*ee*ree, a Land Rover track leads from the Glen Ey road up to 680 m on the spur N of Carn Creagach. You will find it an easy walk from the track end across to Carn Bhac, 5 km from Auchelie. Another bulldozed road runs up Glen Connie, and beyond climbs up Allt Cristie Beag (Criosda, *Cree*ostyee or swift) to 740 m in altitude, S of Càrn Liath. Two of the many ways of exploring these lonely hills begin at Bynack and at Fealar Lodge.

Glas Tulaichean 1051 m (3449 ft). Glas Tulaichean (Glass *Tool*ichan) or green hill, is a beautiful shapely top with two fine corries of steep grass and a little broken rock, and many long ridges which give grand walking on springy turf. A good route comes from Dalmunzie hotel at 370 m in lower Glen Lochsie, then up Allt Ghlinn Thaitneich to Glas Tulaichean (9 km, 690 m ascent), and back 7 km down upper Glen Lochsie to the hotel. You can also easily combine the ascents of Beinn Iutharn and Mam nan Carn with Glas Tulaichean. In Victorian times when deer stalking was in its heyday, a railway, which still exists, was built to take the shooters up to the now-ruined lodge in Glen Lochsie.

Càrn an Righ 1029 m (3377 ft) is locally called Carn *Ree*, meaning hill of the king. A great round green mass, it lies off the main chain of hills, so walkers seldom visit it. From Glen Ey you can reach it from Mam nan Carn (2½ km) but have to drop and re-gain 250 m of altitude on the way. A recommended route is to climb it along with Beinn Iutharn Mhor and Carn Bhac from the Glen Tilt path via Fealar Lodge. At the bridge over Allt a' Ghlinne Mhoir on the road to Enochdu, 3½ km S of Fealar, you are standing at about 600 m with Carn an Righ rising straight above (2 km). A more gradual route takes the path running up Allt a' Ghlinne Bhig to 780 m, between Mam nan Carn and Carn an Righ. At 550 m, Fealar Lodge is the highest occupied shooting lodge in the Highlands and one of the most remote. Fealar (Féith Làire, Fay-*laar*) or mare's bog-stream, lies in a beautiful, sheltered, fertile green basin surrounded by lonely bare hills. As well as coming in to Fealar by the long road over the hill from Enochdu, you can also reach it by a 3 km path from Tilt which starts NE of the bridge over Tarf, or else from Bynack by an old short-cut NW of the lodge to Allt Garbh Buidhe.

Climbing routes

Although plenty of rocks give interesting scrambling and even – at the head of Glen Callater and Caenlochan – some sporting climbs, the routes are mostly rather contrived as you can usually escape along grassy or heathery ground or broken rocks nearby. This is true even above Loch Kander at the biggest cliff in the area (200 m); the best buttress there carries many grassy ledges which make climbing indefinite. In winter, however, many corries give plenty of easy but sporting Grade I–II steep snow climbs with some ice, Loch Kander being the best place with good snow gullies and buttresses up to 200 m.

Further reading

T. Kyd   The Club at Mount Blair. *CCJ* 3, 210.

H. T. Munro   A summer night on the Glen Shee hills. *SMCJ* 5, 116.

H. T. Munro   The Cairnwell and Glas Thulachan groups (Guide Book articles). *SMCJ* 8, 167.

Anon. Miscellaneous notes. *SMCJ* 30, 187. Well-organised litter louts caught on Glas Maol.

11

Ballater and Creag an Dubh Loch

Craigendarroch	402 m, 365965
Morven	871 m, 377040
*Broad Cairn	998 m, 240815
*Cairn Bannoch	1012 m, 223825

Access
Buses from Aberdeen.

Accommodation
Ballater has hotels, pubs, boarding houses, a youth hostel, a caravan site, tearooms, a fish and chip shop, and a mountain rescue centre at the police station.

Remote occupied houses and bothies
See next Chapter. Also, many old crofts and other buildings which are partly in ruins give some shelter in upper Glen Gairn, at Morven Lodge, and elsewhere, A small, boulder bivouac lies in the screes below Central Slabs at Creag an Dubh Loch. Allan's Hut 256808 at 720 m was repaired in 1973.

General description
Standing at 200 m altitude in the Dee valley, Ballater (*Bal*ater) is the best centre for Creag an Dubh Loch and Lochnagar, and for exploring much of upper Deeside. The lower hills and big glens in the area are heavily wooded, with a fine variety of river and loch scenery. Here you will find a complex fascinating piece of country where a multitude of low hills and glens generally bars widespread views to the higher Cairngorms and allows only occasional tantalising glimpses of small parts of them. However, the view of Lochnagar is superb and largely uninterrupted, as it rises high above a wide skirt of lower ground on the Balmoral and Abergeldie moors. The valley head up from Loch Muick is one of the wilder places in the Highlands, with

the massive dark cliff of Creag an Dubh Loch rising far above, one of the most impressive rock walls in Britain.

Geology and landforms

Much of the district lies over hard pink granite, for instance on Craigendarroch, Pass of Ballater, the Creag Ghiubhais (*Yoo*is or pine), Geallaig, and Culblean with its disused granite quarries. A wide strip of fertile epidiorite runs through Glen Muick and Morven, patches of limestone occur in Glen Gairn, and the green knobbly Coyle at Glen Muick looks unusual due to its magnesium-rich serpentine. Craigendarroch and the Creag Ghiubhais are two great lumps of ice-smoothed granite, an even better place to see this being the little Cnoc Dubh N of Cambus o' May. Channels that were cut by big rivers roaring off melting glaciers bite especially deeply at the Burn o' Vat and the Sloc of Glen Carvie. The best example of a great mound of glacial drift is at Tom Mor on the flats below the Creag Ghiubhais.

Natural history

The moors support more flowering plants than in most parts of the region. You see few red deer except on the Glen Muick drainage and Corndavon, and the farmers cannot maintain high sheep stocks on even the lower moors, because of hard winters. The result is that pine, birch and juniper regenerate very well, the most spectacular examples being the dense birch scrub at Muir of Dinnet, and the pines coming in above Coilacriech (Keil a *Chreech*) where you will also see one of the highest tree lines in Scotland. A rich variety of pine grows at Coilacriech and the Creag Ghiubhais, and of birch in Glen Gairn, Glen Muick and Dinnet. The biggest alder wood in Deeside stands E of Ballater on the N bank of Dee, and parts of the basin around Morven Lodge are unique in Scotland for their extensive dense scrubs of moorland juniper. The very fine oak woods of Ballater and Dinnet contain a varied ground flora and hold interesting summer birds such as the wood warbler. In summer the wild lupins tinge the shingles of Dee a lovely soft blue colour. Down at Dinnet the two fertile, very shallow lochs (greatest depths 3 m at Davan and 4 m at Kinord) support many waterfowl and a few uncommon insects, and nearby there are interesting marshes for birds beside Ordie and in the varied country of little hills around Braeroddach Loch. On the varied and fertile moors of Glen Gairn and Morven you will find as great stocks of moorland wading birds, grouse and mountain hares as anywhere in Scotland.

Estates

Invercauld owns Gairnshiel, Corndavon, Geallaig and Glen Gairn. Dinnet Estate has Culblean, Morven Lodge and Muir of Dinnet. The Deskry side of Morven belongs to Tillypronie, and the E side of Muick to Glen Muick Estate. All these are grouse moors with hill sheep. The Water of Carvie and the ground NE of Coyles of Mick are owned by the Forestry Commission. The Dubh Loch area and Creag an Dubh Loch form part of a deer forest run by Balmoral Estate; ask permission at the Spittal of Glenmuick from August to October. Deer shooting also occurs on Corndavon and Glen Muick.

History

Loch Kinord is famous for its prehistoric crannog or artificial island, built for defence; it forms the smaller of the two islands in the N part of the loch. Michie, in his popular *Deeside Tales* and *Loch Kinnord*, and in his detailed *Records of Invercauld* gave much information on the history of the district. The ring of low hills around Braeroddach carries many ancient cairns, whose history he also described in *Loch Kinnord*. The old site of Ballater lay near the E end of the Pass, the new village being a planned one which started only in the 19th century on what was then a moor. Byron, who spent his boyhood in Aberdeen, lived in summer at Ballaterach (Bal*lat*rich), the farm on the S Deeside road opposite Cambus o' May (*Cam*as a *Mei*).

Walking ascents

Craigendarroch   402 m (1319 ft). The name comes from Creag an Daraich (Craigin*dar*ich) or rock of the oak wood. Ballater's special hill, Craigendarroch is one of the priceless places of Deeside. Although a small hill with only 200 m of an ascent, it towers steeply above the N side of the town, whose upper houses and school nestle among the fine woods at the foot. Craigendarroch protrudes as an isolated round mass of granite, with small crags and screes above Ballater and with ice-smoothed bedrock on its summit. The biggest oak wood in Deeside covers the lower one-third of the hill on its Ballater side, above which many self-sown birches and pines grow right to the top.

From Ballater's Square, you go 400 m up the Braemar road and turn right at Craigendarroch Road along to the foot of the hill

among some grand old oaks. A path zig-zags up the hill, with a
trend to the left. It continues leftwards, goes right around the hill
above the Pass of Ballater and comes back to where you now stand
by the path that slants up to your right. Roughly at the furthest
NE and SW points of this circular path, two other paths, which are
both signposted 'to the top', branch off uphill and meet at the summit.
A recommended way goes up the left track, then right round the N
side to the end, back up to the top and down by the SW end (3
km). The variety of woodland and other scenery is extraordinary and
the view very fine. On the N side of the road through the Pass of
Ballater rise some steep crags of reddish granite among scattered pine
trees, the grand rocks of Creag an t-Seabhaig (Craikan *Joe*-ick) or
precipice of the hawk (see p 241). In 1974 the fine beauty spot of the
Pass has been marred by massive dumping of earth and gravel.

Craig Coillich (from Creag Cailliche, Craig *Keil*ich) or old woman's
rock, rises steeply above Ballater's Dee bridge. A good path goes up
through a plantation of young pines to the 397 m top, the route taken
by competitors in the hill race at Ballater Highland Games. Craig
Coillich gives a better view of the Cairngorms than Craigendarroch,
but is nowhere nearly such an interesting hill.

Morven 871 m (2861 ft). The Gaelic name was Mór Bheinn
(*More* Vin) or big hill. From lower Deeside, Morven's massive
rounded bulk seems far bigger than the Cairngorms, and it towers
above the Howe o' Cromar to the E. It is the 'Morven of snow'
mentioned by Byron. Unlike the heathery hills around, Morven
looks much greener and more grassy, as it lies on the long strip of
fertile epidiorite rock which runs from Portsoy on the Moray Firth
through Glen Muick into Perthshire.

The direct way from Ballater starts up the Tullich Burn. A signpost at 376972, at the E end of the Pass of Ballater, points to the
right of way path slanting NE through a plantation up the side of
Creagan Riach; later the track goes through natural pines by the
Tullich Burn and heads past the ruined croft of Easter Morven to the
top of Morven (7½ km, 670 m ascent, time up 2¾ hours). For a nearby way up with the same distance and height, you can visit the old
churchyard of Tullich with its sculptured stones and then take the
path E of Crannach Hill. A third way from beside Ballater starts by
the path which climbs from Abergairn near the Bridge of Gairn over
the ridge of Craig of Prony. Round the W end of Peter's Hill it
continues as a Land Rover track coming from the W end of the rocks

in the Pass of Ballater, and goes on over Tom Garchory to the E-W path running S of Morven. On the Cromar side, the top of Morven stands only 6 km and 500 m in ascent from the highest point (370 m) on the public road from Logie Coldstone (*Cole*stin) to Boltenstone (*Bow*tinsteen or *Bow*teez), near some artificial lochs. This road takes a low line over the hills, cutting over to the E of the old drove road of Bad Chrasgaigh (*Chraski*e) which crosses the W side of Craig Glas over to Deskry side at Badnagoach. Another old drove track runs from the public road at 382092 by Deskry side SW for 11 km to Lary in Glen Gairn (180 m ascent). Still another you can find running from NW of Loch Davan to Tomnakiest E of Tullich.

From the top of Morven, you can descend easily westwards into the beautiful lonely green basin around Morven Lodge, and then down Glen Morven to the public road (7 km) at Lary (*Lairi*e) in Glen Gairn. Another interesting way down passes over Culblean to the extraordinary rocky gorge of Allt na Dabhaich (*Dav*ach), translated as the Burn o' Vat (7 km from Morven to public road). This takes you down to the Muir of Dinnet (Meer a *Denn*et, 'e' as in her) with its fine birch scrub and its pair of lovely lochs. Perhaps the finest way back is to walk westwards along the watershed to the big jubilee cairn on Mona *Gow*an (Ghobhainn or blacksmith) and beyond over Scraulac to the 551 m top of the public road over the Glas Choille (9 km). From this watershed, at first you look down NE into Deskry and over the fertile green grazing of the Bunzeach (*Boony*ach), now partly afforested, towards Strath Don. Later this route takes you past the unusual rocky gap at the Sloc (*Sloch*) of Glen Carvie. According to Grant's *Legends of the Braes o' Mar*, the old name was Sloc Cailliche after the supernatural old woman called Cailleach Bheathrach who bit out the Sloc with her teeth while trying to cut a way through for the water on the Dee side to flow N into Don! About 1 km W of the Sloc, beyond Mona Gowan, you look S down Glen Fenzie (Fionnaidh, *Feeng*ee or white one) to the birches of Gairnside. Glen Fenzie was an old short-cut for drovers going from Corgarff via Lary to Ballater.

Glen Gairn. One of the longest glens in the Cairngorms from its source SW of Ben Avon to its exit at Ballater, Glen Gairn is beautiful, varied, and contains many fine lower hills, moors and scrubby woods rich in wildlife. It now looks sadly depopulated, and the many ruins of old farms and shielings give the glen some of its lonely atmosphere. Narrow in its lower reaches, with many birch woods, it widens higher up into a broad valley among bare open moors and gently-sloping far hills. These rise up to the 829 m great brown heathery whaleback of A' Bhó Dhonn (A Voe *Gown*) or the Brown Cow, with no 'Hill' as on the map, and locally called the Broon Coo.

The old drove road called the Glas Choille (*Glass* Choll or green wood), now a public road, runs from Gairnshiel over the Shenval hill to Strath Don. A continuation of it to the S of Gairnshiel, the Sròn Ghearraig (Stron *Yarik*, short nose), goes from Braenaloin up the nose and over the top to Crathie. On the Crathie side of the Sron Ghearraig pass you will see at the roadside, just above where the side road breaks off to Corndavon, Meggie MacAndrew's Cairn, where this old woman died in a snowstorm. Sheep drovers still used the route from Tomintoul past Loch Builg to Corndavon and Crathie as recently as the early 20th century, often stopping for the night at Blairglass farm. Other fine old drove roads passing from upper Gairn to Don are the Camock from Gairn at Easter Sleach to the N over Tom Odhar to the A939 W of Corgarff (8 km, 290 m climb), and the Ca from Gairn at Tullochmacarrick to Delavine and Corgarff (8 km, 270 m climb). From near the highest point on the Sron Ghearraig, a Land Rover climbs up to the 743 m top of Geallaig (*Gyaalik*, no 'Hill' as on the maps), a fine viewpoint and good skiing hill in deep snow. Its SE slopes, which now support dense natural young pine woods, make an interesting descent to Coilacriech and Bridge of Gairn.

Glen Muick. This fine glen, called Glan *Mek* ('e' as in her) is narrow and wooded with old birch and young plantations lower down. Beyond the fine fall at the Linn of Muick, where a salmon ladder allows fish to get up, it becomes wider and barer. A public road runs up the E side to a car park, picnic place and information centre just before the Spittal of Glenmuick at 411 m. Walkers and cyclists, but not cars, are permitted beyond here. In ancient times, the Spittal was a hospice for travellers crossing the Capel Mount (p 265). Beside the keeper's house at the Spittal, the rough road to Allt na Giubhsaich and Lochnagar turns sharply right. Straight ahead, a dirt road continues for 1½ km to Loch Muick. On the way to the loch you will see a signpost pointing left to the Capel Mount over to Clova, an old path which is now a bulldozed road.

Ahead, another bulldozed road which obliterated yet another fine old path now skirts along the lochside through fine groves of birch, crosses the Black Burn, and zig-zags up the 'Streak of Lightning' to the plateau beyond. It then runs along the plateau, in places almost on the edge of the steep drop to Loch Muick. This road goes over the col S of Corrie Chash, beside Allan's Hut at $7\frac{1}{2}$ km from the Spittal of Glenmuick; beyond, a path continues, dropping S down the Style Burn to Bachnagairn. However, instead of using this bulldozed road, a better way for the walker is to take the old path that runs from the Black Burn footbridge along the lochside. At the top of the loch, 6 km from the car park at the Spittal, one branch turns round and over a footbridge to Glas Allt Shiel. The other goes in a long slanting climb up the Diagonal Path to meet the bulldozed road on the plateau.

Loch Muick at 400 m is a fine sheet of water lying in a narrow trench between the hills. Steep slopes with some crags rise from the lochside to the plateaux above, and in this respect it has something of the character of Gaick. In places, the ravines and screes run right into the water. Loch Muick consists of a flat-bottomed basin with water up to 78 m deep, held back at its N end by a barrier of glacial gravelly drift which is topped by a deep blanket of peat. Covering 220 ha, $3\frac{1}{2}$ km long and up to $\frac{4}{5}$ km wide, with an average width about $\frac{2}{3}$ km, Loch Muick excels as the biggest loch of the Cairngorms and the Mounth, and also one of the most beautiful ones.

Glas Allt Shiel, a private locked lodge 4 km from Allt na Giubhsaich and 6 km ($1\frac{1}{4}$ hours) from the car park at the Spittal, was built by Queen Victoria in 1869. It is sheltered by a pine plantation, with a very high stone wall that kept out the deer when the trees were young. The Shiel stands on ground thrown into the loch by the Glas Allt or green burn which bursts tempestuously from a ravine behind. Queen Victoria used to like to spend a night or two here in October, preferably when the hills were white with the first snow of winter. Glas Allt Shiel has undoubtedly one of the most spectacular situations of any lodge in the Highlands. From the Shiel a private road runs all the way down the W side of Glen Muick past Inchnabobart (Insh-na-boe-bart) to the public road near Birkhall.

The Dubh Loch. To the W of Glas Allt Shiel a well made path goes along the lochside and in 3 km and 1 hour you climb about 240 m to the Dubh Loch at 638 m, from which the burn descends in a series of rocky shelves and pools. As you ascend this path, you pass the Stulan (Steallan, *Styoo*lan) or little cataract, a little stream that tumbles down from the hidden Loch Buidhe, lying high above and behind a precipitous face to the N. On the S side, beyond some high clumps of birch, jagged spurs, bluffs and slabs lead up to the stony cone of Broad Cairn, but the finest feature by far stands NW of Broad Cairn where a huge slabby wall of granite cliff rears abruptly above the Dubh Loch. Dubh Loch (*Doo* Loch) or black loch is a good name, as this high NE-facing wall keeps out much of the sun from the loch. You can easily imagine the scene when Queen Victoria's son, Duke of Edinburgh, once swam out into the dark loch after a wounded stag and killed it in the cold water.

The great wall above the loch is Creag an Dubh Loch or, as local folk call it, the Craigs o' the Doo Loch; hence the correct Gaelic spelling should perhaps be Creagan Dubh Loch. With a vertical height of 270 m or 900 ft at one point, and most of the 1½ km line of cliff around 200 m, here stands the highest continuous rock face in the Cairngorms and one of the highest in Britain. The N slope above the Dubh Loch also looks striking, with a big sunny wall of undercut slabs called Eagle's Rock lying to the SW of a 1051 m top, and a fine waterfall leading to the plateau of Am Monadh Geal or the White Mounth behind. The W half of Creag an Dubh Loch is split by the wide scree shoot of Central Gully, formerly called the Black Spout locally. It slants up to the plateau and for a walker makes a fine approach to the top, with no difficulty if you are used to crossing the bouldery screes so common in the Cairngorms. The right-hand side of the gully consists of a spectacular wall of steep, smooth and slabby rock averaging 180 m high, where some of the hardest climbs have been pioneered in the last decade.

Cairn Bannoch 1012 m (3314 ft) and **Broad Cairn** 998 m (3268 ft). From the Dubh Loch you can walk easily into the upper basin of Coire Uilleim Mhóir or muckle Willie's corrie which lies to the W of the big cliffs. A gentle climb leads S on to the green top of Cairn Bannoch, 2½ km from the E end of the Dubh Loch (370 m ascent, 1¼ hours), whose name comes from Càrn Beannach (*Byann*ach) or peaked hill. Once there, you are on a plateau of crisp herbage leading easily ⅘ km W to the 1000 m Fafernie (Fi*ferni*e), or ESE for 2 km to Broad Cairn past the 983 m top above the cliffs of Creag an Dubh Loch. This high well-vegetated plateau, with excellent walking on springy turf, runs for miles SW to Glas Maol and SE to the hills on the S side of Glen Doll.

Broad Cairn, probably a corruption of Càrn Bràghaid or hill of upland, is a heathery, stony, granite hill, strikingly different from the green grassier hills of Callater and Glen Doll on the more fertile schists away to the W and S. From its conical summit, the easiest way back goes down its E shoulder, where you come on a Land Rover track at 860 m leading down to the other bulldozed roads beside Allan's Hut (p 236), 2 km from the summit.

The Coyles of Muick. The 7th Series OS map errs here, as local people use the 'Coyles (*Keils*) of Muick' to refer to the whole range of hills so obvious from Ballater. The highest is simply the Coyle (601 m), a curious peak with knobbly bosses of serpentine and a dark green vegetation. The middle hill in the view from Ballater forms the steep dome of Craig of Loinmuie (Lon*moo*ee), the third one being Meall Dubh (Myal *Doo*). A good way to the Coyle starts from upper Glen Muick, where you can easily climb for $2\frac{1}{2}$ km up from the metal bridge at 328891. It makes a fine walk to go the 4 km along the whole hill range, finishing on Creag Phiobaidh (*Fee*pee) at the E entrance to Glen Girnock (*Ger*nak, 'e' as in her). Alternative ways up are by the Land Rover track passing just W of Loch Ullachie (*Yoo*lachee) to the top of the ridge, or by the forest road going from the metal road bridge at 346936 near Birkhall straight up the burnside to the top of the wood near Meall Dubh.

Cairn Leuchan. The old Mounth Road of Mount Keen starts at the memorial at about 210 m beside the Bridge of Muick near Ballater and runs past Ballintober (no cars) and up the N slope of Cairn Leuchan (*Loo*chan) on the E side of Glen Muick. On Cairn Leuchan you are on the edge of a huge sweep of rolling peaty high moorland and whalebacked hills. A bulldozed road goes S downhill from Cairn Leuchan to cross the headwaters of Tanar and climb again to 680 m on Hare Cairn, where it is merely a stroll E to Mount Keen or S into Glen Mark. Another bulldozed road heads SW of Cairn Leuchan along the watershed almost on to Fasheilach and down Druim Cholzie to the burn SW of the Linn of Muick.

Climbing routes

Creag an Dubh Loch forms the highest and longest continuous wall of rock within the area described in this book (see p 237). This cold cliff faces NE and the granite falls steep and smooth; hence the climbing is mostly hard and the place good for winter ascents. In recent years it and the Loch Avon cliffs have become the main centres for exploration of new hard summer rock climbs. It now has a Climbers' Guide largely to itself (Cairngorms Vol 5, by A. F. Fyffe). Yet the first pioneer, G. R. Symmers, came here only in the late 1920s. J. H. B. Bell next climbed the fine VD route of Hanging

Garden, and the Labyrinth, and then, as on Lochnagar, came a great wave of new ascents starting in the early 50s.

The extremely steep western section is separated from the highest wall of cliff by the wide boulder-filled Central Gully, which slants back at an angle and makes an easy route to the plateau, providing magnificent views of the cliffs. The high precipice to its left carries an impressive curving black slit going from top to bottom, the Labyrinth Groove, which offers a very hard winter route (Grade V). To its left again and high up lies an obvious hanging green hollow called the Hanging Garden, with the vegetated Broad Terrace leading from it across and then slanting down to the foot of South-East Gully to its left. Labyrinth Edge (only VD) is a rather vegetated summer climb up the steep edge to the right of Labyrinth Groove, but makes a grand Grade IV winter climb. Above Broad Terrace towers the very steep Broad Terrace Wall, one of the most imposing cliffs in the Cairngorms. Culloden (hard VS), climbed in July 1967 by A. D. Barley and R. R. Barley from Manchester University, went up a series of overhangs in the centre of the face and excels as an outstanding hard ascent which has repulsed several second attempts. The Sword of Damocles (VS and A3) is a superb corner line on the left of this wall.

Further to the W of Labyrinth Edge, towards Central Gully, stretches a huge wall of smooth slabs called the Central Slabs. This wall was at last climbed in 1964 and later by several other very hard routes (VS) such as Dinosaur and The Blue Max. Dinosaur, which was climbed in 1964 by J. W. Stenhouse and B. T. Lawrie, starts at the lowest slabs and goes up by slabs and cracks on fine clean rock to the last pitch of Labyrinth Edge. The ascent of The Blue Max in September 1967 by B. W. Robertson, A. Fyffe and W. T. Wilkins forced a more direct line up the slabs, starting just to the right of Dinosaur. Another route here, the VS Dragon Slayer which was climbed in 1972, passes up a stepped corner system just to the right of and at a few places actually on The Blue Max, taking a central line through the main overlap. The most popular climbs now are Black Mamba (VS) to the right of Dragon Slayer, The Blue Max, and a combination of the lower half of Dinosaur with the top half of Pink Elephant (VS), so called from the pink streak and groove which the lower part of the route follows, on the left of the Central Slabs.

To the W of Central Gully and high on the uppermost cliffs rises the short but fine climb of Sabre Edge (S). Vertigo Wall (VS) goes up the bigger and wider 120 m wall rising from further down Central Gully; ascended first in October 1954 by T. W. Patey, G. McLeod and A. Will, it was then the hardest route in the Cairngorms and a major psychological step towards tackling the harder slabs below. A later big problem on this upper part of the Central Gully Wall was solved with the ascent in 1965 of The Giant (VS and A2), which starts about 30 m down Central Gully from Vertigo Wall and goes up a prominent series of corner grooves and cracks. Between Vertigo Wall and The Giant, another excellent hard modern-type climb which has become popular is the VS Goliath.

The huge overlapping slabs rising above the bottom of Central Gully were first climbed in a grand pioneering lead by R. W. P. Barclay and W. D. Brooker in 1958, up the superb clean rock of the VS Waterkelpie Wall, which starts from the lowest rocks to the right of the foot of Central Gully and swerves intricately up to the cliff top. The outstanding breakthrough of the 50s was The Mousetrap by J. R. Marshall, R. Marshall and R. Anderson in November 1959, a VS and exposed route with entirely free climbing from the foot of Central Gully directly to the plateau. No other comparable new route was done on the cliff till 1964, since when several magnificent climbs have been made on the Central Gully Slabs. In 1964, a new way was forced up the VS Waterkelpie Direct, which takes a straighter line up to the original upper part of Waterkelpie Wall. There now exist a number of other VS routes, some of them being among the hardest in the Cairngorms; the best climbs are King Rat and Mousetrap (both popular), and the more recent fine ascent of The Predator (which may well become popular). Indeed Mousetrap still remains one of the best in the whole massif; sustained but at no point extremely hard, it goes right to the top of the cliff on grand rock. Of these routes, Waterkelpie Direct starts directly below the prominent Red Wall high up the face, and King Rat (also A2) goes up a series of cracks to its left; Mousetrap lies further left again. These all make direct routes which follow very good lines. Creag an Dubh Loch has become justly famed for its many excellent hard rock climbs on clean, sound, steep granite up a massive face.

On the opposite side of the Dubh Loch, Eagle's Rock is a steep slabby mass of granite. Ignored in earlier years, it nevertheless sports 150 m of fine, clean, S-facing rock. In 1967 several hard summer routes (mostly VS) were made here, pioneered mainly by J. McArtney and D. Duncan (SMCJ 29, 65), and a few more have

49.   Ski touring in January above the Howe o' Cromar, with Mount Keen, the Braid Cairn (further left), Dee valley and Culblean (right).

50. Coming up the last pitch of the Crocodile, on the pink granite of the Longhaven sea cliffs.

51.   The Moine Mhor—the Great Moss. Looking eastwards to Braeriach, Ben Macdui, Cairn Toul.

52.   Unbroken snow in March on the beautiful horseshoe-shaped Fiorm Choire of the Glas Maol.

been added since. Winter climbing has also begun, with the Grade III routes of Lethargy in 1970 up the ice of the watercourse, and in 1971 on Spectrum up the line of corners and grooves immediately to the right of the waterfall. As the wall faces S it thaws early, but in hard frost gives excellent ice climbing.

On the N side of the Pass of Ballater, Creag an t-Seabhaig offers a fine practice ground. There are about 20 routes from 12 to 36 m high, of all grades of difficulty, on dry, rough, pink granite. The crag faces S above the road through the pass and is very sheltered behind the bulk of Craigendarroch to the S and among pine trees growing all around. A colony of noisy jackdaws shares the rock with you. Other small cliffs in the area lie more distant, but some accessible crags give short climbs at the old granite quarries W of Cambus o' May and at the Burn o' Vat.

Further reading

A. Bremner   The Vat (Burn of the Vat). *CCJ* 8, 85.

G. Duncan   The Broad Cairn range (Guide Book article). *SMCJ* 8, 49.

J. A. Parker   Creag an Dubh Loch. *SMCJ* 15, 120.

J. McCross   Some walks from Ballater. *Deeside Fld* 3, 10.

D. Mercer   Waterkelpie Direct. *ECJ* 3, 197.

D. Bathgate   Explanation Giant. *SMCJ* 28, 190.

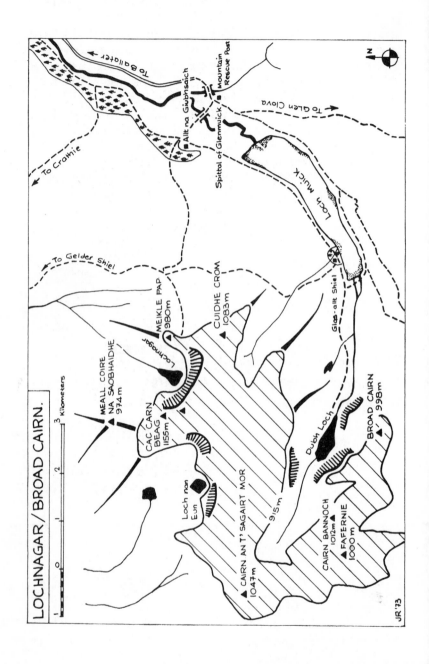

LOCHNAGAR / BROAD CAIRN.

0   1   2   3 Kilometers

N

To Ballater →

To Crathie

To Gelder Shiel

Allt na Giubhsaich

Mountain Rescue Post

Spittal of Glenmuick

To Glen Clova →

Loch Muick

Glas-allt Shiel

MEALL COIRE NA SAOBHAIDHE 974m

Lochnagar

MEIKLE PAP 980m

CUIDHE CROM 1083m

CAC CARN BEAG 1155m

Loch nan Eun

CAIRN AN T' SAGAIRT MOR 1047m

915m

Dubh Loch

CAIRN BANNOCH 1012m

FAFERNIE 1000 m

BROAD CAIRN 998m

JR '73

12

Dark Lochnagar

---

*Lochnagar	1155 m, 244862
*Carn a' Choire Bhoidheach	1110 m, 227845
*Carn an t-Sagairt Mor	1047 m, 207845
The Meikle Pap	980 m, 260860

Access

There are buses from Aberdeen to Ballater, Crathie and Braemar. Public roads go to Spittal of Glenmuick, to Balmoral village S of Crathie, Invercauld Bridge, and Auchallater in Glen Clunie.

Accommodation and other facilities

See Chapters 9 and 13.

Remote occupied houses

Spittal of Glenmuick 307850, Moulzie 283779, Danzig Shiel (locally called Garbh Allt or Garrawalt Shiel) 200903, Auchallater 156882, Bovaglie 302920.

Bothies and shelters

See also p 230. Gelder Shiel 257900 with bunks, open all year. Allt na Giubhsaich 298857 with bunks, locked private hut of Aberdeen University, enquiries to Department of Physical Education, Butchart Recreation Centre, Old Aberdeen. Bivouac 252864 under boulder in NE corrie, holds 3.

General description

One of the grandest hills in Scotland, Lochnagar at once surpasses all other hills in the North East for its variety and its fine setting. Look at it from E of Ballater on a spring day, or from the Old Bridge of Dee E of Braemar. It flaunts far above a complicated mass of lower hills and wooded slopes and valleys. It has so many tops that it forms a small hill range rather than a single big hill. Behind its Ballater face, the vast plateau of the White Mounth stretches for miles to the W and S. It runs out to the great walls of granite above

Dubh Loch and the fine snowy Coire Loch nan Eun above the grand pine forest of Ballochbuie. Best of all, the great cliffs of the cold granite wall in its NE corrie sparkle with snow and ice far into the spring.

Geology and landforms
The rock is a greyish-pink granite; a good fresh exposure after a rock fall lies on the Douglas Gully side of Eagle Ridge in the NE corrie. On the lower hills of Balmoral Forest to the N of Lochnagar, granite boulders are unusually abundant for such low altitudes. The ravine of Clais Rathadan on the way up from Allt na Giubhsaich is a very good example of a dry defile once cut by a powerful glacial meltwater river. Snow occasionally lies all the year round on the White Mounth and on Carn an t-Sagairt but not in most years. Yet an old legend says

> When ye White Mounth frae snow is clear
> Ye day of doom is drawing near

suggesting a colder climate than today.

Natural history
Because of the influence of the schist around the main mass of Lochnagar granite, the hill has a more fertile soil than ground on the pure granite of the Cairngorms. Vegetation is slightly richer, and hill birds and mammals more abundant. Some rare arctic-alpine plants grow on damp shady places in the two N-facing corries, such as blue sow thistle, Highland cudweed and brook saxifrage, and rare sedges on the summit plateau. Big tracts of high alpine grassland and gravelly barrens occur and the mountain azalea thrives more commonly here than on most Scottish hills, its pink flowers making a bright show in June on bare exposed ground. Lochnagar is one of the best hills in Scotland for abundance of ptarmigan, which often perch and take off on song flights from pinnacles on the buttresses.

Ballochbuie Forest contains the largest continuous block of very old pines in the Highlands; Abernethy covers a bigger area but consists mostly of much younger trees, many of which were planted. Unlike the natural forests of Rothiemurchus, Glen More and Abernethy of Spey, it has not been felled in the last 150 years and no big fire has burned in this century. However, the forest has been slowly dying because red deer have eaten all young seedlings for the last century. Fortunately it is not too late, as Balmoral Estate have fenced off three large areas where pines are already regenerating very quickly within a few years; you will see these deer fences on the hillside at the NW corner, to the W of Craig Doin, and a big tract S of the woods of Garmaddie.

Estates

Most of Lochnagar belongs to Balmoral Estate (Bul*more*-il). Invercauld has the Callater side all the way up to Carn an t-Sagairt Mor. The SE and E parts around Glas Allt and from Cuidhe Crom to Conachcraig and Loch Muick are on Abergeldie Estate, for long tenanted by Balmoral.

History

Many artists have been fascinated by the beautiful shapes of Lochnagar, like G. F. Robson who, in his *Scenery of the Grampian Mountains* (1814), gave three etchings of it, and John Phillip who painted Lochnagar as a background in his portrait of the Prince Consort. More famous is Byron's verse, later set to music and ending with the stirring lines

> England! thy beauties are tame and domestic
>> To one who has roved o'er the mountains afar:
> Oh for the crags that are wild and majestic!
>> The steep frowning glories of dark Lochnagar!

When a boy of 15, Byron climbed Lochnagar from Invercauld by the Garbh Allt, accompanied by a gillie (see 'Byron and Deeside: the facts and the legends' by J. D. Symon (1924). *Deeside Fld* 2). Queen Victoria, who loved the hills of upper Deeside, often wrote about Lochnagar in her *Leaves from the Journal of our Life in the Highlands,* and in 1878 she bought Ballochbuie Forest which had been about to be felled. She commemorated its saving by building a cairn on Craig Doin (pronounced Dein) overlooking the beautiful forest, with an inscription recording the purchase and ending 'The Bonniest Plaid in Scotland', from the old legend that McGregor, the last laird of Ballochbuie, had sold it to Farquharson of Invercauld for a tartan plaid. She also built curious cairns on several other low hills between Ballochbuie and Crathie in memory of members of her family, the biggest being the large pyramid to Prince Albert on Creag Lurachain S of Crathie. The track at the head of Feith Laoigh to the W of Gelder Shiel goes to the Prince's Stone, which marks the spot where the Prince Consort spent a night in the open. In those days, when most people spoke Gaelic on upper Deeside, Gelder Shiel was called Ruigh na Ban-rìgh or the shiel of the Queen. Victoria fostered Highland piping at Balmoral, and the tradition lived, as some of the finest pibroch pipers of Scotland in the last few decades have been Balmoral deer stalkers.

Names

The name Lochnagar (Lochna*gaar*, 'o' as in telephoned) properly belongs to the small loch at the foot of the NE corrie, which is marked L. Garr in the map in Blaeu's *Atlas* (1654). A little to the S of L. Garr, the Atlas shows a hill Ben Chichnes. The same name in the forms Benchichins or Binchinnan appears in other early accounts, referring to the whole range between Aberdeenshire and Angus. Some have thought it an English corruption of the Gaelic Beinn Chìochan or hill of little paps. This tallies with the names the Meikle Pap and the Little Pap which still survive. In 1771, Pennant mentions Laghin y gair, and much later Byron wrote his famous poem Lachin y Gair. The name Lochnagar comes from Lochan na Gàire or the tarn of the noisy sound, probably referring to the wind rushing among the crags. Some names of individual tops are confusing on the map, which gives Cac Càrn Beag or little shit cairn for the summit, and Cac Càrn Mór or big shit cairn for the 1150 m top on the plateau. Local people, however, called the summit simply the Ca Càrn, the Ca Càrn Beag being the little point to the WNW at 241863, so prominent in the view from Ballater or Crathie. The big plateau to the SW was called Am Monadh Geal (Um Monna G*yal*) or the White Mounth (pronounced Munth). Ballochbuie Forest probably got its name from the old drove road which went up the forest, next over An Slugan to Callater, and then SW up Allt a' Bhealaich Bhuidhe or burn of the yellow pass, and so to upper Glen Clunie.

Walking ascents to Lochnagar

The usual route from Ballater starts at the Spittal of Glen Muick and from Braemar at Loch Callater, but to see the hill best you should climb one way and go down the other. Time: from Allt na Giubhsaich to the summit and down to Loch Callater, 6 hours by a path all the way. Balmoral Estate allows free access to the top by either of these routes, although neither is a right of way.

From Glen Muick. For roads up Glen Muick, see p 235. A new car park and picnic area lie just NE of the Spittal of Glenmuick (411 m). From the car park a rough private road goes 1½ km NW to

Allt na Giubhsaich, beside a small shooting lodge in a plantation.
Distance: from Allt na Giubhsaich to summit $7\frac{1}{2}$ km or $4\frac{1}{2}$ miles,
total ascent 800 m or 2600 ft, time up 3 hours. The name here comes
from the nearby burn of Allt na Giùbhsaich (Alt na *Gyoo*sich) or
stream of the pine wood. The Lochnagar path starts at the bridge over
the burn and goes up its N bank. A bulldozed road runs from the
lodge itself up the S bank and later crosses to the N bank on the line
of the old path. From here you look up to the bouldery cone of
Cìoch Bheag (Kee-ich *Vick*) or Little Pap which reaches 956 m. To
the right it leads on to the big flat mass of Cuidhe Crom (Coo-ee
Crome) or crooked wreath, named after a snow field which lies late
into the summer on the steep grassy face N of the 1083 m top. Further
to the right rises the prominent big cone of Cìoch Mhór (Kee-ich
Vore) or Meikle Pap. The new road curves above the curious dry
gorge of Clais Rathadan (*Rat*-an) and then continues as a path to a
col at 678 m, where you look down Glen Gelder and over to Ben
Avon. Here another path goes N to Gelder and the Lochnagar track
turns W uphill. To the E of this junction a short climb takes you up
to the fine 865 m viewpoint at the S end of the rounded hill mass of
Conachcraig (*Conna*-chraik), meaning combination of rocks.

The Lochnagar path, now much eroded, heads uphill towards the
gap between the Meikle Pap and Cuidhe Crom, passing on the left
the beautiful spring of the Foxes' Well. Just before the gap ahead,
the path starts to zig-zag leftwards up a steeper slope called the
Ladder. However, you should make a detour here to the gap or even
better up to the Meikle Pap at 980 m, so as to see the magnificent
crescent of crags in the NE corrie at its best, with the dark Lochnagar
far below. You can walk horizontally back along the slope from the gap
to regain the zig-zag path of the Ladder, and so climb up to the
plateau above. The route continues a little back from the cliff top
past the 1045 m col at the Red Spout, a wide open scoop of reddish
gravel where you can easily descend to the loch in summer. The
path now rises to the higher plateau of Cac Carn Mor at a cairn on a
small tor at 1150 m, where the path to Callater comes in from the
left. On the way along the high plateau just before Cac Carn Mor,
you will enjoy diverging to the right, to wander along the cliff top.
The plateau projects out in a few places which give magnificent views
down and along the cliffs on either side. The old name for these
grand cliffs was Creagan (*Craik*an) Lochan na Gàire, meaning crags
of Lochnagar. You look across to the Black Spout, largest gully in the

corrie, which carries a snow cornice in spring but in summer becomes an easy wide shoot of scree. At their highest the cliffs fall 210 m, and screes run steeply below to the loch at about 785 m or 2575 ft.

From the cairn at Cac Carn Mor a small dip follows to the head of the Black Spout and then a short stroll over flattish ground up to the 1155 m (3789 ft) summit at Cac Carn Beag, which protrudes as a great mass of granite weathered into gigantic blocks. On a flat slab close to the highest point stands the indicator built by the Cairngorm Club in 1924. It shows in the N the Caithness hills, in the E Girdleness Lighthouse at Aberdeen harbour, in the W Ben Nevis (with binoculars you can easily see the Great Tower on Tower Ridge), and in the S Ben Lomond, the Pentlands and Lammermuirs, and Cheviot on the English border 174 km or 108 miles away.

From Callater. Distance: from Loch Callater to the summit 10 km or 6 miles, total ascent 760 m or 2500 ft, time up 3¼ hours. You can walk or cycle the 5 km on the private road up to Loch Callater (see p 220). The Lochnagar path starts up the hillside just before the uninhabited lodge beside Loch Callater at about 500 m, and then slants along Creag an Loch, with attractive views down to Loch Callater and the fine corries higher up. (The crags shown on the 1 inch map to the SE of Meall an t-Slugain do not exist. This was probably an error of location for the small broken rocks just NW of the Lochnagar track, at the very head of Feindallacher glen, which do not appear on the map. Also, Creag an Loch is the hill at 193845 near the path, not the hillside 1 km to the NW as shown on the 7th Series map.) From the neck between Creag an Loch and the 1047 m (3430 ft) Càrn an t-Sagairt Mór (Carn *Tag*art *More*) or big hill of the priest, the path slants uphill along the S side of the rounded Carn an t-Sagairt Mor and then drops slightly into the green basin at the headwaters of Allt an Dubh Loch. You now climb easily on to the plateau of Am Monadh Geal (the White Mounth) above 1000 m, and a stroll just N of here takes you to the 1093 m point of the Stuic, commonly called the *Stoo*ee. This rocky buttress almost divides into two parts the wide western Coire Loch nan Eun (nan *Yain*) or corrie of the loch of the birds. To the S of the path here rises the 1110 m Carn a' Choire Bhoidheach, highest point of the White Mounth. You now continue along the grand high plateau and finally climb 100 m to Cac Carn Mor. There you should go E to the cliffs to enjoy the magnificent view which comes suddenly and contrasts with the long walk over the flattish plateau.

Other routes. Allt na Giubhsaich and Callater are tourist routes with good paths. Other routes described below make finer ascents, though they lack paths in places and thus are suitable only for those with more experience; ask for permission from Balmoral Estate or the keepers, as deer stalking may be in progress. For courtesy, you should also avoid these other routes when the Queen is on holiday at Balmoral, usually from mid August to the end of September.

From Glas Allt. Distance: from car park at the Spittal of Glenmuick to Glas Allt Shiel 6 km, to summit 11 km, ascent 780 m. One of the best routes to Lochnagar climbs by the path that zig-zags up the Glas Allt or green burn behind the locked lodge at Glas Allt Shiel (p 236). Giving grand views, it takes you up a fine steep gorge with broken rocks where Glas Allt thunders down in fine falls towards dark Loch Muick. You now come out on a peaty plateau at 600 m; $\frac{1}{2}$ km beyond, a path turns right, across the burn, and leads above the Monelpie Moss to meet the Allt na Giubhsaich path between the Meikle Pap and Conachcraig. Your path to Lochnagar goes between the Little Pap and Creag a' Ghlais Uillt straight up Glas Allt to 960 m, becoming indistinct above where the burn forks. If you slant up to the right above the right fork, you come to the cliff top at the Red Spout.

From Ballochbuie. Distance: from Bridge of Dee to the top by Blackshiel Burn $8\frac{1}{2}$ km (8 from suspension bridge) with ascent of 840 m, by Carn an t-Sagairt Beag and the Stuic 11 km. One of the most varied approaches comes by Ballochbuie Forest. From the W end of the Invercauld Bridge at 185910 a private road runs past the S end of the Old Bridge of Dee to a cross roads at 188905. Go straight across, and then straight across the next cross roads at 194899 by a road that takes you to the Falls of Garbh Allt (*Garra*-wolt) or rough burn. These forest roads, which lead through beautiful natural pine forest, were carefully made in Victorian times; they contrast sadly with the ugly bulldozed roads now being torn out on the hills. The special character of Ballochbuie, which makes it the finest although not the largest area of natural pine wood in Scotland, lies in its many glens and shoulders, some quite steep, where the carpet of pines rises up in places on to the hill crags themselves. Only when you walk right through it do you become fully aware of the rich variety of the forest and its seemingly greater size.

You can also reach the Falls of Garbh Allt from a white suspension footbridge (private and sometimes locked, ask for permission) beside the main road. On the S side of the bridge you take the right fork, and then after ⅓ km turn left; after another ½ km, go straight over at the cross roads at 199900 by the road running uphill beside the rushing Garbh Allt. An iron bridge spans the Falls of Garbh Allt. Here you will enjoy a wonderful view N down the roaring stream, framed by pine forest, to the Invercauld flats of Dee and beyond to snowy Beinn a' Bhuird.

From the Falls, which you reach by a path diverging slightly from the road, go back to the road and up it for a short distance to 197895. Here a new bulldozed road starts uphill to the left, snaking far up the Feindallacher (Feith an t-Salachair, Fain*dall*acher) to about 600 m, near where Allt a' Choire Dhuibh flows in. From there you climb easily by a path running up the Smuggler's Shank to 930 m, and then breast the shoulder between the two burns on to the 1044 m Carn an t-Sagairt Beag. A stroll follows along the plateau to the edge of the cliff and the Stuic (see p 248).

From Gelder. Distance: from 264942 to Gelder Shiel 5 km, to summit by the Lochnagar Burn 10 km or 6 miles. The finest route for seeing the NE corrie starts from Gelder Shiel. At the village of Balmoral S of Crathie, on the S side of Dee, leave your car beside the hall along the road E of the shop, and then walk up the private road leading uphill from the shop. It passes through the steep-sided gap of Dubh Chlais (*Doo* Chlash or dark furrow) between two wooded hills, and then up the moor of Glen Gelder (*Gail*der). About 1 km before the Shiel, a new bulldozed road goes straight ahead to 650 m altitude, stopping about 1½ km N of where the Allt na Giubhsaich path turns at the top of Coire na Ciche. However, the best approach from Gelder is to walk up the Lochnagar Burn to the loch, a route which brings the grand corrie ever nearer and more spectacular. You can then reach the top by the scree shoot of the Black Spout, or by the easy bouldery ridge of the Sneck o' Lochnagar just W of the corrie cliffs. Avoid the slope further W, immediately to the N and NE of the summit, where dangerous wet slabs shelve away precipitously and a convex steep slope to the E often becomes prone to snow avalanches. If you intend to return by Ballochbuie, you should bypass this steep section by first heading ½ km WNW from the summit, and then either descend N to the 974 m Meall Coire na Saobhaidhe or else go down the Blackshiel Burn or over the nearby Meall an Tionail (Myal *Tshaini*l) or lump of the meeting.

Walking in Lochnagar's corries

The NE corrie has been described on p 247. The W corrie or Coire Loch nan Eun shows a different character, less dramatic but nevertheless beautifully remote and arctic-like with its great snow fields and high blue tarns. Loch nan Eun lies at just under 900 m, below the rocky promontory of the Stuic, and makes the summer home for an unusually high-nesting colony of common gulls. Round the corner to the W hide two tiny tarns, the larger called Lochan na Feadaige and the smaller Lochan Tàrmachan, meaning the tarn of the golden plover and tarn of ptarmigan respectively. Sandy Loch lies to the N at just over 790 m. Across the plateau SE of the Stuic you will find the high, shallow, green Coire Boidheach (Cor *Boi*-ach) or beautiful corrie, which is a favourite haunt of hinds and their young calves in late summer. To the E of the Dubh Loch, Coire an Loch Buidhe drains into the secluded, hanging tarn of Loch Buidhe. On the N of Lochnagar, Coire na Saobhaidhe (*Si*vee) and further N the Glas Choire are smaller corries in the complex and rough terrain between the summit and Gelder Shiel.

Climbing routes

The main climbing haunt of the North East has been Lochnagar where the 1962 Guide recorded 60 routes in the NE corrie alone, with about 10 more since then. The symmetrical cliffs of Creagan Lochnagar, rising to 210 m or 700 ft, have two massive side walls at either end, flanking a central section of cliffs. This central part stretches between Douglas-Gibson Gully (obvious on the left half of the cliff, with scree running up it far above the rock on either side) and the great scree shoot of the Black Spout further to the W. In 1893, Douglas and Gibson climbed the Black Spout and its Left-Hand Branch, and Tough and Brown ascended the rather vegetated, dangerous and circuitous face route of Tough-Brown Traverse two years later. Raeburn, Rennie and Lawson made the first ascent of Raeburn's Gully in 1898, now a classic winter climb. Much later, from 1927–34, G. R. Symmers and W. A. Ewen pioneered many gullies and chimneys, and in 1941 J. H. B. Bell and Miss N. Forsyth followed with Eagle Ridge, which was a major breakthrough on an open face, away from the grime and damp common in many of the gullies. He found it 'for difficulty, narrowness and steepness altogether, superior to any of the well-known Ben Nevis ridges'. Then in 1949 began the great wave of modern routes, especially on snow and ice.

To the left of the straight gash of Douglas-Gibson Gully rises Shadow Buttress B, with Polyphemus Gully on its left side. The fine winter route of Polyphemus was pioneered in 1953 by K. Grassick and H. Bates; it becomes especially good when snow does not bury all its ice pitches. To its left you will see the open face of Shadow Couloir where another grand winter route – Giant's Head Chimney (VD, Grade IV) – goes up the right hand of the two chimneys in the couloir. Left again stands Shadow Buttress A and then the Central Buttress which terminates the left or E end of the main wall of crag. Douglas-Gibson Gully itself, although dangerous and unpleasant in summer, makes a magnificent Grade V winter climb. Its first winter ascent by T. W. Patey and G. B. Leslie in December 1950 spearheaded the main breakthrough in high-standard winter climbing in the Cairngorms. The upper wall frowns very steeply and icily, topped by one of the biggest cornices in the district. To the right of Douglas-Gibson Gully, Eagle Ridge (S) forms one of the best climbs in the country by a defined and sustained line up fine steep granite which at times tapers to a narrow crest; it also makes a magnificent hard winter route (Grade V).

Along to the right of Eagle Ridge rises Eagle Buttress, of which Eagle Ridge forms the left edge. The next main feature is Parallel Gully A which has become a popular winter route (Grade III). On its right, Parallel Buttress (S), first climbed by J. H. B. Bell and W. H. Murray in 1939, offers one of the better rock climbs in the corrie and makes a very hard Grade V winter ascent. Parallel Gully B shows as a vertical slit further right; the last of the major gullies to be climbed on Lochnagar, it gave a VS first ascent in June 1952 and a fine Grade V winter route in February 1958. To the right of here, the 210 m Tough-Brown face swoops up as an imposing sheet of steep slabby granite. Several routes lead up it, but a new standard has been set with Mort (VS and A2) in 1968, and in 1970 by the even harder nearby Post Mortem (VS and A3), which were both climbed by M. Forbes and M. Rennie. From below the centre of the slabs, Mort goes up a groove on the line of a fault tending to slant slightly to the right. The nearby Post Mortem, starting at the same spot, takes a more direct line up the centre of the Tough-Brown face. Although a few pegs were used for direct ascent, nevertheless the rest of the climbing on these routes is free and extremely hard. The right end of the Tough-Brown face ends with the well-defined Tough-Brown ridge (Direct Route) whose first ascent came in 1941 by J. H. B. Bell and

Miss N. Forsyth; about a third of the way up it contains a VS pitch up steep slabby steps.

Immediately to the right of Tough-Brown face you will notice the obvious left-slanting Raeburn's Gully, originally climbed by H. Raeburn, J. Rennie and H. Lawson in 1898. Since a rockfall in 1940 it has been VD, wet and loose in summer, but in winter it makes a popular Grade II–III climb, varying in difficulty according to how deeply the snow covers the ice pitches underneath. The far wall beyond Raeburn's Gully forms the crag of Scarface whose lower part becomes heavily iced in winter. On the Raeburn's Gully side of it you will see the extraordinary steep slit of The Clam (S), a remarkable climb where boulders jam the outer walls of the slit.

The next main feature to the W is the huge mass of the Black Spout Pinnacle jutting well out from the main cliff, a fearsome 180 m mass of steep slabby granite and one of the most impressive crags in Scotland. The first ascent of the original Route 1 (MS) by D. A. Sutherland and W. D. Brooker in August 1949 gave an impetus to exploration of Cairngorms rock climbing; although it is not a clean summer climb because of much vegetation, and thus few climb it in summer now, it was the first of the open and very steep face routes to be pioneered by the local Aberdonian climbers. It avoids the very hard lower slabs by slanting back on to the Pinnacle from 50 m in height up the Black Spout, to reach the Springboard, a platform tucked in above the slabs. Route 1 gives beautiful views, and in winter makes a grand, hard, Grade V ascent which is now very highly regarded as an ice climb. The fine direct line up Pinnacle Face, which starts about 10 m in height up the Black Spout from the lowest rocks and joins Route 1 about 30 m above the Springboard, forms one of the harder summer rock climbs in the massif and was climbed first by J. Smith and J. Dennis in September 1955. It proved a very hard Grade V climb on the first winter ascent in 1966. The Link (VS) which goes up Pinnacle Face to the Springboard and then by a major new variant on the right side of the face, was the hardest route on Lochnagar until the ascent of Mort; it ranks similar in excellence to Eagle Ridge. Further right still, Route 2 (S) on the Black Spout Pinnacle starts higher up the Black Spout than Route 1 and joins it after an unusual horizontal traverse above the Springboard.

To the right of the Pinnacle, the Left-Hand Branch of the Black Spout diverges from the Black Spout about half-way up and goes straight on to the plateau. An easy gully with a huge chokestone, it featured in Tom Patey's parody

> Of all the climbs on Lochnagar
> The Black Spout is the best by far
> While from the Ballochbuie
> You can always climb the Stuie
> But the pitch to make the experts blanch
> Is the chokestone in the Left-Hand Branch!

Between the Left-Hand Branch and the Black Spout itself soars the bold buttress of the Stack, a popular 100 m climb (VD) with a fine variety of pitches on clean granite in summer, and a very hard (Grade IV) icy route in winter. The Black Spout is a wide easy scree shoot which provides grand views of the cliffs, and in winter makes an easy Grade I snow climb at a 40° to 45° angle. In good conditions it gives a grand glissade and it has been descended on skis in granular 'spring' snow. To its right, the first buttress is Black Spout Buttress (M) which offers a good, steep, but easy climb for a novice on granite. Further to the right the rocky knob of the Gargoyle protrudes from the plateau rim. The ascent of Gargoyle Direct (VD), which finishes beside the Gargoyle, gives one of the best and more popular of the summer climbs on Lochnagar. The section above the midway terrace goes up grand dark clean granite in the sunniest part of the whole corrie.

In Coire Loch nan Eun to the W of Lochnagar, you will see fine corrie and snow scenery but only broken rocks. The jutting nose of the Stuic (*Stooee*) provides an interesting summer scramble and a sporting (Grade 1) way up to the plateau in winter.

Further reading

J. G. Michie   The Benchinnans. *CCJ* 2, 34.

J. A. Parker   The horizon from Lochnagar. *CCJ* 10, 359.

H. Alexander   The Lochnagar indicator: its building and unveiling. *CCJ* 6, 53.

H. T. Munro   Dark Lochnagar. *SMCJ* 2, 190.

G. Duncan   The Lochnagar group (Guide Book article). *SMCJ* 8, 49.

A. G. Hutchison   Lochnagar (its geological history). *Deeside Fld* 3, 15.

W. M. Alexander The place names on and around Lochnagar. *CCJ* 16, 60.

W. H. Murray 1947 *Mountaineering in Scotland*. One chapter on first ascent of Parallel Buttress.

J. H. B. Bell 1950 *A Progress in Mountaineering*. Chapters on first ascent of Eagle Ridge, and on Cairngorms climbing and hill walking in general.

J. H. B. Bell Some variations and discoveries on Lochnagar. *SMCJ* 23, 32.

T. Patey Parallel Gully B, Lochnagar. *SMCJ* 25, 115. Describes first ascent.

T. L. Fallowfield Winter on the Stack. *CCJ* 17, 9.

W. D. Brooker The Pinnacle again. *SMCJ* 26, 229.

T. Weir Lochnagar. *SMCJ* 27, 21. Winter ascent of a very hard variant of Parallel Gully A.

D. Lang Eagle Ridge of Lochnagar in winter. *SMCJ* 29, 163.

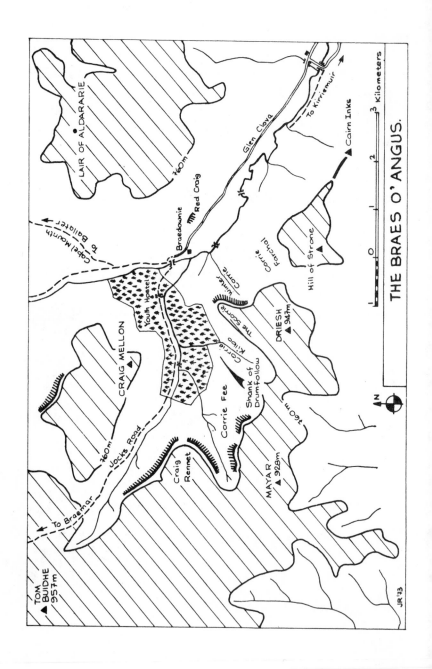

THE BRAES O' ANGUS.

TOM BUIDHE 957m

To Braemar

Jocks Road

160m

CRAIG MELLON

Youth Hostel

Craig Rennet

Corrie Fee

Shank of Drumfollow

The Scorrie

Corrie Kilbo

MAYAR 928m

160m

DRIESH 947m

Hunter Corrie

Forfachal Corrie

Hill of Strone

Red Craig

Braedownie

Cairnwell Mounth to Ballater

Glen Clova

To Kirriemuir

Cairn Inks

LAIR OF ALDARARIE

160m

N

0   1   2   3 Kilometers

JR '73

13

The Braes o' Angus

Ben Tirran	896 m, 373747
*Driesh	947 m, 272736
*The Mayar	928 m, 241738
*Tom Buidhe	957 m, 214788

Access
There are buses to Edzell, Kirriemuir and Blairgowrie. Public roads go to Glenprosen Lodge, to the bridge just N of Braedownie at the top of Clova, to Hunthill Lodge at the top of Lethnot, and Loch Lee Kirk at the top of Glen Esk.

Accommodation and other facilities
There are hotels, boarding houses, pubs, and fish and chip shops in Kirriemuir, Edzell and Blairgowrie, and a hotel and pub at Milton of Clova half-way up Glen Clova. You will find youth hostels at Kirriemuir and at Glendoll Lodge at the top of Glen Clova. The Carn Dearg Mountaineering Club has a hut in upper Glen Clova which holds 12; enquiries should be sent to J. Brown, 609 South Road, Dundee. The Retreat in Glen Esk (tearoom) is one of the better folk museums in Scotland. At Red Craig beside Braedownie, below the rightmost of the three main sections of cliff, 'A well-known cave under the jumble of boulders slightly left and below the South-East Crag provides rough accommodation' (Climbers' Guide No. 5). Its name is the Hole o' Weems.

Remote occupied houses
Moulzie 283779, Glendoll Lodge 278763, Spittal of Glenmuick 307850, Tulchan 185723, Hunthill Lodge 475722, Gleneffock 454788, Glenprosen Lodge 292680.

Bothies
Jock's or Lunkard Bothy 234777 at 700 m beside the path of Jock's Road. Allan's Hut 256808 at 720 m, N of Bachnagairn.

General description

From the broad flat farmlands of Strath More and the town of Forfar (*Far*far) you look up to a fine rampart of hills rising abruptly from
the plain, the grand Braes o' Angus. Their old name was Bràigh
Aonghuis, and Machair Aonghuis referred to the low plain below.
Into the Braes cut several long, roughly parallel glens where the
rivers flow SE to the sea, the finest glens being Esk and Clova
running into the rivers North and South Esk. Their head streams
drain from the great medium-level tableland shared with Lochnagar
and the Glen Clunie hills of Aberdeenshire. Glen Clova has its own
special character. Such a deep trench was cut here that many crags
line its sides. These, the steep broken slopes, the brilliant fertile
green of the hillsides, and the farms far up the glen floor, all look
very different from most glens in the North East. Visitors often
remark on how Glen Clova resembles the grassy, steep craggy
valleys of Argyll or the Lake District. Some of the crags come close
to the road, like the spectacular Red Craig on your right just before
you reach Braedownie. The glen's unusual atmosphere has been
heightened by the new dense plantations of conifers at the top, which
make it look even more alpine and less like most hill country in NE
Scotland.

Geology and landforms

Most of Glen Clova lies over schist, with some gneiss, diorite and
epidiorite, rocks that look very different from the granite of nearby
Lochnagar. The Clova rock feels smoother, and has many small in-
cut holds that climbers find more reliable than tiny holds on the
granite. On the N side of the glen you will see a remarkable series of
five hanging corries, two of which have fine corrie lochs at Loch
Wharral and Brandy. Glen Clova itself is a great U-shaped trench
with steep sides, typical of glacial cutting. The great peaty plateaux
which almost encircle Glen Clova and Glen Esk form one of the
biggest tracts of medium-level plateau in the Highlands.

Natural history

The corries of Glen Clova, especially in Glen Doll, contain some of
the best known places for rare arctic-alpine flowers in Britain. They
grow best on the fertile crags, up on ledges out of range of sheep and
deer, and there the scrub of rare arctic willows is also especially fine.
The district has, however, suffered much from the ravages of selfish

commercial gardeners and private gardeners and collectors. The best places for rare plants – mainly the corries on the W side of Glen Doll – now form part of the Caenlochan National Nature Reserve which stretches W to Glas Maol and Glen Shee. Because of the fertile rocks, the hills look much greener and grassier than in most of our region. Even the heathery parts are richer in other species of flowering plants. Dotterel and dunlins nest on the high tablelands and peat bogs, and eagle, raven and peregrine on a few remote crags. After being almost extinct, wild cats have greatly increased in the Angus glens, where they are now commoner than foxes. On the low ground of Angus, the vale of Strath More is one of the outstanding places in Britain for wintering wild geese, which come here in thousands. Other grand places for wild duck and geese are the Loch of Lintrathen, the marshy Loch of Kinnordy just W of Kirriemuir, Duns Dish E of Brechin, and the fine mud flats of Montrose Basin. Magnificent red sandstone cliffs rise NE of Arbroath at Red Head.

Estates

In Glen Clova, Balmoral owns Bachnagairn and the Forestry Commission Glen Doll; both are deer forest. Further down Clova at Rottal and in lower Glen Prosen stretch the grouse moors of Airlie Estate. Much of upper Prosen and the ground on the little glens W towards Glen Isla belongs to the Forestry Commission, which has planted big woods of conifers on the lower slopes. Invermark around Glen Mark and Loch Lee also forms deer forest ground, along with the top of Glen Lethnot (Hunthill). The rest of Glen Esk and Lethnot are grouse moors, mostly run by Dalhousie Estate Office. Hill sheep graze the whole area.

History

In the 1880s the owner of Glen Doll tried to close the public road by the Tolmount to Braemar, but the Scottish Rights of Way and Recreation Society successfully fought him, and in 1887 the Court of Session upheld this historic Mounth Road. People then were used to walking straight over the hills to travel from one place to another, instead of driving far around them. On the Lair of Aldararie, a hill reaching 832 m in altitude NE of Braedownie, the local people of Glen Muick used to meet their neighbours from Glen Clova and Glen Esk every year to compete at Highland games on a green near the flat summit. Until recently, when some selfish person removed them, you could still see the stones that they used for 'putting the shot'. In 1973, Jimmy Stewart, 88 year old ex-keeper on Glen Muick, told the writer how he remembered as a boy seeing people walking there to compete. It was in nearby Glen Prosen that Edward Wilson of Antarctic fame wrote some of his scientific works, and here Captain Scott came to discuss with him the ill-fated South Pole expedition. The district has many other interesting associations, described by Fraser (1963). Below the mouth of Glen Lethnot, the road SE to Brechin passes over a broad ridge between two low hills called the Brown and White Caterthuns, which remain as very fine examples of hill forts from the Iron Age.

Walking Ascents

Ben Tirran, pronounced *Turr*an (896 m, 2939 ft), is the highest hill on the N side of Glen Clova, rising E of Loch Wharral. The highest point has the old name The Goet (*Gote*), Ben Tirran being the slightly lower bump on the Clova side to the SW. From the hotel at Milton of Clova, a pleasant way up leads by the path straight up for $3\frac{1}{2}$ km and 620 m of an ascent past Loch Brandy (Branduibh or raven-black) to the 870 m top of the Green Hill, whose hollows become a favourite skiers' haunt in winter. From Green Hill you will have an easy walk along the plateau for $2\frac{1}{2}$ to 3 km to Ben Tirran, passing on the way the Craigs of Loch Wharral. A quicker but poorer way to Ben Tirran goes by a bulldozed road which starts from Wheen 4 km further down the glen and runs up to 450 m in altitude, below Loch Wharral at about 625 m. Once on top, away from the steep glen side, you are standing on a long plateau parallel to the glen, with many tops that rise as mere bumps. To the E and NE you will see a great contrast; here the plateau shelves very gradually for miles into remote peaty uplands with meandering streams and twisting lower glens, a difficult country to navigate in when mist and snowstorm conceal the few landmarks. If you start from Ben Tirran or the Green Hill, you can walk easily along this plateau into the wide open valley of Water of Unich (*Yoon*ich) away to the N and NE, and down to Loch Lee and Glen Esk. The plateau also rolls far to the E across vast high moors into the gentle upper valley of the Water of Saughs and over to Glen Effock. Distance: from the Green Hill to Unich stables $3\frac{1}{2}$ km, to Inchgrundle W of Loch Lee 8 km either by the stables and the Shank of Inchgrundle or else by White Hill, Muckle Cairn and Skuiley to Loch Lee Kirk at the public road end 12 km.

Driesh 947 m (3108 ft). Drìs or bramble place. Above Brae-downie (Bri*doon*ee), the sharp rocky 766 m peak of the Scorrie (from Sgòr or sharp point) thrusts out boldly as an outlier of Driesh, and looks one of the finest features of Glen Clova. The glen forks at Braedownie, right to Moulzie and upper Glen Clova, left up White Water to Glen Doll (Dol, pronounced Dole, or meadow). Craig Mellon stands imposingly between them. If you cross White Water by the bridge at Acharn just E of Glendoll Lodge, you will find the Scorrie (pronounced *Scurr*ie) a fine ascent. At the top you skirt the cliffs of Winter Corrie, which is an error on the map for the local name of Corrie Winter. You can stroll easily from the top of the Scorrie to Driesh (3 km distance and 690 m ascent from Acharn, 2 hours up).

A less steep route begins by crossing the bridge ½ km SSE of Braedownie and goes easily up the open grassy Corrie Farchal which lies between Driesh and Bassies. From the top of the corrie at the Sneck of Farchal, at 703 m or 2308 ft, a fence runs W to Driesh and Mayar, and E and then ESE to Cairn Inks. On the Glen Prosen side a bulldozed road now climbs to the 633 m top of Lick immediately S of Driesh, and forestry roads up to 570 m in altitude SSW of Cairn Inks. If you intend to descend from Driesh, or for that matter any of the hills ringing Glen Doll, remember to plan ahead and choose a way down that avoids clambering through the dense plantations. Unpleasant at any time, these are extremely wetting after rain and very difficult in darkness.

The Mayar 928 m (3043 ft). The *May*-yar. The 3 km walk from Driesh takes only an hour as you drop a mere 140 m between them. You can also climb Mayar directly by the 'Kilbo' or 'Kilby's' path up Corrie Kilbo (*Kill*bo), but forest covers the lower slope to about 500 m. The path then passes up to the plateau by the Shank of Drumfollow, which forms the long grassy shoulder that separates Corrie Kilbo from Corrie Fee. An even better way up is to go 1½ km up the road W of Glendoll Lodge, cross the bridge over White Water, and walk up a forestry road which leads towards Corrie Fee (from Fiadh or deer). A path continues up the plantation to the grassy floor of this grand, extensive corrie. Immediately to the S of the fine waterfall at the top, you can reach the plateau without difficulty and so stroll over to the top of the Mayar (5 km from Glendoll Lodge, 650 m ascent). On the Glen Prosen side, a bulldozed road goes from the ruin of Kilbo at the top of the glen, past Cairn Dye and up to 830 m at the fence on the watershed W of the Shank of Drumfollow.

From the Mayar you look S into the head of Glen Prosen, W into Glen Cally (*Caal*ie) and Glen Isla, and NE to Glen Doll. A great high tableland stretches NW and then N, so you can stroll easily to the NW for 3 km to Dun Hillocks (shepherds' hut, often locked), or for 5 km to Meikle Kilrannoch (Cùil Raineach or nook of ferns) and then NE over to the Jock's Road path and so back down Glen Doll.

Tom Buidhe   957 m (3140 ft). Tome *Boo*ee or yellow knoll. A short detour from Meikle Kilrannoch takes you to this point, 3 km from Dun Hillocks and 6 km from Mayar. Here you stand in the centre of the great tablelands, and can appreciate the comment of Sir Hugh T. Munro – the originator of our 'Munros' of today – 'So elevated and flat is the range that a straight line of 10 miles could be drawn from Creag Leacach to the Meikle Pap of Lochnagar, and, except for about half a mile on each side of the Tolmount, the elevation is everywhere above 3000 ft, while even at these points it only falls to 2863 ft and a dogcart could be driven the whole way.' Some find these uplands dull and featureless, but although at first sight they do seem uniform, if you pay closer attention and come on return visits you will find them all very different, with many varying kinds of terrain and vegetation. Getting to know the individual complexity and the sheer extent, spaciousness and peace of this wilderness is to realise its special character and charm.

From Tom Buidhe you can easily walk $1\frac{1}{3}$ km over to Tolmount, 3 km to Cairn of Claise, $5\frac{1}{2}$ km to the Glas Maol, $4\frac{1}{2}$ km to Broad Cairn, or $9\frac{1}{2}$ km to Lochnagar; the choice in all directions from this central point on the tableland is great. If you are returning to Clova from Tom Buidhe, a good way goes E by remote Loch Esk, down to the ruined lodge of Bachnagairn and its old larches beside green meadows, and so to Braedownie (10 km).

Walking routes in the corries

The corries of Clova have great variety and more interest than some of the hills around them. On the N side, Loch Wharral and Loch Brandy are remarkably big corrie lochs in wild cirques with broken crags behind. Further W, the Corrie of Clova forms a fine bowl with faces of broken rock, and round the next corner to the W of Ben Reid, so does the similar Corrie Bonhard (Coire Bun na h-Àirde, Bone *Hard* or foot of the height). On the S side, you will find Corrie

Winter well worth a visit. A good way goes straight up the Gourock Burn that leads into its precipitous screes and dark broken rocks. Corrie Fee to the W is the finest of Clova's corries, with beautiful green meadows, waterfalls and long stretches of crags. On the NW side these end in the bold face of Craig Rennet (745 m), round the corner from which the crags of the Dounalt stretch westwards to the next burn. Beyond, the long line of crags continues by Craig Maud, ending beside the Jock's Road path. At Bachnagairn, one of the most beautiful spots in the area, broken crags lie above the green West Corrie, opposite to the steep cliff of Juanjorge which soars abruptly on the N side. This improbably Mediterranean-looking spelling seems an obvious anglicised corruption, and one pronounces it Gin George as in English gin and George.

Other glens of Angus

Although of little interest to a rock climber, Glen Esk excels as the loveliest glen of Angus and has some grand wild country for hill walkers. Its long twisting course surpasses most Highland glens in variety, with fine old birch woods, bright green bracken, bare heathery hills, river shingles and linns, and prosperous hill farms. Higher up stretch vast plateaux of peaty moors, wild glens with rugged cliffs, and high stony hills. At the foot of the glen, above Gannachy Bridge, you leave behind the flat lowland of Edzell (*Aid*zil) and very abruptly enter Highland country. Walk W of the road at 589728 and turn S, to see one of the finest river gorges in the North East at the Lowps o' the Burn, where Esk hurries through a long, magnificently wooded ravine.

At the top of Glen Esk, beyond the public road end at 261 m beside Loch Lee Kirk, private roads continue to the NW up Glen Mark and westwards past the ruined old Castle of Invermark to Loch Lee and Glen Lee. Both glens are steep and craggy, the 687 m Craig Maskeldie (Ma*skai*ldee) being a particularly fine sharp peak as seen from Loch Lee. Immediately W of the Craig lies a fine gorge at the Falls of Unich, where a path takes you up on to the plateau at Falls of Damff, $7\frac{1}{2}$ km from Loch Lee Kirk. You can also reach the plateau from the house of Inchgrundle (Innis Grunndaile or meadow of good foundation), by a bulldozed road which goes up the Shank of Inchgrundle. It continues on the line of the old footpath to the Unich about half-way between the Falls of Damff (Damh or stag) and the ruined Unich stables. From Inchgrundle a path also climbs by Skuiley further to the E, right to the top of the 826 m Muckle Cairn which stands 3½ km ENE of the Green Hill (for continuation to Clova see p 260).

The private road to the stables at the top of Glen Lee continues as a bulldozed track to 725 m on to the Muckle Cairn to the NW, which is a different hill from the higher Muckle Cairn SW of Inchgrundle. A private road also runs up Glen Mark to the cottage at 320 m at the top, from which a bulldozed road goes W up the glen to just past the tarn of Carlochy (Car*loch*ie). Upper Glen Mark is a lovely green glen with beautiful pools and rapids, surrounded by steep hillsides and crags, the Craig of Doune being especially imposing. Balnamoon's Cave lies at 396833 on the S side of Mark, among rocks about 20 m in height above the river; an old Jacobite's shelter, it is grassy on top, with a narrow vertical door and with its sides built up by stones. From either the upper Mark or Lee, you can easily walk over to Glen Muick. Distances: from public road at Loch Lee Kirk 445803 to Lee stables 8½ km, by Muckle Cairn and Creag na Slowrie to Spittal of Glenmuick 16 km or 10 miles, 500 m ascent. From Loch Lee Kirk to Glenmark Cottage 4 km, via Glen Mark and the Burn of Fasheilach to the Glen Muick public road at 328889 by a bulldozed road going down from Druim Cholzie 17 km, 400 m ascent. There are endless other possibilities for the hill walker keen on exploring for himself.

Between Glen Esk and Glen Clova, Glen Lethnot (Lethnocht or naked-sided) and its West Water form a long narrow valley twisting up into hilly grouse moors. The public road ends at Hunthill Lodge, but beyond the lodge a Land Rover track runs far up the remote Water of Saughs (*Sachs*, North-East Scots for willows); up there you are on the high ground with Ben Tirran to the SW, while to the NE the secluded Glen Effock falls steeply with several broken crags to Glen Esk. Distances: from the public road end near Hunthill by the Land Rover road to the Shank of Donald Young 5½ km, to Ben Tirran 11 km, 600 m ascent. From Hunthill by the track up Water of Saughs to the Shieling of Saughs 9 km, to the Green Hill via White Hill 14 km. From 492729 in Glen Lethnot N by the Whisky Road over the Clash (Gaelic Clais or furrow) of Wirren to Tarfside 7½ km, 200 m ascent.

The next glen to the W is Glen Ogil (*Oge*-il) behind Noranside, a short little glen with planted woods, a reservoir and rolling grouse moors. Next you see Glen Clova, and almost immediately to the W of its entrance at the deep beech woods of Cortachy (*Cortachie*), the long Glen Prosen also opens out to the plain. The attractive lower part of Glen Prosen has natural birch woods, and higher up becomes bare and wilder where it drains the S sides of Mayer and Driesh. Glen Isla, westernmost of the Angus glens, is described in Chapter 10.

The Mounth Roads

Two well known Mounth Roads go over the hill from Glen Clova to Deeside, the Capel Mount to Ballater and the Tolmount to Braemar (for the Mounth Roads from Dee to Glen Esk, see next chapter). The Tolmount has the more rugged scenery of the two and is also a much higher and longer route than the Capel Mount.

Capel Mount. Pronounced *Caip*il Munth, this name comes from Monadh Chapull or mounth of horses. Distance: from public road end near Braedownie to county boundary 4 km, to car park at Spittal of Glenmuick 10 km or 6 miles (3 hours), total ascent 500 m but only 350 m if you start at the Spittal. At the bridge N of Braedownie you come to the end of the public road at about 260 m. A locked gate stops cars from using the private road to Moulzie (*Mùillidh*, *Moo*lee or mill place). About 1 km up, the Capel path slants through a plantation to the right and then zig-zags up the bare hillside above to the plateau. The next 4½ km of peaty plateau are marked by posts, with the highest point at about 695 m or 2275 ft, and the path changes to a bulldozed Land Rover road for the descent to the public road near the Spittal of Glenmuick at 411 m. A finer route, 5 km longer, goes further up South Esk Bachnagairn in its magnificent setting of larches and green meadows surrounded by high crags and waterfalls (footbridges N of Moulzie and at Bachnagairn). From here a path climbs to the top of the plateau at about 720 m beside Allan's Hut, and then continues as a bulldozed road zig-zagging down to Loch Muick beside the Black Burn. You can also vary this descent by taking the path down to the head of Loch Muick (see p 236).

The Tolmount. The name is derived probably from Doll Mounth, pronounced *Tole*munth. Distance: from public road end past Braedownie to the end of the road in Glen Doll 5 km, to county boundary 9, to Loch Callater Lodge 15, to Auchallater 20 km or 12½ miles (5½ hours), total ascent 690 m but only 570 m if you start at Auchallater. This route begins in Glen Doll, where you can walk along the road past the youth hostel at Glendoll Lodge and later up a bulldozed road which runs well up the glen to 560 m. At the road end you stand in a very fine secluded spot, with craggy faces and steep hillsides rising all around. Straight ahead, the main stream comes down a narrow ravine, steep and rocky, but for a climber worth scrambling up. The path now slants to the right up the hill, avoiding the ravine and going above the smaller stream to the N of it. This steep part is called Jock's Road, said to be named after a John Winters (*CCJ* 12, 220). The path climbs past Jock's Bothy and around Cairn Lunkard above it to the plateau N of the main stream, and then goes gently upwards to the highest point at just over 910 m or about 3000 ft, on the Crow Craigies. Passing through the shallow dip at 883 m to the E of Tolmount, beside a broken fence, it then descends fairly steeply into Coire Breac (Cor *Brech*) towards Glen Callater, down grass amongst scattered broken rocks. You now pass the fine Coire Kander on the W side of the glen, and go along the E side of Loch Callater at about 500 m to Loch Callater Lodge, where a private road leads to the locked gate at Auchallater on the public road up Glen Clunie, near Braemar. Walkers unaccustomed to navigating in mist and snow should avoid the Tolmount in winter as the path crosses a big tract of exposed high plateau with very few landmarks, where several people have succumbed in storms. However, to the experienced hillman the Tolmount in snow makes one of the finest winter crossings of the Mounth.

Climbing routes

In Glen Clova, Red Craig beside Braedownie has for long been the main climbing ground on a clean dry face of diorite rock, with many short routes from 15 to 55 m high which vary in standard from M to VS. Twenty Minute Route (M), Flake Route (MS) and Parapet Route (S) are particularly good. Further W rises the conical rocky mass of the Doonie where new 60 m VS routes have been climbed in the last few years (*SMCJ* 29, 65).

Corrie Fee extends far as a grand wild cirque with crags of schist and epidiorite or hornblende gneiss, but much of its rock is too broken and vegetated for fine summer climbing; however, in winter snow and ice the gullies and buttresses give good ascents. On the S face of the corrie, the route called Romulus and Remus (VD) which mounts up the highest rock from the bottom to top, offers good climbing but may seem somewhat contrived as you can escape off to easier ground. The left part of this buttress ends at an obvious gully called Look C Gully, a summer stream which becomes a fine winter ice route. On its left the next obvious trough forms B Gully; B Gully Chimney, which goes up B Gully and then forks left up a chimney, is another watercourse that gives a good winter climb on ice. The short 60 m of The Comb (D) makes a popular summer rock climb on the far right of Corrie Fee's S face, and was hard on its winter ascent in January 1973. On the N wall of Corrie Fee stands the impressive 210 m crag of Craig Rennet, but its rocks turn out to be ill-defined and broken, as are the schist cliffs of Corrie Winter and those at Loch Brandy and the other corries on the N side of Glen Clova. However, under snow and ice all these crags give plenty of sporting climbing of Grade I–II standard, reaching quite high ascents on the bigger cliffs at Craig Rennet and the Scorrie Buttress of Corrie Winter. On Juanjorge the crag looks more defined, with some good steep diorite rock and a couple of recorded climbs, but they are rather short, reaching not over 90 m high. About 2 km to the WNW of Bachnagairn a bigger sheet of rock occurs on Craig of Gowal; although it lies back at a lower angle, its central part has given a 190 m VS climb on clean granite slabs (*SMCJ* 29, 193).

In Glen Esk, Craig Maskeldie makes an interesting sporting route to the plateau in winter when snow and ice cover the considerable amount of vegetation. Other rocks on the Eagle's Crag N of Unich and in Glen Mark, although looking impressive at a distance, turn out to be broken, rather short and fairly heavily vegetated in summer. Try to avoid these small broken crags in all the Angus glens in spring and summer, as they are the nesting places of scarce and much-persecuted birds of prey.

Further reading

H. T. Munro   The Braes of Angus (Guide Book article). *SMCJ* 8, 125.

J. Scrimgeour   The Glen Doll Right of Way Case. *CCJ* 12.

Guide to the district of Glen Clova.   *Grampian CJ* 1937, 14.

D. Fraser   1963   *Guide to the Glens of Angus and Mearns.* Standard Press (Montrose).

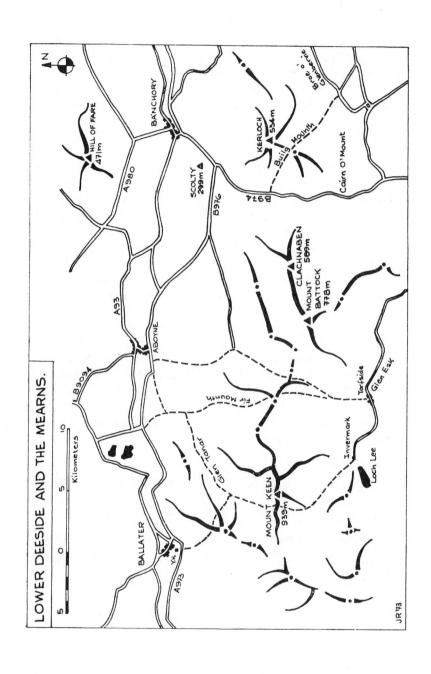

LOWER DEESIDE AND THE MEARNS.

N

Kilometers
5   0   5   10

HILL OF FARE
471m

BANCHORY

A980

A93

SCOLTY
299m

B976

KERLOCH
534m

Builg Mounth

Cairn O' Mount

Glen Dye o

B974

CLACHNABEN
589m

MOUNT
BATTOCK
778m

Fir Mounth

Tarfside

Glen Esk

A93

ABOYNE

B9094

Glen Tanar

MOUNT KEEN
939m

Invermark

Loch Lee

BALLATER

YH

A973

JR '93

14

Lower Deeside and the Mearns

Cairn Mon Earn	378 m, 782919
Kerloch	534 m, 697878
Clachnaben	589 m, 614865
Mount Battock	778 m, 549844
***Mount Keen**	939 m, 409869
Scolty	299 m, 678939
The Hill of Fare	471 m, 672028
Mortlich	381 m, 535017

Access and accommodation

Air, rail and bus services go to Aberdeen, and buses from there to Banchory and Aboyne. Hotels, boarding houses and bed and breakfasts are numerous, and youth hostels occur at Aberdeen and Ballater. An automatic petrol machine is at Kincardine o' Neil (Kin*cairn* a *Nee*-ill). Many shooters' huts stand on the moors but this is not 'bothying' country (see p 26).

General description

This chapter describes the hills of lower Deeside from Aberdeen to Dinnet, including the E end of the Mounth and its southern braes that fall towards the Mearns and the wild North Sea cliffs of Kincardineshire. As you come N by road or rail through fertile Strath More and the Howe o' the Mearns (from Maoirne or stewartry, How i' the *Mairns*), the Mounth gradually hems you in against the North Sea until before Aberdeen you have to rise over its eastern extremity of peaty moorland near the cliffs of Nigg. The commercial air flights to Aberdeen from the south pass low over the area and give a good appreciation of the vast extent and loneliness of its rolling, bare brown moors and hills, which are tinged a powdery pink in August and September from the myriad heather flowers. Although it lies so near the towns, much of this hill country is less visited by people than any other part of Deeside.

Geology and landforms

This part of the Mounth consists mainly of pink granite in an extensive mass stretching from Mount Keen to Glen Dye and Cairn Mon Earn; the Hill of Fare forms another, smaller mass of pink granite. The ground near Aberdeen lies over grey granite, where the colossal 150 m hole of Rubislaw Quarry reaches well below sea level, having until 1972 produced many thousands of buildings in Aberdeen. Gneiss occurs on the fine sea cliffs at Souter Head and Nigg, whereas S of Stonehaven (Steen*hive*) the fantastic vertical cliffs of Fowlsheugh (Fowls-*hyooch*) are composed of conglomerate. Many deposits of glacial drift have formed hillocks and valley ridges, such as you will see to the SE of Strachan (*Straan*). Meltwater rivers from glaciers filling the Dee Valley cut the fine dry ravines at the Slug, Mount Shade, and the remarkable $1\frac{1}{2}$ km-long gorge at Slack o' Birnie E of the Cairn o' Mount.

Natural history

The hill ground supports the most extensive stands of uniform heather sward in Scotland; heather thrives in the dry climate here and on the well drained granite soil. A vast low moorland bog once covered most of the ground S of Aberdeen and good patches of it still remain at Red Moss near Netherley (Nether*lei*) and also nearer Aberdeen. Glen Tanar (Tanara, *Tan*ar or noisy stream) holds one of the largest stretches of natural pine forest in Scotland and moreover one of the few where the young trees are regenerating well. New natural woods of young pine have grown up on heather moorland at Forest of Birse, Glen Tanar, Finzean (*Fing*in) and Kerloch, more extensively than anywhere else in Scotland. Near St Cyrus, many southern species of plants grow on the unusually fertile, sheltered and partly-inland sea cliffs of andesitic lava. For wild animals, naturalists find the notable features to be the pine-forest insects and birds of Glen Tanar, the richness of moorland birds, and the very densely-populated sea-bird colonies at Fowlsheugh (Fowls-*hyooch*).

Estates

There are many small ones. The larger ones that cover most of the hill country include Fasque Estate for Glen Dye (locally pronounced Glain-a-*digh*), Dunecht Estate for Birse and the Hill of Fare, and the separate estates of Glen Muick, Glen Tanar, and Ballogie which lies E of Glen Tanar.

History

The area is rich in ancient remains. Below Kerloch you will see fine circles of standing stones near Garrol Hill and West Mulloch. Nearer Stonehaven, beside Auquhollie up from Rickarton, a standing stone bears an ancient Ogam (ancient Celtic alphabet) inscription; nearby are a few circles of standing stones, and further E the site of an old Roman camp at Raedykes. In the wood E of Raemoir by the B977 road stands a handsome stone monument erected by the Deeside Field Club, commemorating the Battle of Corrichie (Cor*reech*ee) which was fought higher on the Hill of Fare in 1562. At Corrichie the army of Mary Queen of Scots, led by the Earl of Moray, routed the Earl of Huntly in one of the many religious squabbles of the times. In the Mearns the kirk of Auchinblae is dedicated to St Palladius whose name appears again in Paldy Fair, a market that used to be held on the moor across from Glenfarquhar Lodge.

The lower hills and crofts of Drumlithie were the home ground of Robert Burns, who was born at a croft there and only later moved to Ayrshire. Nearer the beautiful old kirk at Arbuthnott, J. L. Mitchell, who later wrote under the pen name Lewis Grassick Gibbon, spent his childhood. His fine descriptions in *Sunset Song* and *Cloud Howe*, the first two books of the classic trio forming *A Scots Quair*, are essential reading for anyone wishing to understand the upland folk and their countryside in the area described in Chapters 14 and 15. Banchory was the birthplace of Scott Skinner the 'Strathspey King' who composed and played fine reels on the violin, and the town now has one of the best-known group of Strathspey fiddlers in Scotland. From Banchory the unusual granite tor on Clachnaben looks very prominent to the SW. The old local legend to explain it was that, in the midst of a row with his wife, the Devil tore up the rock from the valley and flung it to the top of the hill where it crushed and killed her.

Walking ascents

Near Aberdeen. The Mounth ends in the tiny hills covered with whins and blaeberry behind Kincorth, above the S suburbs of Aberdeen (Aiber*deen*). Some Aberdeen town folk call them 'the Gramps', which is the only common use of 'Grampians' that the writer has come across in the whole region. Just W of Loirston (*Lor*iston) Loch to the S of Aberdeen, the Blue Hill gives very fine views up to the Cairngorms and carries a hill indicator. Another indicator stands on the low heathery rise of the 265 m Brimmond (*Brem*on, 'e' as in her, and no 'Hill' as on the maps), to the SW of Dyce Airport; it has now been disfigured by a bulldozed road from the N and by radio aerials.

You will enjoy many fine views of the higher hills from the farmlands of lower Deeside. Just E of Durris off the S Deeside road, the side roads to Ashentilly and Denside give magnificent panoramas; you can see most of the Cairngorms including Cairn Toul, and a complex multitude of lower hills round to Bennachie and Buchan. About 400 m up the Slug road from the Dee bridge at Crathes, you will notice a very fine view of Ben Avon and Beinn a' Bhuird; you look right into Coire an Dubh Lochain of Beinn a' Bhuird, a corrie remarkably well hidden from most places. Perhaps the finest of the far views of Ben Avon is from the roadside at Garrol Hill. In the low country of the Mearns you can easily reach an excellent viewpoint at Garvock Hill between Laurencekirk and St Cyrus, looking over to the very long line of the Mounth.

Cairn Mon Earn 378 m (1241 ft). As you go inland W from Aberdeen, this is the first obvious hill in the Mounth S of Dee. A gently rising, boulder-studded cone, it stands close above the Slug Road from Stonehaven to Banchory. The lower slopes of Cairn Mon Earn (Mun *Airn*) have been afforested, but opposite a lay-by on the public road at 779911 a path leads from a locked gate for 1 km up to the top. An easier and more gradual route (3½ km, 180 m ascent) goes by the gravel road (locked gate), which starts at 780909 and winds round to the Aberdeen side on the way up to the top, which bears a radio aerial and fire lookout. The coast, lowlands and Deeside look very fine from here, and you can see into Garbh Choire Mor and Sgor an Lochain Uaine, a particularly well-hidden spot which is invisible in nearly all distant views.

Kerloch 534 m (1754 ft). Local people pronounce the name Ker*loch* ('e' as in her and 'o' as in bone). This hill gives views down slopes of heather to the valley of Dee and S over the vast brown moors to the North Sea. The easiest way up – every way involves heavy going with peaty slopes and long heather – starts from the Strachan–Stonehaven road at 699916 from which a Land Rover track goes S well up the hill to 706887 (4½ km, 410 m ascent). An interesting descent takes you on the W side to the old Brig o' Bogendreip in Glen Dye down through a fine, natural young pine wood.

Clachnaben 589 m (1900 ft). Locally called Clochna*bain*, with 'o' as in bone, the name comes from Clach na Beinne or the stone of the hill. With Bennachie it ranks as one of the most familiar hills in NE Scotland, hence the couplet

Clochnaben and Bennachie
Are twa landmarks frae the sea

Clachnaben is well known because of the great granite rock which sticks up for about 30 m like a gigantic wart on its E side near the hilltop. From the Cairn o' Mount road at 649869 you can climb up in 1½ hours (4 km, 400 m ascent), passing S of Mount Shade and visiting its impressive dry ravine on the way. Another route comes from the N by a path which leads up the Burn of Greendams to the top (5 km, 440 m ascent). A third way is to start just W of Spitalburn at 645847, cross Dye by a footbridge, go up the rough road to Netty Hill and then to the top (4 km). You can reach the summit of the granite tor almost on the level from the hilltop behind.

Mount Battock 778 m (2555 ft), called Mun *Bat*ak. This shapely hill with its domed top stands high over Feughside (F*yooch*) and Glen Dye. A good approach comes in from 542907 at the public road beside Burnfoot in the upper Feugh. On the way to Burnfoot, you should stop just W of Woodend to see the fine naturally-re-generating pine woods there. Near here an old path to the peat mosses runs up to Glaspits and further E another from Bucket Mill mounts high on Peter Hill. From Burnfoot, a gradual climb up the moor takes you E of Cock Hill and past the remote tarn of Loch Tennet to the stony and mossy top (6½ km, 630 m ascent). Mount Battock is notable in being the furthest E hill in Scotland where ptarmigan nest. The most impressive approach (11 km, but heavy going) lies up the long valley of Aven (Aan); you leave the public road at 613923, cross Feugh at a footbridge, climb past Bogmore to Aven, and then walk up Aven's fine long rocky ravine.

You can also climb Mount Battock fairly easily from Glen Esk, an approach that gives grand views on the way up. North of Millden a rough road leads to the old farm of Blackhills, from which you can climb easily N over Allrey (*Al*arie) or NW by Mount Een (Mun *Theen*) to the top (6 km, 640 m ascent). There are now bulldozed roads around Mount Battock. One goes from Mill of Aucheen in Glen Esk up the Hill of Turret to about 460 m on Hill of Fingray, 5 km SE of the summit. Another starts to the W of Charr Cottage in Glen Dye and climbs to about 580 m in altitude, W of the Hill of

Badymicks and just over 3 km from the top. This last approach enables you to appreciate the wild moorland plateau in this district.

Mount Keen 939 m (3077 ft). Monadh Caoin (Mun *Keen*) or pleasant hill. To see this shapely cone at its best, and one of the finer views of Scotland, go to Tillypronie on the Dinnet–Strath Don road; from here it soars magnificently above the woods and farms in the great bowl of the Howe o' Cromar. The Mounth Road from Ballater to Invermark (p 281) goes over its high W shoulder by a wild bare route. A more varied way comes in from Glen Tanar to the SW of Aboyne, by the public road to a car park at about 180 m altitude beside Glen Tanar House. From there a rough road runs beyond Etnach to the Shiel (11 km up, 180 m ascent, 2¾ hours), a locked hut that stands almost at the foot of Mount Keen. This road is a right of way for walkers and cyclists but a locked gate keeps out cars. It leads through part of what is now the finest tract of rapidly-regenerating natural old pine-juniper forest in Scotland. From just before the Shiel, a bulldozed road climbs on the old Mounth track to 930 m; beyond, the old Mounth path continues on and another path forks left to Mount Keen's stony granite summit (3 km from the glen road E of the Shiel, 560 m ascent, time up 1¾ hours). On the way up you bypass the damp rocky corrie called the *Cor*lach (not Corrach as on the maps), which lies curiously low down on the N side of Mount Keen.

You will find it easy walking along the 2 km E from Mount Keen to the 887 m Braid Cairn (200 m ascent), locally called The Braid Cairns. Although it looks a rounded dome from Cromar, Braid Cairn seems a long sprawling lump of hill when seen from Glen Esk and Laurencekirk. It rises high above the vast peaty plateaux, locally called the Leg o' Moss, which stretch SE over the Hill of Saughs towards Tarfside and form one of the more notable tracts of wilderness in the area. From the Braid Cairn, grand walking on dry, wind-scoured dwarf heather takes you along the line of tops E to Mount Battock. These tops, bounding the great basin N of Tarfside, form the Glen Esk skyline which the local 'glenners' call The *Rigg*in, meaning the ridge. One of the best ways of climbing Mount Keen starts in Glen Esk; you go up Glen Mark, take the Mounth route (p 281) up a bulldozed road to 670 m, and then walk by a path to the top.

Scolty 299 m (983 ft). Local folk say *Skole*-tee, probably from

Sgoltaidh or splitting. With its prominent tower and conical shape, Scolty is one of the best known and easily recognised hills of lower Deeside. It rises close above the town of Banchory (Beannchraigh, *Bang*chree, or place of river bends or peaks). Go to 692950 where a gate leads to a forestry road forking right or to a path forking left. Both routes finish as paths up through the woods to the upper heather moor and so to the top (2 km, 220 m ascent), where the view is very fine for such a low hill. The big plantations of Blackhall stretch N to the River Dee and W to the Commonty and the Shootin Greens on the road from Potarch to Feughside. A marked forest trail starts at 633943 on that road, which was once one of the most important cattle-droving routes on the way to the Cairn o' Mount.

The Hill of Fare   471 m (1545 ft). *Helafay*-ir, 'e' as in her, from Fàire or horizon ridge. Standing isolated from the farmlands N of Banchory, this flat-topped hill contains a remarkably big area of moorland plateau and sends a number of shoulders far out to enclose little wooded glens. For its low height, it forms an unusually complex hill, almost a miniature hill range, and gives fine spacious views. The road to Hill of Fare from Banchory goes through a marshy depression with reeds and willows near the house of Loch-head. This reminds us that, before the land was intensively drained, the Loch of Leys (*Leiz*) once stretched far to the E of here, joining up with the Loch of Park in a great wetland of lake and marsh. Many tracks now lead on to the Hill of Fare. From 685993 W of the T-junction of roads at Raemoir (probably from Ruighe Mór, *Ri*-more or big cattle run), an interesting route goes N up past the old castle at Cluny, then by a hill road which winds through some old trees skirting Craigrath, and so to the wide plateau on top (6½ km, 380 m ascent). Another good way up comes from the N side at 703058, past the old castle of Midmar and Craigshannoch above the Gormack Burn (Gormag or little blue one) by forest roads and an old peat track to Tornamean and so to the summit (5 km). To the NE of the Hill of Fare, the little hill of the Barmekin (*Bar*mikin) near Echt gives a grand view of the low country and carries an ancient circular fort on its summit.

Mortlich   381 m (1248 ft). Mór Thulaich (*More*-tlech) or big hillock. This is the conical hill rising above Aboyne (A-*bein*). An interesting approach starts up the road E of the Loch of Aboyne, past a fine old churchyard to the grassy slopes of Queen's Hill, and so to the top (2 km, 240 m ascent) with its big cairn, where you will see a fine view of Deeside and Glen Tanar. To the E lies Auchlossan, once a loch, then drained, and later a loch and marsh in the 1960s until it was drained in 1972.

Hills north of Cromar and Tarland. Mortlich is the SE extremity of a curving band of hills that enclose the wide fertile bowl of the Howe o' Cromar (How a Cro-*maar*). North of Mortlich rises the slightly higher Craiglich, easily reached in 1 km (180 m climb) from the A974 road at 526063 at the gap called the Slack, where you get a magnificent view up Deeside. On the other side of the Slack rises the higher hill of Pressendye (Praiss en *Dei*). A public road runs from Tarland (*Tar*lan) to 465074 beside Davoch, locally called the Dach, from which a path takes you to a saddle W of the summit. The path is part of an old drove road from 468134 near Towie to the Davoch (8 km, 330 m ascent). At the Davoch, the old drove road called the Lazy Well Road comes in from 425109 near Boultenstone (6 km, 100 m ascent). Between the two runs a third drove road starting from Culfork at 455114 with another variant at Mill of Culfork, and then over Green Hill to the Davoch. Local folk call this hill ridge between Lazy Well and Pressendye Maalie *Waat*, probably from Meallaidh Fhad or long little lump, but absurdly anglicised in some maps to 'Molly Watt's Hill'.

The Mounth Roads

Many paths, once called roads as they were the best roads then available over the hills, lead across this eastern part of the Mounth. Between the coast and Glen Muick near Ballater, there are ten main Mounth Roads. Most of them have variants spreading out fan-like at either end towards different settlements on the low ground.

History

During his attempts to conquer Scotland, Edward I and the English army went N to Aberdeen in 1296; he probably took the Cryne Corse Mounth, as he stopped at Glen Bervie and Durris. By the track from Glen Tanar over Belrorie to Dinnet stands a memorial stone put up by Sir W. C. Brooks who was a former owner of Glen Tanar; its inscription says that Edward also crossed the Fir Mounth but this is doubtful. Until the 1870s some families farmed upper Glen Tanar, but when Brooks bought the glen he cleared them all out. He erected the imposing tower beside the Brig o' Ess at the end of the glen road beside the South Deeside Road, which erroneously may suggest that the road to Glen Tanar House is private. Brooks also erected the many curious memorials, quartz pillars and wells that are so much a feature of the Glen Tanar area, as well as many houses of warm red granite and unusual design for the district.

Harvesters from Tomintoul once used the Mounth Road over Mount Keen a lot on their way to Trinity (*Tarantie*) Fair at Brechin. Walking by the Lecht to Don, they then crossed by the Glas Choille and Glen Fenzie to Glen Gairn, over the Mount Keen to Invermark, and next from Tarfside over the Clash of Wirren to the West Water and Brechin. Many people travelled by the Fir Mounth while carrying timber and resinous torches from Glen Tanar to the south, and all the Mounth Roads from the Capel to the Forest of Birse were in heavy use till the mid 1800s for taking illicit home-still whisky to Dundee and Perth.

Near the top of the Fir Mounth flows St Colm's Well, one of many places in NE Scotland visited by that early Christian missionary. The Tinker's Cairn near the well marks where a tinker murdered his wife. At the trial in Aberdeen, one witness was a Tarfside woman at whose house the couple had called on their way over the Fir Mounth. The man denied he had ever been there, but when the witness said she had given them a drink of milk, he exclaimed indignantly that it was only whey, a fatal remark!

The Causey Mounth and the Elsick Mounth. These went from Aberdeen and Peterculter respectively, to Stonehaven, over what was then a stretch of bleak moors, bogs, stony ridges and peat mosses. The name Causey comes from Causeway, locally pronounced *Cassie*. Although much of this ground has been turned into farmland, fragments of these lowland moors and bogs still remain, the soil is poor, and here the E end of the Mounth presses close to the cold North Sea.

The Slug Road. From Gaelic Slug or gullet. The Slug Road is now a tarmac road from Banchory and Durris to Stonehaven, cutting E of the rocky gullet that gives this Mounth Road its name.

The Cryne Corse Mounth. Probably Crion Crasg or little crossing. This Mounth Road goes from Durris to Drumlithie on a line just W of the Slug. Distance: 8 km from 762916 to 764841, ascent 230 m, time 2¼ hours. Go to 762916 on the Slug Road, where a private road beyond a locked gate runs uphill on the same line as the original path, towards a television mast. The mast rises for 300 m from the shallow basin E of Mongour (from Gabhar or goat), and is a familiar landmark especially at night when its red lights are visible a long way off.

From 765904 you hold to the left past Red Beard's Well by the old disused track which descends towards the afforested valley of Cowie (Collaigh or hazelly) Water. You can follow forest roads across the valley and up the other side to the old tracks leading to the Brae of Glenbervie (*Bairvee*).

The Stock Mounth, pronounced *Stoke* Munth, from Strachan to Glen Bervie. Distance: 10 km from 699916 to 759838, ascent 260 m, time 2½ hours. Several tracks from Pitreadie, Moss-side, Midtown and Garrol Hill join at Tod Steen, at 715881 on the E flank of Kerloch. Here you follow the old Mounth Road into the peaty basin at the head of the Sheeoch Burn (Sithich or fairy), then into the head of Cowie Water and up to Leachie Hill where the track descends to the Brae of Glenbervie. The slopes of Cowie Water are now afforested but you can travel by new forest roads.

The Builg Mounth, from Glen Dye to Glen Bervie. Distance: 11 km from 652873 to 736819, ascent 200 m, time 2¾ hours. The Builg Mounth starts from S of Scolly's Cross in Glen Dye, crosses Dye by a footbridge to Heatheryhaugh, and then climbs up the Builg Burn S of Kerloch. Over the top, it goes down the shoulder of The Builg and into the headwaters of the Bervie (Bearbha or boiling) Burn. There you should take the forest road as the plantations in this glen are huge and thick.

The Cairn o' Mount, locally called The Cairn a Munth or The Cairn, is now the public road from Banchory to Fettercairn and Brechin. Although reaching only about 450 m, it runs across a bleak exposed plateau and often becomes snow-blocked. One of the most important of the Mounth Roads, it had the beautiful old Bridge of Dye as early as about 1680, and also a spital (Gaelic Spideal or hospice) at either end of the high moorland section; one stood at Spitalburn in Glen Dye and the other uphill from Clatterin Brig in Glen Saugh. In earlier times the Cairn o' Mount was also often used by armed forces on the march.

The top of the Cairn o' Mount is one of the best viewpoints from any road in Scotland. Here you stand right on the edge of the main Highland fault and look steeply down to the uniform sweep of flat green farmlands to the S, whereas to the N and W you see a complex jumble of brown heathery hills and glens inside the outer boundary of the Highland rocks. This contrast, as you reach the summit of the road, comes as a great and sudden surprise. To the E, N and W, vast peaty heather moors stretch out to bare rolling tops. Snowy

Lochnagar, rising beyond the great high plateau of the Glen Esk hills, looks like a peak rising from an undulating subarctic tundra, as in Dovre Fjell or Iceland. To the S, a huge expanse of fertile low farmland in the Mearns and Strath More sweeps far down to central Scotland and out to the North Sea, often glittering in the sun. On a good day you can see the Firth of Tay beyond the Sidlaw Hills, the Bell Rock lighthouse, the E tips of Fife beside Tentsmuir and St Andrews, the Fife hills of Falkland and Lomond, and the Ochil Hills and Earn valley. On the clearest days you can see beyond Fife to the Firth of Forth, the Isle of May, the Pentland and Lammermuir Hills beyond Edinburgh, and the Scottish coast as far as St Abbs Head not far from the English border.

At the S end of the Cairn o' Mount the road drops steeply to Clatterin Brig. The big house on the hill to the E is Glensaugh Lodge (*Sach*, from North-East Scots for willow), which has for long been one of the farms of the Hill Farming Research Organisation. Shutting off Glen Saugh from the Howe o' the Mearns rises the bulky brown Strathfinella Hill. The road to Auchinblae runs past Loch Saugh, one of the extremely few lochs in Kincardineshire. It continues on through Strath Finella (Finnghuala or white-shouldered woman) and the Glen of Drumtochty, which are steep-sided and thickly wooded with tall dark spruces, larches and other conifers. Indeed the scenery is quite unlike the open sweeps of farmland and hills so characteristic of the Mearns.

The Birse Mounth. This runs from Birse (Berss, 'e' as in her, from Am Preas or the thicket) E of Aboyne, to Tarfside. Distance: from 536966 at Birse to Glencat 3½ km, to Feugh road below Ballochan 6½, to county boundary 12, to Shinfar 16, to Tarfside 19 km or 12 miles, total ascent 700 m, time 5¼ hours. The Birse Mounth goes over the low hill to Glencat, and over the next low hill to Birse Castle and Ballochan (*Ba*lochan) which stand at the W end of the public road up Feughside from Strachan. At Ballochan the valley of Feugh leads S, and the route now runs up the W side of the stream, coming out past the gap of the Sloch to the col between Tampie and Mulnabracks. A fine view opens out here into the great circular basin of Glen Tennet and Tarf, round to the hill of the Rowan with its monument. The track now descends S to the unoccupied farms of Glen Tennet and down to Tarfside.

The Fungle. This goes from Aboyne to Tarfside in Glen Esk. Distance: from Birsemore to Ballochan 8 km, to county boundary 13, to Shinfar 17, to Tarfside 20 km or 12½ miles, total ascent 690 m, time 5½ hours. From 529974 at Birsemore beside Aboyne, you walk SW along the wooded loch-side to the little glen of The Fungle; a slightly shorter but less attractive way in comes by the road to 523972. About 2 km up from Birsemore you come to the seat at the fine viewpoint of 'Rest-and-be-thankful', above a grand slope of natural pine wood with many interesting dead trees. The route then passes the cottage of The Guard, goes on to a moor with a very good natural regeneration of scattered young pines, and later joins a rough road that comes in from the farm of Newmill to the NE. At about 425 m you cross a flat shoulder before descending to Ballochan at the head of Feugh. From here the route to Tarfside is the same as by the Birse Mounth (p 279).

The Fir Mounth, Am Monadh Giuthais. This makes the most varied of the Mounth Roads crossing from Deeside to Tarfside. Distance: from 472982 on the Dinnet public road to Millfield 2 km, to county boundary 12, to Shinfar 18, to Tarfside 21 km or 13 miles, total ascent 690 m, time 5½ hours. The old road started at Dinnet and passed over Belrorie Hill to the Tanar bridge above Millfield, a place which is now on the public road up Glen Tanar from Brig o' Ess. Just S of the bridge above Millfield lies a meadow where the landowner Brooks cleared out the unfortunate farmer and erected a private chapel. The road now curves uphill above the Burn of Skinna (Sken*aa*ie); be careful not to take the other road far up beside the river. You next enter a great bowl of magnificent pine-juniper forest, and then climb on to the open hill of Craigmahandle (Craig-ma*han*il) and beyond to the plateau. Passing St Colm's Well, the route goes right over the 723 m top of Tampie and then drops down a Land Rover track to Shinfar and Tarfside.

The Mounth Keen. Monadh Caoin (Munth *Keen*). This fine crossing goes from Ballater to Invermark in Glen Esk. Distance: from the mouth of Muick to Pollagach 4½ km, to Tanar 8½, to county boundary 11½, to Glenmark cottage 15½, to public road at Invermark 19½ km or 12 miles, total ascent 840 m, time 5½ hours. You leave the public road at 366947 beside the bridge over Muick. Turn left here up the dirt road that starts at the memorial at about 210 m, go past Ballintober, and then at the next junction keep uphill into the larch wood. The old path, now a bulldozed estate road, passes at about 585 m between Cairn Leuchan and Craig Vallich (Bhealaich or pass), and dips into the peaty headwaters of the lonely open basin of the

Pollagach (*Pool*ach) Burn. Here it becomes a path again, which rises to 600 m before dropping to cross Tanar SSW of Etnach, near the site of the extinct ruined hamlet of Coire Bhruach. You now climb on another Land Rover track to 930 m and continue beyond by a path up to about 770 m that skirts to the W of the upper cone of Mount Keen. The route next leads gently downhill and then steepens to zig-zag down the Ladder to the cottage of Glenmark at 320 m. Below the cottage a stone memorial over a well commemorates Queen Victoria's crossing of the Mounth here in 1861. On the last and very fine part of the route, you walk down the E side of rocky Glen Mark to the public road at 445803.

Climbing routes

You can enjoy scrambling on small broken rocks in many places, but no good high natural crags exist inland. The tor on Clachnaben is of steep, fairly holdless rough granite, giving a number of interesting routes including all the chimneys (see *CCJ* 10, 145), as well as several miniature ridges and some crack and face climbs on the wall. Beside Allt Deas to the SW of the Shiel in Glen Tanar stands a curious hidden rock face of schist which gives very short climbs on a steep wall with small holds. Several disused quarries offer short, hard climbs on granite. Now that the Rubislaw Quarry at Aberdeen has gone out of use, its 140 m walls of grey granite will become more stable and already they offer several hard rock climbs, first ascended in 1971 (*SMCJ* 30, 72). Water fills the floor of this and several other old quarries. The smaller cliffs on the coast at Souter Head and Cove to the S of Aberdeen have long been a very popular climbing ground (see Further Reading) giving good short routes of all grades of difficulty on excellent clean gneiss. For a short distance from about Cove Bay S to Clashrodney a section of higher granite cliffs offers the grand climbs at South Cove. The many sea cliffs further S remain largely unexplored, with altered grits on the wild indented coast from S of Cove to Stonehaven, and sandstones from Stonehaven to St Cyrus.

Further reading

A. Cruickshank & A. Copland   The Blue Hill. *CCJ* 1, 29.

R. Anderson   Mount Battock and Clochnaben. *CCJ* 1, 138.

A. Copland   The Brimmond Hill. *CCJ* 1, 219.

J. Cruickshank   Mountain indicator on Brimmond. *CCJ* 9, 1.

H. T. Munro   The Braes of Angus (Guide Book article). *SMCJ* 8, 125.

G. M. Fraser   Glen Tanar. *Deeside Fld* 3, 29.

A. Bremner   Surface geology of the Strachan basin. *Deeside Fld* 3, 45.

G. M. Fraser   The Hill of Fare. *Deeside Fld* 3, 56.

Anon. Blue Hill indicator. *CCJ* 12, 122.

Anon. The Glen Tanar Right of Way Settlement. *CCJ* 13, 42.

A. Watson   Three mountaineering incidents at Aberdeen. *ECJ* 3, 59. Ascent of Marischal College tower and other events.

Etchachan Club 1969 *Rock Climbing Guide to the North-East Coastline of Scotland*. Up-to-date account of the routes on the cliffs at Souter Head and Cove, S of Aberdeen.

R. J. Grant   Rock climbing on the North-East coastline. *CCJ* 18, 26. A personal assessment of some of the routes in the above Guide.

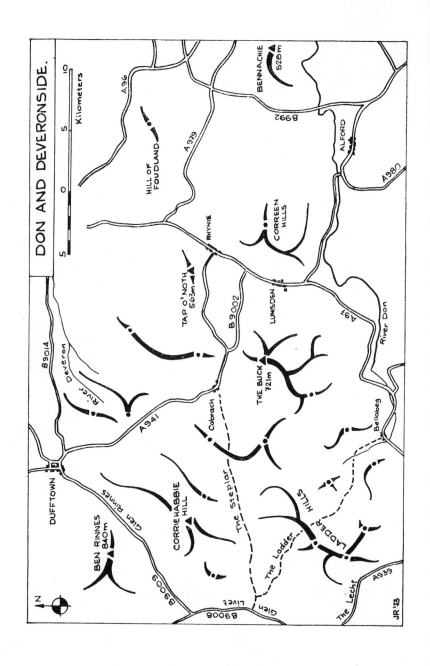

DON AND DEVERONSIDE.

Kilometers

N

BEN RINNES 840m
DUFFTOWN
B9009
Glen Rinnes
B9014
River Deveron
A941
CORRIEHABBIE HILL
Cabrach
The Steplar
LADDER HILLS
The Ladder
Glen Livet
B9008
The Lecht
A939
Bellabeg
River Don
A97
LUMSDEN
THE BUCK 721m
B9002
RHYNIE
TAP O' NOTH 563m
A941
HILL OF FOUDLAND
A96
A979
CORREEN HILLS
B992
ALFORD
A980
BENNACHIE 528m

JR '13

15

Don and Deveronside

Bennachie	528 m, 663227
The Tap o' Noth	563 m, 484293
The Buck	721 m, 413234
The Bin of Cullen	321 m, 480642
Mormond	234 m, 964573

Access
Rail and air services go to Aberdeen and rail from there to Inverurie and Huntly, two towns near Bennachie and Tap o' Noth. Public roads and buses run up the main valleys, and close by the fine coastal cliffs. On Donside, buses go to Bellabeg.

Accommodation
Youth hostels are available at Tomintoul and on the S bank of Don at Corgarff in Strath Don. You will see many shooters' huts on the moors, but this is not 'bothying' country (see p 26).

General description
This chapter covers a very extensive area in the valleys of Don and Deveron, and also mentions the coast. The shorter Don ('o' as in bone) flows E, parallel to Dee but N of it. Both rivers enter the sea at Aberdeen, a name which comes from Oban Dheathan or mouth of Don (Deathan, river deity). Deveron, joined by its two main tributaries of Bogie and Blackwater, flows NE to the Moray Firth at Banff. The name Deveron, pronounced *Div*erin, has come from DubhÉireann meaning black Ireland. No hill in this lower area reaches 900 m but the scenery of these valleys is pleasant, the low hills show much variety and the coast offers the finest sea-cliff scenery on Scotland's mainland E coast. Although not as grand as Deeside, Donside has fine river, hill and woodland scenery, and richer farmland, or, as the old verse went

> Ae mile o Don's worth twa o Dee,
> Except it be for fish an tree.

On Donside, Deveronside and Strath Bogie (Stra *Boe*gee), the many small farms give a softness to the countryside which has gone from the now uninhabited higher glens around the Cairngorms. From the farmlands of lower Aberdeenshire and Banffshire these low hills look far more prominent and are thus better known and loved by most of the people than the much bigger hills further inland.

Geology and natural history

This area is so extensive and varied that there is space here only to mention its most outstanding features (for more details, see the Forestry Commission's booklet *Forests in NE Scotland*). In passing, one may note that most of the hills in Donside, Deveronside and Glen Livet lie over schists, diorites, limestones and other rocks which break down into more fertile soils than does granite. These low hills support a richer variety of plants than the granite low hills of Deeside, and also larger stocks of wild birds and mammals. Bennachie makes an exception, being an isolated mass of granite. On the farmlands, the vast rookeries at Hatton Castle near Turriff (*Turr*a), at Straloch, and in other woods are the biggest in Europe. On the coast, you will find outstanding places for wild duck and geese N of Aberdeen at the Ythan estuary and its nearby Meikle Loch of Slains, and further N at the grand Loch of Strathbeg (Stra*beg*). The Ythan estuary is a very fine place for wading birds, and the nearby Sands of Forvie hold the biggest colony of eider ducks in Britain and great colonies of terns, as well as supporting an unusual plant community of crowberry and 'reindeer moss' lichens growing on sand dunes. You will see very large numbers of sea birds on the wild cliffs of Troup Head, Lion's Head and Pennan Head on the Moray Firth coast.

Estates

Mostly small, they are too many to mention individually. All the moorland and hill ground in the area described in this chapter is grouse moor, Glen Fiddich and Blackwater W of Cabrach being also deer forests. The Forestry Commission owns most of Bennachie and large tracts N of Morven, NW of Rhynie and elsewhere.

History

On a bare hillside in upper Strath Don stands the old Castle of Corgarff. Here occurred the gruesome tragedy that features in the ballad 'Edom o' Gordon', where Margaret Forbes and her family were burned to death in 1571 during a clan feud between the Forbeses and the Gordons (see also 'Corgarff Castle', by W. D. Simpson, *Proc. Soc. Antiqu. Scot.* 1927). Kildrummy Castle lies further down Donside, about 16 km W of Alford; it is one of the best Scottish examples of a 13th century early castle.

D. Gordon (see Further Reading) recently retold how Bennachie used to be a commonty or common land for the use of all the people to dig their peats, quarry stones and graze their stock. Then, during the early 19th century, when the population soared and land was scarce, squatters settled on the SE slopes and a Bennachie community grew there. The nearby lairds pushed an order through Parliament to divide up the commonty between them and to charge rent. In Gordon's words 'Known as the rape of Bennachie, it brought a poem from William Thom, the weaver poet of Inverurie. The lairds' leader was Dalrymple of Logie. Thom's lampoon described the great boon they had all enjoyed, and all their great commonty had meant to them and ends

Bennachie has become but a pimple,
Upon the nose of Sir Hugh Dalrymple.'
Subsequently, many who could not pay rent on this very poor land were evicted, and the community later died out by voluntary emigration.

At the Well of the Lecht, by the roadside, an inscription from 1754 records that 'Five Companies, the 33rd Regiment, Right Hon. Lord Chas. Hay, Colonel, made the road from here to the Spey'. In spite of the references to Wade at Tomintoul, this road was not constructed by Wade who left Scotland before the 1745 rising. About $\frac{3}{4}$ km up the glen to the E of the well stands a forbidding dark building, the remains of an ironstone and manganese mine which the York Buildings Company worked here in the 18th century; horses carried the ore in panniers to Balnagowan in Abernethy where it was smelted with charcoal from the Nethy forests.

Glen Livet and Tomintoul are Roman Catholic country in a predominantly Presbyterian region. To the SSE of Chapeltown, at the Scalan (Gaelic Sgalan or hut), a school was run for training Catholic priests during most of the 18th century. These were years of intimidation; several times the army broke the place up, and in 1746 it was sacked on orders from the infamous Duke of Cumberland. But the college survived, later to become Blairs College in lower Deeside.

About 1 km below the Well of the Lecht on the other side of the stream of Conglass (*Cong*lass) or dog burn, you will see a ruined cottage. Here, in June 1920, occurred the Topliss affair which was something of a sensation then in the peaceful North East. An ex-soldier called Percy Topliss had murdered a taxi driver in Hampshire in April 1920 and then disappeared. Later, a man who was supposed to be a wandering labourer arrived at Tomintoul and began living in the empty cottage; local folk paid no heed until he started tearing down the woodwork for kindling his fire. On 1 June, the Tomintoul policeman and two neighbours went to the cottage. A revolver shot rang out and two of the party were badly wounded, whereupon the man fled. From the description, it became clear that Topliss had escaped from Hampshire to this remote spot in the Banffshire Highlands. Five days later he was seen on the road between Carlisle and Penrith, and when challenged by a policeman he drew his revolver. The constable retreated for armed help and there followed a fight on the road, when Topliss was shot dead.

Walking ascents

Bennachie   528 m (1733 ft). Pronounced Bain a *Hee*. Although not much over 500 m high, Bennachie ranks as one of the best known hills in all Aberdeenshire. Standing high over the 'fairm-toons' of the Garioch (*Gee*ree) and the further low farmlands of Buchan, Bennachie is the first hill to be seen by North-East fishermen nearing land on their way home to Aberdeen. Many who have never had the pleasure of seeing Bennachie or of exploring this hill so dear to Aberdeenshire folk will have heard the sad old song that runs

Oh! gin I were far Gadie rins,
Far Gadie rins, far Gadie rins,
Oh! gin I were far Gadie rins
At the fit o' Bennachie

(Gadie, pronounced *Gaa*dee, is the stream on the N side of the hill, running into Urie.) Many know the song as a bagpipe tune, the regimental march of the Gordon Highlanders. From N or S the long ridge of Bennachie with its prominent tors resembles a series of breasts, and some have taken the name to be Beinn Chìoch or hill of paps, but this has been disputed by others (see p 21, reference to Alexander 1952).

Bennachie forms not so much a single hill as a 5 km-long ridge with a series of distinctive tops. The highest is the 528 m Oxen (*Ow*sin) Craig, but the best known and by far the finest is the slightly lower easternmost point called the Mither Tap. A great mass of granite crowns the Mither Tap, which makes it easy to identify from afar and gives Bennachie a character greater than that of many higher peaks. The Forestry Commission has planted the lower slopes with conifers which are hard to walk in if you stray off the cleared paths. Bennachie has always been a popular hill, and in recent years visitors have greatly increased. In 1973 a local group called 'The Bailies of Bennachie' was formed to look after the hill.

On the N side of Bennachie a widened road leads from 1 km W of Oyne (pronounced Ein) past Ryhill farm to the 'Back o' Bennachie car park'. From here, a path that was completed in 1973 by the Forestry Commission leads S through the woods to the top of Oxen Craig (2½ km, 370 m ascent), and another path breaks off in the wood to go E of Oxen Craig towards the Mither Tap (3½ km, 1½ hours). In late 1973 the Commission also started to make a brand new path from Oxen Craig to the Mither Tap. A second approach comes from E of Oyne where a widened road leads to a car park at 692244; this lies near the old fort of the Maiden Castle and the very fine sculptured stone called the Maiden Stone. From this car park a path runs SW and then winds up to the Mither Tap (2½ km, 330 m up), the last part passing through a huge 4½ m thick circular wall of large stones which form the remains of an Iron Age fort. From the Mither Tap you will enjoy a very fine view of the North East's windy coastal tip and of its vast tracts of moorland and hill ridges.

The Mither Tap stands up sharply from the S side beside Don. One of the interesting routes from this valley starts from the top of the glen N of Millstone Hill, a point which you can reach by forest roads (car park at Woodend SE of the Mither Tap, distance to the top 3½ km). A second good approach from the S side comes in N of Monymusk beside the ruined castle of Pitfichie; you can cross Don by a footbridge at Ramstone, just below Paradise Wood with its fine old larches and pines. The easiest route through the forest then goes around the W of Millstone Hill and up the Birks Burn to the Bennachie path which climbs N from the neck between the two hills.

The Tap o' Noth   563 m (1849 ft). Lying between Deveron and its eastern tributary of Bogie, the Tap o' Noth (Tap a *Noth*) looks a prominent cone with a flat summit. The blunted top comes from a circular wall of vitrified masonry, where the firing of a wooden Iron Age fort was so hot that it melted and fused the stonework. It dates from the same period as the vitrified fort on the little green hill of Dunnideer near Insch, whereas the conspicuous archway of Dunnideer Castle dates from much later in medieval times, though largely composed of material from the older fort. The quickest way up the Tap o' Noth starts at the A941 road from Rhynie to the Cabrach; a track winds NW from Howtown and then E to a fire lookout on the top. The valleys and moors to the N now form the heavily wooded Clashindarroch Forest. Another interesting place near here is the strange moor with its many weird rock outcrops and little hills N of the B9002 road from Lumsden to the Cabrach.

The Buck 721 m (2367 ft). Local people usually call it the Buck i' the Cabrach. You can reach this graceful pointed hill quickly by going to the highest point on the Rhynie–Cabrach road and then for 1 km S along the B9002 road to Lumsden. From here the Buck's summit lies 2 km along the fence to the SW (310 m ascent). A beautiful fertile green cone over rich andalusite schist, it gives fine views over the vast moors of the Cabrach basin to the W.

Donside. Although less grand than Deeside, Donside from Monymusk onwards shows a soft beauty and much variety. The river continually bends around the base of wooded hills or laps the edge of pleasant green haughs. At Corgarff, some of the highest arable farming in the north of Scotland occurs on the S-facing slopes. Here the road goes over the Cock Bridge, locally called Coke Brig, crossing the little stream of Allt a' Choilich or burn of the cock. On Donside you will see scores of interesting little hills and glens and vast moors, with a rich wildlife and offering fine views. By Don, a few 500–570 m examples are Lord Arthur's Cairn and the scrubby Coiliochbhar (Calyi*vaar*) N and S of the beautiful oak woods of Littlewood to the W of the Howe o' Alford (*Aa*furd); the pointed Ben Newe (*Nyow*) E of Bellabeg; and the Baronet's Cairn overlooking that lovely sweeping bend of Don beside Lonach. These and innumerable others offer plenty of fine exploration.

The Lecht Road. An Leachd, the declivity. This is now the public road which goes from Cock Bridge at 402 m in Strath Don, over the hill to Tomintoul, and which often features in the news after it has been blocked with snow. Although its highest point at about 645 m altitude, 1 km S of the watershed, lies slightly lower than the Cairnwell road's approximate 670 m, the Lecht hills usually receive more snow, height for height, than Glen Shee or the Braemar hills. The road climbs steeply above the Allargue Inn (A-*lairg*) and then reaches a flat top which gives a very fine and unusual view of the E and NE sides of the Ben Macdui–Cairn Gorm plateau, of some of the Loch Avon cliffs, and particularly of the great bulging flanks of Ben Avon. The road drops from this flat top before climbing again over a broad col, and then descends steeply to the burn of Conglass. Half way down on the E side of the road you will see a lovely, reedy tarn called Lochan gun Doimhne (goon *Doin*) or tarn without depth, the opposite of the 'bottomless loch' stated in earlier editions. The road then crosses Conglass, and near the corner below the bridge it passes the Well of the Lecht on the way down to the breezy uplands of Blairna-marrow (Blàr nam Marbh or dead-men's moor), Glen Conglass and Tomintoul.

The Ladder Road (*Laidrom*). This old right of way is the shortest walking route from Strath Don to Glen Livet and Tomintoul, taking you over an interesting range of rolling hills, the Ladder Hills. Distance: from public road at 339158 NW of Bellabeg to the Chapeltown of Glenlivet 13 km or 8 miles, total ascent 440 m, time 3½ hours. A public road from Bellabeg (Baile Beag or small farm-town) goes up Nochty Water (Nochta or naked) and over the hill to Glen Buchat. Leaving this road just before Torrancroy, you turn into the secluded upper glen of Nochty, and walk on a road through a Forestry Commission plantation to the ruined croft of Duffdefiance at about 385 m. It got this strange name from a crofter called Lucky Thain who came over the Ladder from Glen Livet to squat here; by the time Duff, the local laird, challenged him, he already had a house up and its 'lum reekin', so he sat there successfully in defiance. From Duffdefiance you climb by a bulldozed road for 180 m on to a long plateau. The road ends at 595 m where you come to the old path leading to the summit at about 735 m, near a cairn. On the far side the route drops down by the Ladder Burn to the Braes of Glenlivet, a wide open green basin surrounded by heathery hills, once well-populated but now with most of its crofts in ruins. The name Glen Livet (*Leev*at) comes from Lìomhaid, meaning polished or glittering.

After 1945 the Forestry Commission planted up much of the lower moorland in Glen Livet, around Tomintoul, and in Strath Avon, a district which was remarkably lacking in wood previously. They planted small patches of conifers that sheltered the farmers' stock, and their forest roads gave the farmers access to turn some of the moor into grass. Here the marriage of forestry and agriculture did not alienate the farmers, and the patchy landscape with round wooded hills and green fields amongst them gives this once bare area a pleasant character, indeed, one that is unusual in Scotland.

Monadh an Fhàraidh (*Mon*achan *Aar*ie) or the hills of the Ladder. From the highest point on the Ladder right of way, a short walk SW takes you to Carn Mor, which at 804 m forms the highest of this long range of the Ladder Hills. These broad hill tops bear a crisp lichen-rich vegetation, with vast peaty hollows between them where many golden plovers pipe mournfully, and a few dunlins scream in late spring. This makes grand ski-touring country, which you can easily reach from the top of the Lecht. The 792 m Carn Ealasaid (*Caarn Als*itsh) or Elizabeth's hill is a fine viewpoint 3 km on the W side of the county boundary on the Lecht. On the E side, snow lies long in Coire Riabhach (Cor *Ree*-ach) or brindled corrie, where a tractor pulls up skiers on a rope tow in spring.

The Steplar Road. This old right of way goes from Glen Livet over the hills through the Blackwater deer forest to the Cabrach. Distance: from Chapeltown of Glenlivet to Cabrach kirk 17 km or 10½ miles, total ascent 420 m, time 4¼ hours. From Chapeltown, take the path by Burnside of Thain to join a rough private road that curves along the side of Livet to the ruined Suie (Suidhe or seat) on a grassy knoll. To the SE, the steep narrow valley of the Kymah Burn (Caime or crookedness) and the broken rocky face of the Eachrach stand out prominently in this countryside of gentle rolling slopes. Beyond Suie the road carries on up Glen Suie to a col at about 520 m, and then zig-zags up W almost over the top of Corryhabbie Hill and down into Glen Fiddich (*Fitt*ich) and Glen Rinnes. From that col, a track descends to Glen Fiddich Lodge and so down the glen road to Duff-town. However, the old Steplar route breaks off as a track to the right just after Suie, climbs easily to between Cook's Cairn and Cairn na Bruar at about 600 m, and then contours round for 1 km. Avoiding the track which breaks off to the left and leads to Blackwater Lodge, you descend straight ahead to Blackwater which winds along the bottom of a wide open glen. The chief impression 'here is one of great loneliness, low rolling hills and bare moorlands, with not a scrap of wood or green ground in sight, and the whole scene made more weird by a solitary granite tor, rising like a ruined keep on one of the distant hills' (Alexander, early editions of this Guide). At about 400 m you cross the upper Blackwater and then climb up to the summit at approximately 540 m, beside Dead Wife's Hillock. Ahead now you suddenly see the Cabrach which lies like a huge cup below, surrounded by low hills and studded with many crofts and farms that are now mostly deserted. This great bowl is the Hich (high) Cabrach, whereas the Laich (low) Cabrach lies further down Deveron. The name Cabrach means 'abounding in cabers or tree poles', revealing that this now bare treeless bowl was not always so. Dropping downhill, you soon come to the old houses of Aldivalloch (Allt a' Bhealaich or burn of the pass) the scene of the song 'Roy's wife of Aldivalloch'. Here you come to the road leading to the Kirktown of Cabrach at about 320 m, from which you can motor down Deveronside to the Grouse Inn in the more wooded Laich Cabrach, and so to Dufftown. The historic Steplar path continued from Kirktown of Cabrach on to Rhynie by the route now taken by the tarmac road. From Aldivalloch, an old drove road goes S to 356178 in Glen Buchat (10 km, 200 m ascent), and another further E runs from the Cabrach kirk S to 411173 in Glen Kindie (11 km, 250 m ascent).

Hills of the North-East Lowlands. Several well known isolated low hills give fine views over the broad farmlands and coast. Among the more notable ones are the pointed Bin of Cullen (321 m) beside the Banffshire coast, which gives a magnificent view across the Moray Firth; the rounded Knock Hill near Keith; and the Fourman (*Foremon*, no 'Hill' as on the OS map) rising steeply above the rich woods of Mayen by Deveronside. The hills of Foudland and of Culsalmond (Cul*saa*mon) or Tillymorgan carry large old slate quarries beside the Huntly-Aberdeen road. Furthest out of all, in the very tip of windy Buchan stands Mormond (Mór Mhon, *More* Mon or big hill) rising to 234 m near Fraserburgh. Mormond, one of whose summits has now been disfigured by tracking aerials and buildings, is well known for its white horse and white stag, which are made of white stones on opposite sides (S and N) of the heathery hillside. Many more will know it because of the fine old Buchan ballad 'Mormond Braes'.

The coast. The coast of the North East has a rich variety of fine sea-cliff scenery. In Banffshire, most of the many miles of cliffs are of Dalradian slate, and to the E of Macduff some fantastic sharp slaty ridges run horizontally out to the sea. You come to the finest cliff scenery along the 120 m crags near Gardenstown and Troup Head, and at the vertical red sandstone walls of Pennan where there are huge steep stacks and spectacular ridges. The higher grounds of Fishrie S of Gardenstown and Windyheads Hill S of Pennan give particularly fine distant views of the hills described in this chapter,

as well as beyond to the Cairngorms and across the Moray Firth
to Caithness.

Climbing routes

On Bennachie a number of tors or large warts of granite project from
the hill. A few fine steep outcrops on and near the Mither Tap
provide short but sporting routes on dry, rounded, weathered granite,
from M to VD in standard. Smaller tors on the Buck o' the Cabrach
and the many weird little outcrops near the road from Lumsden to
the Cabrach offer good boulder problems when the high tops become
enshrouded in bad weather. Various disused quarries in the district
offer the only other rocks, mostly short. However, the coast more
than makes up for the scarcity of natural rock inland. The slate cliffs
E of Macduff give short but interesting climbs on smooth rock with
small holds, especially unusual on the fantastic sharp ridges going
out to sea. The rough pink granite cliffs of Longhaven (Lang*hei*ven)
just S of Peterhead are now very well known for their excellent rock
climbing. You will feel quite a mountaineering atmosphere among
Longhaven's varied amphitheatres and ridges where some of the
walls even face inland. When bad weather comes to the hills you can
have a grand short winter day there. The place is also excellent in
summer, when the climbing becomes more carefree on the sun-
warmed red granite and when the smells of sea-thrift flowers,
campion, salt water and sea-bird dung all add to the unusual character
of the place. A guide by the Etchachan Club describes all the routes
(see Further Reading).

Further reading

R. Anderson   Two Donside hills: Coillebharr and Lord Arthur's
Cairn. *CCJ* 2, 92.

A. Galloway   The Club at Bennachie. *CCJ* 2, 373.

R. Anderson   Glen Fiddich and neighbourhood. *CCJ* 3, 22.

S. P. Gordon   Corgarff and its hills in winter. *CCJ* 5, 233.

Etchachan Club 1960 *Rock Climbing Guide to the Cliffs of the
North-East Coast of Scotland.* Includes some notes on the cliffs from
Banff to Fraserburgh, and early accounts of the pioneer climbs at
Longhaven.

Etchachan Club 1969 *Rock Climbing Guide to the North-East Coastline of Scotland.* Up-to-date account of routes on cliffs from Peterhead to Cove.

D. G. Gordon   The Bailies of Bennachie will protect and preserve the Garioch's great heritage. *Turriff Advertiser,* 4 May 1973, 2.

R. J. Grant   Rock-climbing on the North-East coastline. *CCJ* 18, 26.

AMENDMENT 1980

New maps

The Ordnance Survey has published new, maroon-backed maps on a scale of 1:50,000 (about $1\frac{1}{4}$ inches to one mile) to replace their old one-inch to the mile maps. The first series has the same contours as before, the old information in feet being merely transposed to metres. They give a few new roads, new houses, and new forestry plantations, but omit most new hill tracks and most new patches of natural woodland. If your old one-inch sheets are still in reasonably good condition it is scarcely worth buying the new first series maps. In the area covered by this guide, the new first series numbers are 27, 28, 29, 37, 38, 42, 45, 53 and 54.

However, the new second series maps have been completely redrawn after new survey, and give far more precise detail on contours and other features that exist on the ground but did not appear in the one-inch maps (or the first series new maps for that matter). Contours in the second series are every 10 metres, and most new hill tracks and patches of natural woodland are shown. The second series is by far the best set of large-scale maps ever produced for the Cairngorms, and we recommend readers to buy them. Navigating with them will be much safer than with the old maps, as they show some small cliffs and steep slopes omitted in the old maps.

In the area covered by this guide, the only second series maps are numbers 35, 36, 43, 44; these four cover the whole of the main Cairngorms massif and most of the other big hills in the area. They extend from Calvine west of Blair Atholl to Mount Battock near Banchory, including Beinn a' Ghlo, the Glenshee area, the Angus glens and Lochnagar. They also stretch north over most of the Spey Valley as far north-west as the Carrbridge area, and east from there past Grantown to Glen Livet, the Lecht, and the Dee east to Kincardine o' Neil.

Green-backed maps on a scale of 1:25,000 (about $2\frac{1}{2}$ inches to one mile) have also been published by the Ordnance Survey. These are like the second series 1:50,000 sheets, only at a much bigger scale. For anybody who wishes more precise detail for any purposes, they are outstandingly good, their sole drawback for climbers and walkers being that each sheet naturally covers a smaller area of countryside. The special Ordnance Survey Outdoor Leisure map on The High Tops (Cairngorms) published in 1974, is on this scale, but covers a bigger area than usual because the sheet size is much bigger in this one case. The green maps are available for most of the hill ground in the area covered by this guide, and only the maps for some of the lower hills have yet to be published.

Tracks and paths

A track has been bulldozed at the top of Glen Gelder, so there is now a bulldozed track from near Gelder Shiel all the way to Allt-na-giubhsaich Lodge in Glen Muick. A path runs from west of Lochan Buidhe on Ben Macdui, along the south-west corner of Cairn Lochan and down to Coire an Lochain (marked on the green 1:25,000 map). Another path runs along the top ridge of Meall a' Bhuachaille and Creagan Gorm at Glen More.

Telephones and mountain rescue

A public telephone has been installed at the stable 100m. north-west of Derry Lodge. Another is at the Spittal of Glenmuick, inside the ranger's hut (on opposite side of the road from the keeper's house). A vacuum-packed casualty bag has been put in the first-aid box in the Corrie of Lochnagar.

Guides

A new climbers' guide to routes on rock and ice (Vol IV-V), for Lochnagar and Creag an Dubh-Loch, was published by the Scottish Mountaineering Trust in 1979. In 1978 the Etchachan Club published an up to date guide to Sea-cliff Climbs in the Aberdeen Area, covering the coast from Peterhead to north of Stonehaven, available from Marshall, 306 George Street, Aberdeen, and from bookshops in Aberdeen.

Huts, buildings and bridges

A fire has destroyed the little good shelter that still remained at Geldie Lodge. Bynack Lodge and Ruigh nan Clach in lower Glen Geldie are in ruins. The Carn an Tuirc ski hut at 172809 has been demolished. There is now a cafe at the top of the Lecht road between Strathdon and Tomintoul. The footbridge over Glas Allt Mor at 036987 in upper Glen Derry was dismantled in summer 1979. The former road bridges at 038933 at Luibeg and at 040934 over the Derry Burn no longer exist. If you are coming down Glen Luibeg and heading for Luibeg, you will have to walk down to the road bridge over Lui at 041933 when the rivers are high. If heading for Derry Lodge you can cross Derry Burn by the footbridge further up the burn at 041935.

Errors

The 1975 edition said the poet Robert Burns was born at Drumlithie near Stonehaven, but it was Burns' father who was born there; Rabbie was, of course, born at Alloway near Ayr.

INDEX

The names of rock routes, most low-ground features, and also most access points, bothies and other such items now easily available in the sub-headings of the Introduction and the Chapters, are omitted from this index, which concentrates on the main hills, corries, glens and cross-country routes.

Stock Mounth 278
Strath Avon 90, 92, 93
Stuic 248, 254
Suie 292

Tap o' Noth 289–90
Tarf (Tilt) 181, 182, 183

Tolmount 221, 222
Tolmount (mounth) 220, 265–6
Tom Buidhe 262

Wells of Dee 147
White Mounth 248
Winter Corrie 261, 267

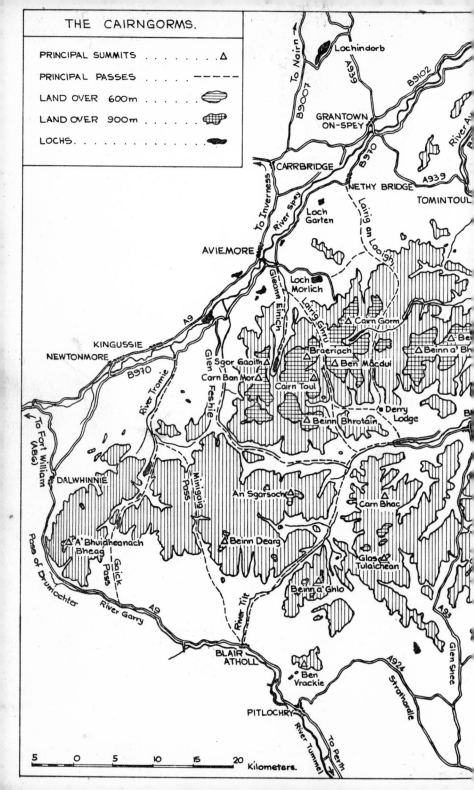